THE COLLECTED POEMS OF ROLAND MATHIAS

Roland Mathias

THE COLLECTED POEMS OF ROLAND MATHIAS

Compiled and edited
by
SAM ADAMS

UNIVERSITY OF WALES PRESS
CARDIFF
2002

© the collected poems, Roland Mathias, 2002
© introduction and notes, Sam Adams, 2002

British Library Cataloguing-in-Publication Data.
A catalogue record for this book is available from the British Library.

ISBN 0-7083-1760-X

All rights reserved. No part of this book may be reproduced, stored in a retrieval system, or transmitted, in any form or by any means, electronic, mechanical, photocopying, recording or otherwise, without clearance from the University of Wales Press, 10 Columbus Walk, Brigantine Place, Cardiff, CF10 4UP.
www.wales.ac.uk/press

Published with the financial support of the Arts Council of Wales

THE ASSOCIATION FOR
WELSH WRITING IN ENGLISH
CYMDEITHAS LÊN SAESNEG CYMRU

Typeset by Mark Heslington, Scarborough, North Yorkshire
Printed in Great Britain by MPG Books Ltd, Bodmin, Cornwall

Contents

Foreword	vii
Acknowledgements	viii
Roland Mathias: A Biographical Sketch	ix
Introduction: The Development of the Poetry of Roland Mathias	1
List of Poems	53
The Poems	59
Appendix	289
Editorial Note	293
Notes	294
Select Bibliography	374
Index of Poem Titles	377
Index of First Lines	380

Foreword

This edition is part of a series of publications, sponsored by the Universities of Wales Association for the Study of Welsh Writing in English, bringing together collected editions of Welsh authors writing in English. The field has received relatively little attention in the past and it is hoped that, with the republication of major literary works from earlier this century and before, critical interest will be stimulated in writers who will handsomely repay such attention. The editions are conceived of on scholarly lines and are intended to give a rounded impression of the author's work, with introductions, bibliographical information and notes.

JOHN PIKOULIS
General Editor

Acknowledgements

I owe a very great deal to the vision and support of the Universities of Wales Association for the Study of Welsh Writing in English, which not only endorsed my proposal that the short stories of Roland Mathias should be returned to print but also encouraged this larger undertaking of editing his collected poems. The two volumes together represent virtually the entire creative output of one of the key figures in Welsh letters in the twentieth century. A special debt of gratitude is owed to Dr John Pikoulis, the general editor of this series of publications, who gave valuable guidance, suggested aspects for development and read and reread the introduction and notes with a keen critical eye. Whatever blemishes remain are entirely my responsibility.

The editorial department of the University of Wales Press has once again given meticulous care and attention to the processing of the text through its various stages to publication, and I am immensely grateful for all the help, always cheerfully supplied.

Above all, I acknowledge with heartfelt thanks the cooperation of Roland Mathias throughout the time I have been engaged on this task. He has been ever benignly patient with my clumsy efforts to achieve a proper understanding of the complexities of his art and thinking, ever ready to offer advice, reminiscence and materials that would assist the project. The long conversation about his work, extending over several years, has been a rare privilege and an unforgettable experience.

Roland Mathias: A Biographical Sketch

1915 – Roland Glyn Mathias is born 4 September at Ffynnon Fawr, a farmhouse (now demolished) in Glyn Collwn, above Talybont-on-Usk, Breconshire, the home of his mother's parents. He is the eldest of the three children of Muriel (Morgan) and Evan Mathias. His mother, brought up on the farm, had gained the Higher School Certificate at Brecon Girls' School and for a time had been a pupil-teacher at the local primary school. His father, brought up in Llanelli but of peasant stock from Rhos Llangeler, Carmarthenshire, had been educated at the University College in Cardiff and trained for the ministry at Coleg Coffa in Brecon. At the time of his son's birth he was serving as a chaplain with the South Wales Borderers in the Dardanelles.

1916 – Revd Evan Mathias, struck down by dysentery, is shipped home from the Dardanelles. He is mentioned in dispatches for his tending of the sick and dying on the hospital ship. On his recovery, he joins the forces on the Western Front, where he spends the remainder of the war. In 1918, he decides to stay with the army instead of returning to the Congregational Church at New Inn, near Pontypool, where he had begun his ministry.

1920 – Early in the year, Evan Mathias's wife and two children join him at Cologne, where he is attached to the Chaplain General's office. Their first home is an apartment on the top floor of a mansion overlooking the Rhine. From a high window the young Roland Mathias observes the passage of shipping on the river. He begins to acquire German through contact with the family's German maid and commences his education at the army school attached to the Black Watch regiment.

1923 – Evan Mathias is posted to Bulford Camp on Salisbury Plain and the family return to Britain. Roland attends a private school for children of officers billeted at Amesbury as well as wealthier local families. His German, once fluent, begins to slip away. He is socially ill-at-ease among his fellow pupils but already showing signs of intellectual superiority.

1924 – In July, Roland's father gives him a copy of *The Lone Tree Lode* by Captain Owen Vaughan ('Owen Rhoscomyl'), a Western yarn with a Welsh narrator. In retrospect, he claims that the book gave him a consciousness of his own Welshness and a 'first introduction to Anglo-Welsh writing'.

1925 – In September, Roland begins his career as a boarder at Caterham

School in Surrey, an independent school with a strong Congregational tradition. Although homesick at first, he makes rapid progress in his studies, winning prizes on the way.

1926 – Revd Evan Mathias is posted to Aldershot and for the first time buys a house for the family. The poet's mother never comes to terms with army life.

1927 – Evan Mathias spends a year on a tour of duty with the British Expeditionary Force in China. His children regard him as irritable and rather forbidding. They feel perfectly self-sufficient without him.

1929 – Still not fourteen, Roland Mathias gains the London Matriculation. In September he enters the sixth form at Caterham and participates fully in school life, taking a leading part in clubs and societies, writing for and co-editing the magazine, making a considerable impact as an actor and singer and earning house colours at rugby and hockey.

1933 – With distinctions in history and French in the Higher School and Intermediate Arts examination the previous year, he goes up to Jesus College, Oxford, to read history, where he flourishes, academically and in extra-curricular activities. Posted to Catterick, his father rents a family home nearby at Richmond. During six years in Yorkshire, father and son draw closer, often walking together in the woods and on the moors, but Muriel Mathias's antipathy to soldiering has by this time crystallized into an inflexible pacifism.

1936 – Roland's First-class Honours in history earns him a college prize. Among the books he buys with the prize money is Edith Sitwell's *Aspects of Modern Poetry*, which he later says made him aware of 'the concept of "texture" in poetry and the conflict of ideas and attitudes in contemporary writing'. Elected an honorary scholar of the college, he embarks on historical research on 'The Economic Policy of the Board of Trade 1696–1714' which, in due course, gains him a B.Litt.

1938 – In September, his teaching career begins at Cowley Boys' Grammar School, St Helens, Lancashire. He joins the St Helens Rugby Union Club, plays in the back row of the scrum and becomes club secretary.

1940 – In June, Roland Mathias appears before the Lancashire and Cheshire Tribunal for Conscientious Objectors and is registered for non-combatant duties in support of the war effort. His appeal is turned down but he refuses to comply with the decision and continues to teach his sixth-form students, though (at his own suggestion) without pay. Revd Evan Mathias, longest-serving chaplain of the 'United Board' (Combined Free

Churches), and with the rank of colonel since 1928, retires from the army. The house in Aldershot is sold and a new home found in Brecon. There, the strength of his wife's puritan convictions and extreme pacifism are a continuing source of tension.

1941 – Roland Mathias comes to trial in September for refusing to attend a medical under the Armed Forces Act. He is sentenced to three months' imprisonment with hard labour, which he serves partly in Walton and partly in Stafford Gaol. On release in November, he again refuses direction to civil work in support of the military.

1942 – In January, he begins teaching at the Bluecoat School, a boys' grammar school of ancient foundation in Reading. In the autumn, he is twice directed to work (as a farm labourer and for the Great Western Railway in Didcot), again refuses and receives a three-month prison sentence. Pupils and some of the staff of the school contribute to a fund to pay a fine and obtain his release. His first volume of poetry, *Days Enduring*, is published by Arthur H. Stockwell Ltd but attracts little attention.

1944 – Roland Mathias marries Mary Annie (Molly) Hawes, daughter of an Oxfordshire farming family. They make their first home in Reading. With a friend, Pierre Edmunds, he founds and co-edits a local arts magazine, *Here Today*, and contributes poems, a short story and literary criticism to it. Keidrych Rhys selects his 'Balloon over the Rhondda' for his anthology *Modern Welsh Poetry*, his first appearance among recognized Welsh writers in English.

1945 – Molly Mathias gives birth to twins. Conscious of his family responsibilities, the writer leaves the Bluecoat School for a better-paid temporary post at Carlisle Boys' Grammar and commutes daily from a rented house in the outskirts of Gretna, on the north shore of the Solway Firth. He finds an outlet for his acting ability in joint staff-pupil drama and a local amateur dramatic society production.

1946 – In September, he becomes a permanent member of the staff of another boys' grammar school, St Clement Dane's Holborn Estate. He again involves himself in extra-curricular activities at the school, particularly drama, and continues writing short stories and poems, mostly during school holidays. The poems appear in *The Welsh Review*, *Poetry London*, *Wales*, *Life and Letters To-day* and *The Listener*. His second volume of poetry, *Break in Harvest*, is published by Routledge and reveals a distinctive voice with concerns for landscape and history.

1948 – He is appointed headmaster of Pembroke Dock Grammar School and immediately sets about raising the academic and cultural expectations of pupils as well as taking part in all the developments he instigates. He becomes an important member of the town's arts and drama societies and, in the years that follow, commits a considerable portion of his energies to chapel, community and cultural affairs in south Pembrokeshire.

1949 – In the spring, he makes his first appointment to the staff of the school, recruiting Raymond Garlick as a teacher in the English department. Soon after, he is influential in founding the magazine *Dock Leaves*, the first number of which appears in the autumn under Garlick's editorship. As a writer, Roland Mathias appears in all but two of the twenty-two numbers of the magazine before its name is changed to *The Anglo-Welsh Review*. In his many contributions, he emerges not only as a poet and short-story writer of substantial achievement but as an outstanding scholar and critic.

1952 – Roland Mathias's third volume of poetry, *The Roses of Tretower*, is published by Dock Leaves Press. It reveals the virtuosity and muscular energy of his mature voice, the strength of his Christian convictions and his capacity for critical self-analysis. Reviews of the book acknowledge its considerable strengths but also earn him a reputation for obscurity.

1956 – *The Eleven Men of Eppynt*, his only volume of short stories, is published by Dock Leaves Press. The book contains his entire output in the genre with the exception of a few anecdotal tales from his earlier attempts at short fiction and three later stories rooted in family relations.

1958 – Mathias leaves Pembroke Dock to become headmaster of the Herbert Strutt School, Belper, in Derbyshire.

1960 – In October, arriving at Brecon on a half-term holiday visit, he finds that his father has suffered a stroke earlier the same day. While he is close to his mother, they have little in common, but his relations with his father have been strengthened and deepened with the discovery of a mutually stimulating intellectual challenge and many shared interests. *The Flooded Valley*, his fourth book of poems, is published by Putnam and attracts a number of favourable notices.

1961 – He succeeds Raymond Garlick as editor of *The Anglo-Welsh Review*, a commitment that he will sustain until 1975. A Schoolmaster's Studentship at Balliol College enables him to spend a term at Oxford, where he completes research on an uprising among Catholic recusants at Whitsun, 1605, in Archenfield, part of Herefordshire close to the border with Monmouthshire. The topic has occupied him intermittently for almost twenty years and later inspires several poems.

1962 – In July, the poet's father dies and is buried in the hillside graveyard of Aber chapel, near Talybont-on-Usk. The occasion forms the basis of the elegy 'A Last Respect'.

1963 – *Whitsun Riot*, the outcome of his research project, is published. A stylish and absorbing exercise in historical detection, the book is widely and favourably reviewed.

1964 – In September, Mathias takes up the headship of King Edward VI Five Ways, Birmingham, a boys' grammar school of ancient foundation. Though less conspicuously involved in extra-curricular activities, he pursues his educational aims with undiminished energy and succeeds in raising standards.

1967 – Elected to a second Schoolmaster Fellowship, he spends the spring term attached to the English department at University College, Swansea, where he meets Vernon Watkins, also completing a fellowship in the same department, and lays the foundations of a critical appreciation of the other's work.

1968 – He receives a Welsh Arts Council award for services to writing in Wales.

1969 – He receives a Welsh Arts Council bursary and resigns from the education service. He and Molly move to a new home in Brecon (close to his widowed mother) which, with extraordinary prescience in view of the writer's interest in Celtic culture, the previous owner has named 'Deffrobani' (an allusion in the *Book of Taliesin* to the original home of the Welsh people). Mathias begins his second career as full-time writer.

1970 – He co-edits *The Shining Pyramid and Other Stories by Welsh Authors* with Sam Adams and gradually earns a reputation as a lecturer, commissioned contributor to literary journals, committee member, occasional broadcaster and lay-preacher. He is appointed visiting lecturer at the universities of Rennes and Brest. *The Anglo-Welsh Review* and the scale of his own contributions to the magazine grow remarkably. He contributes 'Meetings with Vernon Watkins' to Leslie Norris's memorial volume *Vernon Watkins, 1906–1967*.

1971 – His fifth book of poems, *Absalom in the Tree*, is published by Gwasg Gomer. Though the critical response is slow and not unmixed, recognition of his stature as a poet emerges. He becomes visiting lecturer at the University of Alabama, USA, where he writes an autobiographical essay for the first volume of *Artists in Wales* (ed. Meic Stephens). His seminal essay on Vernon Watkins, 'Grief and the Circus Horse', is published in *Triskel One* (eds. Sam Adams and Gwilym Rees Hughes). 'An Act of

Significance', a long poem about the discovery of America by Madoc, prince of the house of Gwynedd, is broadcast by the BBC.

1972 – *Absalom in the Tree* is awarded the Welsh Arts Council's poetry prize. He contributes a major article, 'Thin Spring and Tributary', on the origins of Welsh writing in English, to *Anatomy of Wales* (ed. R. Brinley Jones) and begins a correspondence with David Jones that will culminate the following year in publication in *The Anglo-Welsh Review* of Jones's last completed work, the poem 'The Narrows'.

1973 – His research on the shifting linguistic boundaries in Wales is published as 'The Welsh Language and the English Language' in *The Welsh Language Today* (ed. Meic Stephens). He recruits Gillian Clarke as co-editor of *The Anglo-Welsh Review* and begins a five-year stint as chairman of the English-language section of Yr Academi Gymreig.

1974 – His monograph on *Vernon Watkins* in the Writers of Wales series is published by University of Wales Press. He lectures to the Powys Society on the poems of John Cowper Powys.

1975 – He contributes 'The Caseg Letters – a commentary', a detailed study of the literary relationship between Alun Lewis and Brenda Chamberlain, to a special number of *Poetry Wales* (ed. Sam Adams). 'In Search of the Silurist', an early excerpt from his research into the family and personal history of Henry Vaughan, is published in another special number of *Poetry Wales* (ed. J. P. Ward).

1976 – Roland Mathias resigns his editorship of *The Anglo-Welsh Review*, by this time the longest-lived of any English-language literary journal in Britain. With Sam Adams as co-editor, he publishes *The Collected Short Stories of Geraint Goodwin* and, as editor, *David Jones: Eight Essays on his Work as Writer and Artist*. He takes over as chairman of the Welsh Arts Council's Literature Committee, a position he will retain until 1979.

1978 – He begins his long and painstaking work as a major contributor to *The Oxford Companion to the Literature of Wales* (ed. Meic Stephens, 1986), initially in the researching and drafting of many entries and, as the work approaches its conclusion, in reading and rereading the whole text. He undertakes reading tours in the USA, visiting universities in New York State and Washington, DC, and returns to the University of Brest, where he writes several poems on Breton themes.

1979 – Another long-held interest is brought to fruition with the publication of *The Hollowed-Out Elder Stalk: John Cowper Powys as a Poet*, the first book-length study of the writer's poetry. He contributes a survey of

'Literature in English' to *The Arts in Wales 1950–75* (ed. Meic Stephens). His sixth book of poems, *Snipe's Castle*, including the broadcast poem 'Madoc' and a sequence, 'Tide Reach', conceived as the libretto for a cantata celebrating Pembrokeshire, receives lengthy and considered reviews and earns him the recognition he has long merited.

1980 – *Snipe's Castle* is awarded the Welsh Arts Council's prize for poetry. He becomes chief reviewer of *Ninnau* ('The North American Welsh Newsletter') in addition to reviewing regularly for *British Book News* and *The Anglo-Welsh Review* and occasionally for the other magazines based in Wales. '"The Black Spot in the Focus": A Study of the Poetry of Alun Lewis' is published in *The Anglo-Welsh Review*.

1981 – His essay 'David Jones: towards the holy diversities' is published in the *Transactions of the Honourable Society of Cymmrodorion*. David Jones's *The Narrows*, with an introduction by Roland Mathias, receives its first separate publication.

1982 – An article, 'Channels of grace: a view of the earlier novels of Emyr Humphreys' in *The Anglo-Welsh Review*, brings together key features of his thinking about a novelist he has long admired for posing moral questions about man's knowledge and understanding of goodness.

1983 – *Burning Brambles: Selected Poems, 1944–1979* is published by Gwasg Gomer.

1984 – He delivers the Annual Gwyn Jones Lecture on 'The Lonely Editor: a Glance at Anglo-Welsh Magazines'. The anthology, *Anglo-Welsh Poetry, 1480–1980*, the product of a collaboration with Raymond Garlick, is published.

1985 – Roland Mathias is awarded an honorary doctorate by Georgetown University, Washington, DC. A collection of his literary criticism, *A Ride Through the Wood: Essays on Anglo-Welsh Literature*, embracing those writers who have meant most to him in the canon of Welsh writing in English, is published by Poetry Wales Press.

1986 – In May, in the midst of a hectic schedule of writing, lectures, readings and committee work, he suffers a stroke. A great deal of work is set aside, including a book-length study of the poet Henry Vaughan. He begins the task of putting in order the accumulated papers of a lifetime in literature.

1987 – Large-scale work undertaken before he fell ill continues to appear – *Anglo-Welsh Literature: An Illustrated History* and two chapters on the

Civil War in the *Pembrokeshire County History*, as well as other contributions to several books and journals.

1993 – New poems by Roland Mathias begin to appear in *The New Welsh Review* and *Poetry Wales*.

1996 – His seventh book of poems, *A Field at Vallorcines*, is published by Gwasg Gomer. Molly Mathias dies suddenly in November.

Introduction: The Development of the Poetry of Roland Mathias

The pages that follow make sparing reference to the circumstances of the poet's life, the salient facts of which are presented in the biographical sketch that precedes them. Rather they concentrate upon the poetry, the early influences that shaped it and its stylistic and thematic development. This approach possibly has the disadvantage that links between the writer's life and his art are insufficiently highlighted. Certain characteristics of the poems are readily explained, however. The multitude of historical allusions, for example, are what one would expect from a poet who had read history at Oxford and who subsequently gave a good deal of time to research in specific periods. Mathias is also interested in genealogy, a closely related field of study. That his father's family is frequently the subject of poetic meditation may be explained by several factors, including the affection he felt for his uncle, David, his father's brother, the attraction of the strong contrast between the origins of the clan on the 'squatters' moor' of Rhos Llangeler, Carmarthenshire, and their later achievement and last, but by no means least, the intellectual stimulus provided by his father when, during his student days at Oxford, the poet began to know him better.

From the earliest poetry, Mathias's response to the Welshness of especially his father's family and to the rugged topography of Wales, mountain and coastline, identify him as a Welsh poet. National consciousness, however, as distinct from awareness of Welsh roots, is not a feature of the first four volumes of poetry, whereas several poems in the fifth, *Snipe's Castle* (1979), disclose an overtly patriotic stance. We cannot be sure how his long exile (all but ten of Mathias's first fifty-four years were spent outside Wales) affected that sense of Welsh nationality which, by his own account, he acquired early, but it is reasonable to conclude that this change was a consequence of his quitting teaching to settle in Brecon in 1969 and becoming active in cultural affairs in Wales during the 1970s, the decade of the first major debate on devolution.

Readers may ponder upon the genesis of certain other features of the poetry. In the mature poems there are many expressions of his sense of unworthiness compared with ancestors and living relatives of his father's family, compounded by the irony of his more comfortable existence, and of his concern with the nature of good and evil and guilt

Introduction: The Development of the Poetry of Roland Mathias

in the sure knowledge of his own susceptibility to the latter. These clearly have much to do with his sensitivity as an observer (a role for which exile had fitted him) and, broadly, to his upbringing and the strength of his Nonconformist belief, but beyond that one can only speculate.

Although they contribute in various important ways to the writing, none of these ingredients of his life or habits of thought made him a poet. From the beginning, he was in thrall to the power of words, their sound, meaning and rhetorical potential. He is not an assiduous user of dictionary and thesaurus, as some critics have suspected, because he has little need of them. Gifted with a retentive memory, he amassed an unusual vocabulary that includes rare, obsolete and dialect words, and in his poems he shapes this personal reservoir of language almost as though it were a malleable medium.

The writer's mother, who had briefly been a teacher in the primary school at Talybont-on-Usk, taught him to read, as we learn from the semi-autobiographical short story, 'The Rhine Tugs', which describes his infant fascination with the tugs he watched from the window of his parents' apartment overlooking the river:

> He could not remember when he had not run from breakfast to jump one–two on the couch and up to his seat over the world; his mother would call him to read. But the words were lost in his mouth and he could not find them for thinking of the little tugs below.

He was soon, by his own account (in his *Artists in Wales* essay), 'reading avidly'. The formal education that followed, first in army children's schools in Germany and later at a school at Amesbury, Wiltshire, close to Bulford Camp and the army training area of Salisbury Plain, confirmed in him a love of stories. From the same source we know that identification with the self-declared Welsh hero of a rattling Western yarn, *The Lone Tree Lode* by Owen Vaughan ('Owen Rhoscomyl'), his father's gift for 'a good first year's work at school', brought an initial consciousness of his own allegiance to Wales. His bookishness did little for his standing among fellow pupils but left him and his 'word-haunted memory' isolated at the top of the class.

Throughout this time, and in the years at Caterham that followed, whatever experience he acquired of poetry was that which was considered appropriate for children in English schools. This was itself conditioned, at secondary level, by school certificate examination set books. It would have been the same, of course, had he been educated in Wales. When he began writing poems himself, his style was 'highly-coloured romantic' and his models were 'Tennyson and Arnold, with an

Introduction: The Development of the Poetry of Roland Mathias

argumentative muscle or two from Browning'. In the *Artists in Wales* essay he recalls his English master at Caterham saying 'that my work was, as to matter, very competent, but that he "could not stand" the way I wrote' (p. 165). The criticism did not stop him writing poems, entering school poetry competitions and, in due course, co-editing the school magazine. English was his favourite subject and it was only the freak of his doing rather better in history than in English at the higher school certificate that persuaded him to read history at Oxford. Speculation about how different his creative life, his poetry, might have been had he read English is as pointless as it is interesting. What we know is that reading history gave him another dimension on which to exercise his intellect and, later, his creativity. It also gave him access to the distinctive flavours of the language of other periods, and intuitions about historical characters whose designs and desires were awaiting discovery in official papers or self-portrayed in their journals and letters.

The question of early influences on Mathias's writing is important. Contrary to the impression that might have been given by the quotation from the *Artists in Wales* essay above, he knew little of the Romantic poets. A suggestion that a few of his more sensuous verses, such as 'The Stars Above' (25), might owe something to Keats he rejects out of hand ('I never knew him'), and it is clear from the incomplete draft of an essay on Wordsworth he was writing about the same time as 'The Rhine Tugs', which contains an allusion to Wordsworth in France, that he read *The Prelude* for the first time in the early 1940s – and was unimpressed. In any case, the *Artists in Wales* essay does not tell the whole story. In a note that he contributed to *Poetry Wales* in 1978 (13, 4) he wrote:

> Awareness of the poetry of Edward Thomas came to me, in some sort, very early. *Poems of Today, 2nd Series*, which was a set book for School Certificate ... contained 'Out in the Dark', 'Roads', and 'The Penny Whistle'. Of these the first, with its unusual stanzaic formation and oddly hanging last line, was alien to my experience and I recollect that I approved in no more than moderation of the other two ... It is perhaps galling to have to admit that Flecker, Newbolt, Charlotte Mew and Walter de la Mare were more to my taste then, but every reader must need begin from the ethos in which he grows up. (p. 112)

Following one of our conversations, he wrote down the titles of poetry anthologies he had read first at Caterham, expanding slightly the information contained in the *Poetry Wales* 'Note'. They included *An Anthology of Modern Verse*, published by Methuen in 1921, *Poems of*

Introduction: The Development of the Poetry of Roland Mathias

Today, 2nd Series, a publication of the English Association dating from 1915, both of which were still being read in secondary schools in the 1960s, and *Georgian Poetry 1916* and *1917*, edited by Edward Marsh, published by H. E. Monro's 'Poetry Bookshop'. He had also, he said, 'read and re-read' A. E. Housman but 'couldn't do anything with it' (that is, though he admired Housman's poetry, he could not or had no wish to emulate it). He spoke in rather similar terms about Hopkins in an interview with Cary Archard (*Poetry Wales* 18, 4, 1983): 'I began to write influenced by Gerard Manley Hopkins, with whom one obviously couldn't compete. Anyway, that would have been going up a direction that couldn't be followed any further' (p. 61). Hopkins's poetic expression of faith, albeit at the polar extreme from Mathias's Nonconformist Christianity, was an obvious attraction but did not offer a template. The effect of his use of rhythm and language went deeper and, as we shall see, manifested itself later.

In the meantime, the principal models for his writing were poets of the Victorian era and the Georgians. A glance at any of the anthologies mentioned above will be enough to convey the selected poets' commitment to regular metres. There are only four unrhymed poems in Methuen's *Modern Verse*, for example, and none in *Poems of Today*. Rather like the art students of his day, who spent a great deal of time acquiring the basic skills of draughtsmanship, Mathias practised assiduously the metrical forms and poetic devices that were the stock in trade of Tennyson, Browning and Rupert Brooke, and of older contemporaries like Newbolt, Masefield, de la Mare, Charlotte Mew, W. H. Davies, Gordon Bottomley and John Drinkwater. James Elroy Flecker (1884–1915) he remembers with particular affection. This is not altogether surprising when one reads in the Methuen anthology (where Flecker rates five poems to T. S. Eliot's one):

> Evening on the olden, the golden sea of Wales,
> When the first star shivers and the last wave pales:
> O evening dreams!
> There's a house that Britons walked in, long ago,
> Where now the springs of ocean fall and flow . . .
> ('The Dying Patriot')

'The New Miracle' (31) appears to carry faint verbal echoes of Thomas Hardy's 'The Darkling Thrush' and 'Afterwards', both frequently anthologized, the latter in Methuen's *Modern Verse*. In a bleak image that foreshadows the poet's mature vision, it compares the sights of the countryside in early spring, still half-held in winter's grasp, with London streets decked for a coronation.

Introduction: The Development of the Poetry of Roland Mathias

> The gaunt old cheek of earth
> That last I saw is smaller grown
> And softer, lulled within a veil
> Of leaves. The rutted lanes
> Are leafy confines that align
> A whipped sky of wind. Dull coronets
> Of buds blur on the spiring dusk
> And blow to green.

The free verse and the textural effects of alliteration and assonance illustrated by the lines quoted (the repeated consonants l, s, b, d and the vowel sounds of 'lulled', 'rutted', 'Dull', 'buds' and 'dusk', of 'cheek', 'leaves', 'leafy' and 'green', and of 'align' and the curious epithet 'spiring') identify a poem that differs somewhat in style and feeling from the majority in Mathias's first book, *Days Enduring* (1942). Any similarity with Hardy, however, he declares coincidental. That he has no more than a superficial acquaintance with Hardy's poetry is surprising, not least because both from time to time employ a similarly knotty and muscular language sprinkled with dialect and archaisms to work out complex and tangled ideas. If I did not already know a line such as '. . . the unseen waters' ejaculations awe me' to be Hardy's (from 'After a Journey'), I might well accept it as Mathias's.

Most of the poems in *Days Enduring*, one or two surviving from his school days, the bulk from his later Oxford years (a few first published in the Jesus College magazine) and the beginning of his teaching career, were written under the spell of Georgian prosody and diction. One specific debt can be identified. The religious poetry of Francis Thompson (1859–1907), neglected now, had a large following in the first half of the twentieth century. 'In No Strange Land' with its epigraph 'The Kingdom of God is within you' (one of three poems by Thompson in the Methuen anthology and one of six in *Poems of Today* where, curiously, title and epigraph are reversed) had a typically powerful hold on its readers:

> The angels keep their ancient places; –
> Turn but a stone, and start a wing!
> 'Tis ye, 'tis your estranged faces,
> That miss the many-splendoured thing.
>
> But (when so sad thou canst not sadder)
> Cry; – and upon thy so sore loss
> Shall shine the traffic of Jacob's ladder
> Pitched betwixt Heaven and Charing Cross.

Introduction: The Development of the Poetry of Roland Mathias

Mathias reproduced the regular stanzaic structure in every detail in 'O World Intangible' (35), the title itself a phrase borrowed from Thompson's poem.

The notion of writing poems to mark the New Year (1, 6, 37) might have derived from Gordon Bottomley's 'New Year's Eve, 1918' and Rose Macaulay's 'New Year 1918'; the significance of the date attached to these anthology pieces would not have been lost on a young man with much energy, high ambitions and strongly pacifist beliefs, who saw calamity approaching as the 1930s unwound. There are also poems – 'Declaration of War' (41), 'Blitz in Manchester' (45), 'Café Parting' (49) – that are in an unrhymed, basically iambic form (though not blank verse) rather like that favoured by another of the anthologized poets, Walter James Turner (1889–1946). Otherwise the effect of the Georgian poets was broad but pervasive. Their brand of pastoralism, their often intense response to the natural world, held a strong attraction for one already in love with landscape but, above all, at the beginning of his own creative journey, it was the appeal of their traditional lyricism that drew him, especially as they are represented in the anthologies, which tend to omit their longer narrative and dramatic work. It is hardly necessary to add to the examples already quoted further illustrations of Georgian poetic language, but they can be multiplied many times from any of the poets named – Brooke's 'A Faun a-peeping through the green', 'Sweet water's dimpling laugh', 'voices that do sing' and 'washen stones', for example; the frequent preference of 'thy', 'thee', 'thou' and 'thine'; use of the abbreviated forms, ''neath', 'o'er' and so on. All are characteristic of the mainstream of poetry, at least at the start of the 1930s.

Almost exactly two-thirds of the poems in *Days Enduring* have rhyme, the vast majority within a regular stanza form. Many of these have been turned out directly from the Georgian mould. While accomplished metrical exercises, they are often emotionally empty, expressing only a general sentiment about the passage of time, as in 'New Year, 1935' (1); love, as in 'Joy and Faith' (2); melancholy, as in 'Long Abed' (4); weather, as in 'Moorland Thunder' (5); trees, as in 'The White Poplar' (34); and flowers, as in 'White Peonies' (9):

> The scent of peonies in June
> Is redolent of dusk,
> Of sorrow, and a jangled tune,
> Of heartbeats hid in lettered rune,
> And musk.

Introduction: The Development of the Poetry of Roland Mathias

> And as I sit they glimmer white
> Above the vase's blue;
> Their cream-pale scent o'erhangs the night,
> The murmur of a spent delight
> And rue.
>
> Their tint-edge folds betray no woe,
> But only jewelled tears,
> A whispered sigh it must be so,
> A laden longing for the slow
> Slow years.

Elsewhere, the sun is 'o'erlain' with clouds; a place can be 'A paradise enow ... embalmed new from Lethe's pool'. The young poet sees Cardigan Bay ''mid wavelets twinkling smiles' and he has a sentimental view of dying, with 'a steadfast smile as one at peace / Looks toward eternity'; 'dead' rhymes with 'unnoticed'.

There are examples enough to prompt the thought of parody, but the poet has no such intention. He is simply full to the brim with words that are occasionally at odds with the emotion of a poem, like the 'heartbeats hid in lettered rune' above, trying his strength with lyrical forms and often, at the same time, projecting more than a hint of romantic melancholy. The sentimentality, a characteristic of many of the early poems, and the romantic self-image, without irony, are far removed from the self-critical, mock-heroic or anti-heroic stance that was to be adopted in his mature writing. This is not to deny that both the young man's pose and the poems themselves possess a good deal of charm. Some of the best poems in *Days Enduring* employ Georgian mannerisms and formality with persuasive freshness. One such, 'Evening in Saundersfoot' (38), was composed during a Pembrokeshire holiday in August 1938 when, after more than eighty unsuccessful applications, he heard that he had been appointed to his first teaching post. It is a brief, rather Audenesque, narrative about unexplained signals from ship to shore at dusk. Another, 'Tower on an Evening Sky' (43), which has a similar tightly structured lucidity, is a prayer for strength, not to fight but humbly to withstand whatever may befall.

Alongside the formal lyrics in *Days Enduring* we find a small number of poems that are different, though still imitative. In 'To My Uncle David' (7) – one of a handful of poems about the poet's favourite uncle – and 'On Hearing Richard II, Broadcast by the O.U.D.S.' (8) the model is seventeenth-century dramatic utterance. Both have a basic ten-syllable line, in the latter with occasional rhyme. However, the most striking development is from work in which the imagery, like the metre and diction, is influenced by the poet's reading to that in which it is the product of personal experience and observation. The latter begins with poems about young love lost or waning that date from 1936, but is most characteristic of those written in the turbulent period 1939–41. In several that chart the progress of his emotional life there is still a measure of self-dramatization, but less affectation. A few of these, 'Now Starlight Knows You Not' (23), 'The Stars Above' (25) and 'For Marjorie' (48), have complex metres and rhyme schemes; though unrhymed, 'Café Parting' (49) and 'Blitz in Manchester' (45) also have metre. Others, such as 'Parting' (20), 'Dusk' (24) and 'Lament for Cassandra' (47) are in free verse. In this variety of forms we see the first signs of an attempt to vary metre to suit the subject. He would become a constantly inventive maker of stanza forms that are not imposed but arrive with the subject and the drafting of the opening lines, and he welcomed the challenge of sustaining the metre to the end of the poem. This delight in technical virtuosity is as obvious an attribute of his first book as it is of his last.

Perhaps inevitably, it is the violation of normal life wrought by prison that produces the strongest, most memorable images. Advanced drafts of some of the poems concerned appear in Mathias's Notebook in red ink, the first, 'Inter Tenebros' (50), an expression of indomitable faith annotated 'Walton Gaol, Sept. 1941'. After almost sixty years, the experience of what he described to me as Satan's kingdom ('the pit, the nether lines') remains as fresh in the poet's mind as it does in that first prison poem and in those that follow it: 'Vista' (51), 'Bars' (52), 'Wishes from Walton' (53), 'Cries in the Night' (54) and 'Fagenbaum' (55). Images of the sights, the sounds, the menace and monotony of prison are contrasted with the few signs of ordinary existence that penetrate its walls and those savoured, tantalizing memories of life outside:

> Desires upon my slate
> And seven-squared days that bleach and crack
> Between the wells and balconies
> And concrete exercise –
> How can you give me back
> Those gilded weeks and back
>   the breath of Wales . . .

'Bars', from which these lines are taken, consists of two eleven-line stanzas with an identical rhyme scheme (the rhymes of the second and the fourth line running through both), and a very similar syllabic pattern of long and short lines. The poem weaves images of prison life and a longing for freedom into an intricate web of sound and rhythm.

Introduction: The Development of the Poetry of Roland Mathias

Mathias's First-class Honours in history in 1936 earned him a college prize. Among the books he bought with the prize money was Edith Sitwell's *Aspects of Modern Poetry*. In his *Artists in Wales* essay he records how this made him 'aware of the concept of "texture" in poetry'. He presents the experience as a turning point in his development as a poet: 'what I wrote from that moment was in very vital respects different' (p. 166). The first product of his study of Sitwell is 'Knapweed' (26), a single sentence in the form of an eccentrically rhymed poem of fifteen lines all of eight or ten syllables. Rhyme, and occasional half-rhyme (unusual in this book), is one element of the poem's texture, which manifests itself also in repetitions – of letters (l, m and s conspicuous among them); of sounds and gradations of similar sounds ('crown . . . round . . . known . . . now . . . new . . . sun . . . man . . . mounds . . . noon's . . . deploy . . . plays . . . Rhine . . . again'); and of words ('new'). The whole poem, and the final four lines in particular, are knitted together by a combination of these effects:

> . . . till the sun
> Blinding the man into boy
> Beats on the mounds; at noon's deploy
> He plays the robber by the Rhine again.

The poetic resurrection of childhood experience is common enough but this treatment of the theme, which subjugates memory to linguistic imperatives, is far less so. It points the way to the development of a style in which verbal texture is a characteristic feature and language may be bent and compacted to serve the poet's purposes. That the development proceeds discontinuously should not surprise. It is in any case difficult to trace through *Days Enduring*. Although the poems appear broadly in the order in which they were written, their chronology is uncertain, for some that are thematically similar have been grouped together regardless of the date of composition and one or two were misplaced as a result of the publisher's whim or error. ('Café Parting', for instance, appeared between the prison poems 'Cries in the Night' and 'Fagenbaum' and has been moved in this edition.)

Nevertheless, towards the end of this first collection are two poems, 'Pastorale' (63) and 'Balloon Over the Rhondda' (64), which mark a clear step forward. The sound effects illustrated above are deployed in them too, rather more subtly in the former, but the predominant tone is unaffected and playful, markedly different from that of the poems that precede them. 'Balloon Over the Rhondda' was published in 1943 in the London-based journal that consistently welcomed Welsh writers, Robert Herring's *Life and Letters To-day*. It describes aerial

Introduction: The Development of the Poetry of Roland Mathias

manoeuvres of an unusually humorous cast for wartime. The observers are Sunday chapel-goers, among them the poet and his father. The self-portrait of the former is unflattering: he is a callow young man, unsuitably garbed for the occasion in green corduroy and conscious of the reproving looks of the deacons but unmoved by them. The poet's delight in texture is evident in the intricate sound patterns of the opening lines, where the repetition of consonants and consonant clusters (t, c and sc), and the chain of vowel sounds ('Tabor ... door ... corduroy ... green ... spleen ... tweak ... peak ... seen ... capping ... scalp ... scamper ... noise ... boys ... evacuees ... teasing') provide a jaunty tune to accompany the action:

> We had gone down to Tabor, to the door
> My corduroy a green
> Tug at the ministerial spleen, a tweak
> At the white scarf-knot, peak in pocket seen
> Capping the diaconate,
> In time to scalp the noise
> And scamper made by boys, evacuees
> With paper aeroplanes the teasing wind
> Forced down behind the chapel rails.

'Balloon Over the Rhondda' was subsequently included in the Faber anthology *Modern Welsh Poetry*, edited by Keidrych Rhys (1944), which placed Mathias for the first time in company with Idris Davies, Alun Lewis, David Jones, Emyr Humphreys, Vernon Watkins, Ormond Thomas (John Ormond), R. S. Thomas and Dylan Thomas. However, he knew nothing of the work of his fellow contributors and would continue largely oblivious of it for some time to come.

The poet now considers 'Pastorale' the better poem, indeed, the best thing in the book. It is related to an earlier, and more serious, prose account of a bus journey from Merthyr Tydfil to Brecon (see Notes p. 302) that contains several clues to the origins of images that appear in the poem: 'little Caesar' in the opening lines casts a long Roman shadow to the end of the poem; the 'well-sprung flight' of the bus has its echo in the final lines quoted below; the 'sizzling heat', the 'bare shoulders' and the 'sheen on the shoulders of the Beacons' are common to both; the poem's 'crosses in the valley' have far greater significance in the prose piece, where they are shown to mark the graves of people from mining communities. The time would come when meditation on the harshness of such lives would become a defining characteristic of Mathias's poetry.

The choice of the French word *pastorale* as title is mysterious. The poem presents a contrast of town and country, but without the deeper element of criticism of the former one might expect in conventional pastoral writing. Perhaps the poet's English studies had been abandoned before he could gain that understanding. Those in French, however, might well have supplied a suitably loose working definition of pastoral romance as essentially comedy, and that is what we have in 'Pastorale' – a light-hearted, playful treatment of a journey along a familiar route.

The poem reveals him enjoying the company of his fellow passengers on the bus. The ordinary folk who mount and dismount are characterized and the conductor, Daio, who knows them all, has a leading role. There is just a hint of the mock-heroic in the telling of the tale, but the poem has a quality of human warmth and sympathy that distinguishes it even from those previously noted as dealing with chapters in the poet's emotional life. The language is playful, too, the imagery more complex, more concentrated, more ambiguous:

> So to the pinprick roofs and
> Voiding the motif, voices, mountain sun
> We pressed a hundred springs across the pool,
> Clipping our odorous texture with a punctual knife,
> Dragging the toga of the higgledy town.

This is a long way from the traditional craft of rhyming stanzaic verse and a clearer demonstration of the poet's enjoyment of language for its own sake. Closely viewed now at the end of the journey, the roofs of the town are etched as sharp as a pin, as they rise 'higgledy'(-piggledy) up the side of the hill in toga-like folds. The talkative human cargo, part of the pastoral 'motif', along with its collective memory of the sunlit mountains, has bounced on the bus's 'hundred springs' across the 'pool' of Usk, itself fed by a hundred springs, to arrive and disembark (with a punctuality as neat as the conductor's clipping of tickets) in Brecon, close to the confluence of Roman roads and overlooked by a Roman 'gaer'. Leaving the odours of the crowded and overheated vehicle, the passengers themselves for a time become town-dwelling toga-ed citizens. The passage is impressionistic, its rhetoric an ornament of understanding rather than an impenetrable barrier.

Enthusiasm for *Days Enduring* was largely restricted to friends, family and pupils of the Bluecoat School in Reading. Its publisher, Arthur H. Stockwell, whom Keidrych Rhys (in a note to Mathias) declared 'a crook', did little to publicize or market the book. It was, however, noticed by Patricia Ledward (in *Poetry Review*, July–August 1943) who thought it 'authentically tuneful' and commended its 'vigorous economy and . . . nice adjectival originality' (p. 244). That apart, it attracted as little attention as most other books in those early years of the war. With the confidence inspired by the appearance of his poems in *Poetry London*, *Wales*, *The Welsh Review* and *Life and Letters To-day*, Mathias sought an established publisher for his second volume. *Break in Harvest* was added to Routledge's 'Broadway House Poetry' list in 1946, alongside volumes by John Heath Stubbs, Norman McCaig, E. J. Scovell, Geoffrey Grigson and Alex Comfort. 'Balloon Over the Rhondda' and 'Pastorale' were, understandably, given a second airing, but the book is dominated by three themes, often in combination: love, landscape and history (on the broad canvas of events distant in time as well as those more narrowly focused on the war and the poet's family).

Here, too, we find clear evidence of the influence of Hopkins on Mathias's poetry in 'Fulwell' (76). The title is the name of a Cotswold hamlet and the home (Fulwell Farm) of Molly Hawes, who would become the poet's wife, where there is a leafy lane, a 'grave dolmen' nearby and, significantly, a well. It is to this spot that he has come 'from far' (that is, Wales) to find multiple symbols of his love, concluding with the chaste reflected moon, waiting in the depths for the dipper that will draw it up.

> O mine, O tension in the main
> Unmoving helplessness, O pain
> Untenable but shaped as round
> And equal as the ungiving ground,
> How may I hold, then, tell me,
> Hold this great drop from the sound
> Of misery, keep me so that I feel
> Not empty, not feel passionless and punished?

These linked sounds, their urgency, their insistent resonating, and the questing, questioning tone, recall 'The Leaden Echo and the Golden Echo', which Hopkins subtitled 'Maidens' song from St Winifred's Well'. Much as the golden response of Hopkins's echoing well gives assurance of divine love, in 'Fulwell' the 'great drop', both a measure of depth and the epitome of life-giving water, stands for earthly affections. Images of love as a wound that, like the well, can be opened and closed or as a communion of water that brings spiritual inspiration ('come to the sharing / The drop pentecost' – though he promises a quiet response rather than an apostolic speaking in tongues) belong to traditions of religious ecstasy.

The poem seems driven by intense emotion but the pell-mell of it is

Introduction: The Development of the Poetry of Roland Mathias

cunningly crafted of rhetorical devices, repetition at several language levels again prominent among them:

> No one but you and you bold
> Can lean chafing the worn edge and peer
> Where numb the noticeable orb is cold
> And moveless, under the ledge the moon
> And the water near.

The reversal of normality that sees the beloved 'chafing the worn edge' of the well rather than being grazed by it, the construction 'moveless', the choice of 'noticeable' as epithet for the observed moon, the rearrangement of the expected order of words separating 'numb' from 'cold' and from 'orb ... moon', which are both qualifiers, and the placement of the preposition 'near' after the article and noun rather than before them, all contribute to an individual rhetoric.

Rhythm also contributes to the texture of the poem. The interaction of this with the chiming of words strongly suggests a poet whose work is mediated by the human voice. The dramatic qualities of many of the poems throughout this collection repeat the point. The notation of stresses (thus: – / — /) alongside the developing text in occasional drafts suggests that the lines were spoken aloud, or at least rehearsed in the mind's ear, in the act of composition. Mathias's recent handwritten observation on 'Hillside' (89) that he was 'doing things with rhyme and anapaest' confirms his interest in the number and position of stresses in the line. His early models in Georgian prosody would certainly have encouraged this and provided him with technical confidence and efficiency.

As with the revelation of the importance of texture, it was from Edith Sitwell's *Aspects of Modern Poetry*, particularly her chapter on Hopkins, that he gained fresh insight into the flexible use of rhythm. Even in his schooldays at Caterham, Mathias could not have failed to admire Hopkins for his intellectual and moral qualities, but the little of his poetry in the familiar anthologies would have served only to reveal that he, too, had served an apprenticeship in conventional metres. Sitwell showed there was a great deal more of instant appeal in his language.

Sitwell's opening statement – 'since [Hopkins] worked his discoveries to the uttermost point, there is no room for advancement, for development, along his lines' (p. 52) – is echoed by Mathias's remarks to Cary Archard in the interview mentioned above (p. 4). Drawing on the 'Author's Preface' to *Poems (1876–1889)*, she goes on to explain 'sprung rhythm' ('feet of from one to four syllables, and for particular effect any number of weak or slack syllables') and so on, and writes about the powerful realization of Hopkins's subjects

> ... produced not by a succession of images alone, but by the movement of lines, by the texture, and by [his] supreme gift of rhetoric. It should be realized that rhetoric is not an incrustation, a foreign body which has somehow transformed the exterior surface of a poem ... it is, instead, an immense fire breaking from the poem as from a volcano. (p. 53)

She quotes Herbert Read (from *Form in Poetry*) on Hopkins's invention of words (such as 'shinelight' and 'firedint') 'when his sensibility finds no satisfaction in current phrases'. W. H. Gardner (introducing the Penguin selection) identifies other features of his language: the readiness to take liberties with conventional grammar, the use of alliteration, assonance and internal full- and half-rhyme to create a sound texture that is an integral part of the rhythm, the rearrangement of the conventional positions of words, the employment of archaic and dialect words, the creation of compound words, the unconventional use of words (for example, nouns as verbs), the juxtaposition of colloquial and incantatory language. All are features of the style and diction of Roland Mathias's own mature poetry, yet it is only a very few poems ('Fulwell' notable among them) that have any recognizable indebtedness to Hopkins, so completely and naturally were they assimilated into his own voice. Indeed, what his acknowledged admiration for Hopkins's poems seems to have done is to release the resources of language he already possessed from his voracious reading and his study as a historian of archive materials for the creation of a personal rhetoric. Despite the strength of his adherence to the Nonconformist cause, recognition that he was incapable of sacrificing personal ambition and devoting himself to his faith to the extent Hopkins did may have contributed to the self-deprecation that characterizes a number of his more important late poems.

Mathias rejects the suggestion that his use of alliteration and assonance is influenced by a familiarity with *cynghanedd*, the system in Welsh prosody demanding strict patterns of consonants and internal rhyme. His education in England provided no such opportunity for study, and the influence of his father, who was well informed on the subject, was not strong during the poet's formative years. All the evidence confirms that, if he knew little of Welsh writers and writing in English, he knew far less of them in Welsh. Yet those elements of his style that perhaps resemble *cynghanedd* were already well established when he was writing the poems in *Break in Harvest*. It might be argued that he imbibed a feeling for Welsh metrics from Hopkins; if so, it was unconscious.

Although no other poem in *Break in Harvest* has quite the qualities of 'Fulwell', sound texturing is a constant, done occasionally in stanzaic forms that recall his first book but with greater complexity. In 'Evening: Unloading Wheat' (85), for example, the two five-line stanzas have rhymes that link the first word of the first line with the last of the second and the second syllable of the fourth line with the last of the fifth. In the first stanza also, 'logic' rhymes with 'magic' and 'hours' with 'wars'; a similar pattern is sustained in the second: 'elevator's . . . craters' and 'stars . . . wars'. As usual, alliteration augments the tune. The stanzas, too, are linked by rhymes at the end of the fourth line ('weapon . . . imprison'):

> Sesame, word of logic, or wild guess
> Towards this mandate's golden brown economy,
> Open my hand with magic, work no less
> Than Mars with this so-grained weapon
> To build unanswerable hours beyond the wars.
>
> Beneath, the elevator's spinal rattle
> Clutches the off-cart shock in an engrossing sheath.
> Christen the craters of this mind, my battle! –
> I fork off what my feet imprison,
> Tugging my guts out that the assembled stars may mark.

The poem does not present difficulties once the situation is understood (wartime, the poet in the fields helping with the wheat harvest and, unaccustomed to the effort, colloquially 'tugging [his] guts out' while the stars assemble to watch) and the common relationship of 'sesame' with both bread and magic recalled. The texture and highly structured form of the poem exemplify the poet's technical virtuosity. It is one example among many throughout Mathias's poetry of his pleasure in overcoming difficulties created by his initial casting of lines into metrical patterns of daunting complexity.

The 'love' poems in *Days Enduring* were all about partings. In this second book love is celebrated against a background composed of landscape (Cotswold, in the main), the inescapable fact of the war and a heightened sense of history. 'For M.A.H.' (77) is an exultant love lyric expressed largely in terms of historical characters and events:

> Walls cannot hold the wind against me now:
> I am the one to walk the rows at Tew

> Believing jasmine breathes the shape of you
> And Lucius Carey makes you his first bow.
>
> I am with Hampden in his ragged charge
> Hoping for Chiselhampton held or down:
> I ride with Bushell into Oxford town
> To mint the college loyalty in large.

The Notes (p. 307) explain the allusions. They expose the narrative of the past as a context that was constantly present in the mind of the poet and available, like personal memory, as another kind of texture to lend depth to his writing. 'Enstone Rock' (74) elaborates the story of Thomas Bushell (who is also the happy recipient of God's bounty in Mathias's short story 'Digression into Miracle'). The location is very near Church Enstone, where Molly was born, as is Ditchley, one of Oxfordshire's grandest eighteenth-century mansions.

'Prospect of Ditchley' (94), which describes the neglected park of the great house and is similarly rich in historical reference, provides a further example of the poet's metrical craft: the first four lines in each stanza rhyme *abba* and the first word of the third line rhymes fully with the last word of the fifth. The Thames Valley landscape of 'Lowbury Hill' (91), with its contemporary evidences of war, is steeped in the blood of battles past, going back to the Romano-Celtic period and the Anglo-Saxon invasions. 'In This Cold Room' (90) brings the war into Molly's home, where the pictures on the wall of barbarism in Roman arenas offer a mute and obscure echo of 'Armageddon over the first cloud'. Fatalism is the only possible response:

> Now when our part is life we must proffer it,
> Here in this room, out of the picture,
> To the arm and communion of death.

'Drover's Song' (71) introduces a Welsh historical dimension. The reader may assume 'Dafi Jones o Caio' is a generic drover but, as a significant figure in Nonconformism (see Notes p. 304), he allows the poet to celebrate his faith while demonstrating his technical virtuosity. No one could doubt that this jolly, atmospheric rendering of a piece of fairly recent history, with its almost regular rhyme and several levels of repetition, is meant for performance.

'The Ballad of Barroll's Daughter' (72) is the first of two long narrative poems set in the Welsh March (the second, 'The Roses of Tretower' (114), is also in ballad form); they are essentially about conflict between father and daughter over the latter's choice of lover. In 'Barroll's Daughter', Margaret defies and deceives her father in order to marry

Introduction: The Development of the Poetry of Roland Mathias

Tom Lenthall, an illiterate, brutal womanizer who cares more for his horse than for her. Rejected by her father and soon repulsed by her violent husband, she flees, taking her baby with her, and survives by becoming a servant wherever she can find work. In due time, her daughter follows her into service. The story of the wretched Margaret is the stuff of old-fashioned melodrama. It is also a piece of family history, as the concluding stanzas tell us:

> In Battle churchyard is the stone
> And long she has been lying,
> The Christian whose molested life
> Was happiest in her dying.
>
> The servant-girl was my great-grandam,
> With half my heart I court her:
> In prancing blood the other half
> Checks out on Barroll's daughter.

The poet's sympathies are with Margaret and her daughter, but the rough sexuality in the colloquialism 'checks out' is the poet's acknowledgement that the 'prancing blood' of Tom Lenthall also runs in his veins. The poem has become a vehicle for self-analysis.

In *Break in Harvest*, the rehearsal of family history is established as a major theme in Mathias's writing, as much in sober admonishment of personal frailties as for its intrinsic interest. With variations, it recurs in 'Grace Before Work' (86) and 'London Welshman' (69) – for which the short story 'Block System' offers a complete gloss. 'London Welshman' is a portrait of Shon, a 'squatter's child', carpenter and member of the extended family from Rhos Llangeler who has set himself up as a dairyman in London. His desperate longing for home is cloaked by a pathetic pretence of satisfaction ('Ah! This is the place . . . This London'). His business is profitless and his only haven from the misery of a precarious and humdrum existence is his memory of childhood, his only reassurance the knowledge that no one in London is interested or cares. If there is a moral here, it is implicit in the fate of Shon, who is ashamed to admit failure by returning to the Rhos, and in the sympathy of the writer.

From 'Grace Before Work' we learn that the conjuring up of ancestors, actually the historian's careful mapping of his family tree, is an obligation the writer must accept or else turn his back on Wales ('go home / No more'). The physical characteristics of his father's family, 'dark, long-headed men', are identified here for the first time and will be reiterated often in poems and short stories, just as their

Introduction: The Development of the Poetry of Roland Mathias

Nonconformist faith practised in the simplest of Independent chapels will be celebrated. His self-deprecatory image as 'The last-born, least-bred herb twopence / Of the soil' will also be repeated, though not in the same words, along with a sense of his unworthiness of the richer rewards life has brought him compared with that first antecedent, Thomas, the carpenter of Maengwyn, 'to whom fell / Much less of tack and harvest'.

In the language of 'Grace Before Work' we see how the assiduous exercise of metrical skills and Hopkins's influence developed the muscular strength of Mathias's poetry. The rhythm of the lines is based on a variable pattern of stresses. The sound texture is woven of occasional end-rhymes, including 'fixity . . . prolixity', half-rhymes ('germ . . . warm . . . harm'), internal rhymes ('unbettered . . . unlettered'), and the lingering echo ('more . . . moor . . . doors . . . door', 'Floor[cloth] . . . door'). The diction admits archaisms ('simples', 'plenish'), unusual words ('exordium') and compound ones ('fine-win dreams', 'bed-silver Usk', 'backbreak past'), one at least doubled ('last-born, least-bred').

The bounds of conventional syntax have been stretched. The poem begins, as it were, in the middle of an elliptical sentence, part of a confession or catalogue of faults: 'Then in remembering I do not enough / To integrate the present with the past.' In the next three lines the rhythm is preserved by a rearrangement of word order, separating 'I' from its qualifying phrases ('The last-born . . . soil'); in the process, the archaic 'plenish' loses its infinitive marker ('I must try . . . plenish). The imagery is often compressed and occasionally ambiguous. The general meaning of 'Making the cast with simples' is sufficiently clear: it is part of the self-imposed injunction to recall, conjure up, the ancestral past, but the use of 'cast' (albeit as a noun) hints at both magic and the sowing of seeds while the herbal 'simples' relate to his low estimation of himself as the 'last-born, least bred [twopenny] herb' to spring from that soil. The strange rhyming constructions 'exordium of fixity' and 'saved landlords from prolixity' give the reader pause, but 'fixity' is a synonym for permanence and 'exordium' for a beginning, though it is used out of its usual oratorical context; 'prolixity' suits well enough the constant nagging of tenants by landlords, not extended to the squatters on the moor. The lines that have Thomas Maengwyn, founding father of the line, 'spread on the certain tenter / Floorcloth of fine-win dreams, bursting the door / Higher above the mud identical' simulate, with sound and image, the wonder of the achievement of building a house on common mud and raising a family that would reach out into the world. They also challenge the reader to engage imaginatively with phrases like 'certain tenter', another unexpected rhyme (with 'carpenter') which

Introduction: The Development of the Poetry of Roland Mathias

alludes to the firmly fixed hooks on which the humble tapestry of the family's dreams is hung, and then to visualize how the height of the doorway rises with the elevation of the family's aspirations.

The 'rank discomfiture of green' in the second paragraph is synonymous with 'the scum of the forests' in R. S. Thomas's later poem 'Reservoirs'. This section compares the relatively fertile landscape around Brecon, where his parents had moved after his father's retirement, with the barren moor that was the lot of 'the first builder'. The final six lines are self-instructive: the poet, who in his easier life represents the best hopes of his peasant ancestors, must memorialize them so that, by his desk labour, they too may have some part in the more comfortable present.

'Grace Before Work' demands to be read aloud for the release of its incantatory power. In this as well as in its subject and message it resembles many later poems. It contributes to the assessment of *Break in Harvest* as transitional for, with this book, the foundations of Mathias's poetic career are laid. Henceforth, readers would be familiar with the characteristic features of his voice and his major themes.

Break in Harvest was reviewed quite widely in Wales and England. Pennar Davies, broadcasting on the Welsh Home Service (28 April 1947), considered the book too 'elusive and exacting' to be dealt with adequately in a few minutes, but recognized the poet's 'highly personal style'. He thought Gerard Manley Hopkins was probably 'his chief master' and described Mathias first as 'a poet of moods, subtle and complex moods of hope and melancholy and doubt and longing' and a little later as one 'of contemplation . . . lost in the midst of the wonder and terror of the world'. The *TLS* reviewer (19 April 1947) imagined he saw 'a tug in [Mathias's] poetry between two idioms, Welsh and English' that made language for him 'a more intractable medium' (compared with other Routledge poets), but could still conclude 'There is solid promise in this volume'. E. P. Thompson, the historian, in *Our Time* (June 1947) thought Mathias 'a poet of pale transient moods' who, at his most successful, 'achieves neat water-colour sketches . . . But he tries to do more, and there is obscurity here as well – springing not from any complexity but from lack of poetic stamina and intellectual guts.' Writing in *Tribune* (25 April 1947), Naomi Lewis detected ' a fresh and pleasant manner, suggesting, in a general way, Edward Thomas'. At first, her reading of the poems suggested that the poet 'is not bookish' but 'presently there are hints that this is an illusion. "Fulwell" and the attractive "Prospect of Ditchley" are not naive

Introduction: The Development of the Poetry of Roland Mathias

poems. And [quoting from "Lowbury Hill"] there is the Hopkins-echo.' She concluded:

> The suggestion of concealed poetic sophistication makes it difficult to guess how his work will develop . . . But this collection should please those who like their poetry cheerful and pastoral, for Mr Mathias gives the impression of being neither tortured nor doomed, and prefers the sunlight of Wales to the cold stone. (p. 19)

Virtually all the reviewers grasped some aspect of the poet's art and intention but even the most sympathetic could not perceive his religious commitment and the essential seriousness of his examination of himself, especially in relation to his forebears.

Mathias's salary at the Bluecoat School in Reading was £100 per annum. As a young married man whose wife had recently given birth to twins, he badly needed to make some progress in his teaching career. Jobs were still hard to come by, but he secured a temporary post as junior history master at Carlisle. Thus *Break in Harvest* ends with 'Going' (95), a poem from the summer of 1945 about the poet's family 'out on a tangent from the torn circle / Of friends', travelling in a jolting lorry to a new home in the north. Their destination was a small house, one of a row built originally for 1914–18 naval personnel, on the outskirts of Gretna, close to the shore of Solway Firth. It was a far cry from the Cotswolds and Reading. As he travelled by bus daily the nine miles to Carlisle, the landscape of this northerly region imprinted itself on his mind.

The poems that begin Mathias's next book, *The Roses of Tretower*, 'Solway' (96), 'New Year's Day, 1946' (97), 'The Lurking Ancestor' (98) and 'From a Bus at Crosby, Cumberland' (99), reflect that desolation. Though still stitched together with rhyme, they have structures somewhat less wrought than those in the previous volume. Nevertheless, they display familiar features of the poet's rhetoric. In 'Solway', for example, we meet alliterative texturing; rearrangement of word order at the imperative of rhythm ('The restless claw-marks on the shore of birds'), which simultaneously affords a duality of meaning; visual and aural imagery that incorporates word play ('Wall holds the cropped farm up', 'the slapped tide lies') and idiosyncratic and bookish diction ('perorate', 'vogue', 'paltered'). There is, too, the striking metaphor of the unstoppable 'ego' of the tide and (surely with horse-drawn conveyances in mind) the image of a cloud streaming away from the mountain as 'Skiddaw and his cabby's breath'. The historian's feeling

Introduction: The Development of the Poetry of Roland Mathias

for place is, as ever, complicated by his sense of the past, but here the figure called up, Paul Jones (see Notes p. 312), is no mere decoration but, with his 'turning knife' (his propensity to change allegiance), suggestive of the theme – as is the tide 'ego' metaphor. The poem describes the affliction of change for both old and young. The teacher, on his way to school, meditates on his pupils, their voices breaking, growing to rebelliousness and vice, and on the ironic (or hypocritical) condemnation of wayward youth by the old, who were themselves no different.

Three further poems draw upon the landscape of the Solway Firth and the sentinel hulk of Skiddaw to the south, 'The Lochmaben Stone' (104), 'The Mountain' (105) and 'Searching Spring' (106). The Notebooks show that, although the first was 'roughed out' in Gretna, the last two were written some time later, 'The Mountain' during the Christmas holiday, December 1946–January 1947, and 'Searching Spring' at Easter 1947. By this time the writer had returned to a permanent teaching post in the south and was living in North Harrow, Middlesex.

There is then no immediate reason for the unremitting gloom of much of 'The Mountain' before the great reassurance of 'Comfort ye, comfort ye, my people' begins the riposte to what Mathias described to me as the 'jeremiad' of the first fifty-five or so lines. Clearly, the poem owes a great deal to his experience in the north. Here again are explicit references to school ('I / Am busy with catcalls in the expected quiet'; 'I come home slowly with a careworn mouth') and also to his temporary post at Carlisle and the family's rented accommodation ('The piece I paid for grows its galls . . . shortened lease'), although in the context of the rant ('O for all stiffer pedants . . .', etc.) that precedes and includes these lines, they might easily be mistaken for images of some other human affliction.

In the opening sections, the raw topography of the shoreline symbolizes a state of mind penetrated by Christian doubt:

> I have been here in the fields a year
> And never felt so far, desperately
> Far from the course of Christ
> And of His star.

The distant peak represents the 'counterspirit', God's promise of mercy to the sinner who repents. The prayer that ends the poem, 'Give me the punishment that saves, / A mountain ministry, appraising Lord', is a passionate plea for a life dedicated to worthy toil. Failure to achieve or live up to this aspiration would remain a constant thorn in the all-too-

Introduction: The Development of the Poetry of Roland Mathias

human flesh, a motive for self-deprecation and theme for poetic contemplation.

There is no escaping the bleakness of 'Solway' and the other three poems that open the book, all written directly out of the Gretna experience. They surely reflect the poet's state of mind as he strove to come to terms with the place, his own precarious position at Carlisle Grammar School and his pressing family responsibilities. In conversation, Mathias has been concerned to show that life in Gretna was by no means as dismal as the poetry would seem to imply. He quickly made new friends in the north and was successful as a teacher, to the extent that, though a new and temporary member of staff, he would from time to time discipline the classes of a colleague (hence 'busy with catcalls in the expected quiet'). He helped organize extra-curricular activities for the boys, took part in a staff-pupil drama production and performed in a play that was staged by a local amateur dramatic society.

As we have seen, the Gretna poems were completed between September 1945 and May 1946, mostly during school holidays. This creative spurt owed a great deal to his success in catching the eye of J. R. Ackerley, distinguished editor of *The Listener*, the journal of BBC radio broadcasting, which then played an important role in artistic and cultural affairs. Mathias's success in placing 'Solway', the first of his poems to appear in the magazine, may have influenced the tone of most of the other five that followed in quick succession. More generally, however, he was not at this time (or at any other) a prolific writer; the consuming busyness of the school term allowed him little scope for composition. It became his habit instead to write poems and short stories, or at least to polish earlier drafts, while holidaying with his parents in Brecon or at the home of Molly's sister in Offenham, near Evesham.

An interest in Thomas Bushell, the historical character first encountered at Enstone, later prompted holidays in Aberystwyth that allowed him to visit the National Library and explore the old silver mines nearby. These studies ended in disappointment, because the research on the silver mines had already been done by others, though they contributed to Mathias's creative output in prose and, as we have already glimpsed, in poetry (see p. 16). Brecon holidays gave him opportunity to visit the hamlets and walk the hills and twisting byways of the border zone of Gwent and Herefordshire (even now little changed), where he pursued his interest in the fate of Catholic recusants at the beginning of the seventeenth century. This interest was stimulated by his serendipitous discovery of the existence of relevant documents in the published catalogue of the papers of Robert Cecil, marquis of

Introduction: The Development of the Poetry of Roland Mathias

Salisbury, at Hatfield House, no more than ten miles from Offenham, at a time when he was seeking an intellectual way into Wales even though he could not yet return there to live. After some twenty years of intermittent effort, this research led to *Whitsun Riot,* a splendid example of historical detection, as well as a number of distinctive poems.

Several poems in *The Roses of Tretower* are, as it were, by-products of the poet's topographical and historical familiarity with the southern March: 'Olchon' (110), 'Craswall' (111), 'Thomas ap Richard of Doier to the Tower, These' (113). All three were seemingly begun at Brecon in August 1947 and completed soon afterwards on the poet's return to Middlesex. To these we may add 'Coed Anghred' (130), which belongs to April 1951. Craswall and the brook and valley of Olchon are near neighbours, some six miles as the crow flies south east of Hay-on-Wye; the Black Hill rises between them. Another five miles or so due east lies the Golden Valley and the northern area of the 'commotion' among Catholics in 1605 that is the subject of *Whitsun Riot*. Landscape and history are also central to 'Olchon', which celebrates a place that may well have been a modest centre of early Nonconformity. The poem is an affirmation of the welcoming embrace of the writer's own faith, conveyed in the inviting imperatives 'Go on a step' and 'Come ... Nothing is wanting but the child's / Wide trust'.

The hamlet of Craswall can claim more tangible ecclesiastical links, but Mathias did not visit its ruined priory and the motive of the poem is not religious. We have seen how, as a child, he became aware of his Welshness. His sense of belonging, particularly among the roots and branches of his father's large family, was heightened by exile. 'Take me over the Border', a prose essay published in *The London Welshman* (January 1961), traces a route that passes close by Craswall and offers an extraordinarily vibrant sense of coming home:

> And so it was that ... I murmured to myself, long before the border was officially marked, 'This is it.' And felt it in the spine and along the edge of being ... Sometimes I school myself to forget it, to let myself be surprised, even to be lost in talk and to come alive un-noticing. But the plan never succeeds. Spine and tongue will not let it, if will eye.

'Craswall' has the same theme and the same intensity of feeling, although the expression of it is tightly controlled, so that readers can be surprised by the discovery in the final stanza that 'This is the boundary ... [where] ... nightingales / Struggle with thorn-trees for the gate of Wales'. The 'road down' is that leading home.

'Thomas ap Richard of Doier to the Tower, These' was the first thread wound into one of the most idiosyncratic strands in Mathias's work, the direct poetic interpretation of history. The diction on this occasion is not imitative of seventeenth-century speech or writing; later poems touching upon the same episode and in a similar mode would be more coloured with archaisms and syntactical ruggedness. The aim is to offer a ballad-like account of the aftermath of a historical event. Though the title suggests an epistolary form, there is nothing in the poem to support that premise. The 'letter' is of course pure fiction. There are fewer difficulties in it than the poet's rhetoric sometimes affords and it is sufficiently meaningful without recourse to historical references. In any event, should the reader – or the listener – expect instant and total intelligibility? Is it not enough that we get, in this instance, the gist of armed conflict, the unsuccessful defence of 'the true faith' and the threat of death hanging over the defeated leader? This was clearly the poet's intention, because no prose gloss was added to the text. Although the Notes (p. 317) explain various particulars, it is doubtful whether the poem is any the better for them. One might observe in passing that, in *Whitsun Riot*, 'Vaughan of New Court in the valley' is more properly identified as '[Rowland] Vaughan of Whitehouse' – a reminder that the poet's sense of language and rhythm overrode his concern for historical precision.

'A Letter' (125), a product of the summer holiday in 1949, marks a considerable advance in this epistolary mode. Again the poem rhymes, but subtly; some are half-rhymes and, because of the prevalence of run-on lines, part of a trick of vernacular informality. The language mixes the colloquial ('Eight years ago come Tuesday'; 'Mad you had made me, Ellen Skone'; 'Well that was it!'; 'As a matter of fact, and my close / Friends do tell me . . . '), a scrap of dialect ('scrallion') with the linguistic invention of 'talked my tongue out of duty', 'the whole cliff laboured under frown', 'Brawned out a bit', 'a twenty-oner', and flashing images such as 'Big as a brown wind', 'the sun came down / Like a bakestone'. Put simply, it has a distinctive voice, compounded of irritation and desperation, which is and yet is not the poet's own. Read aloud, it has the tone of a letter. The poem also exemplifies the dramatic quality often observable in Mathias's verse, which might remind us of his experience as an actor and his ease in public performance. Attributes such as these, occasionally hinted at in the earlier books, are now handled with sureness and complement his control of extensive resources of language.

'Remember Charlie Stones, Carpenter' (126) belongs to the same summer of 1949. By this time, Mathias was settled in Pembroke Dock but exploration of Breconshire and the border continued, as on the occasion of the visit to Capel-y-ffin that inspired the poem. This was taken in the company of an artist friend, Eric Peyman, the illustrator of *The Roses of Tretower*. Given its theme – the inevitability of death and dissolution, and the unknown destination of the soul – the opening section is strangely playful in tone. The ambiguities of the question that opens the second paragraph bring the reader up short. The 'proportions' of Charlie the carpenter are both those of his being and of the artefacts he has created, and judgement is passed on them in a frame of 'time' that is earthly for the one and eternal for the other.

Like a change of gear, the question starts the poem's engine running on a new note. As the language gathers biblical echoes, the tone becomes liturgical, incantatory:

> Or did this bowl
> Of hills burn like an August offering to the Lord
> So that your soul cursed it
> Three times with force and was afraid,
> Prating as ill as I?

This elicits a response that does not satisfy, for the body melting underground does not see or feel, and the question is rephrased – 'Are you bound there, Charlie? By one or many?' – God or Satan? Of course, there can be no answer. The poem ends with the enigmatic rattle of a coin in a collection box and a sober (if obscurely expressed) recognition of common mortality. The imagery, the occasional archaism, the mix of colloquial and incantatory, the linguistic inventiveness, the compression and muscularity and increasingly dense texturing of the verse as the poem reaches its climax all pronounce it characteristic of the poet's maturity.

The Roses of Tretower has a good deal more to stimulate the reader responsive to linguistic virtuosity. 'Hawk' (115) and 'Freshwater West' (123), less complex than 'Fulwell', share the latter's varieties of rhyme, its strong rhythmic pulse, its alliterative and onomatopoeic patterning. The landscape and weather of 'Hawk' are characteristically Mathias ('Grey clouds . . . Buffet and Jehu-crack' and 'cart-tracks stiff and red / Pointing like chapped fingers from the gate'), while 'Freshwater West' describes and, in movement and sound suggests, the clash of sea and land. Neither poem, however, is merely descriptive. The borrowing from Donne in 'Freshwater West' ('Broken like sand from off the human coast') emphasizes its allegorical reference to the ebb and flow of life while the 'Cruel, nonchalant' bird of prey suggests 'nemesis', death falling upon the meek and innocent. They are further examples of poems that serve the writer's thought-provoking purposes.

Mathias's liking for the metaphorical presentation of ideas is illustrated most clearly by 'Riddle' (129), a series of images representing

Introduction: The Development of the Poetry of Roland Mathias

stages in the life of man and, more particularly, of the poet himself as he struggles to tame his garden in an 'urban tower', his new home at Pembroke Dock. The writing is a little less oblique in 'Judas Maccabeus' (102), a poem on the same theme and employing the same allegorical approach as the short story 'Saturday Night'. It describes a performance of Handel's oratorio at The Plough, the historically significant Congregationalist chapel in Brecon, which his father and, much later, he himself regularly attended. The title poem of the book (114) began as a short story bearing the same name, 'The Roses of Tretower', and has a romantically supernatural climax. An extensive range of rhetorical devices, including allegory (admitting at the close an element of Christian mystery), is employed in its ballad-like retelling. The poet's interest in the Vaughans of Tretower extended from the early 1950s to 1986, when illness forced him to suspend his fresh biographical study of Vaughan. The particulars of sunshine, grave mound, yew trees in 'On the Grave of Henry Vaughan at Llansaintffraed' (108) owe a little to Mathias's feeling for place, another constant that emerges clearly from a survey of his poetry, but the poem is more notable for its display of the development of his linguistic powers, culminating in the exultant incantation of the third stanza.

'The Tyle' (131), 'The Flooded Valley' (116) and 'Returning' (132) have much the same purpose as 'Grace Before Work' (discussed on pp. 17–19), confirming the poet's self-appointed role as memorialist. The first stanza of 'The Tyle' presents another admission of guilt that, in his pride (engendered by a comfortable existence), he does not sufficiently acknowledge his debt to those who laboured long for small returns before him. 'The Flooded Valley' shares a number of circumstantial details with the short story 'Ffynnon Fawr', which fictionalizes his return to his birthplace. The mobile 'boots' in the line beginning the second section, for instance, are a lively extension of the story's 'boot, obese with the pressure of bones and mud', standing before the empty fireplace in the bedroom of the derelict farmhouse. The poem, however, speaks for all the dispossessed families ('Kedward, Prosser, Morgan') whose life and livelihood in Glyn Collwn are now marked only by chapel tombstones (see Notes p. 319). The power of incantation is again released by textural devices and other elements of the poet's rhetoric, such as the syntactical reorganization of the penultimate line to separate 'poor' from 'stone', the noun it qualifies. The episode that inspired 'Returning' is the poet's return with his own children to The Tyle, the first farm of his grandfather Joseph Morgan. The visit took place in 1951, three years after the composition of 'The Flooded Valley', but its theme is much the same: the sense of loss, of grief at the severed connections with the past and of the need to celebrate 'God's hosts', the departed in the Lord, who in 'shoot and stem' live still.

In September 1952, angered by a cock-eyed review that perceived links between *The Roses of Tretower* and the prose of Cledwyn Hughes and Rhys Davies, Mathias wrote a letter to the editor of *Poetry* (the magazine of the British Poetry Association) in which he specifically denied the 'Welshness' of his writing other than as it might occur because 'the reflections of the author are aroused by a feeling for place'. He had lived in Pembroke Dock for four years, and had played a major part in the founding of *Dock Leaves*, the most important contribution to the development of Anglo-Welsh writing in the 1950s, but he did not see that his own poetry, which he considered 'metaphysical', had 'any real concern with people, community or social feeling, in a way that one could conceivably define as Welsh'. (His family roots were clearly another matter.) This may seem perverse but it was the case as he saw it. He had grown up in exile, visiting Wales only for holidays while he progressed through a stereotypically English education at independent school and Oxford. He had taught, until Pembroke Dock, only at schools in England. All the influences that bore upon him, not least the poetry he read, were English. Yet he had a profound inner certainty of belonging to Wales. There is a tension here, but the Welsh March is temperamentally his home and being on the border, both insider and outsider, is constantly creative, as many of the poems show.

It was the first, and last, time he wrote to complain about a review. Largely through exercising his own critical faculties for *Dock Leaves*, he was even then learning about Anglo-Welsh literature and preparing for his role as one of its major apologists. Through the 1960s, in lectures, articles and (subsequently, as editor of *The Anglo-Welsh Review*) editorials, he argued the merits of Welsh writing in English and denounced its absence in the curricula of schools and higher education institutions in Wales and its neglect by London-based publishers and reviewers. He sought, too, an improvement in the standard of literary criticism in Wales, and in his own reviews and essays provided a model of the scrupulous attention to texts that became more usual once Anglo-Welsh writing had gained greater academic respectability in the University of Wales.

Poems included in *The Roses of Tretower* had first appeared in a variety of magazines with wide reputations at home and abroad, including *Wales, The Welsh Review, The Listener, Outposts, Poetry Chicago, Poetry Commonwealth* and *Tribune*. The book was published by Dock Leaves Press and printed by Gwasg Gomer, thereby beginning a long association with J. D. Lewis and Sons Ltd. It was, in the main, approvingly reviewed, though the erroneous perception of indebtedness to Dylan Thomas, from A. G. Prys Jones (in the *Western Mail*) and R. S. Thomas (in *Dock Leaves*) among others, must have been galling. R. S. also raised the 'vexed question of intelligibility', while conceding that certain poems presented 'an individual attitude in a fresh way' and used language that was 'taut and robust', unlike the 'flabby insipidity of much contemporary verse'. Richard Church, in the *Observer*, wrongly thought the 'elaborate build up' of the verse forms owed 'much to the laws of Welsh prosody', but saw in the poems 'the expression of a lively mind, vigorous and ruthless'. 'This is odd, abrupt poetry' he went on,

> that makes 'the listening spine creep to the brain' (a characteristic line). It has 'rocks and stones and trees' hurled round in it, symbols of moods and thoughts that make a harsh mental scenery, but often impressive, intimidating, with outbreaks of beauty like sunshine through evening thunder.

Norman Nicholson (in *British Weekly*, 25 December 1952) declared the book had given him much pleasure. 'If poetry were read today, he would surely be popular', he wrote:

> he reflects the contemporary sensibility in a way which is not outside the scope of the contemporary reader. For instance, he has an eye, quick, particular, peculiar, like that of a modern painter . . . He has also . . . an ear for contemporary speech and for that cross-stitch of rhyme and assonance which binds the lines together.

Mathias himself ensured that it reached the hands of some whose views he respected. Glyn Jones's response was typically disarming: 'What you write always impresses me as the work of a true poet. I am sometimes insincere in my judgements, usually out of kindness of heart, but I never say anything as specific as that without meaning it.' Gwyn Jones, who had accepted some of the poems for *The Welsh Review*, wrote to say the volume had given him much pleasure,

> because I so much admire and enjoy your poetry. It is a *damned* sight better than that of many enjoying fancy reputations merely because their friends control various review columns . . . I thought strongly as I was reading your poems that your voice is your own. Your idiom and language, the turn of phrase and rhythm, sound like *you*. The poems are distinctive.

R. S. Thomas's review is intriguing. He rarely accepted reviewing jobs and probably took on *The Roses of Tretower* as a favour to the editor of *Dock Leaves*, Raymond Garlick, with whom he was on friendly terms. He reveals his alienation from fellow writers in Wales at the outset by referring to Mathias (only two years younger and earlier in the field as a published poet) as 'one of the younger members of the, by this time, tatterdemalion school of Anglo-Welsh writers'. The tone of the review is stiff throughout and, where it is not critical, it usually offers faint praise. One of the few favourable observations is that Mathias 'is conscious of Wales as a different country from England', wherein we recognize a poetic preoccupation of the reviewer. What surprises most, since he was both practising poet and Anglican priest, is that Thomas does not once acknowledge the many poems in the book that have Christian themes or allusions.

In his role of man of letters, which began to develop soon after his arrival in Pembroke Dock in 1948 and grew exponentially following his return to Wales in 1969, Mathias gave far closer attention to Thomas's poetry than he received in the *Dock Leaves* review. He concentrated particularly on the other writer's religious philosophy, which was the theme of the article he wrote for the R. S. Thomas special number of *Poetry Wales* (7, 4, 1972) and was returned to in the reviews he wrote subsequently. He invariably recognized Thomas's great strengths as a writer but could not conceal his disappointment with some of the religious and moral messages the poetry conveyed: 'I should have liked to feel that through the struggle of a poet who is also a priest (and who wasn't quite so glib about equating the two functions) I was being shown something that might be my struggle too.' (Review of *H'm*, *The Anglo-Welsh Review*, 21, 48, 1972, pp. 201–3)

There are two other points of contact. Both Mathias and Thomas wrote poems about Maesyronnen, the dilapidated 300-year-old chapel in Radnorshire. Mathias's 'Maesyronnen' (61), the earlier, is in part inspired by the evangelical spirit that spread from the place and records the historical antipathy of the Puritan founding fathers towards the Anglican Church. Thomas notes 'the stale piety mouldering within' and is more interested in birds singing in the rafters. Much later, in 'Sir Gelli to R.S.' (184), Mathias adopted the persona of a figure he knew well from his research in connection with *Whitsun Riot* to correct an unsympathetic portrait in Thomas's 'Sir Gelli Meurig (Elizabethan)'.

We can draw no conclusion about the relationship between the two writers on the basis of either poem. Nor is there much to be made of their different views about Welsh culture and identity, except to observe that, characteristically, Mathias challenged his own instincts of national exclusivity and found them flawed (for example in 'Porth Cwyfan', see page 41). But there is no sense here or elsewhere of mutually repelling poles. As poets, each steered his course without reference to the other. For his part, although as a critic he was obliged to consider them, as a poet, Mathias denies ever looking over his shoulder at the attitudes adopted by his near contemporary to religious belief, morality and society.

By 1960, when his next collection came out from Putnam, the poet had already been two years in a new job at Belper, Derbyshire. *The Flooded Valley*, advertised as his first book, though actually his fourth, contains twenty-five poems that had appeared in *The Roses of Tretower*. Eight new poems represent the years 1952–60. These include, however, foreshadowings of developments in thought and technique that were to gather momentum through the 1960s. They are rhyming poems that display the range of the poet's distinctive rhetoric. In several, the compression of language challenges the reader, although concern with the process of ageing and the awareness that brings of the proximity of death emerges clearly enough from virtually all. They are, too, outdoor poems, their melancholy arising from a meditative interaction with landscape, ancient churchyards and a dilapidated mansion.

The poet recollects that the impulse of 'An Age' (133) was an outing with his children to pick blackberries at Cosheston, Pembrokeshire. That fact has no part in the poem, but the unacknowledged presence of the children has a great deal to do with awareness of age for one who, as a child, himself picked blackberries. For once it is an autumn poem with the conventional association of fruitfulness, but the 'envelope' (a frequent metaphor for the containing air, light, atmosphere of a scene or event) 'has let an age escape', his unconsciousness of the toll of years. 'Conversation at Stackpole Head' (137) is an internal debate about time and man's ignorance of the coming hour of his departure. The rhetorical devices in 'Marston Sicca' (139), not least its uncommonly archaic diction, give due warning of the concentration and seriousness of its contemplation of death-in-life. 'Cascob' (141) has in it something of the matter and, in the shaft of colloquial levity ('For two pins / I'd leave in a hurry'), something of the manner of that other graveyard poem remembering Charlie Stones (126). The same question of whether the soul ascends to God or goes to the devil is repeated here, in a physical and metaphysical borderland, near Offa's Dyke, where the church belfry stands on a pagan 'druid's mound'.

Anticipating the elegiac current that runs strongly through the poems of the next decade, 'For Warren Davies, Two Years Dead' (143) establishes the poet as self-appointed 'remembrancer' of those whose lives were worthy of celebration. The syntax, imagery and style of the poem are complex but do not obscure the portrait:

> ... the clematis
> With which you set our hill court in purple
> Twice is page again, and up the lattice
> Creeps. How slip, how preening cast of yours, can it recouple
> This switch of land to you and greenly in it
> Grapple your ailing hand?
>   It was cold,
> Cold of a Sunday morning early in Church Street
> When you turned in your sleep, and old
> Morning, at last unmanned, curtained his gold.

The Editorial Note (p. 293) explains the inclusion in the present volume of a further four poems that were omitted from *The Flooded Valley* but, even with this addition, it is not a large harvest for the later years at Pembroke Dock. Perhaps poetry had been further squeezed into a corner of the writer's life by the demands of the local community and, for a time, by short story writing: *The Eleven Men of Eppynt and other stories* was published in 1956.

The influence of Putnam, a London-based publisher, obtained a fresh set of reviews, some in respected metropolitan newspapers and journals. It is at this point that certain analytical views and descriptive terms begin to crystallize around Mathias's work. In the BBC radio *Bookmark* programme broadcast on 12 October 1960, Raymond Garlick spoke of the poet's language as 'taut, sinewy, knotted, drawing rarely exercised words into its stretch and flexure'. The poems, he thought, were 'an expression of an uncompromising, analytic and highly individual sensibility'. The *TLS* reviewer (30 September 1960) noted the 'exact imagist portrayal of Welsh town and country scenes' and then elaborated:

> [but] clear descriptive power is not an end in itself in the best of Mr Mathias's poems. There, the few taciturn, rather stoically unhappy references to himself give another point to the details of the scene around him. They are not simply symbols of his moods, they are real things; but one sees that he is driven to this hard appreciative looking at them because he feels their slight beauty is all that there is ... [his] sound play ... is equally fine for his purpose.

Elizabeth Jennings, writing in the *Guardian* (21 October 1960), was equally impressed:

> Mr Mathias looks at landscapes and sees not a tranquil collection of forms but a gathering of diverse energies ... This is a violent and vivid world. Even when [he] writes about people, he sees them more as potential sources of dangerous energy than as compact and orderly

personalities ... *The Flooded Valley* is a forceful and disturbing collection of poems.

Qualified praise came from the *Observer* (18 December 1960) where Al Alvarez considered it an uneven book:

> His theme is mostly landscape: landscape made odd and upsetting by the eye of the beholder, yet upset also by his fragmentary rhetoric ... [The] mixture of trite poeticisms with touches of genuine subtlety ... is typical of Mr Mathias's hit-or-miss style. At one moment he can be striking the weariest rhetorical postures, then suddenly he will pull out a line or two of real poetry.

With far more space at his disposal, Glyn Jones (in *The Anglo-Welsh Review*, 10, 26, 1960) could illustrate his generally enthusiastic response to the book. He remarks first the poet's technical skill and 'mastery of whatever language he wishes to use' and his adherence to 'strictly contemporary themes':

> I don't mean H-bombs and space travel ... but what happens in the heart, mind and imagination ... you couldn't find more poetic subjects than these anywhere. That is, when someone so accomplished, so skilful, so sensitive and aware as Roland Mathias handles these themes, the result is poetry. (p. 72)

While praising the poetry as 'the sort, once you give yourself to it, that won't leave you alone', he also expresses his disappointment that it occasionally leaves him baffled. He begins the charge oddly:

> His work lacks on the whole a superficial glitter, the verbal interest which would make it attractive to those repelled at first, perhaps, by its rather austere obscurity. For [he] is too frequently a bit of a baffler. His greatest fault is a sort of massive impenetrability. (p. 72)

Similar critical views continued to be expressed for some time, notably by Jeremy Hooker in his article 'The Poetry of Roland Mathias' (in *Poetry Wales* 7, 1, 1971). While perceiving that the writing 'enacts the hesitancies and complexities of a conscientious mind', and accepting Glyn Jones's view (in *The Dragon Has Two Tongues*) that its 'opacity' arose from an 'unremitting concern for truth', Hooker thought 'full critical justice perhaps requires the less generous observation that this opacity can be infuriating'. The article is not entirely negative. Indeed, it attempts to provide a balanced view of the poet's strengths and weaknesses but the weight of criticism levelled against those passages of compacted language and metaphor, integral to the poetry, is severe:

Introduction: The Development of the Poetry of Roland Mathias

> Among the poems in Roland Mathias's three important collections there are some that can be understood only with a degree of concentration exceeding even that which Shakespeare in the language of *Troilus and Cressida* demands. (p. 8)
>
> *Break in Harvest* ... is in parts almost as maddening to read as the period apocalyptics that for a time claimed even Vernon Watkins ... [The] same syntactic and imagistic originality that sustains ['Pastorale' and 'Balloon Over the Rhondda'] also overreaches itself, becoming tortuously compressed and oblique to the point of incomprehensibility. (p. 9)

The reference to 'the period apocalyptics' is erroneous or misleading, for they were no more a part of Mathias's poetic education than they were of Dylan Thomas's, who was also invoked by reviewers from time to time. In conversation, Mathias's response to these and other such comments is impatient. He expects the reader or listener to be sufficiently attentive at least to gather the broad meaning of a poem and to find intellectual stimulation in the display of linguistic effects rather than being deterred by them. If scholars want to unravel the knottier tangles of his rhetoric, that is their business. In this respect, the comparison with Shakespeare is apt.

The twenty-three new poems composed in the decade following *The Flooded Valley*, though numerically unimpressive, have remarkable qualities. But, again, we have to ask why there are so few of them. His Notebook II shows that a change occurred in the routine of writing poems during this period. In earlier years it was a swift affair; no matter how complex the versification, poems would be finished in four or five drafts, having emerged in substantially their final form in the first. The poems of the 1960s tended to be roughed out and put aside, often for several months, before being amended and usually worked on once or twice again some time later before they were considered finished. This more protracted, discontinuous process was partly a consequence of his professional devotion to his job as headmaster at Belper and then Birmingham. Partly, too, it came of the burden of editing *The Anglo-Welsh Review*, which he took over from Raymond Garlick in 1961. But most of all, perhaps, it was because he found it increasingly difficult to find the frame and the words he needed to express emotions and ideas that were deeply personal to him, and to be honest to his ascetic Puritan conscience. Indeed, more copious writing might have become incompatible with the poet's sense of what needed to be said: he wrote no more poems than he wanted.

Introduction: The Development of the Poetry of Roland Mathias

Mathias's upbringing locked him, happily though often assailed by doubt, into a lifetime of service to Christianity. His steadfast Nonconformist outlook has always been central to his existence. It may seem strange, therefore, that religious themes and images are uncommon in the poems of *Days Enduring* ('Inter Tenebros' being a striking exception) and *Break in Harvest*. However, they appear frequently and in a variety of contexts in *The Roses of Tretower*, where death constantly haunts life and faith is ever besieged by doubt. The poetry of the ten years or so that followed is yet more overtly and completely dominated by questions of belief and morality. The habit of self-deprecation, quietly revealed in earlier poems, is clearly manifest in the context of these Christian concerns. When *Absalom in the Tree*, Mathias's fifth collection of poems, was published in 1971, it won a Welsh Arts Council prize and prompted a close critical reappraisal of his work.

'Brynafan: First Light' (146), begun in August 1961 and completed in November 1962, sounds the keynote. The poem is richly textured: rhyme and half-rhyme, internal and at line-ends, carry a subtle tune while alliteration and assonance fill out the chords. The imagery is highly compressed. It confirms that Mathias paid little heed to reviewers' complaints about the density of his rhetoric. The experience that gave rise to the poem was a single night's sojourn at a cottage in Ceredigion owned by his brother, Alun. It opens in ventral darkness beneath the curving cruck ribs of a bedroom directly beneath the roof. The thickness of night is metaphysically linked to the dark inner workings of a full, and inhuman, stomach. This oblique imagery works as much by the power of suggestion as by direct comparison. The impression it creates almost subliminally is of unpleasant ferment and mischief in the darkness before dawn. It also confounds a man on the borders of wakefulness with a fox on the hill that is no ordinary creature of the night but 'tod on his heap / Of ages', a symbol of man's endless capacity to get up to no good. The question for the man/fox is whether he can 'pick / Heaven out beyond the cotton hill' of bedclothes or wait for the 'recovery of tricks', that is, pursue the godly way, or follow the path of the devil. In the second section, with the coming of first light, the phantasmagoria dissipates. The fearful choice offered by darkness is perceived to be unreal; no ill has been done. Day arrives in primal innocence (though the skeletal aspect of the personification is a broad enough hint that things are not all well), like a newly born kid seeking the teat. In full day, '*he*', the whole man, revives, with all his faults, and a longing to live forever, or at least long enough '[for] a last crack at ill'. At first sight, the wish of the final line seems to be for time to carry on the fight against evil. But it is ambiguous. Mathias now says it has the

Introduction: The Development of the Poetry of Roland Mathias

opposite meaning, a last chance to do ill. The sequence of consonants mimicking snapping bones in the first lines ('Within the cruck the night / Is thick') is echoed at the end by the phrase 'last crack', which underlines the poet's conclusion: even in full light there is something of the night about all of us. Use of a metaphysical conceit that merges the identity of man and animal is not confined to this poem. It can be seen also in the snipe/man of 'Snipe's Castle' (181), for example, and, more broadly, in the complex allegory of 'Brechfa Chapel' (187). The constraints of an almost regular stanzaic structure and the extraordinary compression of 'God Is' (158) are warning enough of the emotional intensity that drives this poem. It was largely written in August 1968, while the poet was headmaster at King Edward VI Five Ways, Birmingham, and about to start his last year in the profession. The biographical reference is pertinent: it is the 'sleek' heads of pupils he has in mind in the second stanza of self-indictment, and the book-lined room in which he '[sits] so long' is the headmaster's study. He stands accused by God of equanimity ('my tranquillity') in the acceptance of his failure as a teacher (working 'against the grain' of Christian belief) to raise children in the faith. Although the poem ends with an exclamation mark, the last couplet, responding to the accusation, is clearly a question: are prayers for righteousness and grace not enough? He already knows God's answer.

Inner moral conflict is the theme of these two poems and, unexpectedly, of 'Not Worth the Record' (160), which Mathias wrote for the Welsh Arts Council's 'Dial-a-poem' service. What callers made of it is difficult to imagine, though texture and linguistic compaction are not the problems; rather, it challenges listeners because it addresses them directly and demands their own moral and intellectual response. The poem underlines the poet's conviction of his guilt and of his double failure – both to resist sinful intent and to commit the sin intended: 'What I have willed / Has rarely happened, just / As rarely as beneficence / Was my full choice.'

'The Fool in the Wood' (163), one of the group of poems arising out of a residency at the University of Brest in April 1970, concludes with a similarly harsh verdict on his inadequacy as a believer and his propensity for glibness. He sees himself unlike Salaun, the Celtic saint whose entire faith resolved itself into 'four Breton words ... two Latinate'

> ... slower to look
> Piercingly at the cost and bloat
> I have of words. Four, two, less

> Than a fraction of one is their sure
> Count Godwards, alas, for lack of a pure
> Heart and a praising gentleness.

Sins of omission and commission, the sinful thought, somehow more reprehensible because the sinner is fearful of the deed, inactivity, backsliding, failure to be strong in the true cause: these invite the severest of censures and, in the face of them, the poet does not seek to spare himself. His own sense of unworthiness, alluded to earlier in connection with 'Grace Before Work' (p. 18), returns with redoubled force in 'They Have Not Survived' (156), which concludes:

> For this dark cousinhood only I
> Can speak. Why am I unlike
> Them, alive and jack in office,
> Shrewd among the plunderers?

'They Have Not Survived' is an elegy to the 'generations of rigour', as they are termed in the short story 'A View of the Estuary'. It contributes to the pervading elegiac tone of the book, for loss and death are themes that constantly return, whether the poet surveys graveyards in Breconshire, the Borders or Brittany, or the deaths of biblical characters, Holy Fools, communities and ways of life or of close friends and family.

As we have seen, the screwing up of moral courage and the intellectual effort involved in the confessional poems about his failings in the faith predicate a complex poetic response. The writing in these poems (the earliest, 'A Last Respect' (147), dating from 1962) is more subtly textured and the language more relaxed and less rhetorically tangled, the imagery less metaphysical, than is commonly the case in *The Roses of Tretower*. This does not mark a new line of development, for readily accessible poems were always part of Mathias's resourceful modulation of language and imagery to fit the subject. 'Sarnesfield' (148), for example, has familial, historical and colloquial dimensions; it invokes a wry humour to cloak its consideration of mutability and is threaded with imagery of sun, gilding and heraldry. Its subject demands a complex response and the outcome is a poem that stylistically resembles 'Remember Charlie Stones, Carpenter'.

Although the poet's linguistic resourcefulness still admitted a measure of textural embellishment, a plain style best suited a trio of elegies all very different one from another but alike in being loving tributes to the departed. All have a kind of grandeur that arises from language that has a liturgical resonance and sweep:

Introduction: The Development of the Poetry of Roland Mathias

> ... all
> But the elm and the brass handles had air
> About it and petals flying, impassioned as
> Wings, an arc of will prescribed, mounting
> And Sion crying, quick in the eyelash second.
> ('A Last Respect')

> How long is it,
> David, long since your loins were water,
> Since you were a carpenter, wed, kept shop,
> Were poor and a theologian ...
> ('For an Unmarked Grave')

> All will be
> Grass and haze as so many times before
> Till some tight-lipped wave, beating from Greece,
> Ranks past the incoming locals and in a trice
> Lands with deadly importance on your shore.
> ('Some Tight-lipped Wave')

The elegiac mood is sustained by that most melancholy meditation on decrepitude and death, 'A Letter from Gwyther Street' (159) and even by 'Departure in Middle Age' (149), a poem of exile and loss.

As with the earlier books, historical references are plentiful in *Absalom in the Tree*, from the first poem, 'Chinon' (145), to the last, 'New Lease' (167), with its allusion to Llifiau, the Pictish warrior mentioned in the *Gododdin*. Two poems continue the series of reconstructions of historical episodes. 'Indictment' (155), a poem Mathias often performed at public readings, is a reminder also of his enthusiasm for the stage. Like the earlier poem 'A Letter', it has a distinctive tone of voice, in this case one that carries us into the midst of a courtroom drama. Its source is among the documents studied in the course of research for *Whitsun Riot* (see Notes page 334), but the language is the poet's own, a convincing imitation of early seventeenth-century diction. 'For Jenkin Jones Prisoner at Carmarthen, these' (161) takes us forward in time to the turbulence of the Civil War and the Restoration. Within an epistolary frame and a more formal stanzaic structure, it affords a further demonstration of diction that mimics that of the seventeenth century. The language, sententious, erudite, rather ponderous, and the slow rhythm of the long lines, provide a tone-portrait of 'H.V.' – Henry Vaughan. As well as his sense of history, both poems reveal the wide range of Mathias's linguistic and stylistic resources and his command of dramatic utterance.

Introduction: The Development of the Poetry of Roland Mathias

Reviewing *Absalom in the Tree* in *The Anglo-Welsh Review* (21, 47, 1972), Peter Abbs saw both 'successes and dangers attendant upon . . . historical excavation'. Among the successes he mentions the two poems considered in the previous paragraph: 'the poet projects himself into an historical figure who then becomes a living narrator, talking with the convincing and urgent rhythms of speech'. Others, considered failures, '[descend] into empty bombast [and] an unpalatable mixture of cliché, abstraction and rhetoric' (p. 202). The habit of self-deprecation, which began early and developed from book to book, he terms 'embarrassed'. Robin Fulton, in *Planet* (10, February/March 1972), thought the language manufactured: 'if the signs of effort are visible we accept them as a testimony of the craft: hence the frequent inversion, the occasional archaism, the neatly set gem culled from the dictionary that never seems to be far away', although, he conceded, 'this addiction to the resonance of his own language is qualified by a spare kind of self-regard, a self-questioning and discrimination which survive at times in spite of the means employed'. He went on to illustrate linguistic usages that 'block the reader's view entirely':

> The temptation seems to be to use shorthand at all costs . . . this is not the same thing as writing economically, for often the complication exists only at the verbal level. Thus the clumsy device of using one part of speech as if it were another . . . The habit of putting together an abstract and a concrete, one of them (often the abstract) being genitive seems to die hard with poets who made heavy use of it in the forties. (pp. 81–2)

Jeremy Hooker took a different view. In *Poetry Wales* (7, 3, 1971) he wrote of 'a remarkable individual awareness of words, of their sound and meaning at once, so that the pattern of sound as it bears a direct relationship to the complexities of meaning is the principal technical feature of his work'. He went on to make an intuitive link between the poetry before him and that of Hopkins:

> The poem that enacts meaning through the use of the sensuous and kinetic qualities of words, as if words and their arrangement were the organisms, objects, and actions they symbolise, belongs to an important tradition in English verse. Hopkins contributed his own intensely physical experience of spiritual reality to the tradition at the same time as he made it embody a potent Welsh element; and it seems to be on the basis of this tradition that Mathias's instincts have led him to form his own highly individual style. (pp. 97–8)

Elsewhere in a review that amended the stance he had taken in his earlier article in the same magazine (see p. 32), Hooker wrote of the

Introduction: The Development of the Poetry of Roland Mathias

poet's turning his writing 'into a process of radical self-questioning' and testing 'with great humility his own "achievement" (as a maker, as a man) against the life and work of those he truly respects'. He saw in poems like 'God Is' 'urgent and remorseless expressions of [the poet's] disquieting scrutiny' of himself, and in those on historical themes examinations of 'the nature of right action in the light of a sensitive conscience'. Of the more directly personal poems, he considered 'Sarnesfield' and 'A Last Respect' 'easily among the finest poems [he had] read by a contemporary for some time'.

The final poem in each of three of his published collections marks a significant juncture in the poet's life. *Break in Harvest* concludes with 'Going' (95), about the journey north to Carlisle/Gretna, *The Roses of Tretower* with 'Returning' (132), in which the exile revisits with his own children the farmhouse that had been his grandparents' home, and *Absalom in the Tree* with 'New Lease' (167), a poem about 'The Wells', the dilapidated cottage at St Twynells, Pembrokeshire, that Mathias and his wife bought and brought back to life. The poem is significant for its characteristic self-directed irony at his coming with mercenary intent to acquire a piece of the 'captor / Country', the land that has captivated him, and for its underlying sense of national responsibility. To let the cottage (which the council official who inspected the property declared 'Done for') tumble into dereliction would be for him 'punishable', an offence against his duty of maintenance. Renewed experience of Pembrokeshire would make a significant contribution to subject matter in the next book of poems, *Snipe's Castle* (Gomer, 1979), where the nature of patriotism would be an important theme.

The fair copy of 'New Lease' is dated 10 December 1970. The next text in the Notebook is 'An Act of Significance', the original title of the long poem broadcast by the BBC in 1971 and printed in *Snipe's Castle* as 'Madoc' (188). Although the fair copy is undated, composition of its 634 lines is likely to have extended some months into 1971. The 'Welsh Indians' has been a research interest of the poet for over fifty years and, when a reading and lecture tour took him to the University of Alabama, he made the most of the opportunity to examine the relevant records on the other side of the Atlantic. Notwithstanding the views of professional historians, his own research convinced Mathias of the fundamental truth of the story. The BBC's commission enabled him to put the gathered material to use. The Notes (p. 350) identify the sources of the poem, locations and historical figures.

The setting of 'Madoc' is an American Indian heaven where characters from different centuries address one another in language that is refined, measured and portentous – a plain enough language of heaven to stand alongside those idiomatically coloured speeches or letters from other times and places that had long been part of the poet's repertoire. The issue of history versus mythology, which might have offered a dramatic, if obvious, framework for the entire narrative, is confined to the speeches of John Evans and the stern accusations of 'A Voice' (which may be the poet's own) in response, that Evans was a traitor and a liar. Instead, the poem takes as its theme the preservation of national identity. Under attack from Indian tribes, the followers of Madoc split into two ideological camps. Gwenllian represents those who would fight to the last to keep a distinctive culture pure, and Riryd the men who, seeing defeat inevitable, are reconciled to mingling blood, language and traditions with their enemies. The historical outcome posited by the poem is the survival of Welshness at the expense, or in spite, of its dilution. 'Madoc' is more than a dramatic summation of the story of the Welsh Indians; it is an allegory of the survival in decline of the language and culture of Wales in the twentieth century.

Several poems touch on the same or a very similar theme: 'Snipe's Castle' (181), 'Is it the Same Country?' (176), 'To a Tombstone Fragment in the Garden Path' (186) and, most powerfully, 'Porth Cwyfan' (171). Together they represent a substantial shift in the poet's engagement with the 'matter of Wales' from that denial of concern for Welsh 'people, community [and] social feeling' in his letter to the editor of *Poetry* (see p. 27). His patriotic sense of belonging had been considerably strengthened when he returned to live in Brecon in 1969. Editorials in *The Anglo-Welsh Review* through the 1970s reveal his increasing espousal of Welsh causes in literature, the arts, politics and society. A greatly expanded circle of friends throughout Wales ensured that issues of language and culture were constantly before him. He began his essay 'Pe medrwn yr iaith . . .', translated into Welsh and published in *Y Faner* in February 1980, by expressing his regret that, for all his attendance at evening classes, he still could not speak Welsh:

. . . a minnau ag awydd mor gryf i fedru siarad Cymraeg, a throi mewn cylchoedd le'i siaradir, a chael yr ymdeimlad o fod 'i fewn' yn y Gymru etifeddol.

(and I with so strong a desire to be able to speak Welsh, and to move in circles where it is spoken, and to have the feeling of sharing fully in the heritage of Wales.)

Rarely, however, are emotions, even as strongly felt as these, allowed unquestioned into his poetry.

Introduction: The Development of the Poetry of Roland Mathias

The habits of rigorous self-analysis and self-blame jostle with instincts of patriotic exclusivity in 'Porth Cwyfan'. It is June, but the weather is unseasonable – 'cold, the wind / Bluffing occasional rain' – more like autumn, the season of many of the poems. The crusty language and imagery ('dried fribbles of seaweed'; 'the tide's mouthing'; 'A closed-in, comfortless bay'; 'a small / Inevitable tragedy, the umpteenth / In a sinuous month') conjure up a morose mood for which the reason is simply stated: 'I can call nothing my own.' The barking of the terrier, symbolic guardian of the place, reinforces a sense of alienation that is not to be dismissed by a colloquial aside, for he cannot relate to the island and its ancient church. He has only a superficial knowledge of its history but when, 'suddenly angry', he conceives of his little historical learning as a shibboleth to exclude English tourists, it is only to realize, a breath later, that their 'tripright' is as sound as his. The poem offers an antidote to views about tourism and the influence of the English in Wales held by R. S. Thomas.

In a note to me, the poet points out that the man with a Lancastrian accent on the beach 'might have been a Cymro' with his roots in old Cumbria. We do not need to know this, though, to understand the poem. It is accessible at first reading, and with no reduction in linguistic colouring, although this is subtler than that of earlier poems. Half-rhymes and the high proportion of run-on lines disguise the regularity of the stanzaic structure and contribute to the illusion of the poem as an informal sharing of impressions and ideas conveyed with the rhythms of everyday speech. Plain style is mixed with colloquialism ('What in God's name is he / Guarding that he thinks I want of a sudden?') and verbal invention ('wind / Bluffing occasional rain'). The imagery conveys strangely dislocated sense impressions, from the 'branchy / Shifts of voyage' to the cliff 'Eaten by sand' and on to the 'quaking field', the 'few wild settles' in Cwyfan's chapel and the poet's 'blundering walk'. All have fallen under the influence of the 'sinuous month', even to the tombstone that lies 'skew-whiff' in the graveyard. The metaphorical integration of the whole is underpinned by the verbal echo of 'tipwhite', describing the sentinel dog, and the 'tripright' to the island conferred by national identity.

Technical virtuosity is again a feature of *Snipe's Castle*. Rather more than half the poems in the book have rhyme, a round dozen of them in stanza forms. In 'After Christmas' (168), 'The Anchorite' (179) and 'On Llandefalle Hill' (182) the poet set himself metrical challenges similar to those of earlier books. 'Burning Brambles' (175) is in rhyming couplets and the long, coiling lines mimic both the torsion of the vegetation and the melancholy process of meditation upon 'the smell of a life ill lived as it passes down wind'. It is a poem in which the act of flaying the physical garden of foetid and spiteful vegetation and clearing household rubbish has a psychological parallel in uncovering the sins of the past and self-excoriation. Lines such as 'It is an old covert, the fuss / Of discovery long muted' and 'black bottles rainy / Yet stoppered, a heap of old sins without consequence, save / Deep in the land's heart' give us pause, not least because Mathias's habit of inversion allows 'land's heart' to be read also as 'heart's land'.

'Brechfa Chapel' (187) lifts the theme of spiritual self-interrogation to a broader but no less gloomy landscape, where a lake cast in shadow loses light 'bitterly', the dreaming swan on its island 'takes no note' and the air is full of the cries of gulls with their 'bankrupt hatred of strangers'. The darkening scene, the indifferent swan and the 'militant brabble' of scavenging birds allegorize the condition of man without religion. Stones in the graveyard tell of the light of faith once carried far and 'held steady' but not now, as the 'black half-world' encroaches and 'Bleaks by the very doors' of the chapel. When the poet uses an expression as powerful as 'The hellish noise it is appals' we know he does not do so lightly. The threat of evil is real and imminent. To the harsh and unavoidable question, 'Is the old witness done?' there is a lonely answer: 'Each on his own must stand and conjure / The strong remembered words, the unanswerable / Texts against chaos', but in the prevailing darkness of this poem it is not a message of hope.

The final lines of 'A Stare from the Mountain' (169) may allow the possibility of grace, but it is by no means certain. The texturally complex fifteen-line sentence that begins the poem describes the scene. It is 'half-leaved' autumn again, late in the year, the ploughed furrows 'already stiff in their winter / Folds'. The setting sun casts a glow on the landscape, but through the poet's head, exposed to the cold north wind, run 'the frozen / Questions that the poles demand', questions of sin, guilt and God's forgiveness. The sudden appearance of a mountain pony, its outline illuminated by sunlight, so that it seems 'Marked with redemption from a hidden / Source', prompts self-examination for similar signs, 'a gleam / Lining my own shadow'. The stark honesty of the perception 'nothing there / Satisfies' is offset for a moment by a glimpse of the town and its smoking rubbish-tip 'taken by sun and arked, / Burning its pages from the Domesday Book'. Whether this doomsday vision is of man hell-bent on self-destruction or inspired by hope of the new ark of promise we cannot tell.

For an unambiguous expression of faith in God's love the reader has to wait until the final poem in the book, 'Laus Deo' (189, x). The climax of a Pembrokeshire sequence written as the text of a cantata (but not performed because the music, by David Harries, was never completed), it draws together the threads of history and celebration of this favourite part of Wales for him. It has many of the familiar characteristics of Mathias's writing but now used freely, fluently and transparently. The textures of repeated sounds and words are suspended on an open weave of rhyme, half-rhyme and internal rhyme; the diction includes unusual and archaic words; onomatopoeia, personification and synecdoche are among its most frequently used rhetorical devices. All contribute to the poem's verbal inventiveness:

> Hard hands have not kept it, this puissant
> And sacred endeavour, nor high
> Heads either this old domain.
> It is one engrossing work, this frail
> Commerce of souls in a corner,
> Its coming and going, and the mark
> Of the temporal on it.

Thematically it presents a fusion of love of Wales and love of God, the country's 'Maker / As careful of strength as / Of weakness' and with an incantatory power that gathers strength towards its 'affirmative' conclusion.

In combining beauty of style and image, 'Laus Deo' is unexpectedly serene. Interviewed by Cary Archard (in *Poetry Wales* 18, 4, 1983), the poet said:

> I'm certainly suspicious of beauty. It isn't merely that my Puritan upbringing has always made me feel that Keats's dictum about beauty and truth was horribly wrong. My first response is always one of suspicion of anything that intends a larger gesture, particularly when it is a larger gesture which is intended to exemplify beauty. Beauty itself doesn't save. The most disgraceful Nazis, for example, appreciated beauty. So . . . I am rough, if you like, but seeking in the end to make some smaller point which I hope is more honest. (p. 59)

As a poet of landscape, creatures (especially birds), plants and natural phenomena, his writing rarely provides evidence of deviation from this rough honesty. The harsher conditions of autumn and winter are his choice of weathers, mountains and rugged coastlines his characteristic habitat. In *Snipe's Castle*, 'Fool's Fingers' (172), 'The Damson Tree' (180) and 'May-Trees Climbing' (183) are among a baker's dozen of poems that contribute in various ways and measures to the large stock of imagery that renders nature a fitting expression of the Puritan conscience. Landscape is often numinous in Mathias's poetry, but the

Introduction: The Development of the Poetry of Roland Mathias

God present in it usually appears to be as indifferent as the red, rutted soil stiff with frost.

The book also takes further the development of certain characteristic themes. Of the poems concerned with family, 'Is it the Same Country?' (176) looks back once more to the harsh existence of the squatters of Rhos Llangeler, his father's forebears, whose simple lives are both an example and reproof to one who comes 'deer-stalkered, by the coining road / From England and nowhere'. 'Blue Blood and Englishmen' (178) has a less usual subject: his mother's father, Joseph Morgan, who believed he had cause to distrust Welsh-speakers and preserved a vision of descent from a noble English line which his historian grandson proved to have been exaggerated. One of the poet's own children, soon to depart on a two-year tour of voluntary service overseas, is the cause of concern in 'In the Swiss Jura' (173), a poem whose intricate stanza form and mix of allusions and rhetoric betray the strength and complexity of the emotion that inspired it. 'Sir Gelli to R.S.' (184) returns to the familiar historical ground of *Whitsun Riot*, with the usual mix of dramatic utterance and mimicry of much older language but with the fresh aim of correcting the unsympathetic view of 'Sir Gelli Meurig' offered by R. S. Thomas (see Notes p. 348). As well as its references to the array of characters and events depicted by the artist, 'Memling' (185) provides a gloss on the poem that precedes it: 'The history we choose speaks largely of ourselves'. 'La Tène' (174) reflects Mathias's fascination with the surviving artefacts of the Celts, but that is only the starting point for meditations on his own work and on the cheapening of experience that is a consequence of tourism.

In 1980, *Snipe's Castle* gained the poet his second Welsh Arts Council award. There were few dissenting voices among the reviewers. Richard Swigg, writing in the *Literary Review* (12, 21 March–3 April 1980), thought 'Tide Reach' celebrated 'those who stay to work the land and reap the result ... with music of acute, singular robustness' and acknowledged the poet's 'rigour and individualistic intelligence'. He was less appreciative of 'Roland Mathias in his double role of grumbling malcontent and blessed peacemaker – the mixture of the prickly and the conciliatory that makes up his kind of Anglo-Welshness'. The 'self-mockery' he observed in 'Is it the Same Country?', he thought, might put in a claim 'to the status of moral honesty, but the poet can no more pursue it than he can occupy with confidence the critical standpoint of "Brechfa Chapel". Much of the poetry's quirky obduracy ... seems to arise from a taut sense of impotence rather than the reined-in awareness of power showing itself from time to time' (p. 25). Leslie Norris in *The Powys Review* (II, 6, Winter/Spring 1979–80) thought the poems 'although not without some typically complex passages . . . more direct than those in any previous collection' and went on to argue that it is not the thought or the poetic forms that present difficulties 'but [the poet's] stern honesty and unshifting insistence on giving us the very kernel of his meaning'. Norris also responded to 'the wonderful visionary quality of [Mathias's] observation' and declared him 'by nature and training a historian, and by temperament a religious man':

> In poem after poem, Mathias creates the natural world with almost unfailing sensitivity, and in language which is itself a declaration of sensuous delight, rich in texture, often unusual in vocabulary; but his essential message is that among those fields and with those people, he is alone and without comfort. The friction between the strength and controlled pleasure of the writing and the stark bleakness of the message creates a most moving situation. (p. 87)

In *Snipe's Castle*, the review concluded, 'he seems to be stating the fact of his nationality with almost every line he writes, implicitly and explicitly'.

In *Poetry Wales* (15, 3, Winter 1979–80 pp. 130–8), Peter Elfed Lewis saw Mathias's poetry as 'decidedly intellectual, despite his delight in tropes and verbal inventiveness, and . . . also more socially committed, more centrally concerned with Wales'. He testified to 'the close-knit intricacy of his work, its verbal density and rhetorical richness, its syntactical complexity, and its finely argued intellectual coherence' and suggested that the historical allusions in poems such as 'Memling' and 'Sir Gelli to R.S.' succeeded 'in communicating at an emotional level despite their contextual difficulties'.

Burning Brambles, Mathias's 'Selected Poems 1944–1979', published by Gomer in 1983, afforded critics an opportunity for re-evaluation. Anne Stevenson, in *The Anglo-Welsh Review* (75, 1984), characterized his work as 'above all a poetry of verbal dexterity', later adding, '[a] good deal of the interest inherent [in the poems] is to be found in the lessons of their amazing versification'. She remained disconcerted, however, 'by [the] referential nature of many poems like "Porth Cwyfan", together with the poet's apparent unwillingness to give away secrets'. This, she thought, 'must be held to blame for the poet's relative obscurity outside Wales'. For her, 'such progress as there is [from *Break in Harvest* to *Snipe's Castle*] takes the form of increasing lucidity – or seeming lucidity – coupled with a greater density of reflection'. 'There is a hunted quality about Mathias's best poems,' she concluded, an edge of bitterness which is indistinguishable, sometimes, from an overwhelming and poignant sadness. But there is humour too. The poems must be read again and again, for they are more than their surfaces, and description is the only way in ... Certainly Mathias is one of our major poets, easily in a class with Geoffrey Hill and Seamus Heaney. (p. 100)

In his review article (*Poetry Wales*, 21, 1, 1985), Jeremy Hooker, who from being the most trenchant critic of the difficulty of Mathias's writing had become his foremost apologist, responded to Stevenson's reservations:

> Syntax and verbal texture are conspicuous features of his style, and both serve meaning. At the outset, in many of his poems published in the 1940s, there is troubled and partly occluded poetry, in which a strong emotional impulse is impeded by its means of expression, and the very eloquence is inarticulate. This is probably due in some degree to his extreme consciousness of the poem as an artefact, and his preoccupation with the madeness of verbal texture, which owed much to his reading of Hopkins and Browning, and despite the marked independence of his mind, it is probably due in part to the poetic climate of that decade ... Later, increasing skill has made verbal texture one of the main sources of pleasure in his poetry, but when combined with his essentially qualifying voice, which is bent on being truthful at all costs, in a largely non-colloquial language, it can also make considerable demands on the reader. (pp. 96–7)

For the most part he concentrated on religion and the quality of language in the later poems. The 'main springs' of Mathias's poetry, he said, are 'memory and guilt':

> the Puritan conscience engendering his conviction of personal inadequacy also involves the most radical questioning of all man's actions, works and motives. In consequence, his strong impulse as a praise poet, born in gratitude to particular people, who have given him his inheritance, is partly thwarted by his Puritan consciousness of sin, and wholehearted praise comes through only rarely in his poetry. But when it is released, it flows [as in 'Laus Deo'] with singular purity and force. (pp. 94–5)

'Mathias is a moralist', Hooker adds, 'concerned with what God asks of him personally and of man in general':

> His conviction of sin is acute, leading to self-dislike: 'the smell of a life ill-lived' of 'Burning Brambles' is typical, and throughout his poetry

the temptations of the flesh are felt and bitterly regretted. He asks in 'The Mountain', 'Give me the punishment that saves', and in a much later poem, 'The Green Chapel', . . . 'the fear within / Is worst, the horror of separation / From meaning', so that physical and spiritual torment, in a condition of penitence, is at the heart of his poetry. (p. 100)

By way of a discussion of the historical poems, the article concludes:

Many poets of his generation have looked to London; he has remained true to the Romantic rediscovery of an original Christian value: that life here and now, or there and then, in the individual soul and in the particular community is as important as life anywhere at any time. (p. 101)

Mathias's last book of poems was published by Gomer in 1996, seventeen years after *Snipe's Castle*. There had been no let up in the rather stately pace at which the poems of his maturity were produced, or change in what had become the usual manner of composition, but the unusual lapse of time before the appearance of *A Field at Vallorcines* was caused by the stroke he suffered in May 1986.

The first nineteen poems in the book were written between November 1978 and May 1985 and, with the single exception of 'Grasshoppers' (208), had first come out in magazines from Wales or further afield, including the United States and Australia. Of the remaining ten, written between December 1991 and July 1995, only the six 'Spoon River Anthology' poems had not been published in either *Poetry Wales* or *The New Welsh Review*. Breaking with custom, perhaps in response to the not unkind strictures of Anne Stevenson, the poet added explanatory notes on the text (which are reproduced, and in some cases expanded, in the Notes to this volume). Continuing the practice of his earlier books, however, he arranged the poems largely in chronological order of composition. Those written after his illness do not betray the many hours of labour that went into their making but do reveal changes in his highly individual style and rhetoric, for he has not fully recovered his verbal inventiveness and metrical facility. They still have the capacity to pull the reader up short:

> When I was jaunty
> And unafraid, the river hill was
> Dinas, staining the right bank

> With shadow, canvassing the sticks
> About the edge.

When it is required, that distinctive actorly tone, too, remains available:

> I speak what I believe, and
> Do. It is not
> Everything that the Lord knows
> In his panoply of cloud.
> Look at me, Caleb.
> It's time.

And he continues to draw upon an enormous range of historical and topographical reference. The general reduction in the density of poetic texture remarked in relation to *Snipe's Castle* holds for *A Field at Vallorcines* but it is as much as ever a key feature of poems like 'Onset of Winter' (190) and 'Aber' (191):

> Such anecdote
> As I have requires the emphasis
>
> Of this tumbled close, the tossing waste
> Of hill, the sombre rain coming on
> At tea-time. No quicker motion, not even haste
> Of words need leap to show.

The frequency with which stanzas end with run-on lines, as above, betrays the craft that lies behind the appearance (or sound) of fluent informality that is a feature of the collection.

The concerns of family, mutability, history and landscape and the lessons the natural world has for the conscientious observer penetrate the book as fully as those that preceded it. There are further examples of metrical accomplishment, as in 'Ronan' (206), and especially 'Tŷ Clyd' (192), where the complexity of the stanza form is again an indicator of the emotional intensity of the creative process. The only way, it seems, to achieve objectivity sufficient for contemplation of the irony of 'Tŷ Clyd' (Cosy House), which explores the tensions in the relationship between his parents and in his relationship with them, is by ratcheting up the technical demands of the poem. For similar reasons, poems about family that appear metrically uncomplicated often demand a second look. 'Expiation' (197), for example, another view of his maternal grandfather (originally entitled 'A Sort of Expiation' though with no less certainty that amends were being made for his unflattering portrait in 'Blue Blood and Englishmen') has a regular pattern of end and internal rhyme barely perceptible until the poem is read aloud.

Introduction: The Development of the Poetry of Roland Mathias

The same is true of the title poem of the collection (203), where in all but one of the triplets a rhyme echoes from the middle of the first line to the end of the third. Although the setting of 'A Field at Vallorcines' is in the Swiss Alps (as the poems remind us, the poet and his wife frequently holidayed in the mountains of France, Switzerland and Austria), it was actually written some weeks later at a hotel in Nefyn, in north Wales. Its direct description of place conveys an impression of writing *en plein air* while Molly was painting the scene, as often happened, but it is actually an example of emotion recollected in tranquillity. It is a late love poem. Compressed description, highlighting significant details in the alpine landscape, leads to the quietly triumphant assertion in the final triplet of the strength of a lasting relationship in the face of all the vicissitudes of life.

The emblematizing of creatures and natural phenomena assumes, if anything, greater significance in this final collection. 'Signal' (196) brings together the subtleties of a rhyme scheme that the silent reader might miss and verbal repetition that functions as a kinetic image of falling leaves in its allegory of life dwindling to the grave. On its dappled surface, 'Terns at Rossnaskill' (201) describes the behaviour of seabirds, but words and images associated with warfare prepare us for its universal message of the arbitrariness of death in a world seething with life. These are readily accessible poems, as (once any historical allusions are explained) are the great majority in the book.

Perhaps the most riddling, despite the acknowledgement of the title's biblical source, is 'They, Without Us' (199). In a note to me, Mathias described how it was written: 'The poem came out of the blue in a field beyond Seefeld [Austria]. Molly was painting at the time – a whole day. I think only a few alterations were necessary when I retyped it.' The dramatic style is instantly recognizable and the topography close to the poet's Brecon home; the poet's own notes identify the historical figures named in it. There is a playfulness about the poem that disguises its serious purpose, which unfolds when we realize that the 'soldiers' are Christian soldiers and that 'Crwys' is not necessarily the Welsh-language poet of that name ('Peredur' had appeared in the drafts); he may well be an Everyman, earmarked by God's saints for recruitment to the faith.

'They, Without Us' is one among several poems that are dramatic utterances. Four of the six 'Spoon River Anthology' pieces come into this category. Perhaps the most impressive is 'The Steward's Letter' (193). As Mathias's notes indicate, the persona adopted in this case is that of Paul Delahay, whom we have already met in connection with 'Indictment' (155). Here, in a letter to his master, the tone is different.

Introduction: The Development of the Poetry of Roland Mathias

The text is a somewhat altered version of an actual letter addressed by Delahay to the elderly Lord Burghley. Early drafts of the poem dating from January 1979 (it was completed a year later) are accompanied by a notation of the number of stresses in each line and, in a few places, by observations such as 'one stress too many' or, in the fifth stanza, 'one line missing'. The strange (to our eyes) seventeenth-century orthographic conventions were reintroduced at the second complete draft. As a recreation of the language and manners of another time, it is the apotheosis of the poet's various ventures in a genre that is his own.

Reviewers welcomed *A Field at Vallorcines*. Robert Minhinnick, writing in *The New Welsh Review* (36, Spring 1997, pp. 85–6) praised the poet's 'imaginative wrestling with history, so that the past leaps alive into our midst', and found 'technically intricate poems [possessing] a clarity that will surely place them among the most accessible examples of his verse'. In *Poetry Wales* (33, 3, 1998, pp. 21–6), M. Wynn Thomas thought the book 'all the more a triumph in that so many of the poems . . . are of vintage calibre, and . . . all the more moving in that from the very outset the experience of ageing is factored into the writing by various unaffected means'. His painstaking and insightful analysis included consideration of the religious and moral core of Mathias's art and the idiosyncrasy of his 'astringently mannered writing'. 'Part of the poignancy and power of *A Field at Vallorcines*', he concluded,

> is the feeling it generates of one who has grown old in the service of values and beliefs that the world has increasingly held to be foolish. The dignity and consequentiality of Mathias's achievement as a poet is, however, rooted in his unwavering determination to make poetry rhyme with principle. (p. 25)

Mathias is his own harshest critic, whether in questions of belief or morality or writing. In the Cary Archard interview he said:

> I always begin to suspect myself when I catch myself making a rhetorical gesture. I have put aside poems when I feel I am getting into this bigger thing which I feel is largely composed of empty rhetoric. I had a poem on the stocks (now discarded) intended to celebrate a walk in Switzerland last year. I knew I wanted to make some larger significance out of the beauty of the day as the poem went on, but couldn't stand myself doing it. (p. 59)

Fortunately, the manuscript was preserved along with the others from the early 1980s and it appeared in *A Field at Vallorcines* as 'Grasshoppers'. Notebook III provides a further gloss:

Introduction: The Development of the Poetry of Roland Mathias

The idea of 'Grasshoppers' came to me whilst having lunch by the Rhinerhorn, in September 1982. The third copy was the one that was tucked in my Poetry Notebook III in October. I didn't feel that it was quite the thing that I wanted.

In September 1989 we climbed the Rhinerhorn again, and found the grasshoppers exactly in the same place. In 1991 I tried to make the whole design work, but my ability was not sufficient to make any changes. In June 1991 a fair copy was made in Deffrobani.

Given the beauty and clarity of the poem, its gentle meditative tone, the ease of its speech rhythms and the magisterial strength of its message, it is hard to conceive what dissatisfied in 1982. Harder is the realization that he would write only another half-dozen poems before his illness in 1986. Although not his final utterance, and not representative of his metrical and linguistic inventiveness, the closing lines of 'Grasshoppers' serve as well as any to represent the essential qualities of Mathias's thought and writing at the height of his powers:

>   It is right
> To climb as we can, to the limit
> Of will. To do less
> Is unworthy of such sun, such far
> Blue purpose as the distance is,
> Folded back and back, fainter
> And fainter always, surpassing
> Peak with peak, till the day
> Is what we can never be and scarcely comprehend.

The Poems

* not previously collected or published

DAYS ENDURING and other poems (1942)
1. New Year, 1935
2. Joy and Faith
3. Sunrise at Even
4. Long Abed
5. Moorland Thunder
6. New Year, 1936
7. To My Uncle David
8. On Hearing Richard II, Broadcast by the O.U.D.S.
9. White Peonies
10. In Frimley Woods
11. Sunset Over the Sea
12. Memories
13. Rissersee
14. Against Jericho (June, 1936)
15. Sundew
16. Hiraeth
17. Days Enduring
18. Sea-moods
19. The Fall of the Year
20. Parting
21. Grains of Sand
22. October Sun
23. Now Starlight Knows You Not
24. Dusk
25. The Stars Above
26. Knapweed
27. Under the Shadow
28. The Past
29. Good-Friday
30. Passers-by
31. The New Miracle
32. Storm
33. Youth
34. The White Poplar
35. 'O World Intangible'
36. On Newport Reservoir

List of Poems

37. New Year, 1939
38. Evening in Saundersfoot
39. The Forest
40. Lines Written on Hearing of the Invasion of Poland (September 1st, 1939)
41. Declaration of War (September 3rd, 1939)
42. Dream
43. Tower on an Evening Sky
44. Pax Nobiscum
45. Blitz in Manchester
46. Nepotism
47. Lament for Cassandra
48. For Marjorie
49. Café Parting
50. Inter Tenebros (Even Here)
51. Vista
52. Bars
53. Wishes from Walton
54. Cries in the Night
55. Fagenbaum
56. Night on the Brecon Road*
57. The Close*
58. Credo*
59. Oxford Castle*
60. Slow Meeting*
61. Maesyronnen
62. Worm in the Brain
63. Pastorale
64. Balloon Over the Rhondda
65. March on the Mountains
66. End-piece

BREAK IN HARVEST and other poems (1946)
67. The Bearers
68. Beacons
69. London Welshman
70. Llyn Bodgynydd
71. Drover's Song
72. The Ballad of Barroll's Daughter
73. Whitewater
74. Enstone Rock
75. Ladysmock*
76. Fulwell
77. For M.A.H.
78. Prayer Before Marriage*

List of Poems

79. Last Happiness
80. Kidmore End
81. Requiescat
82. The Cauldron of Diwrnach Wyddel (A Poem for the D-Days)
83. The Lament of Little Gwion
84. Mirror
85. Evening: Unloading Wheat
86. Grace Before Work
87. Pontwillim Plough
88. Subite
89. Hillside
90. In This Cold Room
91. Lowbury Hill
92. Crossing into Peace
93. Break in Harvest
94. Prospect of Ditchley
95. Going

THE ROSES OF TRETOWER (1952)

96. Solway
97. New Year's Day, 1946
98. The Lurking Ancestor
99. From a Bus at Crosby, Cumberland
100. In Offenham Church
101. Evening
102. Judas Maccabeus
103. The Path to Dinas
104. The Lochmaben Stone
105. The Mountain
106. Searching Spring
107. Bablockhythe
108. On the Grave of Henry Vaughan at Llansaintffraed
109. Drought
110. Olchon
111. Craswall
112. Camp by the Windrush
113. Thomas ap Richard of Doier to the Tower, These
114. The Roses of Tretower
115. Hawk
116. The Flooded Valley
117. Morning: New Jerusalem
118. A Winter's Day
119. Pas Seul
120. Pas de Deux

List of Poems

121. Towards Pencombe
122. Spring in Weggis
123. Freshwater West
124. Afternoon in Water Street
125. A Letter
126. 'Remember Charlie Stones, Carpenter'
127. O Tihuanaco
128. Argyle Street
129. Riddle
130. Coed Anghred
131. The Tyle
132. Returning

THE FLOODED VALLEY (1960)
133. An Age
134. To the Muse, Wrongheadedly*
135. The Lost Kingdom*
136. Scithwen Valley
137. Conversation on Stackpole Head
138. Building a House (in Four Movements)*
139. Marston Sicca
140. Orielton Empty
141. Cascob
142. Friends I Have*
143. For Warren Davies, Two Years Dead
144. The Last Days of Heat

ABSALOM IN THE TREE and other poems (1971)
145. Chinon
146. Brynafan: First Light
147. A Last Respect
148. Sarnesfield
149. Departure in Middle Age
150. Freshwater West Revisited
151. For an Unmarked Grave
152. The Least Echo
153. Absalom in the Tree
154. Some Tight-lipped Wave
155. Indictment
156. They Have Not Survived
157. Testament
158. God Is
159. A Letter from Gwyther Street
160. Not Worth the Record

List of Poems

161. For Jenkin Jones Prisoner at Carmarthen, These
162. Under Quinag
163. The Fool in the Wood
164. Au Cimetière de Brest
165. Channel Saint
166. A Celtic Death
167. New Lease

SNIPE'S CASTLE (1979)
168. After Christmas
169. A Stare from the Mountain
170. Squirrel-path
171. Porth Cwyfan
172. Fool's Fingers
173. In the Swiss Jura
174. La Tène
175. Burning Brambles
176. Is it the Same Country?
177. Pwll Llong, Pwll Whiting
178. Blue Blood and Englishmen
179. The Anchorite
180. The Damson Tree
181. Snipe's Castle
182. On Llandefalle Hill
183. May-trees Climbing
184. Sir Gelli to R.S.
185. Memling
186. To a Tombstone Fragment in the Garden Path
187. Brechfa Chapel
188. Madoc
189. Tide-reach   i The Green Chapel
                    ii Guénolé
                    iii Nesta Vows to Escape from the Norman Hold
                    iv Wave and Furrow
                    v His Nurse to Young Harri Tudur
                    vi The Remonstrance of John Poyer
                    vii The Enlargement of Stackpole House: Harvest Time
                    viii The Arming of Aberdaugleddau
                    ix The Soul's Plain Seeing
                    x Laus Deo

A FIELD AT VALLORCINES (1996)
190. Onset of Winter
191. Aber

List of Poems

192. Tŷ Clyd
193. The Steward's Letter
194. The Path to Fontana Amorosa
195. Innocent Dying
196. Signal
197. Expiation
198. Saturday Morning: Appin
199. They, Without Us
200. Cynog
201. Terns at Rossnaskill
202. On Discovering Daumier's 'Don Quixote Reading' in the National Museum at Cardiff
203. A Field at Vallorcines
204. On South Lord's Land
205. Sanderlings
206. Ronan
207. Cae Iago: May Day
208. Grasshoppers
209. Jazz Festival
210. The Lamentation of Marchell
211. I Shall Take the Gig*
212. The Clear Sea
213. Look at Me, Caleb

Half a dozen Poems for the Spoon River Anthology after Edgar Lee Masters
214. Dr John James Williams
215. Mary Jane Robertson Williams
216. Howell Price Williams
217. William Retlaw Jefferson Williams
218. Gwenffreda Cate Williams/Alice Matilda Langland Williams (Alis Mallt)
219. Frederick George Robertson Williams

220. Peter Has Been Digging*

The Poems

1   NEW YEAR, 1935

We know that time slips on unseen, unheard
Amid the panorama of our days and nights,
And passes like a ghost without a word
Between the chattering groups of courtiers and the lights
So gaily bright within that anteroom
Before the throne.
The palace of pleasure
Is the sign thereon.

But still it seemed at this momentous hour
Of stilly quiet, when the ageless feet grow slow,
When time's swift runner at the ebb of power
Hands on his baton, that above the moon's pale glow
There should have sprung a star to mark the tomb
Of years past flown.
But the pale sky above
Had no sign thereon.

2   JOY AND FAITH

Joy is the substance of delight in all things,
In wings,
In the first ray that heralds the sunrise,
In the bubbling sweet that springs
Into love's eyes.

Faith is the substance of belief in all things,
In the springs
Of goodwill that fill the human breast,
In the bell-like voice that sings
'With God be the rest.'

3   SUNRISE AT EVEN

Softly, softly down the carpet of eventide
We crept, frightened by the stillness
And the silence
That pressed us round on every side.

It is not often that the spirit stirs
From out the hardened shell and case of man
To take the air;
But even as the twilight trembled on the firs

And the mist crept upward to the darkened height,
It seemed as though a hand had touched us all
With new-found bliss,
And we had stumbled on the source of inward light.

Old scenes, old melodies had dearer grown,
And all the world was shining with a radiance
Transfiguring
The weakness and the pain that we had known.

4   LONG ABED

How sombre lies the earth against the white! –
That fleecy, joyous billow of the sky
That flows forever on and out of sight
Before the regal radiance which the sun
Casts, as a king his looked-for almony
To all he passes by.

I would that ere the sun goes down in fire
And scatters his last coppers in the gate of night
He would return, and meeting my desire,
Shower for a moment dear his gold on me,
Upon the bed whose heavy folds hang dark –
Dark as the trees, the blackening moor I see –
And sweeping out the twilight of my sight,
Would cast on me the mantle of his ecstasy.

5   MOORLAND THUNDER

Only the sob of raindrops in the grass,
The leaden sky, the runnel's sullen sound,
The sodden measure of the footfall on the ground,
The weary drape of mist at vision's bound
Where rainshapes pass.

A sudden gleam! An azure shore appears
Where thunder rolls his wind-swept waves in vain;
And soon the runnels, swollen with the rain,
Sing loud and clear; the sun so late o'erlain
Smiles through his tears.

6   NEW YEAR, 1936

And so tonight another door will open,
Turn upon silent hinge, and slow reveal
Another of the varied galleries of art
Which we must thread; so hard it is to feel
A joy without a chafing of the heart
For new sights promised! – we cannot choose but part
For that the door will open. We must go.

And when tonight that other door will open
Silent, but in the silence trumpet-loud,
Perforce we turn our gaze from pictures here,
Our comments leave, our jostlings with the crowd,
Our common seat, but lately grown so dear, –
That silent ushering follow, wrapt in fear,
Toward the door that opens. Let us go.

7   TO MY UNCLE DAVID

A smile –
That like a ripple ever widening in the reeds
Makes on and on, to every corner,
Flag and bastion, till the whole expanse
Heaves with the crests and hollows of its merriment –
Broke on his face, and in his eye there came
A twinkle, omen of great deeps translucent
Where moved dim half-shapes shadowing
The mirror of his mind.

8 ON HEARING RICHARD II, BROADCAST BY THE O.U.D.S.

Vacant were we, and dull of eye,
And stumbling heavily through eve's sixth hour;
And one had fall'n asleep for weariness
After long wanderings; while flickering lower
The firelight fell in dour despondency
Upon grim curves and darkened silhouettes
Of huddled figures dim in hollowness,
Upon the bowed heads of stringèd puppets
Lax with unuse; and on the plaited hair
Of one persistent parrying sound for sound
More empty, suited to the shriller blare
Of life's first trumpets; one had left the room
Bent on the common round – the lines of care
Called louder than the musical deep boom
Of voices girding, clashing, dropping slow
From yonder corner darkness – deepest gloom
Of all its dully sisters – where the ruddy glow
Shone from the pilot-light; while against all
The shaken pall, the patter rushing blind
Of sudden sleet, blown by a bitter wind.

A pause. A new note falls upon the strife.
The raging dies. The cruel callousness
Of Richard's tongue gives place to peace
Hard-gasping won, to the slow ebb of life,
The bated words of Gaunt's old gentleness,
And sorrow. Shades of shame and shallowness
That stalk abroad within this blessèd plot,
This throne of kings . . .

The padding of the sleet goes on apace.
The firelight flickers hollow, cavernous.
The day draws in. Is this the end of all?
Tired heads may fall asleep, and face
Their pillow in the silence sonorous,
And others weary in the listening,
But words that measureless yet measured call
Across the years are darkling answered still
By shaking boughs and gleams of sudden sun

That shoot the west. The world its listening
Ceases not, beyond. The trees are tall,
And spring is come. The fervoured waters run,
The land blooms still and dark, unbidden all
Of man. There surges yet that guardian sea
As centuries past it did. The sleet and sun
Fail not. All things await us. What are we?

Within the room the darkness rustled dim
And shadows fell on fallen heads, and night
Veiled tired eyes alike and down-dropped limb;
But still slow-wending words stole stilly on
Beneath the shining of the pilot-light.

9   WHITE PEONIES

The scent of peonies in June
Is redolent of dusk,
Of sorrow, and a jangled tune,
Of heartbeats hid in lettered rune,
And musk.

And as I sit they glimmer white
Above the vase's blue;
Their cream-pale scent o'erhangs the night,
The murmur of a spent delight
And rue.

Their tint-edge folds betray no woe,
But only jewelled tears,
A whispered sigh it must be so,
A laden longing for the slow
Slow years.

10   IN FRIMLEY WOODS

Beyond me and between
The white hardness up on high
Stand the pine-tree boles, brown-notched
And barrelled, stubborn crop of lean

Hard warriors, old in war, who try
To score the chain-mail of the sky
With the spears of ancient symmetry.

Beneath me and around
The bracken that sings in the tread
And the caressing carpet
Solemn, needle-brown, no sound
Disturbs, where soft as on a bed
Laid with the mattress of the dead.
Aeons could cross the brow unnoticed.

11 SUNSET OVER THE SEA

Before the earth was round, or man was tired,
The sun rewarded toil with evening's pay:
The waters were, as now, by sunset fired
Red, beyond Cardigan Bay.

In coracles man hugged the shore, nor knew
The ocean's wider beat, as dim I see
That coaster bound for Trevor, grey on blue,
Lean under Bardsey's lee.

Perchance the reddening arrow of the sun
Shot over darkening waters to the west
Disturbed Columbus as, his labours done,
He musing sat at rest.

Maybe he pondered, laying chin on hand,
And answering glow with glow, pushed out his prow,
Daring to sail the fiery track that spanned
The westering world. But now?

On other coasts beat grey and grey-green seas,
But here the blue, spread south to dim New Quay,
Wears wide a steadfast smile as one at peace
Looks toward eternity.

And now again, 'mid wavelets' twinkling smiles,
The sun glides incandescent on his way

Reddening a path where gleam the western isles
Red, beyond Cardigan Bay.

12   MEMORIES

I travel back to joys unmixed with pain
To stormy days, to days of sunshine, hail and shower,
To hours when mischief ripples stormed and fell
Before the lines of fishing-nets at Porto-Pi;
When nettles stung, and the sharp stubble stood
In battered rows, like little spearmen bold and still;
When rain beat on the roof in frightened sort,
And thankful shivers strained the blankets' soft caress;
When every wood its secret hiding held
And the high lands above the Kiwi situate
Were lonely, vast and lonely, as the plain
Whose silent folds stretched on, and treeless on away.

O then the world was young! Its youngling eyes
Were but half-open, and the unaccustomed glare
That was the sum of things forbade
The singling of the blackened from the fire's red heat.
Then joy was young! and bounded fleetly down
Discovery's rides into the clearings of the world.

13   RISSERSEE

A quarter mile it was the signpost said
To Rissersee; but who amongst us all
Could guess that in the Kreuzeck's darkened flank
So near, a stone's throw barely in the trees ahead,
Lay such a jewelled pocket, bright and silver small?
A bawbee in a fabric fold of rich design
It gleamed alluring from the barren Wank.

To such as white with dust and travel-stained
Climbed the steep way and felt its cornered cool
A silver sea it seemed, spray without brine,
A paradise enow, a heady heaven gained,
A precious drop enbalmèd new from Lethe's pool;

Content was its own mirror, where were pictured forms
Lithe by the fields of conèd Waxenstein.

14   AGAINST JERICHO (June, 1936)

Gone is the plain of Esdraelon
Flat measure of fertility
And peace untroubled by the sight
Of watersmeet.
Gone too the scarpèd heights of Ramleh
Whose passes hardly-gained
Beckoned the stiffer upward thrust,
Endeavour's adolescent son
Distrustful all of steep declivities
And sudden treacherous falls
That bring foreboding Jordan
Too soon in sight. And last
The reeling days behind now hold
The sluggish river, measure of all hopes.
All, all that lay behind, before
Pinned faith upon the breast-high wading
Of Jordan's stream so that the head
Saw still the sun and air and sickened not
With salty aftermath.
Pitiless the valley lay – it brooks no wail,
No creepers to foreknowledge ford.
But now that too lies heavy with the haze
That palls the west.
The sun smites now upon a keener air.
I tread the heights of Moab, watching stony ways
That stonier climb above and clatter on
Past stone and thirsty dust and stone again.
It is no land of full fertility
But sparsity may eke out well in sun and wind.
Endeavour is not blunted and the heart made sick
By an unending fight with sleep.
Ahead lies only sameness
But the stones know peace –
No sudden falls to fear, no terrors in the haze.
In all the way I tread with echoing step
The future holds no dread but of the past.

Jordan rolls sluggish yet, but what care I?
The crossing is done. The East at last!

15 SUNDEW

Maybe in days to come the sun will shine
But never now!
Our wandering summer has forgot his song,
The curtain's dropt, the hissing rain-clouds throng
The sky-scene. May the sun vouchsafe
His anthem, purple on the moors, be mine
Before he takes his bow!

Maybe our eyes are weak not to perceive
The sun in rain –
The dewdrop shotten with the rose's red –
The mirror of the quick to raise the dead –
The grasses' green. Who knows how oft
I'll hear without, before I take my leave,
The beat in the boughs again?

16 HIRAETH

Sir Benfro's silver beaches whisper sweet,
And Teifi's broken water calls aloud;
The lisp of western waves dims through the beat
Of rain in England here. Alone and proud
I lean within the archways of the mind
And listen – listen how in happier hours
The western song was sung, and lonely find
Time's sordid rhythm the softer for their powers.

But there's a clearer call. The vision's dim,
For now the dusk is dropping like a cloak
To hide the Beacons' spurs. The narrow glim
Is flick'ring now (must be) while quiet folk
Go to their rest. Light on the shadowy sill
Leans one, I know, beyond all hope the best . . .
O half a world's 'twixt me and yonder hill,
And half a heaven's lost there in the west!

17 DAYS ENDURING

Four days remain to me, but four – and then
The coast may lie in sun, the swans may sail
Majestic on the Teifi's tidal breast,
The waves may bluff the Island race again
And roll the black of seals, the sun's last zest
May fire the barren cone of Mwnt . . . for me
Four days, to brand my soul nor living fail
To fashion memory.

Tonight I watched the river-mist a-creep
Upon the meadows and the young moon shiver
At the shadow of Preselly's southern stride.
The dusk was full of whispers, joys my keep
Shall grapple . . . Spring will wander on the tide
And answer others' calls, in tears and laughter –
Yet I, when I hear not, though still forever,
I fear thereafter.

18 SEA-MOODS

Wind-whispers
(Passions rage)
But the cool scurry of the sands
Melts into saxifrage.

Gust-eddies
(Dispute palls)
And over Cemmaes bluff green head
Sodden the rain-mist falls.

Sea-volleys
(Peace at last)
While storm has over Teifi's arms
Her battling mantle cast.

19   THE FALL OF THE YEAR

Now that my morning window sees the fields
Afloat with clouds, while farther trees rebuff
Their grey attack, I know that winter wields
A severing steel that patterns poor enough
This life's poor stuff.

I am content it should be as we see,
Nor heed the cold. But mist is as the knell
Of flesh and blood, the gripe of penury
Upon the heart, the muffled passing bell
From earth to hell.

Its vapour islands me, blots out the land
Where one sun-planet shone upon the towers
And trees afield; alone at sunset-stand
I could imagine then our mirrored powers –
Your life and ours.

The blur of distance, memory of hills
Seemed then a happier frame for this long day.
It was not hard to add – (for sorrow spills
Its stupor nightly) – cóntent to its grey,
As warmth to clay.

But now my sunset eyes are lidded o'er,
And vision's shortened by the span 'twixt earth
And heaven. I know no knocking at the door
Except my own. My compass is the girth
Of self-born dearth.

And so this bitter pall must bound my hope,
Muffle my soul's sad unison, and beat
Your words into dank whispers. Here I grope,
Mistrustful ever can your distant feet
Find my retreat.

PARTING

One day of wind (it was my last)
I climbed the Forest, carpeted
With velvet for the bound of little apples
Falling softly. The fern above was mazèd,
Acre-deep, and winnowed by the gales. I felt the air
Blow cold and unconsoling on the ridge
Behind my backward look.
The petty houses set across the vale
(I saw them all), the white hotel, the shining rails,
And Salem set upon its little mound,
Seemed grey and clean and swept.
The earth was billowy, dull,
A swollen face of tears,
Whose heavèd cheeks still moist
Bear witness hurried hands
Have smeared their secret flow
To meet the sudden coming-on of smiling noon.
The nearer hills
Were dumb with insolence,
Bravado born of straining trees,
And clouds to cover their retreat.
Unwise I should have been
To laugh in such a sulky world –
Nor could my farewell day evoke
A sound, or song or sneer, from postured gravity.
I was sorry and alone, and full like
To be the sorrier soon, for that this child
Must have my room, and sprawl and smile
And joy another world than mine.
Youth's tears are all too brief,
And sobs will never see the morning's grey, –
So this young earth, whose thousand years
Lie stored within the anteroom of life,
New-washed and brushed, impatient to resume
His squabble with the sun, constrained himself
To look at me and see me go.
The day's formality had awed us both
Into a tractable and stilted shade
Of discourse, when the voice is low
And stumbles hurriedly in shoals of silence.

I could not bear formality, respect
At such an hour, endure to hear
The shift of restless feet. And so I turned
Unheeding down Cwm Clydach's crabbèd side
Toward my short day's close – and heard afar
The runnels singing with a new release,
And happy outbreak of o'er-burdened birds.

21   GRAINS OF SAND

Eastward there's only the world to see
And north but the cordon's white,
But west is the beat of the heart for me
And the ebb of the sea from the sight.

The song is old as the race is old
And its burden lost to the wise
Who tell by touch the hot from the cold
And stare at the mist in our eyes.

But vision is there. He is purblind who can
Of his own tell the granules of sand,
And contemplate coolly the poundage of man
Nor flicker the scales with his hand.

22   OCTOBER SUN

The year's last levee was a-throng today:
The gates were open, and a courtly smile
Roved from the sober gallery array
Of trees in brown to conscious chequer style
Of field display.

'No mourning by request' had been the word
Sent out, and yellow, brown and green
Stood in the presence with a smile and heard
The rustle that their clouded lives had been
Royally blurred.

23 NOW STARLIGHT KNOWS YOU NOT

The lamps are trimmed again upon my doom
And night must come . . .
The sun that looked just now into the room
Went wan and numb
To bed. He missed your studied upward gaze
To glow his pride:
The chillest spot tonight
Was at his side.

Somewhere beneath this arch of dark mischance
You sure must lie.
I did not see you go, had never a glance
Or farewell sigh.
I only know from out a curtained gloom
Has flown a spark –
Now starlight knows you not
Nor shadow-dark.

24 DUSK

The lees of life
Are left – now you are gone.
My day has wandered to its closing dark
And dulls into a dream . . .
All morning through
Moving from room to room
And street to street I prayed
To glimpse your going.
I did not dare sit down, or read, or rest
For fear of missing you. Calm
Was a nightmare and a dream
Of morrows gloomed by candlelight
Until an end should come . . .
And conversation over coffee-cups
Could not be borne
When you (I knew not when)
Might pass for ever
And a day.
I, like the devils, know
How ceaseless torment sinks into despair

And softens with a shade. The sun
Was on the street at noon and heaven
Could compass all, both you and me
Within one planet. Now the stars are cold
And unreflecting fire.
So unknown I turn
Upon my heel of exile, feel the air
About me maze into an unmocked calm
That pities sleep. Your wake
Still laps upon my drowsing shore
And troubles dreams, but quieter now
And night can hold us all at one again,
The unknowing and unknown.

25   THE STARS ABOVE

Out of the pallor of a dream
I rise to catch the stars apace
Upon their windy voyaging.
The air is soft, this night of grace
And apple to the cheek. I see
The hunt is up, Orion's face
Is set, and Sirius draws up close
To keep the rear. (The hindmost place
Was e'er the one for hot and cold,
For plagues and heats.) But on the race
Or droop to day! Not I alone,
But many, mounting on the dais
Of air, and slumberless, move on
In purlieu of the gloom, the trace
Of moonrays cut. The shadowy point
Of midnight pencils through the space
Of shadows, and a weary wail
Gusts to the watcher's white-lit face
Above, and on the aftermath
Of wingless rush there spins the lace
Of laughter. Insubstantial hope,
The leader in the hopeless chase,
Clutches at the stars' amusement,

Seeing shadows' sharpest pace
Go slipping down into a dream.

* * * * *

Hollo, hollo, feel and follow!
Night about is near and hollow,
Vent of wind and gape of time,
Time itself is mow and mime
To the stress of starry rhyme.
Follow!

26   KNAPWEED

As knapweed, bitter like the plague,
Black head that bears a purple crown
(Fire round the smoky circlet leaps),
Broods always, seen, upon a wind that creeps
By shade and sand behind the town
Round Marienburg, a common man enough
To be a monarch and a mood . . .
So scenes and colours buried in the blood,
Neighbours not known for tens of years,
And scents now under sea, come out to claim
The old allegiance new (the tarnished frame
For the new etching), till the sun
Blinding the man into the boy
Beats on the mounds; at noon's deploy
He plays the robber by the Rhine again.

27   UNDER THE SHADOW

If I could see that all my miseries of heart –
My watch alone upon the minutes' flickering run,
My after-fury at the unsupporting part
Of stiffened tongue in ill, my silence, moment's fun
That outplays patience, ache of mockery's hollow sting –
Were of my weakness always to enjoy a place,
How sooner would my spearless soul, how closer, cling
To Him Who circles each sad tower at its base!

28   THE PAST

   When walls are down and through the wide of air
   The level days of legend glide,
   The groans of Troy from under tussocks strown
   And temeraires, alight upon the tide
   Labour no more alone
   But in me share.

   They fall and whimper at the feet of time
   And time, forgetful, allocates
   An hour, a day, for their forgotten tears
   To shallow vainly at the gates
   He locked himself in years
   Before his prime.

   But Troy and I have into harness gone
   To buckle sorrow to its well
   Of brackish deeps, draw pain enough to pave
   Time's steps into a slipway, swell
   Poor sidling trickles, save
   Dark coming on.

29   GOOD-FRIDAY

   A half hour since
   The air was shot with sun,
   The wind behind the hill asleep
   And gnats a-dance –
   And none
   To shout a warning when there came
   That sudden still of cold,
   The shiver at the back of earth
   Before the storm.
   The sky's bright blue of eye
   Belied its battle-mood,
   But soon
   The flights of snowflakes bluffed the soil
   In criss-cross fury, bearing leaves
   To burial-ground.
   A foster-dark had fallen on the day

Bringing black midnight's spirit all a-chafe
Within the form of afternoon
Into a new dominion.
Moved unawares there came in mind
An omen whiles remembered in the world,
When at the ninth hour of the day
There fell a dark, the temple veil was rent
And all the dead were moved
To mark one passing.
Into this centuried day are come
The gloom again, the riven veil,
The hissing voice of fury – but less fell
In being fallen, turned
To vision sanctified
And spotless, robed without a stain
By that same sacrifice.

30   PASSERS-BY

The days pass quicker than my finger slow
Can count them, days
That jolt and stumble on each other's heels
To rush my checking-place, and go
Into eternal air-dinned ways
Where night their number steals.

Was it on such a fair tall day of spring
As passes now
I saw you last? . . . For named, and written here,
It still is nameless, on the wing
That silence spreads along the bough
Of dreams, in sad arrear.

But such an one as this stayed but to fawn
Upon my breath.
And now they cease to pander, knowing power
Gone from me, step along my lawn
Of shadows to the dark. And death
Will scarce vouchsafe his hour.

31   THE NEW MIRACLE

The gaunt old cheek of earth
That last I saw is smaller grown
And softer, lulled within a veil
Of leaves. The rutted lanes
Are leafy confines that align
A whipped sky of wind. Dull coronets
Of buds blur on the spiring dusk
And blow to green.
The air stirs dully. Grey
And greensweep merge and separate
In silence. Houses are hidden
That were known to me.

I had not seen these things
In London, where
Bulging necks of buildings
Crane to the sun and coloured words
Are winked across the area-ed waste
Till dawn, and coronation hues
Obscure the green, the coronal
Of all our countryside . . .
Yes, I have been in London,
And had not known these things.

32   STORM

Can it be night?
The furrowed window face that views unmoved
So many a winter sorrow with a daylight mien
Like ice itself transparent turns
A troubled look. A few dark leaves
Hang dripping round that puzzled brow
(Stray laurels for a twilight martyr left)
And over candid eye lie lashes
Long with tears
That draggle the distortion to a grey
More groundless, airless, dully at the seam

Than grey goosefeathers
In a witch's dream.

Poor eye of day! – that sees without, within
No straining splendour of a light to share,
No sun to give, no lamp to take
To unaccustomed gloom, and of itself
Has none! – see how it falters, weakly peers
Upon a day unknown and drops
Its darkened tears!

33   YOUTH

As on my birthday, many days ago,
From lonely Penwaundwr I watched the solemn rains
Pass and repass, the fitful sun forego
His choice of moor and pasture, breathing on the plains
Like one pursued, and, staring, saw beside
A hollow 'neath the Fan, of green, with barns and towers
Brown blots upon its flank, where swam a tide
Of steady sun, – so now within these silent hours
I see my life. I have lived islanded
The like from shades, strange heats, and cold of clouded mien.
There has no breathing fear with black'ning tread
Come by me softly before sun-up, clad my green
In mourning, and the world in rags; no task
For matins yoked the early fragrance of the field
To hardened hands and tillage. And ask
What can I more? The dew is gone. The bell has pealed
The morning well-awake, and noonday near.
This elbow of the hill is sharp with sun. And I,
My rest is o'er. No image of the dear
Grey kindliness of dawn must prison me, no sky
To dream my single day adown must pale;
Or late I'll see the dwindling of my treasured gold
In sunset on the hills, and twilight fail
Unhindered into dark, the herald of the cold
And peaking pallor of another dawn.

34   THE WHITE POPLAR

'Who laughed?' said a wind from the west in the dawning.
The poplar, to deprecate ill-will, half smiled
And waved his white hands at the dark muttered warning
From out of the wild.

'I laugh but from light heart' persisted the jester
To lords from the southland pursuing their way.
'Then dance to our lilt and no brawling sou'wester
At noontide' said they.

In pale cap and bells in the moonlight he beckoned,
Grimacing and mocking the mild airs of night,
Throwing alms to the earth with the gesture he reckoned
A master-wind might.

* * * * *

In winter the merriment dwindled, the peeking
Was crabbed by a man to a caper that shamed:
When whispered tones strained to a threat and a creaking
 . . . The jester was maimed.

35   'O WORLD INTANGIBLE'

   Blow hot and cold
   And know me for the foreigner I am.
   Ride swift, ride sure
   And render me an exile in my home.

O elements of fury, pace and wit,
O plagues of ice and passions of the sun,
O hail upon my blinded windscreen hit,
You batten me and bind me into one –

One with my own, my temper and my powers,
An equal unit breasting through a throng
Of lights and darks, of sorrows, airs and hours
My fellows pander to and pass along.

Theirs is no wind and sun, or hot or cold,
No outer world that challenges the blood;
Theirs are discomforts, joys and tears tenfold,
And fortunes fending them from fire and flood.

Their pulses follow at a grumbling span
The mischiefs of this air's far-seated heart.
But I must ever cherish, if I can,
The perfect measure when I play my part –

The sense of movement in a starlit space,
Of body in a symphony of air
That sings and sees no notion of a race
Rolling and buffeting with startled care . . .

Then in some greying evening when the sphere
Is still, and there is no more touch nor tone,
Into the peaces of the soul I'll steer,
Amphibian of the seas around its throne.

36   ON NEWPORT RESERVOIR

I see a ripple on a thoughtless arc, and then
A smokestain crossing the unruffled hill . . .
There goes the sluggard puffing up, the gradient half-perceived,
Up to the final grandeur of a blank defeat. And thus
A pity, should a stranger say,
That box at Pentir Rhiw that pits the face,
The black gape of the mountain's mouth
Forced to a cry.

Words, murmur, words
That now attendant run on patent minds . . .
And yet I'm told the standard's universal,
Effortless, that hoardings of the past
Have shocked our feet into a single path,
Fashioned our gods. Objection, opposition come
From mammonites and fools afraid to look
On beauty, lest they miss their mouths that eat.

The Poems

So let it be.
My portion is as plain, I say
And fellow with the worst, or what you will,
Carved in my eyes that under lids
Count lovely only living as men can
The less to crave.

I pray no pardon then to mourn
The muted line of rubble mounds beneath
The water's level flooring, think
Of infant journeyings by Tyle's fields
With a half-run at dusk, and how
Before this bow in nature's hand was bent,
My father leapt the train beside that box
And downward falling to the farm's dull life
Was happier in that force, that stain, than we
Who silent, numerous, watch beauty's face.

37   NEW YEAR, 1939

The sun, the railings, and the coping shine;
The chestnut, with cold arms and frugal smile,
Leans on the wall with neighbour cheer
For bed and board within.
Hear a low laugh, caressing a cat,
And grinding of boots by the gate,
And the sky (that has played us a roof-tree before)
Falls dark, embarrassed, as a husband does
Who hiccoughs in a game, unable to abate
The beetling drone that drifts across its dark.

And yet today's discomfiture is more than this:
The players all are bunglers now
And dealing in a brighter candlelight.
Between the years, as in a niche, we see
Their fumbled hands held up and played
Unpurposefully, knowing not the end,
But patient as the tulip in its pot
That jerks its head back in the sun,
Crawls on one hand, but always on
Towards an earthen verge.

38   EVENING IN SAUNDERSFOOT

When I remember how I met the man
And eyed the lantern shut toward the land,
Heard curses muttered at the dogs who ran
Too close to me, I sense the message still
Crossing the sand.

Why should he stumble up that balk of black
And swing his stealthy light twice to and fro?
Was that the mast-lamp of a sheltering smack
Lifting the swell? I thought so then, and still
I think it so.

The castle trees, the tunnel's lower dark
Might cover all, I thought. Why should that car
Arrive, its headlights rove to find a mark
In me? And would the last house window's red
Extend so far?

I lingered obstinate that night to blink
The glare that urged me home beyond the sand.
And still I linger. Can it be, d'you think
They smuggle still? Did I, a stranger, spoil
What they had planned?

39   THE FOREST

From copse to copse I leap and hollo
Laugh and then am still –
And look! – my stragglers ranged afar
Come graceless in, together follow,
And windily obey their lordling's will.

Some are but saplings yet, and others
Near as old as I:
These that were born with me have blown
Up to the moon and back like brothers –
Yet in the dark as deadwood dreams may lie.

If in the dawn my dictates sally,
Hazel for kindness first,
A loyal oak for early strength,
Sure on the verge see black fear's tally! –
A cordon of the spindle-tree accurst.

This is my forest: but its sowing
Breath of the night was blown;
The spires ring all its hearts to tears
When I am sad, and stars just showing
Hear in its silly laughter soft my own.

40   LINES WRITTEN ON HEARING OF THE
INVASION OF POLAND (September 1st, 1939)

As short a while ago as seven hours
I thought still, sleepily, of dawn,
Of days ahead, days gone whose dowers
Were left upon my hands unworn.

I had in mind my coming journey north,
New forms in school, a season's fill
Of struggling for the tryline, back and forth,
A winter's striding up the hill.

There was that dreamed-of tackle by the stand
That I would try, the choir I'd join,
And summer with a car, all I had planned –
A work of thanks because my coign

Of history was happy – say I can,
Days in St Helens and in Breconshire
If in their sweetness have not made a man,
On to their midnight still aspire.

But now I lay them down. For to what end
Go past and future? – all I do,
And have done, has no point, no blade to bend
To war. Yet I am tirèd too.

The little store of interest I have built,
And my peculiar laughter, ecstasy,
Are tipped into the common pit of silt
And stupor. What remains of me?

41   DECLARATION OF WAR
                         (September 3rd, 1939)

Down at the station there are pickets set
And waiting for the drafts of men
That tumble off the train. Their uniforms
Are slack, no wire in their caps,
And all grin meaningless at the salute.
'Dragoon Guards? – right!' – and off they go
The wagons camouflaged, driving like mad,
Their dirty brown and grey a dash
Between the kilts and townsfolk in the street
 . . . All day they drive. And in the camp
Are pools for bombs and sandbags banked up high,
A maze of hutments and an earth
That's black with busy ants . . .
The man next door
Lay last night through in Oudenarde,
The barracks over hill, and phoned his wife
That it was quite a lark, a change
From civil crawlings to and fro . . . A change?
Why not? . . . He has no option now
On English earth, no hour to choose
His seven feet for air and light and view
Towards the park. He'll find he has
No rights at all against the massing worms
That violate his frontier. Why,
His crawl is done. And if not that, the lark
Will flutter overlong with all
Its laughter spent. And limitless the air,
Once ally with the earth, will dark
With eagles' wings and sway the kites
Of every careless dream that's in his hold.

42 DREAM

That frail asbestos finger
Whose blue claw
Defied its neighbour flame
Confronted me. And left there came
A milkwhite chanting for the cat.
I could no more
Have moved the lawn for mowers
Than a lazy drat
Would lay the mound of dinner-plates
That slanted up the sky.
And there were cows, I don't know why,
Climbing a tennis-net
To nibble chalk.
Frightened, I thought of Frigga at her wheel
Weaving her final web
And made to stretch my hand . . .
But all its feel
Was baffled by a voice I met
In air. 'Absurd' said this
'To cause a fuss
And make me conscious of your trivialities.'
And then I knew it was my world
But angled, curled:
The cat would never lick the dinner-plates
Nor I my fears, whatever find
I made between the fire and grass,
And either food or I (look either way)
Were only half consumed,
Limply consigned
To wander till these purgatories pass.

43 TOWER ON AN EVENING SKY

Tower on an evening sky
That sails like cloud,
Curls flag and lifts its crows-nest high
To every gale,
I crave aloud

Your calm unbending grace
Clearing the seas:
As Hatto's tower to mice – the place
Of any hold
To eyes like these –

You summon me. Your dark,
Your strength persists,
The unknown jousting at the mark
You win each course
And stay the lists.

I envy you the less
Your palmer strength,
Praying my habit's humbleness
May tower aloft
As true at length.

44 PAX NOBISCUM

The heat that blistered Finger Post
And brought the dust to Dentons Green
Is not more far than this deep plummet-dropping dusk
(That holds from Cribyn fast into this flowering close,
Pluming the heavy-scented budleia
And folding myriad butterflies abed)
From aqueous serenity and Thy shining levels.
Let's not mistake: I am as sheltered there
As here. The little hold I strike for's out of sight
From sward or postern.
I must not think this blossom air
And plum-nosed dusk a-peering down
My boundless friends.
The worms lie in this garden too
And gnaw their dividend from every rose.
The feudal strain has not grown weary yet:
War is man's rightful service to his lord:
All else is fear, which has no rights.
Up in the furrowed heat men knew their pains
But here
The flesh cries blood and soil brings up a rose.

... I must not weary, Lord: Thy rose is sweet
As peace, but peace not of the heart.
Lighten my toil to bring that larger peace
Lofting like sunlight on the Beacon slopes
To every treasure walled against the wind.

45   BLITZ IN MANCHESTER

I would have said
Do you remember how the light dashed out,
The shuttered glass
Cracked right across,
And dressing-gowns lit up to dogged tea
Beneath the stairs
To the accompanying gallop of the guns? ...
And in the morning how I picked a way,
Shambling through splinters to the station ramp,
Between the burning pillars, under sagging roof,
To see no trains:
And shivered lastly on a lorry
Going west, with twenty-five aboard,
Into the greying day? ...
But that's not what I mean.
And if I say
I see still how your heart leapt
To syncopate each crash,
Making a stormy rhythm in my life,
The white, your face
Across the dying anger of the fire,
And the low sofaed whisper of your tone
Stifling the umbrage of the skies,
You will understand ...
These, these persist and mope
Though many nights come on
And madden down upon my dreams.

46   NEPOTISM

    High founts that play in the sun,
    Lions at court –
    Long scaffold poles creep with the grain,
    Point with the facade one
    Into a mystery of jagged pain.

    Black-outs break loose for the day,
    Limber the dead –
    Tenement windows blink their rental,
    Washing's down, there the stray
    Bulk of the pole horizontal.

    Wood calls to high-leaping wood.
    Has it no right?
    What balk can unuse bring? O then
    Watch for the buttressed good,
    The creeping masts of unimagined men.

47   LAMENT FOR CASSANDRA

    The mood of many nights
    Dim in September lanes, pausing
    Beside the pale of you,
    Is come again.
    And now I am alone.

    The musing moon, the comforter
    Needing no eyes,
    Climbs to the tree, my lonely tree
    Upon the arming Allt.
    I wander, shadow of myself beyond
    And dust upon the hedge.

    O carrier of tales gone grey and old
    Take up your epic now
    And cosen time again.
    See, he remembers how the motes would comb
    A thousand beams and bend them all
    Upon the pale of you

And be content!
(I did not notice dust.)

I feel the wind. The moon is gone.
See where a star
Runs for a refuge over Cray.

48   FOR MARJORIE

Foam at the Skerries heel
A column on a hill
The peace of the uncovered little land
So still.

Paddles splash in a gill
The keel's scrape on a stone
Laughter undoing her curls to the war
And its own.

Richmond and old mother Môn
Are reeling in a song.
Only you could have kept them singing
So long.

49   CAFÉ PARTING

The soaking rucksack at the table leg,
The leather squeak of protest when the wet
Came sliding in and we
Not parted yet by more than public eyes
Leaning to mingle elbows, petrified
Lest moving once we should not be the same.

All morning rain had fallen persistent, cold
Stunning the land. The coats piled up, the damp
Import of coffeed drapes
Went creeping by the alcoves. On three sides
We were alone. Formalities with cups
Digestive biscuits and odd drooping jokes

About the saccharine we didn't want
Went packing with a trice, but we remained.
Nothing was over yet
But all of time unlimboed and minute
Had slipped into the mind. Invention tired
And every word had stumbled out before.

Seconds were left, no – hours! to search her face,
To seek assurance that was doubly known.
(Some dunderhead had held
The hands of time unasked.) The rain streamed on
Unerring like the clock. There lay the floor
Red, unabsorbent as the eyes and long

With pools like hers, that mirrored only mine
Redundant as the rain. I rose at last
Impatiently, swept out
The image that became a brushed-up thing
Sleek with the dull perpetuum of the drops.

50   INTER TENEBROS (EVEN HERE)

Here in the huddle of the lowest room
Prescribed for those with nothing in their hand,
No present for their host the state
And nothing for the stewards of the gloom,
No pourboire for the bland
Oiling the doors and printing the last late cards of invitation –
Here in the pit, the nether lines
I feel Thy penetration
Lord.

51   VISTA

Greying of suds upon an earthy white,
The dirty rivulets that wander down
The task of yesterday, tomorrow's right
To bridge another vista of eternity,

Hear in the hollow corridors of sound
The voices whipping on unwilling work:
And sense the idling of the days around
Dragging the step of dull invisibility.

52 BARS

Sun-in-my-window-shine
And skirl of gulls around the stack,
Spire burning up out of the blot of brown
And children's cries –
None of you give me back
My feel of air and back
         my hold of heaven,
For daylight dies
And night is a ten-paned vault of black
Too still to break with words
Too tired for eyes.

Desires upon my slate
And seven-squared days that bleach and crack
Between the wells and balconies
And concrete exercise –
How can you give me back
Those gilded weeks and back
         the breath of Wales
That hunted flies
Yonder upon the hills and hugs the tack
For south? And where go I
In this grey guise?

53 WISHES FROM WALTON

Upon the humbled ear
Behind the bang of pails
The rolling humdrum of a hundred cans
Comes dimming in a chant
The keyless ones command, with wide wake eyes
Descanting from Bootle swells and stops
To Penny Lane or anywhere

Within the lining of a threading purse.
O
To dive and rise and buy the yards
And know
That each penurious foot
Out to the singled end
Is yours
If you can slip the pence!
O
To run!
To move beyond the pallor of these walls
That point the grey between the blocks,
The yellow mockery of the studded door
That cracks its steel into the room!
I pass it only for the strut
Of wired cockerels round a little run,
Flutter to break a heart not wings,
And watch the listless bagging suite
The men in front make upon every bend
Limping unhopefully on
To an unfinal straight.
Air is persistent, ground reverberates:
This is that larger world and we
Are part if we could have it so.
But no!
If I should ask the transports of the sky
The brave lean waves of comfort to my hand,
Bootle par excellence will not suffice
Nor Blundellsands, nor every yard
From here to Lister Drive
To traverse fifty times.
I only want, how little and how much,
The green young dram illusion spills
Upon the unprobed soil
Soaking its adulation, joy
Worlds deep into its dark warm throat,
Deep from the tentacles of care,
Strong from the gripe of rising consternation.

54 CRIES IN THE NIGHT

The train that whinnies at me in the night
Shying the Stafford network gingerly
Turning to cry once more
Remembers other riders from the dark.
The northern belter rackets on
Tautening the reins,
Hurling his iron jeremiad
Across a raucous world.

But he is wrong, the faithful one
Who lingers crying after me.
I count for him so patiently –
Another ten, another eight
The nights must peter soon, I say.
And then his wheels clop on.

55 FAGENBAUM

Follow the ponderous tailor, mark
The bulge of all the Ghettos
At his nape,
His polished cranium
Cast like a globe abruptly on the spine
Circle the plot –
Coat upon oxbody ploughs the round,
The legs creased up
To tease with worsted friction at the knees
Knocking the step.
Always the inner round, the eyes cast down
And belly forcing room.
Silent and shapeless to the hoarse command
Alike and ninety eyes
He draws around, darkening the sun,
Corroding the pile of blackened bars.

56   NIGHT ON THE BRECON ROAD

Turbulent, unbecoming, how this head goes on
To trouble! My only crown is wet
And the imposture of direction is bought dear
In breath, banking a mounting painful debt.
A car's light links the pools. Suppose it means
Persistence, courage, both. Thus the next lift I get
May be another flagrant chariot of wrath.
Wind clapping ears, I pass the county jail
Curious of mumblings in my head. Sing out beneath,
Journeyman free of the gale, of the weather's bounty,
Lacking only your craft. You may tread
Tidily, keeping your symptoms close. Eyes
In a parcel are upon your back. What inmate
Was it laughed? Come pick-my-pocket fellow,
You that drink cocoa and see the bare
Bulb flare yellow, gallantly
Honour my glimmer and despise your star.
Glibly upon the tumbril, tongue, and free man follow
The rain, the lively drummer,
With all the mountains marching in your train.

57   THE CLOSE

Embalm these memories and build
A little tumulus of bedded charms,
My loves unfinished share no harms
The minds of men have willed.

Turn here to find my tearful plot
When under trees I dare the dew to fall
On fancies fretted out, on tall
And fainting bergamot.

Perhaps my world will be so round
That one year yonder I shall pass again
Patient as day, for sleeping men
My feet shall make no sound.

Look then how righteous anger leaps
About the bounds, how soft green sorrow bends
Along the ground, faith made amends
Upon the farther steeps.

And now I go. There is no key.
Will they be mark for vandals where they lie?
Will the shy savour them? Can I
Command this constancy?

58 CREDO

We have remembered now the myth
Of barbarism in the rooted soil,
Causeless vulgarians tying men to trees
Because of black nature flourishing.
What is not near can be
No dropping selfishness of mine
But we have swamps enough that seep
Below this hill. Whose are the roots
Poisoning the burrows?

If we must theorise, where I can cut
The brushwood economic doctrines make
And leave the tree I will,
Lest poor men think a change of attitude
The highest good of all.
I have not come so far and felt the Grace
Line every growth into a pointing tree
Now to survive since soil and site were good
And near below the darkened wood
I should have been a gallows
Weighted to the swing of murderers.
Some thirty years convict me that
I have not sought my God, all-penetrating sun
Rain, wind and dew, enough
But still the incomparable seasons of His Love
Dissolve around. I and the hill are one.
Men's shadows are themselves.

59   OXFORD CASTLE

         The oldest building in the town, they said,
         Its glory that its views confine
         The guests to cattlemarket, lines for goods
         And posters of the war; so mine
         The loss in five short Oxford years I quite
         Forgot the charm of playing with trains,
         Beating cows about, guessing the height
         Of walls legs braced; my gain I understood
         How when the butter's to the fore again
         These things shall lift us into nationhood.

60   SLOW MEETING

         Down Kendrick hill I must admire
         What dainty prescience the sobered earth
         For all her seedlings feels, what falling glow
         In all her stems afire
         When sunning's done. How can there no
         Soft contemplation come to bay? –
         All my friends say.

         Beauty constrains me. Silence so
         My silence shall be, and the emphasis
         On trite divinity the agile crowd
         Waiting the easy *mot*
         As trailer to the day will sip
         Can never trill its way aloud.
         My loves have a beginning in the dark
         Hand missing hand, avoiding so
         The crowded levels of acquaintanceship.
         I never look as I go by.
         Never reply.

61   MAESYRONNEN

         Across the field, beyond the lordly hedge,
         One side as anciently toward the poor,
         The long white chapel leans, a living pledge

Left by the men who broke their Babylon,
The staple of the state.
But now the roof with four blue feet of sky,
The half blocked up with boards, lifts ominous:
A blackened stove with scaly tenebrate
Climbs roundly to the beams: and boxed nearby
Lie dusty hymn-books only ten years old
To indicate the poor and present few,
The incubus
Of braver days.
This angle hides a stiff-necked family pew:
One worthy on his haunches saw the lips
That poured forth assonance of truth, the while
He balked with thick eclipse
Dry contemplation of the undevout.
This oaken pen would hide his children too,
The sidelong smile,
The bag crackling uncomfortably out
And little hands drumming the sermon through.
Here at this curious benchèd table sat
In controversial quorum, face to face,
The leaders of the faith.
Beside the door, in that more cumbered place,
The stranger man, the last uncertain lout
Hunched quickly on his form the cheap machine
Has planed to poverty. In front set out
One hoary bench, thick as a quarried flag
And sagging with the dropsy, bellies back
Into an older age.
Upon the pulpit board new bossed with black
Gleaming with gold leaf, gallant as a page
On which the day's illumination falls,
Start out the names of tens of serving-men
Who launched the lighted Word within these walls
Three hundred years ago, who flung the gage
Downhill across the Wye.

Stand by the door. Be silent, see
Jogging evangelists come in aflame
And seeking men stride out of Breconshire.
Now it is Lord's Day evening. Hear the free
Sonority of Welsh come hushing out

Over the nodding heads, the English psalms
Of a believer with a Hereford name
Choiring the neighbourhood.
Up many a lonely cwm for miles around
The disputatious climb, mouthing the good,
To rack the Church and curse Her Popish springs.
Now by each lonely fire the ashes sound,
The finger in the Book falls on the text
Weighing the household sin. And lo who sings
The penitential round . . .

This was the anvil. Now the sparks beat out
In darker hammering and a little dust.

WORM IN THE BRAIN

Rain in the trees
And in the furrows hissingly
Sour on the breeze
Crabbing the green breath at the gate
Bogging with squalid spate
The gambo lumbering heavily
Humid with drashings for the barn
From raining trees.

Slant on the pane
And roses picking at the sill
Worm in the brain
Wheedling the pinkish text aslant
Spotting the smile my aunt
Hangs happy on her portrait still . . .
All that I love I would pull down
Down with the rain.

PASTORALE

I came from Merthyr by the Cefn road
Above the crosses in the valley on
Into the uncertain nodding of the sun.
Gently we rubbed the shoulders

The Poems

Burned on the brown divide
Fingering the gloss into the skin
Liquid with scuds of cloud running
Before the imperious light.
Late on its hillock spring and all the lakes
Were breaking with a toss and fret.

Inside the bus the sun drove too
Faint with a forgotten smell of leather
And clothes in coffer. Here close were Cefn folk
Keeping their limber legs for summer hours,
Then hill-farm girls, red heavy cheeks
And struggling bags, an urchin clinging
With the bread at heel.
Press double at the bell and Daio knew them all
With corny wit from crumpled schoolboy cap
To Mrs Morris and her heavy legs,
Parcel for the Twmp and tell old Danny
Three o'clock bus on Friday.
                      So the world
Up to the northern neck
Was bickered into sympathy
And rung up every punctuated ridge.

Beyond the Storey Arms the bus ran down
Swinging on hairwide curves above
A wilderness. Silence was here
And sun and the smooth hum
Of tyres. The heat made
Waspish arcs of sound skid off the hill
And with it rode
The faint unkemptness of the horse.

Soon it began again, the farms below
And Daio's bell to ring the engulfing act.
'Fine for the market, mun,' the double touch
Went nicking in
With every name as pat
As fifteen miles away.
Downward through Libanus old ladies then
And boys with sixpence clutching hotly at the hand
To cross the bridge. Conductor saunters to

His mother's door and disappears.
At home to Daio like the hills.

So to the pinprick roofs and
Voiding the motif, voices, mountain sun,
We pressed a hundred springs across the pool,
Clipping our odorous texture with a punctual knife,
Dragging the toga of the higgledy town.

64 BALLOON OVER THE RHONDDA

We had gone down to Tabor, to the door,
My corduroy a green
Tug at the ministerial spleen, a tweak
At the white scarf-knot, peak in pocket seen
Capping the diaconate,
In time to scalp the noise
And scamper made by boys, evacuees
With paper aeroplanes the teasing wind
Forced down behind the chapel rails.
Sighs from the big seat
Came barely out
Above the scrabble of the eager boots
Climbing the gate
    for paperweight . . .

The tease was bold that night,
Suborns of bigger men had gone adrift:
The little clusters in the street
Sent eyes up to the south
And feet were still:

A silver elephant with wings
Came curveting and lolloping
With a one-sided smile.
He turned and chortled, lay down on his back
And laughed, helpless and rolling.
Up from the east came the stern searing of
The pursuit wasp,
In the ballooning laughter poured
First secondsworth of venom and a silence,

Then the wide curve of steady preparation
And seconds more.
The ears fell back
And all the laughter wasted.
Falling a thousand feet the narrow hide
Pine end hung on
In dumb deflation.
Three other Spitfires flew a higher course
Poured in their angled heat
And passed.
Dying in sullenness
The skin a sagging five miles off
Caught of the glory a few sunset rays
Clung to its thousand feet and stooped
Up to the valley head.
Obstinate blob upon the sky
Bleak with attendant stings
It passed behind the housetops
Uncomprehending and absurd.

'Duw, if that Whitley'd hit 'er
She'd 'a shifted' and the remark
Gave the cloth cap an air.
Speculation soon and hands
Went back in pockets
And the whole street on heels again.

Out of the gateway old Arafna John
Signalman's line of red gone thin
Below the waist in black
Came with the deacons to attack their caps
Cordon their eyes perhaps at green and gawk.
'Whose son is this?' and talk apace
Of the pregethwr . . . Green in the eyes again
And no grace in the pause
(The sunset passed behind the mine) . . .
O could the slow vine be husbanded
The branch sweeping the grass?
Better the doubt than diction
Thinking John he said
'I hope you'll set the world to rights, my son'
And plodded on.
Under the sky they were the dumb who nodded.

65   MARCH ON THE MOUNTAINS

Llanfrynach pool is clear again!
And though above the Caerau hedge
The silver mountain ribs remain,
Deep lie their feeders for the rain
And greening at the edge.

O when the watery minutes sound
Like scampers up and down the pane,
Then with the green swell on the ground
Old March will whip his bluster round
And clear the peaks again!

66   END-PIECE

What's done I cannot do
Again, nor turn my hand
To other task.
And such as wolf my fare,
Dandle their dregs and grandly dare to ask
My poor relation's rights and pedigree –
On this I stand:
My story's silly, but it lives with me
And breaks my bread in all solemnity.

67   THE BEARERS

Wet in the field,
A dull rook preaching
To congregated hecklers in the trees,
And there, behind the text from Maccabees
Red warfare reaching
Into this ground, in upturned blood revealed.

Yet I am home
With handgrip, knowing
Something there is that turns me to the hills,
Some bowel-moving look about me tills
The body going
To growth. I am turned bonewards in this loam.

And when I go,
A burden and bearing,
O long the labour the dark Beacons make
Cloudwise across the south, and me they take
Covertly faring,
An Eginhard over the unfallen snow.

68   BEACONS

Bevel and plume of a graveyard yew
Bevel and plume beside
And two black fancies circumscribe
The canvas. Then the hangers fade
Into the stockstill field. Only the wash
Remains, only the sky-stream ceaselessly
And the burnt peat brown of the peaks
Breaking.

69   LONDON WELSHMAN

Money you'll never see, Shon –
And nearly ten years from
The wood you worked in
Handling the milk.
You can live on now incomplete,
Washing bottles, cornering
The lasting bowler and a country hope.
Your picture's fixed (the moving you despise,
A flicker on the mind that goes),
And still imagining begins
'Wel dyma fi ar y rhos' and
Phrases following about the fields
The squatter's child was favourite at the farm
Old women fifty winters gone
Knitting stockings
For the young moormen – Ah!
Jack Saer with a buzz-saw now
Transposed unwillingly
Into an English version.

Welsh flannel grows into the skin
The countryman was born with
And the great knotting root lives on
Mindless beneath and moving
The meagre hill like a livewood limb
Festooning
Stumps of a smaller age . . .
Almost the moorwise collie coming
The stones in Saron speaking
Loom on the road to London.
'Ah! this is the place' you say
'This London' where
The workers care nothing and
Curiosity is no killer
Of an outside root.
Remembering, I know you mean
To hold your unpeopled hill
And have it move
The quiet of this million-mouthing house.

70   LLYN BODGYNYDD

The world a waste of days
The heart a stone for breaking
Man with a taste for tears
Take of this water and taking
Break moss for the stone
My stone
Bring moss to its breaking.

Toss on the whipping world
The harking wave recover
Man with the slipping soul
Love will touch none but the lover
Move light on the grave
Grave stone
The cold tomb re-cover.

71   DROVER'S SONG

   First to the ford tonight,
   No straggling.
   On with swinging udder, rump
   Drolly, rollingly,
   Niggling rump and tail lowingly
   On where that tump of whaleback in the sky
   Grows out of sight,
   By there the pinfold covert in the wood
   Bachan, in the wood, you follow? –
   A butty's hollo from the Drover's Arms hard by
   We'll halter. Haiptrw ho!
   Life and five sundowns going with us good
   Into the morning, boy, the Maidstone street –
   Ware Dafi Jones o Caio
   Singing grace after his meat.

   Halter the runts below
   The hollow tree:
   Up with the swinging udder, rump
   Drolly, rollingly,
   Niggling rump and tail lowingly,
   Brisk up the rustback by the stump
   Switch her and go
   Down by the rollick pathway through the wood,
   Hold her, bachan, wait my hint! –
   There's Jacky Bint in the Drover's Arms, he'll bump
   A bottle when there's plentyo.
   Come morning and the Farnboro ale for load
   And haiptrw ho! and the ale well stowed,
   Sing for the sun, boyo, sing for your living –
   Leave Dafi Jones o Caio
   Bring his God upon the road.

72   THE BALLAD OF BARROLL'S DAUGHTER

   It is ill dying in the wind
   When sons are hard to know:
   And bad for backs are the Skirrid rocks
   When the last storms blow.

A man may be sad of his goods for long
Before he comes to die
And age deny a quiet heir
To hale prosperity.

With Farmer Barroll's heart for work
The intake from the hill
Weighted his wheels on the ringing stone.
One portion was lost still:

Rocks might dissemble did the eye
Fall on a favoured son,
But Farmer Barroll's girls could hear
The rough shale falling on.

Judith and Ellen had no art
That suitors could discover.
Their's was the farmhand's elder leer
When they looked for a lover.

But all the mind of Margaret
Was in her hazel eyes
Deep as a black-fringed salmon pool
Where the moonwaters rise.

When she looked out from Skirrid rocks
She looked neither near nor far,
Only towards the eastern plain
Where the long-dead horsemen are.

And to the night imponderable
With childless Saturn hiding
'O that the storms may shout' she cried
'So that my love come riding.'

Tom Lenthall in a new check coat
Came to the door at noon;
He was the under-gamekeeper
Who left his charge too soon.

Horses and he had long been known
To blanket down together.

When winter oats was in his gift
The horse could do no other.

The elder girls twisted their lips
At him and were not minded:
They had no use for stable breath
And a lover so short-winded.

But Margaret with a choice of hearts
Mistook the crude intention.
He spoke her hotly in a phrase
Across the old convention.

Looking toward the eastern plain
And the mare beside the door
She honoured the prophetic head
And the habit of the poor.

The door was open. Once inside
A lurcher snaps at table.
Any seed on stolen ground
Perhaps defies the parable.

Walks in the woods came to the point
They must elope together
Before the old man would understand.
Margaret had no mother.

The horns of a new moon appeared
Over the High Wood, waiting.
In red-leaved evening Skirrid heard
The news of that rough mating.

Old Farmer Barroll was at heart
As cowed as any other;
He wailed as quick as a weaning child
Grows tired in sultry weather.

But he turned his money in the wind,
Blotted his will in fear:
His girl was rich with a penny then.
A shilling was too dear

For Tom the under-gamekeeper
Who could barely make his mark.
(Touching this failure with the will,
Tom had not meant to work,

Only to move in when the time
And temper were propitious.
Free of the paddock and the best bed –
No, he was not ambitious.

Horses and he were not apart
For long without a whinny:
Women he left and loved again
Liking the feel of many.)

In May the whispers reached the farm.
Abraham John the carter
Swore they were living Pandy way,
Margaret had a daughter.

The child, he said, was sick one day
Inordinately crying:
Tom Lenthall rode his mare into
The room where it was lying.

Then nuzzling up her great green teeth
(Her temper was his whim)
She plucked the baby by the shawl
Over the frantic rim.

The neighbours hearing Margaret's shrieks
Came running in a moment:
The bridegroom backed his greater love
And wished them all preferment.

The carter paused to some effect.
Such moments were his seeking.
Disaster's dog was Abraham John,
A man lost in the making.

In the crowded climacteric
The child escaped a mention;

The clever horse maintained the floor
Against the dire intention.

This bitter tale the sisters kept
Fast in the loyal locket
Of family grief, defying most
Who might come in and mock it.

But in the kitchen it lay close
And kept the wall from Barroll,
For neither sister had the strength
To argue the old quarrel.

A light air turned the money over,
Tails for the heart of lead:
In making up his last account
He marked his young girl dead.

Most days he brooded in the barn
Making a heart for mammon.
At the front porch Tom Lenthall lurched
Drunk, with another woman.

The dogs were rid of him at last,
His trap wheels went in chorus;
But the brief snapping left unbit
The ridden age of virus.

Old Barroll propped his back up straight,
Hard as the Skirrid rocks,
Making intent provision for
His silent daughters' sakes.

Mistake not, the attorney's hand
Reached beyond mere decease:
Judith and Ellen had no art
To bring their sister peace.

The feckless child, the carter heard,
Grew up and entered service,
Becoming tweeny in the house
Of Mrs Nicholls Jarvis.

The mother, striking from her stars
The lewd saturnine lover,
Ran as the bludgeon rain came down,
Wretched in every cover.

In vicarage and home she hid
Whenever fear was harder.
At last out of the planet's reach
She cursed the horse and rider.

* * * * *

In Battle churchyard is the stone
And long she has been lying,
The Christian whose molested life
Was happiest in her dying.

The servant-girl was my great-grandam.
With half my heart I court her:
In prancing blood the other half
Checks out on Barroll's daughter.

WHITEWATER

Looking down
Ears flat, eyes roving roving
In chalk faces
Down on the flat reflection of the water
Hunting hunting
With the insatiable dogs of dreams,
This is the future
The water and fog-wisp
The chase and the failure
Panting, unfinished
The fields that are limed
And the scarecrow hand
Dropping the present
In dull repetition
In black-spreading ripples,
Dropping our faces
Flat as the moment
Down on the white reflection of the water.

74 ENSTONE ROCK

Beyond this contour
Miserly cross the middle of this wold
And there
The glorious beggar Bushell globed his light,
Lean from the Calf of Man, the oil and herbs
Of parsimony back
In the mustard method his great Bacon taught,
Back in the panorama of his pageboy grace –
And calling Charles, the noble slipmaster
Irritant, Charles, catspaw of envoi voyant,
Engineer O engineer, proved for him thunders
Bird song and waterplay
All in one gainly tragedy
From the mosaic rock.
Out of this pulsing drumhead grew the grant
Of mines in silver Wales
And master, master then, prosperity
In minting with the plume of three,
Prosperity the right to plunge
Along the adits to the watered rock
He knew, plunge from a pageboy hope
Emerge an engineer.

The rock, now can I find it,
Could I but
And climb, having the fear
Of falling, up from the plain
Unploughed nardus of the day
To heights with you, your loveliness, the wind
Sorting the chocolate slopes,
Overseer sun from Ditchley way
Planning the hot plateau for the aerodrome
With the immediate berserk navvy by –

Now could I, could I have some fear,
Some hope of holding, fear of falling,
Bollard the rock and mine
The silver mystery my meaning is
On to the adit end . . .
Leave loyal then

Seeking the peerless now, to this
High landscape cling I and the horizon you.

How, greybeard Bushell, did you bring your Charles,
How hold the listening? Where
In your pamphlet penury I feel
The pageboy linger, plying to his dream,
Here I with no more history
Than midnight seek comparison, malpractising
The sorry repetition my unribboned bow.

Where is the rock? And engineer –
The pigs go mudding in your Glyme.

75   LADYSMOCK

I saw you yesterday in the high hedge
On tiptoe with the tallest violets I know,
With fretted-finger eager frame on edge
Glimpsing the designs in the dust below.
You looked as lovely there
In all my day I found no other dream so fair.

We doubtless in our hotter plodding way
Would tag generic labels on your lilac leaf
With malnutrition mourning border fray
Your delicacy and deplore the peep
You manage at the sun.
Yet how our heated passing gives you food and fun!

76   FULWELL

O mine, O tension in the main
Unmoving helplessness, O pain
Untenable but shaped as round
And equal as the ungiving ground,
How may I hold, then, tell me,
Hold this great drop from the sound
Of misery, keep me so that I feel
Not empty, not feel passionless and punished?

Deep,
Yes, deeper the well the dippers seal
Then open, giving back the wound.

For this is fullness, this. Whoever comes
Can lower nothing that will hold,
Can lift no cold cord off the thumbs
Of gravity. No one but you and you bold
Can lean chafing the worn edge and peer
Where numb the noticeable orb is cold
And moveless, under the ledge the moon
And the water near.

O pain, near pain, how may I hold?
Pain, you that are dear and far,
Here, pain, am I bold and plain;
All of me, full of me, deep of me,
Far and not looking, dear and not caring,
Holder and keeper, your near well daring
Deeper than many, bolder than most,
Wearies with water, the cords and the fraying,
Come, saying, lostheart, come to the sharing
The drop pentecost.

* * * * *

I will speak to the quiet, to you sparing
The tongues my moveless water makes,
To you tossed in the quiet
Beyond the pain.
Now I have seen your lane, your leaves,
The slow quartering of your Cotswold sun
Around the eaves, dusk in the lane
And the grave dolmen by it,
I have brought my pain in a piece,
My groan in a drop, the unrelease run
Great to the well in the quiet
And filling the well there you have forgotten.

I am from far, but you are farther
Behind the silence than I believed,
Not here with the moon and the pain
Of the well.

                    I move. I am still, rather.
Only the moonlight heaved.
The quiet is yours and the slow plain
Song of the heart bereaved.

Come, I am moveless.
Come gather me, waiting
The winter for drawing, the deep for taking
The moon up in heartfuls, me mindless and hating
The heap of wet leaves, the creep of November
Cold in the little lane. Leap, silence, closer,
                              this way, I am waiting
The chafe of your coming
The chill of each member . . . O
Willing the rope and the great drop breaking.

77   FOR M.A.H.

You move in history now and in my gain
Is every heartache out of Oxford ground
That's torn from me and muddied every wound
With the swift pellets of a Cotswold rain.

Your names have music. Wychwood runnels bring
Simple unreason to my rising throat:
Unasked abandon fingers at each note
Arraigning an andante opening:

Walls cannot hold the wind against me now:
I am the one to walk the rows at Tew
Believing jasmine breathes the shape of you
And Lucius Cary makes you his first bow.

I am with Hampden in his ragged charge
Hoping for Chiselhampton held or down:
I ride with Bushell into Oxford town
To mint the college loyalty in large.

Where in the morrow may I find you fair?
Is beauty less than now my heart believes?
A green scythe whispers on. The silence reaves
Only the distant windrush in your hair.

And now the hangdogs gather at the fire,
A grey rain falling and the grotted red
Hissing in sequence.
                    Somewhere keep unshed
                    (O somewhere still!)
The last bewitching tears of Oxfordshire.

78   PRAYER BEFORE MARRIAGE

That peradventurer who breaks at last
Upon a love that laps him simply round
And trusts it, I would be:
I die each hour in a discoloured past
And, sick, cannot call thee.

O cut me this corroding pain,
Knot out the parcel in my nailing hand;
Uncord the truss of misery
And friend me fresh into the helpless land.

These eyes that weary in the ward
Relieve with certainty the best obeys:
If I am chastened, O accord
Those the companion of my care and praise

All that the heart cries out for, rock
For the root of memory, the hoped-for hand
Ringing the shoots. Lord, let us feel
The final mercy Thou, yea Thou hast planned.

79   LAST HAPPINESS

In the wet pageantry tonight deploys
For answer to my calling joys, I write
A parting in the head of midnight's hair
And picture it, there white
And straight as daylight on the dress you wear.

Blue flashing tits went beating up in droves
From tree to tree within the groves. I lose
In the blue streak the blackhead one whose feet
Held sideways to our house
Of plaster. We were placed, we, in that beat

Of wings and sideways in the whirring days.
But we held on. Each life obeys the wind
Beating or hanging in it. Underpinned we
Paused by Penoyre and ringed
The leg of fortitude we had in lee.

Then through this circlet of the years the gay
Breasts passed. A fox-brown comfort lay in fern
Upon the hill-top. The sun in turn, red
With exertion, stopped to burn
The moment for our ember day. Ahead

Lay only flight late to the windways, fast
As our beat was slow. Loth townwards, last to part,
We joined the poor jargon of points, starting
The beat again in heart
In learning peas and pulse were one, a thing

Of unity. Living we held the seed
In hands of promise.
                              Now the need comes, nears
The night of days when purpose not fear's slack,
And these in water swell indeed
Only the weight of tears
Only the deadweight tears calling you back, calling you back.

80   KIDMORE END

I remember agrimony. And the tall
Woolly yellow plant you said you thought
Was mullein, shouldering
The small brushed space behind
The cornfield, and the slope,
The sudden slanting of the perilous ears
Crowding the slattern fence

We climbed to reach the copse,
The ground we held imperfectly against
The industry of ants, brutality of
Harvest-bugs and fear tomorrow's hundred miles
Would bring between us. All's to remember
In this yesterday, when yes, (so seldom now)
Our sun was strong,
Planes prayed like pharisees beyond the grass
And summer stayed. But time with tricks on us
Played shunting minutes in our ears
Dragging our goodbyes to their place too soon
Making us mute in the unending lastness
Of the moment. All I could see
Ran down the vista of my heart at once
And stopped it. You were gone.
But on my sleeve was agrimony's hand
Pressing a rough astringent zeal
For cure, for comforter.

81 REQUIESCAT

I have had no great acquaintance
With death. I hawk no rebate
Of a screamed-out blitz in breath
Heavy with bomb-bursts, bits of men
Disposed about the room and dumb
Amen to the doom, to the night they died.
Wounds I have wished and had
Wide as the tomb my soul cast
Sealed at the door, and danger.
It is past and nothing more, will nothing
More than I know and may shield still.

It is far off, that will, that feeling,
And ordered distantly from the one funeral
Disposed by years to ill effect:
A hill, Trealaw, files of men,
Of workmates, there tens of them walking walking
Hat in hand in columns hot in the sun –
Men, miners, boots in the beat of living
An hour for one beat gone.

The sun, the long sun in the gap
And I, burning to earth for the off-beat,
Listened. So the sun failed, and I,
And listening lost the spot
In time, the break in understanding
Too deep for my young cautery.

Now here in April in the sleeve of spring
Caught up, I listen for the step, the beat,
The thickened off-beat of the soilstopped blood,
Here in the quickened field
With grass and stone,
Quick grass and bounden stone.

It mounts to its determined height
And cut, the stone, in white simplicity.
The little candid chips importantly dispose
A space for reverence. Close to I clear
The mind for mystery, the ear for earthbeat.

The cinerarias, dark-blue wedding flowers,
A fortnight loved and ours for ever, droop
From the cup of stone. Now flower it fresh,
Now group we must the gap and clip new green
To charity. These grasses tower with life
Too tall to stoop and cherish what has been.

I lift my head and look
At the wimpey over the hedge, beyond.
Unprinciple in glasses, bald
As steel, a kite on the edge of silence.
In that guise then, in that guise simply
Sunlight discloses death, no other wise,
Death in the sun. But in the words I know,
In one, I search for silence – now preposing peace,
Those turrets still, on lease to rust
A many month. Yet seven years ago
Distrust was peace, the dropping feet
Left the farrago for the fields alone
And individual holes, the crust
Being thinner then, the cantos short
As life. For then the beat,

The Poems

The thin caught beat of otherwise,
Came through.

Here on the hill toward Heythrop
I wait. The sun burns to the top. A child
Thinking a dandelion as mild and sweet
As bordered pansies set to blow
Their ordered day through turns
The solar wheel, and waiting too
The stone cup fills.

I am sad for the stone, the speaker
In life not known and lost
The seeker for morrows I meet
On my pillow. I am sad
Though no sorrows atone, I grieve
For the sherds of the singer
Though I know no words she sang.

I am sad but the pang leaps up,
Leaps up with the living, the light
Rush of may-grass that thickens
The sight, the cheek of the hare
Who beckons bolt upright
In the thrusting corn.

The ages shrug.
The round sun billion
Miles off warms the mound.
So am I finite (and perpend)
I cannot know nor fear my end.

82   THE CAULDRON OF DIWRNACH WYDDEL
                (*A Poem for the D-Days*)

If a man would cook food for a coward in it, he may wait till Doomsday for the water to boil; but a brave man's meat is ready for him as soon as it is put therein. – *The Mabinogion for Children*

       Met at the high table of history,
       Brave men, brave meat, what else
       Commands idolatry? The man cooking,

The men he stirs
Are all in the heat of the moment
Waiting. The waters of asseveration
Rise. Slowly the ribs turn.

Where are the cowards? Where the bellies
To retch at the raw substantives
Of life? They lived
In Monte Cassino long ago
With Benedict, before the bombs
Found them unseemly, blocking
The hundred ways to Rome.
They lived in Bermondsey before
Their food was cooked in messes
And the street names were changed.
They died and were cold. Look,
Look in the water,
In the pale water the slim shoal
Stirs putrescent. Flame licks, flame,
The mackerel cold of memory.
Stir on, stir.
This is the cauldron of Diwrnach.
This is the cauldron of life.

A meal is the moment. Hot
Is the heat of the cauldron.
Fraternal, wide is the choice
Of collops fetched for the board
Of the mighty, in the wide white hall
Of Arthur. Shake at the meat,
Cold remnant, shake at the sunset.
Quake to the waste and be better
Forgotten. Hot, hot is the blood,
Burning to drink, to flow,
Scabbed over by a solemn thought.
Each man is cruseward to himself,
Stirrer to others. Swirl, swirl, waters –
A brave man prods the ribs.

The water is boiling now
And this is the measure of the cauldron.
This is the measure of life.

83   THE LAMENT OF LITTLE GWION

           The hollows are full
           With the harvest
           And the hills
           Thicken to consummation.
           Yellow strokes
           Of mustard
           Sharpen the light
           Whetting the knives
           The long knives of nobles
           The nails of the people
           Cutting a portion
           In the time of living.

           A heap is the board
           And the people heavy:
           Now is the time
           For the light touch of music.

           But I am a child
           Surfeit with swansdown
           And the smell of honey,
           A riddling child
           Watching the dark
           Elder faces
           And the fingers playing
           'Berwm, berwm'
           On the crowded lips.

           I am a prophet
           Without performance
           Lost from the pillar
           And the dark land
           Of my gesticulation.

84   MIRROR

In that white country
In the white spaces
The cool wych elms leave
In the shaped air
The grey pigeons flying
Remote from their places
Dilate in the heat-
Spiring distance and weave
A thin braid of answer
Replying replying
To nobody's echo or
Pleasure for
Nobody's there.

Dust off the figures
Colour the kerchief
The waggoner hooks
Below the shaft there,
Wake up the sleepers
And listen – the bare sheaf
Of silence stalks near,
Beckons nearer, mouth looks
Solemn at mouther
With nothing to hear.
For these are the keepers
Of the quiet of light:
By shiver and compass
The stook and the horses
In mustard and mallow
And corn-combing hollow
Are under the glass
Of the stone-white air.

Quick touch on satin! –
The glass is bare.
But halo and habit
And cold hearts wanting
The corn and the kingdom cry
'O where? where?'

85   EVENING: UNLOADING WHEAT

Sesame, word of logic, or wild guess
Towards this mandate's golden-brown economy,
Open my hand with magic, work no less
Than Mars with this so-grainèd weapon
To build unanswerable hours beyond the wars.

Beneath, the elevator's spinal rattle
Clutches the off-cart shock in an engrossing sheath.
Christen the craters of this mind, my battle! –
I fork off what my feet imprison,
Tugging my guts out that the assembled stars may mark.

86   GRACE BEFORE WORK

Then in remembering I do not enough
To integrate the present with the past.

Making the cast with simples I must try
The last-born, least-bred herb twopence
Of the soil, plenish my little moor or die
With its denuded symbols and go home
No more. In that exordium of fixity
The dark, long-headed men recovered heart,
Built shacks, saved landlords from prolixity,
Beat tedium out of doors and kept
The chapel bare, unbettered, for eternity's room.
Hope in the squatter's heart was a high door
And life beyond. Disestablishment and doom
Broke on the lintel the unlettered head
Uprising. Till at Maengwyn the carpenter,
Our elder Thomas, pared the wood
To find the bite, spread on the certain tenter
Floorcloth of fine-win dreams, bursting the door
Higher above the mud identical. This was the germ,
The fetus of our state and warm
The flannel shirt that keeps the heart from harm.

Looking at orchard, immense red-
Brown cut of roots ploughed in my lens

And picking out of the bed-silver Usk
Bowed rick, the glint of yellow slopes
Patched with the rank discomfiture of green,
I must recall the rock, the beaten husk
Beneath, and the first builder to whom fell
Much less of tack and harvest. In that sense
The century has done justice to his hopes.

Each has his earth and mulches in it good.
O backbreak past, share in the present's food.

87   PONTWILLIM PLOUGH

Red fresh-turned plough across the gate
Was topped with silver riming:
The ice-caps from the broken hills
Sparkled in the taming.

A corner of that picture flashed
From the cracked Christmas mirror:
I leaned across the gate and said
The artist was in error –

Or that at least he would be so
In any stiff town salon.
Critics should bleed their humours out,
Coldcrops keep the bellon.

The mists come up and pluck the side
And fill the cracking valley:
My wish is with the driven plough,
The blackbird in the holly.

88   SUBITE

The track is invisible
Carrying the hardships of the heart
Into this last phase:
The white lines of our former rulings
Blur in this mistral country, where
The undeterred have praise.

Gone the remembered lane, the mort
Of leaves in the nostril, reek
Of the unswept past:
In this unbroken sweep of sight
Presented purity has time, has place
To bury worm and cast.

It is immense on humbled rick:
The grown wheel is increase:
Over the sad straw
In the yard and the lost years
Of rottenness on the draggled land
Deepens the one law.

Unwanted saviour of the scene
Carrying the cubit cross,
Millennial inch of stature on the mind
Unspotting dross,
It falls through the old sacrifice,
Softspoken, slow:
Softly the few unhurried servants go
Among their kind.
This is the morning I shall wish to find
In all the world – Untrodden world!
World under snow!

89 HILLSIDE

Sharply towards the evening, sharply
Pause the moments, halt the unhearing
Passages of time. Forenoon and brain are deaf,
Out of time with the drum-beats, dropping partly
Because of the echo berserk in the vault.

Ear turns, life turns, twisting nightly
In the tumour of the soil. Wood shoots,
Buds break, poor-relation briar sharp on sleeve
Has time into tripwire, stopping, tightly
Pointing the moment with a pin of blood.

In the mad vault I must dissemble
Pains that are part of a speeding dream.
Only the night O and the tumour pressing
Red in my back makes the face resemble
Passage of tears too and the wet winds pleading.

90 IN THIS COLD ROOM

In this cold room, with the pictures
Of night in the arena and the luminous dead
Leaving the untwisted heaps and the lions
Staring at light,
With Armageddon over the first cloud
Apparent with swords of punishment and witnesses,
This is the moment, in this cold room,
For the socket of bone to tremble,
For the ultimate scar.

This is the moment, now, when no cast of eye
Crosses the lawn and the two fir trees
Topple the unsure sky to rain,
Now when the trampling in the coppice
Crashes the fiery tailfins from the trees
Tossing beyond the strafe and sack of towns,
Now when that hotter patriot runs up with a flag
And smart intransigeance, before the night
Begins, before the indifferent tolerable night.

This our communion is in being cold.
The point of history must lie
Always under the cloud and we rise
Because of it and the eyes searching
Here, in this cold room, out of the picture,
For the feel of the sword on ourselves, on the chosen, the cut
On the untrailed coat, on the head
Of undealt words and the ultimate wound.
Now when our part is life we must proffer it,
Here in this room, out of the picture,
To the arm and communion of death.

91   LOWBURY HILL

Comfort in centuries with broken feet
Limps off this hill of recapture, where meet
Interminable bournes of fight
Mapping the brain. The rules of blood that maze
And wall the sight
Meet here. I gaze
And the spread blood goes back
From the wall, runs hard into the hand
And the brain stops. Only the boundaries stand.

A moment and a cowardly kite
Mews from the clambering wood
(Ham Wood the cloth maps have it) which at last sun could
Straddle the unconcern and flowers
Yellow on the interior common of the hours
And blue with stragglers of anchusa breaking out
From the articulated garden of control.
That sun saw the common whole,
Irreverent to the tumuli of blood and track of boot.
These trees converge in shadow, black years leap
On the evolving flowers. All I can do to keep
The decimal of sun recurring in one day
Ringed with the body and the wood
Fails. Centuries cry and blood.
A speck, the half-life stops with fear
The mewing on the unfinished body bare
Goes on. The flecked trenchant balebird flying
Crosses the ring. The wood is Saxon, Ham Wood, crying
Haggard destruction, homeless flight
In the slack eddy of the smoking night.

The cold Fair Mile in face, the banded swathe
Cut in bought field the Saxons scathe
Is silent, dun. Colour and cattle drain
From the pulmonic vein.
Over the grass is Starveall and the hill
Crawls down to Unhill and the draining well.
Smoke rises straight on the blue breeze
Like breath. Is it an axe I raise
Here in the Roman mounds?

Help for my kin or surfeit of all wounds?
Below on the slope the flag, the red
Flight and the tank-tracks run ahead
Of the older enemy in the blood.
I know. I feel it. Red fear will make me mad.

This air, this time of broken rule
Is terrifying. Only the fool
Remains, the rooted, not-to-be-banished broom
On the surrounded common.
Out of the body then, out yellow, make it a room
For death. The axe and hands are here
The horn of kindred and the bare
Body of the Christian dyke.
Dart hands and dam the flood, bare body strike.
Woden has blessed you once
And twice Ambrosius. These great hearts enhance
The honour of our blood and battery.
Rage wind and carry smoke –
Over the abandoned huts the tattery banner look.
Back goes the foam of faces, back the red wave,
I lust now for the life I gave, I, more all this kin
Of bitten helms and bloodshot men,
Less for the forsworn life than for the bones
Left with the broom beside the swollen Thames.

Down Saxons, wait for wounds,
We drive you cattle off the antlered hill.
Wait for us, stumble, what we kill
Is only red with the spewed edge of our fear.
These are the uncovered bounds
Of brotherhood, walls of the great reward. Clear
Are our points like sainfoin on the slope
Close to the dragon standard, blood to blood. Common the hope
Recurs. Kai has the cross
And the five wounds on Liddington, above the fosse.
Here is Kingstanding in our hand no less.
Over the broom our pride
Hangs in the moment and the wave breaks wide
In the future. Badon will bring the flood,
Blood to the unmapped heart, to the torn heart tears.
There will be comfort yet for twenty years.

92   CROSSING INTO PEACE

The humping bridge that spanned
The stream, the plat of sand in wait,
The sprayer full of tar at stand
With the last spate

Dribbling the wheels, the hiss
The subsiding engine proudly sent
After the sun, to us all this
Was nothing, meant

Less than the soft relief
Of Sulham, or the symbolic weed
Choosing the current like the chief
Of flowers freed

From the outriding leaf and lost
In a chestnut gale. But of these none
Intruded. The hot silence tossed
Up toil, time spun

To tarclots. They were part
Of memory. The high banks had been
Years that had grown there on the heart
And the Pang between.

93   BREAK IN HARVEST

A plane like a fish, leap finished, drops
Over the leafheads. In the copse
Much of the converse stops with rain. The crawl
And tick of the twigs is a wall
And a half-world against the louder strain
Of nerves bundling the brain.
In this compendium willow-herb and sorrel
Wilt slowly, soften the old quarrel.

Beyond the trellis and the lost light
Are the shelf of corn and the white
Wound that the binder leaves. In the crack of the hill

Hide the gate-eyed houses, tapping shrill
Orders by the poles that prick the field.
That was the world, and is. The high yield
It hopes for drags the wound again,
Stanched for this moment by the blinding rain.

94   PROSPECT OF DITCHLEY

The ancient pirouette of trees
And the dropped scent of saunters done
Linger, though stiff decades of sun
Have stepped into this ride. No breeze
Now lifts Capability Brown's dead finger.

Here where the dancers cross, the arms
Of the wayfarer over berried cheek
Steeper than sticks in blood, a blown freak
Of silverweed and John's wort warms
The seed of the grass and the stiffened keeper.

The gallery of heat-haze lifts.
Gibbs's italian is topped with leaves.
Only the grandeur of a memory grieves
Over the park and the great shifts
Of age. The upstart cormorants will not be lonely.

The face of Heythrop with stone eyes
Still looks up the ride, but the younger trees
Wander, and the wayfarers do as they please.
The crowd with blood in their cheeks surprise
The dancers. That is their last line yonder.

95   GOING

The slope is taken with a jerk
And our inclining territory of boxes has the look
Of a cubist picture caught up on a shoulder
And carried out, unceremoniously
Knocked down by the auctioneer.
Somehow at least it does not suit the artist's book.

The lorry climbs and backfires. The last local crest
Rears up defiant in a close farewell.
The house is gone already, lost
In the stalking trees, and the suspicious village
Comes to the clasp too late.
Hands on the tailboard slacken, slowly thumbs
Feel back to the labyrinthine stall,
Nearby dimensions reel and settle
Down on the numb circumference of feeling. All
These last dispositions evade
The gravity of the house and garden. We
Are out on a tangent from the torn circle
Of friends, projected towards infinity
And deafened, lest a heart should harden.

The babies eye the shut ribs
Tearlessly, as though the wood and cloth
Were an enclosure of benevolent concern.
Among the boxes, rigidly compressed,
Some of the older child whom commonsense deplores
Has his strewn nursery of tears
Whose uselessness has never lost them place
In the unrealised lumber of a life.
They are all of a piece, the bone rings,
Bicycles and the six beet I could not bear
To see left in the garden, they are a piece
Of the play interrupted, before bed
On a night in winter when the dark dances like fear
About the hut and the bonfire
And the boy under the Kiwi shivers
Seeing his child heart dead.

All sense is shaken as the lorry roars
Out on the tangent. Think, think
Of sandwiches and rugs, my seat and yours,
Seats without arms along a spinning road.
One white look at the globe we get
And the square fits none of the known desires:
The posts are all leaning backwards
And we spin too fast to read.

As the speed slackens some more solid part
Separates in the mind and soberly
Drops from the flying board and wheel.
To the true orient of the heart in time
It comes, cold to the grave on the hill
Untended, with a dribble of weed
In the vase and little leaves edging
The stone. Here there are months to seed
Before she is quite alone, the woman of grave
And grass. Much will be gone
That she loved, Hypatia and Mother o' Pearl
From the children's boxes, birds' eggs in cottonwool
Out of the trunk in the attic that her dead son
Blew and laboriously scribbled, one by one,
The solemn elephant with broken back
Who long ago took a girl unnoticed
On her first ride from home. Dust
Will gather again in the empty rooms
And on the stone flags silence. Fruit will drop
Quietly round the lawn and the raised tower,
The thud lost in grass. From that hour
No one will come to the hill
Where the key of the house is kept.

  A turn, and the senses mingle
Back in the shaking ribs. This is the common
Now and stones jump singly against the sides.
Stones need not wander when the bread
Abides and the fed
Hounds are home. Jolt
As the lorry may and come to halt
Awhile at The Quiet Woman
There is no stillness now nor sacrifice
Can keep the house. Watch how the road spins.
We are out on a tangent and no device
Avails. The circle is broken.
The great cry begins.

96   SOLWAY

Off the low fields the lagging pools
Slip. The anomalous privet droops. Saliva spills
From the beaks of the huts towards
The restless claw-marks on the shore of birds.

Wall holds the cropped farm up. Spent
In green cake-cuts the turning knife of Paul Jones meant
For creeks the slapped tide lies
Willing to have you think it will not rise.

Solemn as beadles, backed like shag,
Galeenies perorate impatience. Then the vogue
Alters, wind follows word
Across the bounding field a winter sword.

Posture at will, this weapon meets
All faces half-way. The short fronting Sark repeats
The threat against the ramp
And starlings take fright from the rubbish dump.

Beware of Skiddaw and his cabby's breath
For guide. The old have paltered and belie their teeth.
Forgiveness is a beast of broken wind.
Youth has the will to rage, blind

Like the ego brimming in the creek.
Expect no warning when the appalling voices break
And the bent lowers. In this lull
Look, the tossed body of a trimming gull.

97   NEW YEAR'S DAY, 1946

Over the stubble the gulls steer:
    Dark with speech is the outlying tree.
Is it courage coming with the wind of the year
    Or the cry of a baby born at sea?

Tomorrow's hovels are on the hill,
    The foreman's bootmark in the field.

O darkening tree, the hammers are still
   Today of all days, and the doors are sealed

As the year comes in. That stump of oak
   Helpless upon the flooding shore,
That was a tree once and likely spoke
   As loud as you, but it speaks no more.

Over the stubble the gulls steer:
   Dark with speech is the outlying tree.
Is it courage coming with the wind of the year
   Or the cry of a baby born at sea?

98   THE LURKING ANCESTOR

Man hath no centre, but misery; there and only there, he is fixed, and sure to find himself. – *Donne*

   Pain, you come out of this patch
   Of frozen weed, you dwell
   In this rubble of wall-no-more and wall-to-be,
   You pace up and down on the shore
   Violently and are not freed.
   I know you, you are the ridged earth, the husky look
   Of the sky, the shrunken seed
   At the core.

   Men have been born of you, misery,
   Under this hill, in dark
   Winters when only the muttering pylons walk
   And stamp in the fields. You in the greed
   Of groundsel, your long will
   In the hungry handlebar swoop of white
   Gulls on the houses, in you is still
   The gift of the need
   And the answer, O were it the least of your lies
   In despite,
   The mark of the beast in the furrows,
   Of God in the fight.

99   FROM A BUS AT CROSBY, CUMBERLAND

No great tide
In my heart of glass
And the swart divers minutely on the rock
Perish in the wide
Purpose of distance, losing the careful mirror as they pass.

Summer tower
Of glass and sweat,
This is the broker's hill where we have been
Before, though the sour
Ticket is differently holed, though our faint suits have seldom met.

This is the hill
Of the same dry ending,
Try John Peel on the wall, summer like fur
On the tongue that still
Waits for the breeze of words and the season of black fruits pending.

If wall is bound
This time I am over,
Tongue leaping words as my glass heart fashion!
See, father of many backs there, kaffir-opal,
Lickserpent Criffel coiling in the firth,
In the waves look, wound
Cool about Scotland's end and the birth of a faithless rover!

100   IN OFFENHAM CHURCH

Like the lost cheesecloth talent in the parable
One pew keeps off the wooden worms of dark:
What sky there is shakes down from the short
Half-pillars of the pulpit and the face of the marble
Cherub who could have flown but lingered.
On each half-fingered ledge creep flowers, at first
Only a fringe of consciousness, but presently
A black mortality fretted by piercing stone
Crying with a faint evening breath 'I thirst'.
Big yellow daisies dry in a cheap glass
Follow the pitiful gleam. The font by the door

Straggles with gilliflowers dropping like blood
Spilt for patience in a brutal pass.
Easter is over full three days and more:
For the proud generation taken in its bloom
There is still no resurrection, only sudden
Demand and service, the dropped heart on the floor.

101   EVENING

Cool is the plot of evening, consolation
Is pressed out of the currant leaves
Into the lucent quiet with the rest
Of the torn essences the heart receives.
Now the light clusters to the shaken spires,
Clings to the tenderest tips of culmination
Remembering, the riddle of desires
Holds of their dust the feathery concept only
And the faint cargo that they made at first.
Over the blurred green garden, over the thirst of lips
Ponder the bypassed peaks, excursive and lonely
As poverty long forgotten, integrity half understood.
This is the part of evening that the rotten
Stales and refreshes not, feeding on no heart's blood.

102   JUDAS MACCABEUS

The gallery of faces is a cloud
Hiding a thunderbolt. Below stairs feet are loud
In the aisle. The tired unbroken
Smile of the pillars urging the blotched brown
Building inward upon the blown mouth
Alters, tightens upon the sharper breath of youth.
The lines of pressure straighten, tautly the hole of air
Purses and shapes to utterance. Shortly is heard the roll
Of despair, of Israelitish women crying at the wall
Dragging their sorrow like hair
Out of the dropped scalp, and threatening, nearing,
The male tormented morrow and the Syrian yelp.
'How vain is man' seed cries in Mattathias dead,
'How vain', but the grey temples all a-sweat

With effort and the loud planted feet
Of the steady bass fronting the enemy hill give lie
To the feeble tale, the sword hacked with earth shakes
In the furrow, driving the work
Deeper, till the morrow breaks.

'How vain is man' sings the hireling,
Making of vanity a measured sweep,
Then a sword-pass, pricking the word in the middle-leap
Of his art. 'How vain is man'
Runs the part, 'who boasts in fight',
And Maccabeus, every ringlet plain
In place, leans on his sword
Complacent, letting his word-distended face
Swell with humility now that the part is over
Like wind bellying under a canvas cover
And slapping the paunch with pride. Is the rank posturer here
The talking sail, the tongue of cloth, in the pit clapping
For both? Vanity applauding vanity, can one fail
To win? Is any victor over the measure of man?

But rise, rise. Anticipate. Always the present ready
And foretold, always the rodlike serpent raised.
The full throat of effort is not cold
Whether the heart be praised or no. Tear down the notes, be bold
Out of the sky so that the pit
Remember it and lie amazed
At the labouring months, at the meeting years of sweat.
These wear work at their temples, get them tears
Lamenting in time for Israel, weathered eyes
Watching from time beaten to time victorious
Over the swung shoulder of the hidden march.
O are they not ordinary, glorious, hounded, down,
To a crown bidden yet compelled to bone?
Bolder the step now, bounded eyes of the dog
And conqueror range over the pit and rise
Again. The planted feet are familiar and strange,
The listening spine creeps to the brain.
Hair greying, cheek and temple a-sweat,
Israel is down and up, vain but not beaten yet:
Dumb eyes and speaking eyes, lips praying like kings
In exaltation, torment, wrongs past counting or care,

It is Wales, it is Israel, Israel upon the stair,
Grey in the gallery, heavy under rod,
Weary and impenitent, the wanderers of God
In the desert chosen, compost of spine and brain –
Against the pit the pillar and in the pillar sign.

103   THE PATH TO DINAS

A bronze fish breathing a fountain of trees
Fixes the minute in a pool of hours.
The river rattles the stone in his head. Disease
Has taken one leaf and breeze a second
Before the fountain lowers. Nothing is lost
Or forgotten but time and his friends
Who make no amends.

A girl and a soldier pick a pledge
Out of the stone's grasp, out of the grappling field.
A boy in the distance is beating a drum to the edge
Of despair and the bird's eye wanders
Back to the wound half-healed. Lime-wet come
Memory and defeat, feverish guests
For this year's nests.

A tree-creeper bold on a trunk has beak
Salient with straws of faith. Faint underfoot
Is the freakish toothwort toadying, flesh-weak
Pauper of fears with half-jaw fast in
The hidden red-felt root. The two are law
In the moment, by the present pressed
Into seeming rest.

104   THE LOCHMABEN STONE

Out of a day the wastrel wind disparages
Into a week with the hearthstone white with ash
Summer goes blowing a host of idle marriages
Simper and wizened seed and scrambling bush
Into the tide's reach, into the water swifter
Running beyond the bar the daylight after.

Cowering among the bents by Kirtle Water
Thinning and harsh with a portion of salt and blood
Summer is shelterless now, out of heart with slaughter,
Caught in the stupid wounds caked in the mud
Of the margined field. Here in the tide's least evil
Winter the houseless sticks and the stone survival.

At the top of the field were fingertips of barley.
The counsellor stone is cold with a century's face.
Where the moss-troopers came to heel and parley
Should not all counsel be aghast for peace?
This is a cold scoured shore, the whins are ragged.
The shadow across the sun is double-legged.

105   THE MOUNTAIN

I have been here in the fields a year
And never felt so far, desperately
Far from the course of Christ
And of His star.
Over divergent poles the missed
Redemption pales and towers
In the night season. With day the tension
Lowers, and stubborn the ground reason
Works in the fields, labouring to conceal
In the long flowering grass a bruisèd heel.

Thrift built a wall and covered it with gains,
Pink growing wickedly out of a grey tide,
A shored embargo on the least of rains
Running between the arid spirit's pride
And the slow conduit of the source.
In the achievement was an hour, an extra minute,
The only prodigal no husks will now bring home –
Nothing was in it, nothing more than proof
Of death in life, the end to which all come
Whose pad drops off the heel and leaves a hoof.
O for all stiffer pedants and the lame
Let there be time, a second still, to rase
That terrain, beat
The slow graze of ruminating

Death, the gaunt to-fro
Of the corrupted udder pending in the heat
Over the prostrate thirsty and for breath.
The choking fields devour me, I
Am busy with catcalls in the expected quiet.
The piece I paid for grows its galls
Immeasurable and by it
The sweat goes back into the shortened lease.

I come home slowly with a careworn mouth
Talking over the flats, and in the south
A mountain sharp with the sun and blue with weather
Outstares that speech with silence, a symbol, rather
A magnitude that makes the firth
And the huts and the fields a plain, and the days
Of the gaining wall of little worth.
What has no secret bounds can have no quarrel
With the unrealised flats, with the dead ward,
But is their hope and complement, their effort spared.

Over the flattened huts the evening climbs
To the blue peak: I wag my head,
Accept it as a freak, intoning to the height
'Is not the mountain beautiful tonight?'
Though in the carnival of wrongs
Those shoulders carry clouds, this first disguise
Of beauty is accepted as sufficient prize,
A florid peak capping all conversation –
Hardly a climbing matter but a fashion
The wall may mount to if the craze should last
(Art catches nature and defines it fast).
So the ghost glimmers and decays in speech,
Slack day collapses on the farther beach,
The firth lies silent with its wonted fears
And all is as it has been many years.

Comfort ye, comfort ye, my people
Saith your God. Vanishing tower and steeple
Comfort not, but the long peak of air
By its mere station there
Raises a counterspirit from the flat
Failure of fields and makes aware

The scuttling centipede of blinding height.
So the still pointer from despond
Is powerful as beauty rarely is:
The fact of Godhead facing the abyss
Is a strong warrant of the path beyond.

Head in my many hands, I seldom see
More than the worn grass margin of the estuary,
The little pinks of thrift and greys of government
Walling the tenement.
But if a glance, with Adam's collar galling,
Climbs out of surfeit sickly over the sheds,
The rinsed-cup colour of the window
Catches it up, inconveniently up, till the beads
Of the back click and the contriving duller
Light of the wall decomposes slowly
In the fuller white of the firth and the sea
And the lowly islands out of immediate sight
But under the same astronomy.
Columns of gold go up and the gospel laves
The divided pagan shore. Over extravagant
Waves of relief the ruffed clouds draw
Clear from the ends of the frayed
Temper and the wretched proud
Experience. Sudden the sun is stayed
In the arch and the unbowed
Neck flushing fashions the collar anew, in a breath aloud,
Pushing the burden of passions back.
So the incredible angle appeals
To the eye and the tongue in the roof
Stutters the tall sky single
And aloof the hour. The window whitens,
The salt sight has power.
Over the flattened huts the vault
Empyrean and the blue break
Of mountain southward matches the wiser streak.

Polluted hand and prescient eye
Can the brave moment bring together?
Out of this dank disharmony,
Out of this going whither and returning
May there not rise achievement, purpose rather?

Can still the fire be soot and simple burning
Wait on the well-constructed doubt?
The mouse of hunger peeks across the hearth
Once in a month, twice in a week's despair:
Nothing it moves to has a nourishing air
But is the semblance of that crust of earth
The cradle cries for, which at first deferred
Grows dearer, till the teeth tire of mould.
O I am growing old and would have word
Of more than gossamer and graves:
Give me the punishment that saves,
A mountain ministry, appraising Lord,
Give me the counter fit and finger
For the pointers in the pit.
By all that common is and suffers hunger
Compass it, compass it.

106   SEARCHING SPRING

Gravelgreat are the hills and perching
Walls are haggard over pitted ground:
In the red manner of a gash the lurching
Streams collide, leaving shoulders ragged
And sudden like the edge
Of our disaster and grave wound. Boulders
Like roofs are lifted off our talk:
Bushes that ruff the hedge and clothe our seeming
Crack in the night and the strained teeming
Multitude of roots sticks in the sight.
No measure now of things that stalk
And vein the sick flayed province under boots:
I had no notion till the fork dug in
My chiefest covenant was with my skin.

107   BABLOCKHYTHE

The still punts with fishers watching
Knees over hands the meadowsweet and nettle,
Caravans and the quick shacks patching
White and windowed the little

Course of the Thames, are the quiet
Feats of the times, incalculable mettle
Of men without names.

The bus marked *Private* and boys making
Play with the pump on the ferry are fated
Like sickness and nightfall: sharp rain raking
The Chequers is in sort related.
They come of the age of the river,
The stripling stage over, summer dissipated
And life without gauge.

Favour is half aversion. The willows
Leave loosestrife rioting over the paddle,
Camp-following willow-herb and painful fellows
From stoneheaps crowding the middle
Steeps of the bank. The parish
Poor get a drink in the unclassified huddle
Of pension and rank.

108   ON THE GRAVE OF HENRY VAUGHAN
             AT LLANSAINTFFRAED

Sun at arm's length, infant cajoling ball,
And stretching finger full of a hale man's blood,
This is the promise, here the hump and wall
By which the grave yew ghosts continue longer
And in their church of damp have hosts.

In this blind parcel is the portion lost,
The hampered reason, the most potent sin:
Yet the prostrate endurance of this dust
Beyond the rain's dearth, into a light season,
Marks the exacting purpose of the earth.

Man that is God and ghost, fuel and fire,
Factor and master, ephemeral, crossed
Peccator maximus stirring to desire,
Dust shall have shape and sing, in the sun faster –
This hump is Pisgah and each shoulder wing!

109   DROUGHT

The groves are feverish as a dream:
In the massed trees a hum of flies
Mounts to a head, rounding and gathering:
Down in the trickle of the stream
A dipper like an undertaker, a size
Too big for his mourning-dress, tries a bored step,
But when a stone cuts up his watered shape
Whirs into stubby flight and wakefulness.

Honddu, river of the dream,
Divides: its breast-wave barely moves
Struck feathers of a bird, a heron perhaps,
Whose crop is dry in the supreme
Insufficiency of death. Wasting from the groves
The dream and I divide, over the grave's end,
And I, lying where every traveller is my friend,
Cry out of Lethe that my bones are dried.

110   OLCHON

Did a dog bark in Olchon?
Or the grass shout
On Crib y Garth?
Compass about this guarded earth
With ocean or the enchanted
Garden with a sword,
Is not this signal flaunted
Grasswise in the wind and railing
Cries of the hawk, the high unfailing warden
To whom the tired dead confide their work?

Go on a step. Be sure and bolder.
The strict baptist caught in every tree
Is dead. Now no stars uncover
What in their hearts they keep
Or what agree
On the appointed shoulder of the steep.

Does the sun hover
Longer? Do the grass wires hum
On the hillside
Louder with dogma than the dull brass
Agony of long desires?

The separate trees cry generously 'Come',
The green close fields
Talk of my entry in a stride.
Nothing is wanting but the child's
Wide trust, treading on mire and tussock,
And the exalting foot that lifts up dust.

The worldling's cassock trips him in this crack,
The mountains make a rent in his long doubt.
Did a dog bark or the dry grass yellowing
In a great whisper leap
'Believe in Me or else I keep you out'?

111   CRASWALL

With a long stirrup under fern
From a small blast of oaks and thorn
The shepherd scours the circling hill
And the sharp dingle creeping to the well.

A trickle from the canting neck
A pony coughing in the track
Are all the stranger hears, and steep
Among the fern the threading of the sheep.

This is the boundary: different burrs
Stick, stones make darker scars
On the road down: nightingales
Struggle with thorn-trees for the gate of Wales.

112   CAMP BY THE WINDRUSH

Concourse of tents on the plat
And the hot cookhouse tempo
Quickening, the burden of events
Creeping towards an ultimate pot or pan:
A day out of old age, perhaps,
Bustling a little, or the child become man
In a dream in pursuit of a wild
Motion of feet, his own hobbled
And tied: beyond blood heat you know
Is the dream's edge, distinct as the riverside.

The chimney smokes and thought
Reaches its waited stop:
Voices drone and develop, sun
Steps off the landing-stage
Into the river and the prone
Reader loses the page for a quiver
Of reeds in the body's run, yellow
Of lilies riding and the white
Float the arrowhead leaves in the eddies
Urge and follow. Look, look
At the gudgeon's flash, there
On the sand. The eyes submerge
From the book and the five
Senses of land unsteady and swirl
Feverish and cool in the dive
From the bright lash of air.

Stentor cranes
Fantastically over fire and cups,
Pleads for his charges' hire
Against possible rains
Or sun's eclipse, and out of bad reports
Bids a quick conference of willowheads
Define the lesser torts. Today a few drops
Fall: fatigues are done,
The bike-tent empties, the beginner races
Blindly to half-day-shutting shops.
Stentor, alone, feels his part resemble
The shed braces in the village sports.

But in the evening men of standing amble,
The long gout of cities has its hops:
And when the stars are out
Over the ricks and the guy-ropes, the dreamer pities
The night's pale way with hopes
And out of comfort picks his share
In the shire's following crops.

When the hot binder clacks the tune
A choral season is not far to seek,
A harvest of brown backs, a calendar week
In fields where the clocks are blown
To and fro and the fine
Web of weather shifts and parts
As the tonsure of weed lifts
In the water. Feather and reed
Are fond mark and atmosphere –
And being is deed.

113   THOMAS AP RICHARD OF DOIER
TO THE TOWER, THESE

Evening is grey with us, Morgan,
    Mist on the low ground:
Restless we are as coneys
    Who once slept sound.

Sir Scudamore he took you,
    And the bishop white as his bands:
Our sixty pikes close in the valletts
    Would have served your ends –

But you smiled your wisdom, Morgan,
    And went with them to the Tower.
What devil's sky in London
    Leers us this hour?

The mountains despair for Arkston,
    Grave the mound is with prayers:
The tall wood of Treville
    Hides greater fears.

The grey men in the hamlet,
  The weavers of Hungerstone,
Work looms that events have lately
  High overgrown.

Wormbridge is awed and quiet,
   Quarrell in hiding. O
Where are the swords in earnest
  For one more blow?

We have only the words now, Morgan,
   Weapons are slack in our hands.
We run in this sorry evening
  The bishop's errands.

Vaughan of New Court in the valley
   Reveals his receipt from hell:
If evil befall you, fully
  With book and bell

We'll curse him for your sake, Morgan,
   And the candle save for your mass
Who die that the true faith be preserved
  Fearless for us.

114   THE ROSES OF TRETOWER

In the late cousinhood of country ways
   No domineer had more heel on the cant
Than the hill-farm Cynghordy's master, whom to please
   In drink was the wisdom keeping louts and dogs from want.

Lewis was pinched out like a water rail
   Up to the neck, secret and furtive in
A spotted coat hurriedly fastened on the nail.
   No cure of blood wrinkled his curt and fitted skin.

The yellow trap he used on market days
   Looked like a painted bird-tray fixed behind
The pub. Cynghordy Uchaf was a tidy place –
   But a hill-pasture often feels the taunt of wind,

And from the dingle digging at the house
   To the long fenced lawn that scuffled with the trees,
The farm had a garbled life of its own and captive laws
   Working at times for Lewis, livid behind his knees.

Eleanor knew it (none of your Welsh names now
   For Lewis: let a girl understand her place
From the start): often the grove of alders had the low
   Fence in their fingers, sourly shaking it in her face.

Oftener the tangle started and rushed out
   Into a solid shadow on the lawn:
A whistle when the moon had turned her sombre coat
   Brought the girl tiptoe-anxious to her gallant soon.

Son to old Williams Hendre, Isaac's son –
   (Spotty and common in a dark Welsh way,
Lewis had said, picking him with the tone
   Of a smart judge of scab) – but how he came to stray

Up to Cynghordy cannot now be told –
   Only a hedge-matter, grown to trouble, where
The alder trunks on the ridge unlaced under the cold
   Pittance of stars. Eleanor lived with the one fear

That Jacob would not come, the rounding dark
   Make in despite a bush or a protest
Of silence. Between shed and trees was a snapping walk
   Broken in bits of talk and kisses, thumb on wrist

To hush and listen, hist as a branch cracks
   In the tread. Lewis was hidden like a nail
Slap through the helpless feather bed and the spattered sacks
   At its end, widening the formal hole with wind and stale

With drink. If that indeed were the fiend overhead
   Completing his fall, rather than hateful down
Already on his belly boding in the seed,
   Beguiling fever in the sodden dark, the one

Transporting hour was possible, the rough
   Astringency of tongues, the soft recoil

Of fears sufficed. Such niggard time must be enough
   Till the long nail cast off its breathing neighbour file.

The ark of gopher wood was not so kept
   In fight, nor the hands of dark persuaded on
As by Jacob's prayers. How behind Hendre barn love leapt
   On him, to bind fast errands and leave gates undone!

But to Tretower he went one likely dusk
   And milking-time, to the house, the point-device
Of mastery, the face of portent and old mask
   Of corruption, ruined them, but having faithless voice

About the valley, echo in nearby stones
   And a bar sinister prized and over-hot
By many a fire, Cynghordy's not the least. O bones
   Of the single sire, pursue your dust beyond the brute

And flame. Remember the ornaments of breath,
   Conjure them. The dead serf had full defence
Against all but his lord. Speak, bones, consort beneath
   The soil in the daily grave. Consider beauty once

Jacob, because of death, and let that charge
   Deny your legacy of gape and fist.
Get in this feckless garden comfort and at large
   Doubt of your godhead till you meet with Christ.

Bring the world's blooms to love before they spot
   And curdle. What is not, how can it speak
Movingly like the stalk and the petal's bleeding? Cut
   Your roses gravely and make an end. No buds will break

In your talk, Jacob, carelessly as you climb
   To Cynghordy. Yet the roses count for much
In your purpose. Crimson, they are eternally the prime
   Of a season, Tretower's warrant for your match.

             * * * * *

Dark fell: the grey trees jigged like dolls across
   The wall: the ghost of roses ran with him
Like a blue prick of pain touchingly over the grass
   And twitching at gammer twilight's skirt on the world's rim.

The alder thicket on the dingle side
  Fell back, the low fence gave before the brunt:
Cynghordy topped its cousins by a final stride
  Of thorns, but had no guard against the soil's affront.

Counterfeit bush or bear made small remark
  In his ear or brushed at all by Eleanor's:
Her lunar fingers branched above the lifted stalk
  And the arriving petals pricked on into tears.

'Under the wall I picked them, by the gap
  Where the gate is warped.' The wood gave a low sound.
'In the Tower garden.' How the words sagged from the lip
  He hardly knew. Transfixed, empty, he felt the round

Convex forcing of the nail through wood
  And the snap as the slivers break in front of it.
Lewis was coming. Quick. The trees were a trap. They stood
  Aghast. A stick went off like a gun. Wait, wait a bit.

Which way? There, there. God with us. Run. Oh run.
  Out of the dream they peopled on the hill
Dropped Jacob, like a bone to the grave level, sin
  To the common stock. The woman felt the rose-prick fail

In her hand, plain as a scream. Parry as weak
  Is beauty's best, flesh but a vain parade
Of the eyes. Before the wicked fortitude will break
  And the nail's flourish soon call off the brief crusade.

She ran round the cowering house with her powerless rose
  Petals dropping, crying like rods on the stairs,
And up in her room in panic, with the sickly close
  Shut of the pelted sheep clawed from the dip, the fears

Of the stalker mounting, mounting, craftily stern
  And fated like shears, cried quickly out on her,
Out, pull the window sash, save the wretched puling thorn
  And the stray wish of the rose. Out weepingly, honour

Poised there on her sleeve, downwards she bent and flung
  The roses, straight from her palsied grief and red:

Then pent, saw the doorpost flinch at the upward tongue
   And the whole staircase cry reprieve at the nailing tread.

Under the miscreant noise and the slow moon
   The hasty bunch stood upright by a verge
Of lawn, propped by a ledge of grey-as-bethel stone,
   Patient to wait catharsis or the primal urge.

Common incessant rose and uncommon
   Triumph over cross and nail, suppose
The love of life in bones, the beauty born of woman
   Could out of God catch fire, burn and defy the cause

Of death, accepting comfort only like
   A wound, would not the thief in man draw breath?
If the cut rose should root, the sorry thorn unspeak,
   Sword must and nail be satisfied, no other sheath

Than Christ avail and the slow dead decide
   To grow like April from the gravehill. O
World, O last great thirst, O breathless thief who died,
   Such love would sanctify all loves, unsoil below

So many bones without the winter's shift.
   Watch how they grow then, Lewis, how the grass
Lodges them wisely and the God-troubling thorn is left.
   The ground rejects it now, its generations pass.

There unoffending, still without reproach,
   The roses burn against the flagrant earth.
All is to bed now, sinned-against and sinner. Search
   Out of dust and water warrant for a second birth.

* * * * *

Three weeks of summer stalked Cynghordy's hill:
   The cold took Lewis from his parents' bed
Towards the shivered circle of the stars: no will
   Of his unmoulded him, no doubt or latter deed

Troubled his watchful timeless head: a gulp
   Of vinegar mistaken in a bout

The Poems

Was his despatch: cursing his vitals for their help
    The bedlam skeleton seized death and dragged him out.

Jacob, as powerless as the grass, became
    Cynghordy's master in a russet world:
With winter's scissors in and out of frost, the seam
    Curled and ran from the field path like a rage of cold

Straight from Tretower's garden to the hill.
    The old earth opened there, the verge retired,
And in the kindled rut the crimson roses still
    Fired out of soil a creed, out of flint the spark desired.

Blood binding spring to spring and death to life,
    Budding out strength where was a suffering-rod,
Jacob, who cheated birthright and took farm to wife,
    Has in his garden still the wilderness of God.

115   HAWK

There are marks of snow on the goitred neck
Where the cut begins. Grey clouds concentrate
In a mountain hurly-burly shoulder
To shoulder. Buffet and Jehu-crack
Predominate. Slowly the day grows colder.

Already the cart-tracks are stiff and red
Pointing like chapped fingers from the gate.
Above the perfunctory grass a level
Eye-flight off, look, close, rigid
A hawk, irate as a stone, with the squireen's cavil.

The flower's eye narrows, pupil-cold
To the master-pinion, nemesis over the heath.
A handful of lambs new-born and hardly
Able to stand or knuckle herd appalled
Underneath. The span grows in the wind more lordly.

A nearby elm gives a warning creak.
The wind is stronger. Cruel, nonchalant
The grown spanshadow ascends, breasting

In smaller and smaller spirals, beak
Proper and cloudgallant, the black land cresting.

Out of terror only a speck that drives
Quickly before the wind to the shoulder line.
The tracks of the kingdom watch and the hammer
Stops under the hill. Each lamb unshrives
His fellow and fine the day is with a laverock shimmer.

116   THE FLOODED VALLEY

My house is empty but for a pair of boots:
The reservoir slaps at the privet hedge and uncovers the roots
And afterwards pats them up with a slack good will:
The sheep that I market once are not again to sell.
I am no waterman, and who of the others will live
Here, feeling the ripple spreading, hearing the timbers grieve?
The house I was born in has not long to stand:
My pounds are slipping away and will not wait for the end.

I will pick up my boots and run round the shire
To raise an echo louder than my fear.
Listen, Caerfanell, who gave me a fish for my stone,
Listen, I am alone, alone.
And Grwyney, both your rivers are one in the end
And are loved. If I command
You to remember me, will you, will you,
Because I was once at noon by your painted church of Patricio?
You did not despise me once, Senni, or run so fast
From your lovers. And O I jumped over your waist
Before sunrise or the flower was warm on the gorse.
You would do well to listen, Senni. There is money in my purse.

So you are quiet, all of you, and your current set away
Cautiously from the chapel ground in which my people lie . . .
Am I not Kedward, Prosser, Morgan, whose long stones
Name me despairingly and set me chains?
If I must quarrel and scuff in the weeds of another shire
When my pounds are gone, swear to me now in my weakness, swear
To me poor you will plant a stone more in this tightening field
And name there your latest dead, alas your unweaned feeblest child.

MORNING: NEW JERUSALEM

Scarves pull at the throat, a gale
Of stripes for funeral sheet, a fistful
Of feathers and a blow to all hale shapes.
House-smoke like honour's shred
Lies by, curl-papered and abed
Like Sunday folk, then starts and gathers.

This is the corner where the widow lives
Quietly with cancer in her box.
'Are the curtains drawn? Did the milkman get
An answer? We want no nasty shocks.
Go out like an angel on the lawn and look,
Aurora mine. Your place is safe in the book.'

Let the talkers be. Beyond the wall and the curtains meeting
Against infinity there is no choice.
Sneak-thieves quietly pester on the telephone
Hoping there is no answer. And there is none
Beside the separate weak voice repeating
'Leave me alone. Alone. D'ye hear? Alone.'

The talkers emerge and journey, being like-minded, two
And together, wisely out of the wind.

'Fasten the lid, my love, there is no death
That full employment leaves us time to fear.
Transport is ours except for lack of breath.
The lead in feet . . . O now and again, dear,
You irritate. No one blames
You for minding the dirt on the seat,
But at least be firm about it. Draw your skirt
In for heaven's sake and prefer a complaint.
The conductor realises fully what is at stake.
Quite, my dear. That was hardly what I meant.
Our services need improvement at the peak.
The whole world is up, the wild
Men are in Town for the Games
And cut-price touts will press them each to a stall.
Let us do homage first at the Town Hall.
It is winter and time again for the Christ-child.'

118   A WINTER'S DAY

    The blue tide like a lively child
        Ducks at the elder towns on either hand.
    Spoken praises soon can be spoiled
        In an unruly end.

    A puff of smoke pulls the wind about:
        The grey shut faces in fancy halt and shade:
    A second has crossed the planes afloat
        With an expired decade.

    So small a muster of wind and tide
        Will never stir the destroyers up in the reach
    From their mud-plats. Look, only a staid
        Bubble embarks on each.

    The old tide rocks at the turning, mild
        In his ribmarks over the disappointed sand.
    A youngster who did not smile, or smiled,
        Could lose himself a friend.

119   PAS SEUL

    In the grass gold rings
        Gold leaf on every tree
    Nightly a gold piece hangs
        Between my love and me.

    Misgiving in the air
        And in the grass surmise
    There is no other fear
        Than in my true love's eyes.

    Buttons I have and shells
        Will cover that fear over
    Golden the kiss that stills
        The faint heart of my lover.

120   PAS DE DEUX

A purse of silver is lying
Under the mountain's hip as the snow disappears:
The goat and his tether are moved
Twice before evening from fields where others are tied.
O wait for me, death, this is your aide crying
That has a pain at his side.

The scarab's ball breaking
The quarter of winter travels, gathering dust:
Soon after beggarly shoot
Rose and bedeguar treat and remain allied.
O wait for me, death, this is your aide speaking
That has a knife at his side.

121   TOWARDS PENCOMBE

The gate is open and the green ride ends.
Only a rut goes onward in the grass
Between the rough ears and the crannying winds.
This is the country no despair need pass
Unfurnished, nor unless
The chest drops straw is there returning.
Severn mouth over a mass of cloud claps
On all burning converse, and the last
Unanswerable wretchedness rides on for both,
Sorry upon the beast. I hang too by the gate
Of the wood, *The Defence of Guinevere*
In my hand, guilty, double of blood
And afraid, hearing the widows fight
In the fields near and the corn on the graves
Consoling the dead of their end. Queen, parade
Of ruin, crown among the sheaves, out of your reckoning
Was the palled wind and the alarmed apparel of the leaves.
As the bush beats, spires to treachery, so you appear
Beckoning the season forward till the rush
In the combe is red-brown and the clear
Brook in the high land is hushed with reason.
I have your words in my hand, but down
In the fieldway wild you are, white as the swords thrusting

Back through soil's broken front and shield.
The anguished crop is Arthur's and the cry
Rusting along the hedges and bitterly crawling up
Into the hills is his. Camlann is high
And hidden hereabouts and the brunt
Rankles beyond these ridges that no hunt can deaden.

122 SPRING IN WEGGIS

Wind like a trollop darting eerily out of the woodpile,
Trotting along pine-needle paths crying the brothers Grimm,
Leering and pattering snow up, scamping the jackman's tile
For keepsake, witch for a blossom and catkin-kind for a whim.

Corners and hillocks raked and drenched soon to make hay of
    summer,
Sawn trunks lodged and drying where the gully brought them down,
Chalets yellow as buttons in the coat of the brisk sun-comer,
Ahead of the season's baskets, the crocus is almost gone.

Easter flush on the lake and like a flag lashed in the furrow,
And in the shops rabbits anxious with bows and cellophane,
Eggs out of chocolate, painted eggs deliberate out of sorrow
And patient like the magnolia buds to break resurrection's pain.

123 FRESHWATER WEST

Over, break white and wash swiftly
Around this rock where earlier
Suds sand hiding swish and uncover.
Press, press on the slope of glass
Sliding over, over. White and pass
Me, wish peace and deliver
From hope, all you bygones, hush
And recover. Break ground and foam
Over and over, newcomers, beat
And surround, beat and surround
And repeat ad finitum, everyone
Beat till the few and the best of these summers
Of mine are as sand, over

And many and meaningless, far beyond
Hand and all measure, lost whereunder
Danger and no man's cast discover.

Wish. I am hidden already. Have I
A wish? Only for peace in the sudden
Hillock of glass and the green
Lease of the tide. Pass,
Pass on your way, over and over,
Beat and digress and repeat, young
Diver and mass old-white
With frays, press and retreat and recover:
Of your half wish there is nothing lost,
Nothing of praise and success, over
And over spoken, nothing but gland
And flesh, a rushing atomiser
Broken like sand from off the human coast.

124 AFTERNOON IN WATER STREET

The red importance of the winter sun
Muffled up briskly and in office late
Touches the bartering crowd,
Giving a hat to glory and an effete
Milliner the right to paradise. None
Of these faces, none is more ugly
Than God allowed, and yet none wise
Or with more than a child's reward.
It is already too late to weigh the justice done.

The red light fades, the hard
Lines break and pucker from the till
Wide oceanwards, will bound to course
And wave. And children cut to a half-vest roam
Unkept out of doors, red with a cracker
Of sun and white with cinema tinsel.
Count out the knacker and next season's catch,
There are hundreds dying now under this hill and home
And not a few at a watch that no death can cancel.

125   A LETTER

    Eight years ago come Tuesday now I walked
    Big as a brown wind angry from your door.
    Mad you had made me, Ellen Skone, talked
    My tongue out of duty, crossed me more
    That day than I remember. And the sun came down
    Like a bakestone. Well, that was it! –
    The widow lost her lodger in a fit
    Of temper and the whole cliff laboured under frown.
    I am no more a scrallion than I was,
    Brawned out a bit as a haulier over Roose
    As a matter of fact, and my close
    Friends do tell me – God who has
    Caught me enough in a lie prevent me now,
    O now when I want the truth! Friends?
    I have none. None that I trust like the hands
    Of the clock on midnight and the slow
    Matching of your rounded arms.
    I am no fool to harp upon your charms
    Like a twenty-oner, lose my pen in words
    I can hardly spell. But listen, if it affords
    You pleasure. I'm sorry. *Sorry*. Now
    Answer me fairly, Ellen. This is my only throw.
    Must you pretend like a Sunday child from home,
    Play 'tisty-tosty, how long shall I live'?
    The hay is carried and the high tides are come.
    God in heaven, do only young men wive?

126   'REMEMBER CHARLIE STONES, CARPENTER'

    The stream is sultry and a short haze mulls it,
    I in the hooved earth merry as a stick
    Half-peeled and giving the horse-turds ample berth.
    Here, having eaten, what in hysteria can I do
    But wait, as shell and paper wait, myself
    The best time to be thrown away? In every site
    There is some aptitude, some haunched-up niche
    Or bee-hide where the sourest litter
    May so be decorous and quicker rotten.
    Here close at hand too is the fear in which we are all begotten:
    'Remember Charlie Stones, carpenter.'

Were your proportions, Charlie, seen as well
In time as in the Gill
Script spreading your white stone under the seven trees?
Or did this bowl
Of hills burn like an August offering to the Lord
So that your soul cursed it
Three times with force and was afraid,
Prating as ill as I? Over this valley is a well
Beating with water and I do not see it,
The hills are shaped every day afresh with a new hand
And I do not feel it,
Only the sultry dancer under the seven trees
I know and the body's stirs
As it frets to change its ground.
Are you bound there, Charlie? By one or many?
Rattle the church-box louder and detect my penny.
I know too well to remember, Charlie Stones, carpenter.

127   O TIHUANACO

I have prayed askance in the slow cold air, in the cave
Of portentous snow, grievously I have prayed
To the Grass-Eater, cupping my groans to his disk.
I have cried, I his priest, to the copper sky-mask
Of Godhead. He is quiet. Or angry. Or gone south for sacrifice. I am
    afraid.

O Toxodon, Eater of Lush Grass, again the cry
Of custom rises. O Mild One, deign to regard
The grain on the stone turned twice in the meek
Employment of priesthood. Merciful, strike
At the puma-star with your blood-bolt, loose the eyes of your pride
    from ward.

He is quiet. Or angry. Bitterly great rocks hurl
From the yellow puma-face to the puling sea.
The waves froth up. For the priest of the drowned
There is only the desperate cave and coldstoned
Death pressing in. I will free my cloak and lament our fallen city.

O Tihuanaco beloved, these torrid eyes
Braved out the line of craft at your carven quays.
Quick on the sea were your ranging ships
From the cone of Kayappia back to the galley-steps
And bronze was our molten Lord on the cramps and the half-worked stone of the Andes.

Slanting Titicaca, remember, careful water-slope
Seeping towards the salt pans in the south,
Four-Cardinal-Point Country, afford
Me yet grace and you, O Eater of Greensward
Who kept our prayers from the puma and the girdle-tide from our mouth.

Arise, arise, O Tihuanaco beloved,
Your courts uncover to the boundless days,
Your palaces open to all pious races.
Copak, dangerous master of faces,
Come back! I am here, even I, Eoi, come back, you may still have praise.

Days of fasting return, return, with the singers
Careful and clear in the palace cells with their kind
Palms to the Grass-Warming Mildness, making
A hollow of practice. Now they are seeking
Their warmth in the waters apart. They move in the darkness like hair in the wind.

Only the slaves remain, the terrace-tillers,
Livers in caves on the Illimani alone.
What can I feel for these brutes my brothers
And less in the light, when Copak smothers
There in the dark, in the ashes, weeds, water, where greatness and nothing are one?

In a trance I felt it happen – the darkened opening,
The offering unconsidered on the stone,
The ashes falling, then the bent
Of the puma's eye, the furious up-slant
Calling the girdler on to the passes, into the fields of the prone.

Where can I go from the perished, from Tihuanaco
Pallid with friends, from the corpses nudging the wall?
The sun-gate is down and the doormen froth
On the cave's lip like slow bladders of growth
Reaching up from the depths. Chamak-pacha is come, the great
   darkness, covering all.

Only the hail of rock of the puma's hurling
Bitter into the pool of the city's head.
Only the echoes, only the going
Of words from my mouth. There is no means of knowing,
Grass-Eater, if you are angry or beaten now. I am better dead.

128   ARGYLE STREET

A man with a blowlamp clambers opposite
Burning the brown paint off the sills.
The house in chancery fills
The drab street with indecision, and tonight
Even the corgis at numbers two and twenty-seven
Cannot decide to fight. The mainspring
Seems to be loosed in so many wills
At once. A gull on the tufted chimney
Shrills in the tedious light. Across the haven
The hooters sound, and in them work
Deflates, the semblance of plan and the conscious skills.
A question is posed
And not answered. Why
When so much is ended do we still begin?

The man
With the blowlamp has no use for the dark.
The door of the house in chancery is closed.

129   RIDDLE

My first is like a sea-horse, scaled
And hip-shaken now, but wickedly bucked itself
Neither by Neptune's crupper nor out-of-water rider,
Livid as pride and yet a damned outsider

In every nap but one. An enemy had done this,
You may think, before his title failed.
Yet is its strength to burst the earliest element and peer
About and roundabout a new world sun and bring it near.

My last is sightly in his urban tower
Awake while his bonds increase. Matcher of stars
And caterpillar master, he works the state of his alarm
In brass and counterpeace, lest the worm
In his guts persist. Decent an age older
He tires soon. The coffin brings his shoulder
Down, the fire in his hand burns lower.
Is there a thorn stick growing in his newest park?
That will he need to hoist the final work.

Now is the moment when your guess is good.
Wreathe me with berries and I give back blood.

130   COED ANGHRED

Up seven green steps, around a moist
Deploy of cypress, are the graves.
Stiffness in sum. Per contra, then, a haste
Of bramble superscribes and braves
It over spurge, having run
And suck of cross and craving stone.

A day in the pluck of summer
When a reach of apples half-held the trees:
A roan cow reckless of tick or cuckoo-comer
Rubbed at the priest's house: once-sown
Potatoes had the wit to flower
Whitish along the spit of after-hedge
Below the barn: and carefully no power
That contrary sun-up steps acknowledge
Pressed the demand of what is not
And no more tires or sees.

A roughneck robin with an Irish eye
Stepped on a scroll and marked
My small advantage of his territory.

The yard I gave he sternly overtook
Watching me steadily.
'Robin' I muttered, 'Robin Caffrey, look,
I will what a friend can do.'
A pigeon flapping slowly through
The wood, his soldierly bars flashing,
Shortened the sentiment and made it good.

I bent, and with feet pashing
The green spurge groundlings did what I could
With a bramble. A stalking cousin near
Took up the quarrel and drew quick blood.
I stopped. 'God, I shall tear
My trousers sooner or later' I said
On thorns. Let the dead unbury their dead.

131   THE TYLE

In the proud season penitence
Droops like a haulm. The dance
Of ashes frets the arc of sky
Violently, pushing the stars away.

Pressure of water in the ear,
Not so much sound – the near
Intelligence that breaks the hill
Trembles in ignorance behind the shell.

A rounded bush repeats the moon:
White curve and cosened stone
Prison it faintly between boughs
Travelling like a mist towards the house.

132   RETURNING

Above the elderberry bushes and the banks where hens
Scratch, baring the faults of rock and occasional shanks
Of spindle-trees, watch how the lane happens
To dwindle, the knock of the water rises, breaking in
Like an old controversy in the brain. In such a crisis

Of unmaking, with the handstrings tauter
Than in child's time, I come to the house.
The strain of talking is partly excused by the climb,
But the first elements cry nevertheless and walking
Jubilant about on the attic floor peer down
Where the four apple-trees have grown.

A bonnet of ash at hedgeheight, below, a two-yard skirt
Past the butterfly bush and the tumbled bit-white axe-wood
Heap in the path, this is my love and hurt,
Half-rush and obstacle of mind, a mountain humbled
By all her children, yet having flowers to keep and beanfields crying
Contentment to the hours. In no time
But a haste of prying the unspectacled child
In me trots to and fro, measuring attics and spying tins
In streams, wild with comparisons and unaccomplished blots.
On the slope opposite as time begins a horse
Patiently switches in the gorse.

Who was a child has children now in his wake whose elbows press
Manfully upon tears. I am myself, to shake
Back to wariness. If the whole dusk of fears
And the missioner's box mounting the feathered lane with me
Slight and shrinking at bole or bush or the eared shadow of a fox
Slinking, survive in the vile push rotating
The seen half of my world, behind o
Beyond the last wile in the covert, the eyeless lamb
(Was it an eagle, was it, was it?), overt
In shoot and stem God's very hosts groan in mid-shock.
Blood out of them unreds the rock.

133   AN AGE

The blue singleness of summer was in that air
And the bushes hazed after the light
Though it was September gone.
Is it blackberrying, sun
And juice in the hand, or a flight
Of birds shearing over the ferry that holds me there?

The envelope has let an age escape to the sea
And I am old, but not so
Old as Mabon taken from between
His mother and the wall. When
I was young I saw the sun go
Purple on my thumb and birds stand shoaling in the estuary.

134   TO THE MUSE, WRONGHEADEDLY

A neap tide tops my heart, needlessly
Twitching the dried fronds swordlike and about.
I have not spoken since the last year's rout
Was left unrelished on the wasting stones.
I have waited for silence, terribly.

All this is nothing, and the battlements
Of limestone, caverns for the washed-off worm,
May crash the bay down if they need my harm.
I shall not speak. I am older now and proof
To the bone against your blandishments.

135   THE LOST KINGDOM

If you were dead, as I,
Then the drowned kingdom of our stars
Might cry like legend between Cardigan
And Lleyn, catching the half-bards unawares
In their cave. But in all honesty I cannot die,
For all my sickness cannot, nor the discharge hide
In beard or barbary like a camelman.
I could abide in any cramp but this,
Basting the callus freshly with infirmities.

Yonder's my land, a touch away, a glass
Would over my shoulders show it, a ride
Of ants invade it, a neighbour's children pass
Across its fields like cavalry.
There are my mountains under hand, the high
Framework of window has them, every whit
As hawked-at as the tacking moon.

Shadow by shadow I know them, cloud-
Sally over and still as a heart-clot, circuit
Of Salem repeated and The Plough begun –
Loud, loud as the organ, stop by stop
Extended and the whole heart blown.
O summer and kingdom leagured, youth
And love I have lost with mummering mouth!

Senni's counsels, by summer langoured, were light
On your ears, slack his wishes
Described all shallows, called every parapet
Chafe and grooving a shape of tears.
All's one, one, and that not good.
The extravagance of blood
Submerging stone.
Dance, dance all you bushes
The stream beside, foxgloves redden
Your fingers, stiffen and twirl with pride
Of loving, deaden the sound
Of Senni listening. All that washes
Your veins is water. No one has died
Above you, no scent lingers, nothing the warren round.
Dance, you bushes of hazel, go
About, about in your merriment. I
At my window hear you though
The black stars are out. Zealously
Circle and circle, clap in the cloud
Where it breaks. Cry aloud, cry
All the coppice and dance. You are my parish
And young. There is no elder who wakes
Save I, and none to look you askance.

To that high kingdom almost under hand
There's no more ingress than a memory.
On the immediate pupil of the mountain's eye
No iris pool appears, no new
Remark of dew on the cool pasture.
For maldominion am I cast out,
For raging round Trephilip like a fire
In the hazels, like a foxtail in the few
Harvests of youth. I sit now to the knout,
Beyond the crier of further ill, quiet

Against the rage of second sight,
Sill-stayed, bastinadoed, full,
A beast in the next-door pale.

From this house know, as know you will,
My eyes of glass go out, ungoverning
The grave champaign my midgets till.
You shall not pass, whether this winter
Or the one hard on your heart.
You shall not pass, for how much brazening,
No matter for erst regard. My kingdom's yonder and foolishly
Hinterland once both its counsel and calling stream
In rout stands, in travesty fonder
Than the advised fields in grain. You,
Lady fain, never I cast you out.
But now there is no more
No more to do. About, about,
Go turn about. I do not know you
In autumn. It was a summer dress you wore.

136   SCITHWEN VALLEY

I have no stick to poke down in the tank
Cautiously, to clear weed to the blank
Sides. The sun is bantam-brown. I hear
Rather than see lambs spindle at the stone wall near.

There are four kestrels in this single field,
Tweedy hangers-about that the wild
Sun misses. The chug of a tractor below, man's
Conscience in metal, stops at and starts his plans.

Holly and rock come out upon the cheek
Of the field above. Quickly the hot week
Breathes on the hill and passes. What I move
In the tank is slimed and fit for no sheep's trove.

I have a second in the breathing day,
A stop of blood. What other man, away
In a bantam past, bit out a tongue and stood
Shamed and sick on his hillock when the sun was good?

137   CONVERSATION ON STACKPOLE HEAD

Time, if we had a watch, would point to four.
Against the light there wheeling over two score
Blackbacks peddle their reason mewing to the cliff.
Is it worth a guess, that crying, if
I know the bounds of life? Vary the game,
Demonstrate briefly that the lame
Emmet will always trundle in the hoppling last
Flax grain of the nine hestors, how fast
Soever the night falls. Excellent! Depend
On it that is no more than a net whose end
The floats mark yonder under cliff. Even half a man
Could stomach this without a cardigan.

No wind to speak of and the south-east roll
Flattening somewhat. If that hole
Goes past the immediate rabbit to the sea
This limestone headland and the lee
Cliff landward are fretted further by the tide
Than one would think. This side
Is dangerous. See the rocks boiling at the jut
Where the race is. A slip would gut
One soon enough, and the sea feeding round the toe
Step quietly up. Sun coming out, you say? No,
Not if I know it, not in a hundred years, not
In a lifetime. Even this anchusa has the spot,
Winded about the edge and sour. Without a watch
We loose an hour and make a shorter catch.

138   BUILDING A HOUSE (IN FOUR MOVEMENTS)

I
The house is already building
Do what you will.
Label me wirepuller, whitecollar snob,
Aspirant for the upper ten,
Queue-leaper-general,
Corrupter-simple of the also-ran –
All this is chicken-feed,
Corn-cob, fish-heads, yam –

I can afford not to tread on it
Bin or backlane it;
The stones are ample that give you bread.
Your heaps have summer too, riding
Convolvuluslike on the blowy back,
But I can see over them,
I can see Barrack Hill over them:
(Cut out the cackle and the working to rule.
The poet has a basinful
And four feet on the pediment) –
Our house is building
Do what you will.

II
Half of the garden should be sand
By the look of it, what's left breeze-block.
The concrete-mixer makes its own
Conversation, but ha ra rattle and
Presto, despite appearances
To the contrary, the plot will sprout greybeards
And tattle, meaning well, of course.
For one handy with my experience
Wiring should not be necessary
And ditching a work surely
Of supererogation.
But for the long word harried here
The collied syllables
Caught on the long back doctoring
The rigid weekend like a slipped disc
You might have felt a lack of confidence
In so much saying. And that
Would bring in winter to my company
Quicker than concrete cracking the digger's floor
And the doorposts failing.
You are the public and my fractious destiny:
Your carpings kept and treasoned
In the bin resemble you.
Their whiskers grew upon another man.

III
Count this impiety who cannot put
Stone upon stone, pattern upon a heap,

You stained employees of disparagement,
Pity beneath a lid, you cloudbreath
Mongers parsleywhite above,
And who cries *Build* on this, yet does not cry,
Build out of Sodom when the mountain's gone,
Turn to and *build* when the backward cave is gone
And God past pleasing
With the half-goods done?
The beacon lowers and rushes, shoulder heaving
The mason nightblack cully upon his heels.
But the hod makes back, occipitally out of dusk
The ladders rise, and over the polities
The raf comes in, the triumvirs, stepping upon heads
Wide of the beam and humble, with little by
To laugh at the interstellar condescensions
Affecting flight. Morning amazed, the fainter
Clouds disperse, unwinter cumuli
About the lady Preseli's nape,
The staid to-fro disclosers of the oil-veined hill.
Light of the clock a Kuwait tanker
Is hasty enough of waterwork to crowd
Like a nursing animal to the tether side.
Intake and heavily, marked overtime in Gath,
Has temperature as thudding as one day
Can keep. No solids lost, cosmopoles
Piping content before the waking cold.
Over what spectacle shall our stir
Concord? The hard inflection of the estuary,
The charitable Sunderlands currying
The drowned favours of trawlermen, or
The unchinking perquisites of sky?

IV
In the garden yet there is nothing high,
Nothing above a shrublace or a byboot
Babylonica, no hide for the Lord's song growing.
Nothing the sandgrains over but an infant rue
And the dried gruel of a stony spring
Hipping the spade and hopes of a new calling.
Mercy this major plot
And to the shadeless, undeserving
Commonplace of pride and plastercast

Call up the weeks of conscience, seven
By one of grubbing, like God of the Caucasus
And the Barrack Hills. Mercy upon us, hideless
Thou, basin and pediment dasher,
Washer in purple of our rabbity ills.
I have deserved little from the polities,
From proud occasions less. Close to the beacon
Glasses flash and flesh
Lies circled till the hopper fills.
Rab upon rab, I ask it, make my bed
Bitterly or the red hillock yields
Home and five windows on Thy wider fields.

139 MARSTON SICCA

I watch the muster of grasses between the stones,
The wind pitching dead in the porch
As the afternoon passes,
And I feel my free soul bounden, all of a sudden lodged, its habit bones.

There is nothing to say, or have said, now the news has run
Like a rabbit about the apostles
In their yards: not one unread
Apprentice gravelled in his piece will cry covenant with me, never one.

What the poor scholars mutter, the poor I laid
In the gown, I hardly know.
The alphabet I utter
Graves every mound with a title to blame. In its vowels am I too mort and unmade.

I watch the muster of grasses between the stones,
The wind pitching dead in the porch
As the afternoon passes,
And I feel my free soul bounden, all of a sudden lodged, its habit bones.

140 ORIELTON EMPTY

There has been burning, identifiable still
   Behind composure when the shuttered front
Opens its thirteen eyes. I have no leave to count,
   Nor should, as one whom the house knows well.
But to myself this due: the dusk face welcomes me, leads
   Into conversation, asks for scrutiny.
So if I say 'The corner urn needs
   Looking to. Where the guttering drops a new
Course welded in would help', nothing is out
   Of courtesy but the homegoing sun.

Many of the trees are copper, one
   A beech, a Japanese maple another, and the covenanting
Bastions of wood declare a ring
   Burning the reds and yellows into centuries.
The lake is reedy, indistinct with flies:
   Durgi and Soda, gundogs of the Rosebery age,
In this red evening whimper, the cortège
   Halting again at their graverails. Rhododendrons drink
Gapingly like mangrove roots from the nearer bank.
   Of the whole circle there is no one left to thank
For the windbreak, for the island hopes
   Of the heart, for the sickle that blunts and stops.

Up the ride, at the wood's end, is a tower fickle
   With grasses. Kestrels nest where a beldame and her pack
Gamed all her guineas away in a round
   Of parties to dawnlight, foxes going to ground
Before her and the wood shut close at her back.
   A night and a night and only the owl for cock.

The scar has widened, weeping over fire and century,
Reds and yellows falling, by and by
Sodden and historied in leaf and frail.
Outside the circle the sea winds scut and kill.

141 CASCOB

Just here's the middle of a silence that
Has already sung the centuries like a gnat:
The valley's middle too, by the hill sound
Topping the trees. Perhaps the full circle, for the bound
Of the churchyard circles and the black yews
Are markers. Each on the circuit ropes and screws
Giddily, wind having caught it widdershins
At the clock's three. No true arrest. For two pins
I'd leave in a hurry, were it not absurd . . .

Blank wall facing west, belfry of weather-board
Raised on a druids' mound, none of it
Reassuring. Within, a brass of familiars, habit
Of clergy, *pater pater pater, noster noster noster*
Three times for Saturn, *O save our sister
Elizabeth Lloyd from spirits, amen*. Behind
My back a thin mediaeval tongue, the wind
Carrying it woodward, tang and tone.
Service at three. Who is it coming? Afternoon, afternoon.
The thin hymn wavers to the circuit hedge.
The yews grimace at my ear, there, at the edge
Of being. Sister, sister, night follows day
Out of these bounds, loping beyond the yews, away
Giddily over wall and number and ken.
Quiet these centuries. Who is it going now? Amen, amen.

142 FRIENDS I HAVE

A fall, a season running into sleet,
And a new skin receiving none too well
Light for the travelling bones. What's to tell
Of all this northern weather but the feet
Lodged in pools, unkindly more at home
Than the dried poll in fog? Blessing the well
Is customary. With water there's no quarrel
Save that it is not blood. But O the heart dumb
Under this hill rejects it, does but work
In the week as the mole blind, pumps
From old levels (on a shift that damps

And falls have not made mercy of) the dark
Remembered drops, the kindnesses of old
Unshaken friends, making the round
Of Wales. Here, subterranean, is the sound
Steadily of a concourse, cognisant and bold.

143   FOR WARREN DAVIES, TWO YEARS DEAD

How best remember? Shipwright you, quiet, wry
As a hawk, a viking-cast dropped out of conquest,
Averse from talk most when there were gabbers by
And jawed like Magnus at the holocaust.
A crab for history, though, that reared you hard
Where South Hook breaks its point and the pock
Of the fields begins. What was to guard
There but your elders' shins, the proud stock
Of last year's swedes? Better to caulk
And hammer, a foot for each element. Better yet
Rashly, the sun-glimmer white on the stalk
Of cliff wheat, to bolt the herring-set
And sail from Hakin Point into a safer parish
To find a wife. Supple the marriage bond,
Penultimate as life: suddenly it was your wish
To swear out of fervour certainty, terrible and fond.

One of your feet on shore at little cost.
And so, alive in both, to a jig royal in the crowded yard
Chathamward, big with craft. Not grounded, tossed
On the shingle yet, nor ringed up at the hard,
Your Pater tackle held, the homing breeze aroused
A spinnaker, blew the repeat softly on a tack
Up Church Street. Something to be housed,
You thought and grateful, little to lack
With wife and chapel and garden, the chief
Of goods at will. And so, humbly, moods
Notwithstanding, at number twenty-three life
With its prints of sixty years began, its crowds
And sermons and keels. A sight of the water
At Lewis Street bottom, mud as they meet,
The trickling pill and the tide, a daughter
In the wake of two sons, and the breathless feat

Of roses running their course narrowly
Between back walls, these pricked your quiet
Like joys. And, upon a time in summer, slowly
Making to ebb, a trick or two with a boat, and by it
Lawrenny smoking across the tide, a plat,
A temporality of grass left rulerless
In trees. Of all your drift of seconds, these that
You cupped from Cleddau were the last to pass.

You rarely wrote. I am your remembrancer.
Your sort of speaking, though, I cannot snatch
Delicately out of the plain pewed answer
Of meeting. You were no Sunday catch
For clowns observant, no plotter had you cold
As sweat under his armpit, waiting for the drop.
If words were a trap sometimes, sometimes your hold
On them slacker than theirs on you, the prop
Of conscience kept your talking up, some little-wanted
Truth tripped out whatever the great boning jaw
Ungripped and said. No man took you for granted
Who had not bought his bed and licked its straw.

The corner after chapel was our beat,
White-collar jobbers and casuists but for you
Who, twice the age of reason, could defeat
A joke like a friend, and hullabaloo
Break on my chest, cracking in jaw
And context with the best. Shake, shake
In the fingers as you did and claw
Sadly at seedlings you were wont to take
Tenderly, this week the clematis
With which you set our hill court in purple
Twice is page again, and up to the lattice
Creeps. How slip, how preening cast of yours, can it recouple
This switch of land to you and greenly in it
Grapple your ailing hand?
                          It was cold,
Cold of a Sunday morning early in Church Street
When you turned in your sleep, and old
Morning, at last unmanned, curtained his gold.

144   THE LAST DAYS OF HEAT

  About the sill the gritting of the leaves
  Rubs the imperial preference of dust.
  Sahara-like, the margins of disgust
  Step eyeward, degrade what the heart achieves.

  Such heat leaves my significance afraid,
  This tower a bead under a taller arch.
  At whose reproach will the noon parch
  Me, at what proximate these faint colours fade?

  Weeks back I rarely cared for the rain.
  Identity was no more saved by it
  Than bubble by river. But my eye's quiet
  Socket is running now, while it lasts a rhine.

145   CHINON

  The lizards on the wall move
  When I move:
  Shallows in the Vienne
  Colour the tale I have.

  All that was royal once
  Cruel once
  Crowded these towers with
  Heads that have mouldered since.

  Then Aquitaine, England, thick
  Your walls, thick
  With promises your spears.
  O promises are quick!

  Anjou, an arm as long
  As yours long
  Sheeted you cold to bed.
  Shame on a conquered king.

  The lizards on the wall move
  When I move.

All such, having leave of death,
Distrust the reach of love.

146   BRYNAFAN: FIRST LIGHT

Within the cruck the night
Is thick, an animal residue
Of bones and food, the soupy wash
Of a working stomach an hour short of its time
When the light went out for good. To pick
Heaven out beyond the cotton hill,
Have knees for drumsticks and the dead hock
Of day for gnawing, what's this
For tod on his heap
Of ages, waiting for light to tremble
And the recovery of tricks?
Ergo, who's the squint for
But the quickest to fix
And arrive?

Light when it comes
Is a mist from the foot-window
Marking the floor, a cast for the eye
First on the drawn-up ridicules
He lay afraid of, and last
The desperate thin pelt he slavered on,
Fox that wished like man.
In all the gorse-humped hill
Not a fly innocent bone
Is broken yet, no kill there to pick
Over or inheritance cry.

Day comes white of shin, sans flush
Or knowledge of forerunner, a cave
Kid for pap, hazily at grope for this roof
Under which *he* stumps now, mettled up
Again, methusalem with a wish,
Asking that history should lack
Effect from cause just long enough
For a last crack at ill.

147 A LAST RESPECT

The sun, disinterested, summer on either side
Of the watershed, glanced along every road
In the county. It was a weather just
For a last progress, a proportion of death
In the hazels' cardust and the early yellowing
Of the lake trees, of life too, tetchy and pale
In the blown colts that the cold cliff of winter
Would rear into stallions. The processional cars
Had sound, yes, but a small sound like dust
Dropping on dust and the rush of hedgerows
Touched and not touched, a sound like a sigh
Caught in the tunnel of hazels and falling
Back, wheel by wheel, bowing and hollowing
Towards the minor hierarchies of grief.
It was July: there was no want of leaf.
Flowers the shire over were not hard to come by.

The lane was south. Above Cantref hazed green
Shoulders held up the farther points, the pinnacles
Of Sion, and their shimmer was an eye
Over the dying world, a blood that the dead
Plead by and pilgrims when they wake.
The settled dust on the hazels looked less grey
Than the new dust raised as the wheeling drift held on
Slowly towards those mountains, no move
Of mouth or limb. Sure as the heart empties
The last thick syllables dissuade the tongue.

In this hiatus when no stolid ghost respires
All that was left of breath suddenly ruffed the flowers
On the bier ahead. The hearse, its guttural base,
Ground into some declivity of gear and all
But the elm and the brass handles had air
About it and petals flying, impassioned as
Wings, an arc of will prescribed, mounting
And Sion crying, quick in the eyelash second.

Who are you to say that my father, wily
And old in the faith, had not in that windflash abandoned
His fallen minister's face?

148 SARNESFIELD

It came from those trees there, that rapid
Intimidation of shot. Panicking one could guess
The gunner astride a fork, hidden, cartridge-loop
Bellying, his every gap monstrous with eye
And the sudden flick of quiet. Awl and hammer
How they work at the temple, in the second
That the cheek bloods! The pool of graves
Ampled with sun: on its edge stockstill we all
Stood on the gravel, the bead line of us
Drawn goggling, butts an inch or two taller
Than Japanese but as much aback
In this clearing as a shock patrol
Caught whipping out of cover. There, look,
Woodpecker! – up there, high, his exercise
More rational than ours. 'You know
He only drills a dead branch, don't you?'
Being alive was incredibly to begin
Warfare again and justification, as though outside the grave
There were no greater wisdom than to win.

In the sun's pouring nothing stirred.
No grass pricked, elder and yew
Had long stopped shouldering the thicket
And stood there separate. On the tower
The cock was a gold achievement, as full
Of himself and breasted every way at once
As if the sun had left its quartering.
An hour at stand: York Herald in the north-east corner
With a grass-train of Marshalls forming
In his shade: and, at the path's bend
To the worm-eaten porch, a worn flat epitaph,
John Abel on his back, with a flourish
Of markets and the praise of Hereford,
Ledbury and Leominster stilted above him.
Air and mark for long have you, countryman
And King's Carpenter, sun-slant into the worn
Letters of your achievement, while your work
Stands, arched over concourse, high and clear
In the hunching of march towns!

In such still sun all buildings stand.
Any achievement, gold or the seeding
Clock of words, looks every way at once
And satisfies. Of the five travellers one
Stood still in the gold pool, fingering
The mistery in its aery vat, a moment
Gilder and master. Thus in relief high
Noon and happy cast can keep a pigmy safe.

Ten minutes clear of bullet-burst. But woodpeckers
Are never out of mark for long. Suddenly this one
Began to blaze along the achievement's edge,
Shooting the cock full of wry
Machine-gun comment and the tree-bole
Chock of an almost discernible dust. Which
Of the splaying limbs could he so easily tell
Was rotten? In which, sun notwithstanding,
Had he to drill his condemnatory hole?

149 DEPARTURE IN MIDDLE AGE

The hedges are dazed as cock-crow, heaps of leaves
Brushed back to them like a child's hair
After a sweat, and clouds as recently bundled
Out of the hollows whimper a little in the conifers higher up.
I am the one without tears, cold
And strange to myself as a stepfather encountered
For the first time in the passage from the front door.

But I cannot go back, plump up the pillow and shape
My sickness like courage. I have spent the night in a shiver:
Usk water passing now was a chatter under the Fan
When the first cold came on. They are all dead, all,
Or scattered, father, mother, my pinafore friends,
And the playground's echoes have not waited for my return.
Exile is the parcel I carry, and you know this,
Clouds, when you drop your pretences and the hills clear.

150   FRESHWATER WEST REVISITED

After six years this winter has not changed,
Encounter of sea and land, ellipses
Of force that intersect and flow boldly
Into and round each other as though
The air were party to either, *socius*
Only because savage both determine so.

This is no place of secondary forms,
Pretty distractions, heights of cliffs
Or trees, not far-out ships puffing
Irrelevantly of other shores and clashes.
Here the brute combers build the waterhead
And grass girds up the dunes the shock washes.

Away inland one can forget so much,
Ease the elliptical abrasions, bandage, duck,
Sidestep the bull-nosed rushes of a wrong
On right, proffer a parody to the back of it.
This cold October morning lays the action bare:
Sea is, and land, and bloodwreck where they meet.

151   FOR AN UNMARKED GRAVE

It was night at last when he grew weak
And his chest moved him involuntarily
About the pallet. Night too when the whim
Came to corpse him in tussock
And ramping weed. His bones did not need
Much holding, but the hard-tack joke
Racked up like sputum with the cough
Will take more than the clamping mud off
An upland clod or two, more than the sport
Of October wind, to kill it.

I will speak to him here, in Cwmcamlais ground,
The mountains spare and grudging his time
Against their own. How long is it,
David, long since your loins were water,
Since you were carpenter, wed, kept shop,

Were poor and a theologian, companied
A nephew wide over Senni and the nearer
Hill of day? Nothing to tell,
No fossil couplet, no borrowed stone crying
The claim of a life against an era?
You are not worth a second in the slow
Hardening of Wales, only in the sand
Of the fallen cliff that was my youth.

152   THE LEAST ECHO

'Finished, yes. Complete and in order now.
Heavens, no hitch. Just thought I'd let you know.'
Far more than a nostril curl. The whole
Cheek fell disastrously on the pale
Downturn of the lower lip. Each task complete
Precipitated this fall, the bit
Of paper derisively waved, the feat dismissed
From significance. Yet he never ceased
Unnecessarily to report, over and again,
His empty assignments, the filed thin
Victories daily ignored by lesser men.

Always he left his immediate
Superior uneasy, staring for more than a minute
At the tree-lupins stemming the fall
Of soil on the red bank beyond the tarmac. 'Hell!
Wants my job, he does, the devil.
Thinks me a talker, incontinent, fill-
Dyke in every month, chewing the fat
Of my colleagues' achievements. And that
While the work, the inescapable real
Works, hulks on his back.' From this chill
Indictment was no direct appeal.

Power may bring easement but the off
Chance does well enough. Fallen-Cheek, stiff
With immediate acclaim, dissembled, set up his name
In a newer building, stared with phlegm
Across a wider tarmac. His old boss
Florid with Pilsner and the snap release

Pinned on him all the robust claims
He had made for himself. No man's aims
Could be cabined indefinitely in such
A modest opportunity, he said, much
As if he meant it. Let alone a man of reach.

But the real epitaph was less final
If sadly repetitive, all the skill
Of the early couplet at a loss to change
The recurring ultimate jangle. True but strange
That Fallen-Cheek once, with eyes innocent
Of all public praise, finished his sprint
In darkness, bled at his books all night, and first
On all counts, whooped back to Hopkinstown, burst
Open his parents' door and stopped. All
That the silence tripped was memory, the will
To the present, the magnitude of time gone ill.

To have forgotten, that day of all days,
Was incredible, to murder the homilies
In stone on the hill, to disregard
The repetitive dull voices that inferred
Only what they and the neighbouring streets had known
When the three of them had been staid and one
At 9 Victoria Terrace. His Burma decoration,
First in Greats, that mathematical aberration
Of Fifty-One in the Quarter, all these burst
Blindly upon knowing and were dispersed
In its dusty ball without echo, being unsaid.
But from that time he cared for echoes, afraid
In his heart of finding the least one dead.

153 ABSALOM IN THE TREE

Hey, friend, I have been here a long time
Even if by my youth you would not think it.
The blood's half-purple stammers in my head,
My hands and feet are marrowfat, heavy
As feathers, unfit for the delicacies of undoing.
In the past hour impenitently this crown
Of shouldered gold, capillaried from the heart

Upwards, has agreed to let me down a bare
Inch, but understandably I have grown
Too little, even with brain at stretch, for
Ground to reach toe or anklewards to take
The strain. You seem a fellow unlikely to miss much.
Cut me down.

You must have got wind of the battle, man.
I take it you are my age, so bound to know
What the issues are. And now I look
At your sword-hilt and jerkin I can see
You were one of mine when the sun was higher
And the day in doubt. No, don't groan
Or deny the cause. There was a kind of glory,
Wasn't there, in breaking up their axioms
About their prurient heads and one by one
Bawling out the freedoms not to be kept from us
In this age we make? The kingdom, ah the kingdom
Of moods, of our celebratory rage! For its sake
Cut me down.

You are considering what? your prior duty?
But that's a word to keep for those with rules
To break. Are we not opportunists, you
And I, life-tasters for a consummate generation?
But you slip away, the calculating pieties
Abroad in your face. Go, go. David my father, alone
And agonising, will gladden to know of the gold
Alive in this tree, will weep off the sudden lift
Of his eye from the worm and the ranging bone.
But what shall I do with forgiveness? the wry
Face of morality when it is sick? If I'm to be free
For his stock embraces, at least they will have to
Cut me down.

The wood is greener now than at my first hanging.
Ridiculous this freak unjading, happily
Clapping my pudding hands up to the dull
Crawl of the scalp I can barely recollect.
Dismembered, I am still companionable, the avid king
Of a part, coarse lord of pottage and the brown
Sweat-saddle jogging the distances. O I command

Something, yes, the darkness falling across my face
As I swing. Mephibosheth, if you like, grown
Heady, out of place, an arrant mover of trees
By his hair's temper? Yes, that is it. I shake
My kingdom already. Ah, behind me the sticks crack!
Cut me down.

Joab, it wasn't you I expected, with my gold
Tarnished and this arboreal gibe topping
My usual oratory. Old beetle-brow, shudder
Of gall, you showed me how suddenly a blade
Slides under the fifth rib. But tutorially you
Dared not improve on my father, for all your frown.
Didn't I cross your politics too, hear all men
Myself, subject each cause to my cold opinion?
Convention I killed, protocol rather. The crown
Must grasp how much more power by half political
Assassination has than your snickering knifework.
But you look fulfilled, as though you'd picked your hour.
. . . Cut me . . . down . . .

154   SOME TIGHT-LIPPED WAVE
              (for Hugh and Lily Griffiths)

Killed in the bomb explosion en route for Nicosia,
13 October, 1967

Hearing the news from Idris, hoarse,
An undulant like the underwater telephone,
I sat in the outer hall, still strapped in
My unexploded cabin, feeling your Comet's course
Plummet like bedlam from the polities
Into the sea of ancients beyond Kastellorizon,
Your first and ultimate flight one
Catch of innocents for the Minoan savageries.

Out of my porthole I can dimly see
The house at Slade, hay meadow, spit of wood,
Meeting the sea's slap with a jug of mud,
Happily wait your coming. All will be
Grass and haze as so many times before
Till some tight-lipped wave, beating from Greece,

Ranks past the incoming locals and in a trice
Lands with deadly importance on your shore.

155   INDICTMENT

Did you, John Arnallt,
Sitting at table
In your house at Llanthony,
Say to your mother Walcot,
Thomas Poore the Irishman
And Harry Prosser, servant
In livery to the treasoned Earl,
That Her Majesty's kitchen
Was poisonous full of Cooks,
Naming Sir Robart Cicill
A Cook by his mother, my Lord
Bacon a Cook by the same
Error, Mr Attorney-
General Cook another,
And Master William Cook of Highnam
Beyond the Dean Forest
No more than a kitchen porter
Running hither and back
For the better provision
Of a supper of purges?

Did you, John Arnallt,
Coming out of your cups,
Clap this Prosser, murderer
Of one Stumpe of Walterstone
At Sir Gelly's command,
Cheerly on the shoulder, swearing
There should be no more *cawl*
In Wales till the Earl
Your Master should choke
These Cooks with their own herbs?

You are a debtor three
Times over, a turbulent
Fellow whose affrays have given cause
For the Judges of Assize

Long to take bond of you.
And your cousins, Morgans
Of Penllwyn Sarff, no better.
A danger to all good
Governaunce you are, John Arnallt.
I name you to my Lord President
Of the Council at Ludlow
But go not from my house
By day because of your clamour
And much shouting.

156   THEY HAVE NOT SURVIVED

They have not survived,
That swarthy *cenedl*, struggling out
Of the candled tallut, cousins to
Generations of sour hay, evil-looking
Apples and oatmeal porringers.
A quick incontinence of seed
Cried in the barn, a mind to spit
And squat harried the gorse
Into burning, and the melancholy
Rhos burst into plots, as circumscribed
Only as the lean muscle yearning
Carefully for love could lay
Around each house. But of that
Merely a life or two, enough to multiply
Cousins like bloodspots in the wasted
Grass. Then a new swarming, under
An aged queen, before they walked
Their milgis over the ragged hill
They ghosted every shift, farming
A memory of that last-seen
Country that was never theirs.
It was not will was lacking then
So much as instinct, a gift
Of seed for their backyard culture,
A grip on the girl who bears.

They have not survived.
Coughing in terraces above

The coal, their doorsteps whitened
And the suds of pride draining
Away down the numbered
Steps to the dole, they denied
Both past and future, willing
No further movement than the rattle
Of phlegm, a last composure
Of limb and attitude.
For this dark cousinhood only I
Can speak. Why am I unlike
Them, alive and jack in office,
Shrewd among the plunderers?

157   TESTAMENT

I cannot be sure what
I remember, but it was
Not a heroic escape, a grave
Hypocrisy strangled, the cortège
Of deacons stunned by one
Honest stroke. I was the child
Of belief, aching pitifully
In the unready hours
At the wounds I must suffer
When I walked out weaponless
And grown.

They were all heroes then,
All bullyboys kicking the pews
In, stirring their history up
In a pint-pot, jeering
The shabby unmuscled parades
Of the old Model Army.
But I was a little trembling
Fellow who had known love
And saw only greed
And false heart in such great
Drunken tales.

158 GOD IS

    God is who questions me
    Of my tranquillity
    And works against the grain
    To raise up Cain.

    What is this mark I set
    On each sleek head? The hot
    Manifest of dislike or ice-
    Pick of justice?

    What are these books, this room
    In which I sit so long?
    Are we not met to cry
    'Lord, justify!'

159 A LETTER FROM GWYTHER STREET

    This morning, the rain pucker over,
    I crossed Barafundle from the sun rocks
    To the leaf bank westward. It was fine
    And feathery on the uppish wave. My feet
    In lifting sand uncovered an older
    Sun and a captured wind dry-beached a decade
    Ago. But this is October, the salted-down
    Summer of the deckspar, colloped by sea-
    Worms, and the indestructible layabout
    Plastic of the child engineer.

    This evening, such brief spirit sinking, I visit
    Friends. And first to the grave-spit at Llanion
    Where Siân, her W.V.S. uniform in full
    Fold, pairs her ankle-bones to the town. Is there
    A message for Elis, tied to his cot like
    An idiot, his delicate features clouded
    Towards a bad-weather eye? Or Doc, cooped up
    With his leg off? Or Herbie, lopsidedly
    Smiling in the front room, omnivorous,
    History and egg slapped on unknowing cheek?

My footprints this morning on Barafundle
Went in and out of the wave, the fine sand
Darkening at the tide-touch and, as I looked back,
Not a mark of my passing anywhere, only
Sea eating the whiter sift, creaming mouthfuls
Of stick and hampered stone and memory
Trapped there. What remains of companionship
Cannot reach them now, Herbie and Doc
And Elis. No eye-light flickers and signals
Identification on their already buried beach.

160   NOT WORTH THE RECORD

What is it that you expect, caller?
Another voice of aloneness
In a different register, agreeing
Only in discord, so that the scale
Cracks, sharps and flats mobbing
The instinctive harmonies?
I *am* alone but not your ally,
A singer but in no mode of yours,
By my own fault poor and not
Your mobster, a failure in such sort
That all despair can use
Is the name, the notion of it, not
The feel, the pump of the gland,
The genital misdirection
Of fond secretions or the glass
Up, scrawny finger-held, aerating
The idioms of the blood.

You want to be sure of my failure
As the excommunicate prod
And identify the curse?
Herein I cannot help you
Evidentially, for what I know
Is ignorance. Hard by the pillar
I willed down evil and my hand
Pulled back. I quartered the nave
Sniggering and the shearling choir
Climbed to a paean over-

Towering it. What I have willed
Has rarely happened, just
As rarely as beneficence
Was my full choice. How can I
Offer this failure to you
For identification, caller?
And how persuade your truculence
That I no longer will it
Otherwise?

161   FOR JENKIN JONES
       PRISONER AT CARMARTHEN, THESE

My sun, capricious, holds its heaven. I cannot wish you
Well of the morning, Jenkin, who would engage
For no single luminary but riddled stars
Over every common, gorse-fanged and thorn-staked
Stars that gave back fire from the Approvers' gaze
In a governable brilliance. O I could rally you, calling
You coxcomb, fool for all your port.
But as the sun rises and the old insects warm themselves
I lack the heart.

It is not solely that I am older, sick
Of my cause's rectitude in the mouths of grasshoppers.
I know now how it was that Sions Tŷ Mawr
Could be a servitor at board in my own college
Keeping a hungry distance from the gentlemen
Commoners. Already you had speech
Truculent for tapsters, stiff that bread
Should be broken with prayer and thanksgiving,
Action for creed.

Your unshot gravity was something ridiculous, though,
Captain Jenkin. That soldierly dispatch, those
Pistols always primed, the hundred men
Close in the covert an you called. Did you not
Mistake, from earliest trial, the cause you fought for?
Was it this world to win for your soul-starved
Werin or did you faze the track in minding
Postboys and serving-men, losing the kingdom
And the king?

What have you done for the wretched but raise
False hopes? On Tuesday a week I rode
Under rain to the hovels above Morlais brook
Seeking to bleed a woman from distemper. A lad
Called Courage Gronow showed me a flintlock
To the breast, said that the men were off
Raising a rescue for Capten Shinkin, taken
By the ungodly. How long before they hark at the world
And waken?

Truth is not to be cupped and portioned as you pass
The elements down the rows of the new devout.
All such equality as seems to stretch
To the here and now is gross
Misjudgment, your catabaptism a pander simply
To brutes, the gravest acceptance of room
And substance in each idiot head.
The world has put you down for it, as a practice ill-
Considerèd.

And yet I ponder. We never played together,
You and I, as boys, nor said two words
In college. But I know you roared them off,
The dogs sniffing out royalists. 'No poet ever
Sets his feet to a Parliament's measure' was your word
Joking down the Llanddetty men who would take
Teeth to a cloak or a comfit without command.
I know: Mathew Havard told me, choking
Behind his hand.

But hard on Breda and the young king's
Homecoming there was that strange report
Of the holes in the church door at Talybont,
Your furious aim at the lock, and the dozen
Riders smoking westward into the dark. Was this
An end, then, Jenkin, or a new aim other-worldly
Taken? You are a friend of my doubts, an enemy
Who troubles my heart in failing. Fare
You well. H.V.

162   UNDER QUINAG

   Look
   At the grieved leaning of sun
   Over the waves' rim, and the black
   Crocodile islands rolling
   And snapping like curs after this one
   Last offering of the light:

   Reflect,
   When the ray no longer can
   The pyre the disinheritors reject,
   This is our world turning
   Its mountainous face away, man
   Making his destiny night.

163   THE FOOL IN THE WOOD

   Beech-dark each day, brought down
   From the distant, clerestory sky
   By a sly shaft of dawn, a leafy
   Traverse of noon and the flown
   Red kites of evening. In every such
   The man Salaun rejoiced, jaw
   Loosed on his chest, the gadding law
   Of water in his eye, his ugly crotch
   Hoist in a nest of tree. O the high
   Branch was heavenmaze and the forest
   Pool under it cold as the hest
   Of kindred. An old folly
   Adamant, it had parted groan
   And fool, making of speech an 'O
   Itroun Gerhez Mari' gabbled through
   As the day branched and shone.

   When soldiers with an armour glint
   Like midget suns in a half-world
   Lording and jostling, called
   To him roughly in astonishment,
   Seeing a shamble of hair
   And leg and a stalled protruding

Eye like a heifer's suffering
Cozenage, one, big as glory, cut the bare
Gob of a foot with his dagger-point,
Signalling huge as a lie. But the thing
Was silent, only bucking
The leg back to the branch disjoint
With pain, slowly, by will and parry
Making an 'O' that praised
Like a triumph, then the unvarying raised
Cry 'Itroun Gerhez Mari'.

Not even a pelted fool can kill
The cold for ever, and this one
Tumbled at forty out of his sun-
Shut perch, the sap gone still
In the tree, into the thin-iced pool
Of March, his cowslick bound
For the bottom. What skulled sound
There was in a wood full
Of cracks and tremors introduced
A rest in a private chant, stood
In for silence, as silence did
For glory. Villagers, wilder, loosed
From a house-week, dug the grave
And Montfort, close on Auray, was told
By the last troop in the hundredfold
Story of the fool aloft in the architrave.

April passed, May and the woody
Pool put out its harts' tongues
Cheekily. Set amongst underlings
A full beechcast off a lily
Single and never perceived before
Held up a dizzy cup, its white
Believed most of all for the eight
Stamened capitals it bore
From the base of the stoup, a gabbled
'Ave Maria' gold and amened
From a lost face. A restless wind
Busy as the old woodman, rabbled
The curious at the first halloo:
Some Thomas red from a distance

Rooted about the stem and the trance
Of the jaw from which it grew.

Many who spoke much formerly
Crossed themselves and were quiet.
The pool to touch was warmer. By it
The church that Montfort hastily
Swore to build on his rival's
March and the dubious, lost
Anatomy of the fool grew, engrossed
The sky. The king's and other evils
Over the centuries tripped
And fled from the pool, their works
Of malignancy dead. After the plaques
And the pardons I, glib and shipped
Over last, am smart to note
Four Breton words glossed and struck
To two Latinate, slower to look
Piercingly at the cost and bloat
I have of words. Four, two, less
Than a fraction of one is their sure
Count Godwards, alas, for lack of a pure
Heart and a praising gentleness.

164   AU CIMETIÈRE DE BREST

One of the afternoon, misted over the death glass,
Hour when the last dead hammer in their marble,
Look how the sentries sag behind their dark grilles
Easing the skeleton.

These were the paragons, the hydra-limbed captains
Keeping the sun's quick auger from the prostrate,
Hiding the slabbed kin, the coign spidering coldly,
Names long unlettered.

Browned the camellias nursed between the ground-knees,
Rade winds salt them and the sad rout perishing.
Tears are for cherubs captured by the stone hands,
Children of sea-dark.

Crossed swords but blunted, cramped out of service,
Téméraires raked off the once-spirited water,
Do not such armorials, families of grave words,
Catch at the heart-knot?

Speakers in the main street, blaring over crowd heads,
Suddenly call silence, a fugue of bells faintly
Struck in the foundered echo of each clapper
Picks out the cloud dance.

Jaunty arms pointing, Count Russell de Bedford,
Capitaine de vaisseau, Prud'homme, Gérard,
Officers seconded to the darkened flotilla,
Beckon the dance on.

Stone moves like memory, ponderous, deliberate,
Hiding the wound-chafe, the grimace in moulding.
This is the moment, clapping the grilles to,
Honour must celebrate.

L'Amiral Jean Cras, his widow née Tardy,
Passioned in marble, their portion of stillness
Cramps the partings of duty, brutally leaves them
Wounded together.

Dance will not move them, side by side fallen.
Mist fingers the cherubs, camellias yellowing
Drown in the salt-drops. Gérard, Prud'homme,
Where are your steps now?

Suddenly quiet. The fugue stops. A jangle.
Unstereoed speakers boring the crowds on.
Monoprix has it, not *Sigrand,* the swing-doors
Count in the franchise.

Sentries, sentries, if strength was your duty,
What can you purpose yet, Russell de Bedford,
Prud'homme, Gérard, pointing the grape-shot
Clear of your comrades?

Blackened the cadre, the empire pitied. *Ce qui
Reste de l'honneur* at last will permit you,
Valiants at stand here, full length to topple,
Breaking the last camp.

165   CHANNEL SAINT

Ohé
Guénolé
Tower, nave in disarray
Landevennec was a day,
Ghost whose ripple sent the Word
Like a fish away
Softly away

Pardieu
Winwaloe
Have I caught you swimming so?
Nettle, brake under sickle go
Flat on this back, and Dyfed
Braces your tower, blow
By quick blow.

166   A CELTIC DEATH

For once the Latin has an edge
That fits the scene, not so much end
Of cliff or riftland soluble
In a millenial sea as long
Apprehension's washed-over ess
At wake, shivering promontory
Of unease, dropping teeth and
Saliva-ed sand in panicked
Foretaste of the rock's mortality.
Finistère! It is abrasion,
Threat to the veins, the shadowy
Ness long drowned, the terminal
Paid up lesson of impossible
Absence on the seas of myth.
Call it Léon on the braver days
If you will, when the brass sun's
Knocker shines on a wrinkled,
Toothless ocean, vacant, senilely

Innocent of all those swallowed
Molars from the Roman wall.

But here, tossed on Ouessant, roped
To a continent solely by weight
Of recorded wrecks, lighthouses,
And a too-late prattle of weathercast,
What is the news of living save
The guard behind tamarisk, imagination
Tricked to the closer duties, clocks
And faces, the casual floating bevel
Of a bed, a nearer rocking chair?
Each ewe, once lambed, is tied
To a firmer tuft, the cressy winter
Suck of pool and marsh diminishes.
Swifts, rife and scattering the cheer
Of inconsequent larks, settle
Dust on the roof-trees of old crofts,
Wear out a courage that's past human use,
Sly, fanatic, in the end outcast.

Now it is Sunday and the Bugel
Eussa, quayed in the slapping
Baie du Stiff, ships a black wave
Of passengers, mobbed and kissed
Off to their week in the suburbs
Of Brest. Passion is there, without
Speech, in the watchers, children
Too young to be taken, women
With eyes burning indifferent
Backs on the gangway set
Carefully for nonchalance or school.
Above, three coaches, eighteen
Cars and a few velos momentarily
Out of puff confront the steep,
Staccato presences that stop the hoe
In the potato-plot and scratch
The will strapped to the raging tamarisks.
Silence gets wretched terms, a quarter
Hour for the weekly bloodletting.

April is come and the red sea
Has a hint of summer. Only
Grandmothers, stiff with the coiffe
And rheumatics, stand absurd
In the gooseberry patch, rapt
In a habit of Sundays, making no
Move from their lives to see it.

167   NEW LEASE

It's a dead house, he said. Done for.
Why don't you let it lie?
But the naked ashes cry
In the close wind of this captor
Country, impotent fingers snaked
And spread, making that death punishable
For me, that death punishable.

I come to you, house, like Llifiau
From beyond Bannog, crass
As a Pict and no less
Mercenary, a wanderer with an eye
For walls like yours. Weather
And enemy loose will not command us
Lightly, will not command us.

The ashes will spread brazening fingers
Gloved for the summer nights,
A green for the sleights
Of life and garrison. Eye lingers
Not on this new defiance, nor will glimpse,
Till the season bites, our armour gleaming
At dusk, our armour gleaming.

168   AFTER CHRISTMAS

Old berry and old sun
With other scantlings hang on
A bone from the lost tribe
Convivial song

Sloe like the slow minute
Wrinkles on stick: tooth in it
Bites through the fur to plum
Protestant virgin

Dark needle and dark pine
Bed down the trodden cone
A catholic fret for seed
Ground to the maiden

All humours and all wills
Consult the dark: except fools
Trading a whisper that the Child
Is back from Egypt.

169   A STARE FROM THE MOUNTAIN

As the sun slants, the best of it over,
Into the trug of Usk from the summary
West, masking the struts, the wicker rents
With plush, with a stuff of shaded
Greens gentling the upper, thistly fields,
The thicker bush of forest, ploughland
Cuts of red already stiff in their winter
Folds, tricking the human aberration
Into the same still life, a whole
Kindred lit with the right intensity,
Painted safe to a fortunate choice
Of colours, I stand on Yscir mountain,
Head above wind level, hearing the north's
Voice at my nape, putting the frozen
Questions that the poles demand. Fieldfares
Break from a half-leaved oak as I
Walk a few tentative feet. The fetlock
Hairs, the mane, the portly grassblown
Outline of a pony natured white
Shine between me and sun, the animal
Marked with redemption from a hidden
Source. I look involuntarily, all
Of a sudden in need of a gleam
Lining my shadow. But nothing there

Satisfies, nothing anywhere in the sparse
Clip of mountain, only that down
In the valley bottom is a reed-
Plume of smoke fining the rubbish-tip –
The town, taken by sun and arked,
Burning its pages from the Domesday Book.

170   SQUIRREL-PATH

He doesn't know,
That little zany on the lawn
With his smoke-signalling tail and lingo
Like a cock with its mouth full,
Just where he put that nut to pawn.
Indeed, for every pull of grass
Of a growth enough to bruise
Back from the mower when its great
Trespass begins, there's a tidy shell
He's packed against February
Frost, late snow and the slower
Breath of trees. But he's forgetful,
In fact, of all undermost
Things, his mind a tease
In the beech-top, bent on
Chasing Reduncle up the wind
And down the sapling's bole-bark
To the apple's lower
                    branch.
                            Then
For a lark
            they supple from fence
To ground
            and last
                    onto palisade
                            up
With a bound
            up
                    like impudence
Together to the oak
In escalade, up the quick windy mast and back
From the unanswerable weather.

They've worn a path,
Those little zanies on the lawn,
From paved stone to palisade, both
Of them – and their brothers
And cousins and aunts. Fawn
It is, grey at the edges, just
The colours one would expect dozens
Of little bounders, with their tree
Feet and exuberant usages to lay
Across compliant green. They're no more
Killers than I am, but they don't
Sleep for long in the winter – whoever
Said they hibernate must have seen
Them in snowed-over Maine or Vermont –
And their cranial predicate
Is always a leap, from the level
Of grassblades and breath, to a tree-world
Of catamountain life, of devil-
May-care audacity,
     up
From apple to beech
      palisade to oak
          space to space
Shadow to stipple
      spire to pothook
Answering
   each and together
With gibbering tail
      and peaky know-all face
The cries of the windy weather.

171   PORTH CWYFAN

June, but the morning's cold, the wind
Bluffing occasional rain. I am clear
What brings me here across the stone
Spit to the island, but not what I shall find
When the dried fribbles of seaweed
Are passed, the black worked into the sandgrains
By the tide's mouthing. I can call nothing my own.

A closed-in, comfortless bay, the branchy
Shifts of voyage everywhere. On a slope
Of sand reaching up to the hidden
Field or stretch of marram a tipwhite, paunchy
Terrier sits pat on his marker, yapping me
Bodily out of range. What in God's name is he
Guarding that he thinks I want of a sudden?

To the left is the island, granite-hulled
Against froth, the chapel's roof acute
As Cwyfan put it when the finer
Passions ruled, convergent answers belled
Wetherlike towards God. Ahead is the cliff
Eaten by sand. On the quaking field beyond
Low huts, ordered and menacing. Porth China.

Once on the island those last shingle
Feet I came by seem in threat.
Can you, like Beuno, knit me back severed
Heads, Cwyfan, bond men to single
Living? Your nave has a few wild settles
And phantasmagoric dust. And Roger Parry,
Agent to Owen Bold, has a stone skew-whiff in the yard.

Doubling back again is a small
Inevitable tragedy, the umpteenth
In a sinuous month. Now I avoid
The violent pitch of the dog, with all
And nothing to guard, remark his croup,
The hysteric note in the bark. Two dunlin,
Huffing on long legs, pick in and out of the tide.

A man on the beach, a woman
And child with a red woollen cap
Hummock and stop within earshot,
Eyeing my blundering walk. 'Can
We get to the island?' he asks, Lancastrian
Accent humble, dark curls broad. And I
Am suddenly angry. But how is my tripright sounder,
Save that I know Roger Parry and he does not?

FOOL'S FINGERS

Not everything is named, either
For memory's sake or for the marks
In the book. And what's most secret,
Ridiculous in its fashion, has
Often no more of date than
Repeated omens, settings of twigs
Or stones, threatening the week
With another dervish appearance.

There had been snow that the noon
Sun melted. The sloping fields
Still had a snow-rash, the roughest
Grass clumps sparkily topped with white.
The nameless runnel that lower down
Brings a stick or two to Soar's
Unheeding backs like a wet bitch
Shaking herself dropped here
Suddenly through a culvert from left
To right of the road. The walled-in roar
It was pulled me, from habit, to peer
Down at the wintered split channel
And there, all but surfing the small
Blurt of water, hung a line of daredevil
Ice-shapes, onions, pears, inverted cold
Parsnips of ice that the bank's
Promiscuous trickles had dripped faster
Than one frost's icicles. Down
To the very tips they had run
To freeze, these water-joints, these
Drips without knuckles, pompously fived
And bladdered to make fool's fingers –
Not Struwwelpeter's with trumpery nails
But fat shilling digits with the heart's
Cold water blue in the ends. Later
I saw them everywhere, under the field's
Cornice, solemnly hung from a tree-root
Close to the shock of free water
But never quite carried away.
                              I doubt

That the day will stand, but the image
Will, as my heart fidgets off, gloving
Fool's fingers with a different colour.

173   IN THE SWISS JURA

The tree-flanks are meek
And unsettled, the mountain-back near to the bleak
Closure of sky. We talk
As we walk, my daughter and I,
Without check.

Lilies gone brown
In the spear rank over the pasture. They have grown
Since the mowing, their proud
Points loud, reminiscent, their showing
All done.

Black by the firs
Rise ant-heaps, yard-high hives of the toothy dealers
In famine, consumers of vast
Beanstalks past, straw giants grounded, mine
And hers.

Lop as I will
This solemn tarquiniad is early, cannot forestall
The last frail season. If I
Slash high these summer blades, reason
May still

Carry some cords
At parting, behead her careful journey with words.
But pride and reason are not
Pilot and captain, are not tried
Windwards,

Go blind to the seas
Beyond Europe. Gwythyr, prince, whose sword disagrees
With fire, for whom the ants
Are valiants, answer my desire,
Appease

Such stubborn distance,
Upbraid your colonies woefully, call for expense
Of heart, that islands off
The luff coast of Africa, part
And chance

Of your empire over
All emmets, pismires (red truculents moreover),
Obey in the real giant's field
The questing child no father may
Recover.

174   LA TÈNE

Sun blinding back from glass cases, eyes that see black
Bangles and torcs, chasings that should be bronze,
Bosses for dragons' shields, horse-bits, fibulas, beaten-out
Parts for chastity-belts, haftless swords, and one
Pale diadem – it is all angles, unwelcome graces of light
In the blind pupil. The camera, too, is baffled.
Intrusive struts and side-panels, crosses from nearby
Windows, the black, glowing eyes of objects, starts
And fits at the need to be surreptitious, to watch for
Attendants beginning to walk rapidly at the lens, hale
And unfriendly. What are these arts if not official,
Postcard-size or reserved for the ad-men's brochure?
Somewhere, beyond, at the lakehead perhaps, the real
Multi-faceted eyes of the Celts, escaping so much sun
And lure of glass, pull out and intertwine the tips
Of marsh quakers, the bed for each whorl and spiral
Struck, a dull goldfield, in the hammered grass.

Morning is misty, soon to be hot, a blatant part
Of the mirage. But caravans, a chipboard settlement?
These stilted nomads, under-dressed, ape the testy
Ways of that first armed *entrepôt*, all excretions
Warily piped out and the tribe and pasturage
Listed in full in the club-house. And the calmed lake
That mistakenly dropped its level in the frock-
Coated eighties when the Vougas, father then son,
Began to stake out their *fouilles* with the mortised

Posts they discovered, has regretted those few hot summers,
Such gross *bêtise*. It has lifted skirts long since,
Is decorous, formalist, banked. The slimed gleam of metal
No longer starts the skeleton: horse-bit and boss
Are safe, dispersed, arrayed in an academic theme
For Biel, Genève, Neuchâtel. To turn a leaf
Is mischievous in this tidy commote, a grave
Offence against property and the straits of trade.

The setts of the Thielle just here dress back the language-
Line. Apt it is, apt to imagine the Vandal,
Hun, the impossible Goth weakening, settling, taking
This rhine for marker, trading in barley for metal,
Glazing the lake with his dream. At evening the path
Of the sun would swim back to his eye, and far-off
Wotan thunder less readily. Between main and canal
A darker breakwater rides on its stone: picking
A way along it is a stiff-toed tap-dance over and under
Worlds touching and not touching, two sky-blown revolving
Stages that, sticking a while, advance and fract
Back with the season's colds. I search at the terminal
Beacon for the minute that fits, the fragile
Inscribed recognition, but, finding none, settle
Myself as the fact and the gulls are settled, riding
Uneasy water. Farther out one solitary black-headed
Diver, immersed in his habits, remains unafraid
To go deep, not a tittle impressed that cajoling
Sun and mist and contingent waves slily lip over
The slow-worm unguents covering the threaded gulf

A bow-wave runs from the Thielle. A pleasure-steamer
Easing the water-slaps back from a gilt-white prow
Comes abreast, the after-deck prinked with executive suits
And parasols. Close by the pilot-flag a group
Of Swiss matrons, dark to the neck in wide hats, coo-ee
The dreamer they would pass in the street. Holiday,
Transience, it takes this to whoop up the watery peace
They have. The Germans are visible, paddling, cleanly,
Phlegmatically devoted to commerce, their trance complete
And formal, the wheelhouse raying out lakewards
Like a flashed shield-boss. But the Celts? The ceramic masters
Of Europe, the uncompromised chasers whose spirals

Match real with unreal, whose imagined receding faces
Trade with the fox, whose earth-god horns the stag, Esus
Become Cernunnos, where are they? At watch
With the viscous blade in the quagmire, glassed up in Biel
Or Neuchâtel with the barely-recovered sword-hilts?
At Vix, by the early parade of the Seine,
I felt them, flat on their table mountain Lassois,
Scanning the north and the marvelled-at tin
Grounds, passing from hand to hand incomparable
Cub-lipped Etruscan jars, wary and praised
In their chasing, their statuettes in bronze, their dab
Enhancement of death. But here? The camp appears
Quiet, heat-glazed, its somnolent habits
Unreadable. What breath there is comes slow. I feel
In my hands no skill in beating-out, hammering,
Thinning the solemn metals, no means of waking
The mirage of quay to marvels of cargo, of such kinds
As would beckon the Vandals, their minds imagined
Afresh, made full and winning without ponderous
Wars or a creaking formality. These later deals
Of mine are in words: my quick and unshelved wish
Is to sell each one from a mould made new
In the speaking, as day and mood combine, with
Leaves curling lost faces and the throes of old
Tragedy curved into birds and cubs, so well
Are the graves concealed. But the trader's lingo
Hardens, haste keeps the moulds unbroken, the cases
Fill with horse-brass repeated, godlings in jaded
Paste and rubs of armorial bearings, just what
The buyers need to limit rather than baffle
Cost. Across this counter affluent Vandals press
Wanting the plough-teams of their numbered shires.

Is the Celt lost, his antique designs of faith
And mystery tidied-up in this dried-out marsh?
The diver surfaces after a while, complains raucously,
His harsh note scattering the gulls. He has found
Nothing, not even a bottom silt cleft and unhealed
From stag's horn ravage of the remote, undermost
Retributive fury of riddling, bronze-eyed Cernunnos.

175   BURNING BRAMBLES

The sea at a distance glints now and again, as though
This upland corner, puzzled with smoke, had a new heart to show.

But the land is unhealthy, smelling of green-cut bramble
And rotting sticks; bumps in it, bare of all grass, resemble

Boils that the bold rooting whips had crossed, lanced once of their pus
And left, foetid and out of sight. It is an old covert, the fuss

Of discovery long muted: in the back ditch the tins are so many
Rust-flakes that part in the fingers, dusting on black bottles rainy

Yet stoppered, a heap of old sins without consequence, save
Deep in the land's heart where the sods of the field wall gave

Them summons for turbulence. And now there is burning, sullen
Bramble whips dragged a while since to their pyramid, crest-fallen

But free to strike and trip as they can. The one fire catching,
Out of the gusts from the north-west, needs that quick watching

That one cannot give who forks and carries recalcitrant
Loops from the pyre lower down, full in the wind, only intent

On freeing himself and not falling, with the burdened fork
Wide of the body. It is a slow excoriation: the whips work

Back on the hand, mindless as snakes but bitter. And the smoke
Is bitter, making the nose run and the freer arm for its soak

Keep a shirt-cuff handy. Even the flames bite back, leaving
The near scalp smoked and the green rotten smell of the stalks waving

Threats overhead. The clog of leaves and sticks must be left
Momentarily on the ground. It is enough to unpile and shift

The endless loops of this waste, hearing the crackle behind
And knowing the smell of a life ill lived as it passes down wind.

176   IS IT THE SAME COUNTRY?

That edge of rose – there! – to the tender
Cirrus of evening, the singular mirror's bevel
Of strawberry gardens strung out with netted cloud –
Does it persuade me of fruit I have not seen?

I come, deer-stalkered, by the coining road
From England and nowhere, the gardeners pillage me
Strangely, themselves perhaps strangers, without
Regard for the sticks of my father's house, the loath
Dumb churning, under hand chary clink of coppers
In small pockets and the lofty precept that the *gwair*
Rhos cwtta garners. They walk in their netted
Gardens with quick, stained lips, strangers
Alert for other strangers, eyeing this prodigal
Half back from England and nowhere with features set
For the fallen pine-end, the flat of an old house
Lumbered.
              Dangerous, like all chained vagabonds
With no stake in the land, toes stubbing out vilely
From gravelled socks, I come in my vented coat
And ear-flaps, nailing in tracks the prophet
Walked common and scatheless, all forty days and nights
To Horeb, crying that every bush by the squatters'
Verge has a boast, is messaged and hugely on fire.

177   PWLL LLONG, PWLL WHITING

The sea's blue eye and the lobster boat
Glint quizzically. The morning party
Is off to its usual start. Friday and sun
Prepared for a frolic. No conjuror
Needed. Both north and south the guest
Has a feast of cliff-curve and fret-
Line, from Strumble with cloud-hat on
To the blowy dunce-caps of Tyddewi.

But fallen faces are visible too
Close at hand, slate cheeks collapsed
In slack water, stubble hacked off
By the reiver's stroke, lips wry,
Contained as by accident. Only the
Hairline lives, and eyes, total
As war, recall the skeletal aspect
Two Poles had, long-shanked together, harmless
Fun like this no more than exuberant
Noise in the distance shouting the ruin
Of both their lives and of Warsaw.

178   BLUE BLOOD AND ENGLISHMEN

My grandfather, white-faced son of the water-
Bailey – truly his one candescence was
In taking train for Todmorden, quick and uptight
At the words he had ready for a schoolma'am
Recently travelled there (it was a later rein
That had him fast to the Ffawyddog, stony white
With a trade) – saw himself dogged in living, all
Other follies out of count, by a single villain,
Welsh and a-poop with laughing. Welsh-speakers,
Chapel deacons, sycophants, gave him affront,
Had in one moment made their play of him, done
Him ribbingly down. It was enough to be fresh
From Cardiff, taking a farm as tenant, mazed and
Uncomprehending. But one neighbour clown
The first, then all, bid him up stiff and sharp
For milch cows, heifers, hill sheep, hayrakes, gambos,
Item by item down to the oddmost tundish, pricing
His eyebrows out of the market. He was a nervy
Man, the engine often at thrash in his temple,
But skilled with walls and the dressing of house-
Stone when there was no tribulation from jokers,
Mates and their balderdash. At another sale than this
The vendor-widow, mantled in quiet and stooping
Black, would have crossed his mind's eye, even
Spoken a word. But this was an hour and a diddle
He had known all his life, the dirty ribbers
Putting him up, nudging each other in Welsh,

Safe in their sour-smile welcome, seeing him
Lofty, pig in the middle.
                          From then there was one
Offence unforgivable and he made it language,
Preaching it haplessly from greater to smaller
Glat, pleaching his every slope against that alien
Glottis. From so much vehemence there grew release
Only in the fat gallop fields towards Hereford.
Man there was shapely, tongued more like a friend
And born of a higher lineage. Bridge Court he
Searched for, on his few days off: it was an
End and purpose, the keeper mansion where his hurt
Could be salved by gentlefolk, his ancestors
Of the years beyond proof. But it chose
Wilfully to stay hidden, a blue Sunday spoken
Of in the east, from which the intemperate scars
Of the tongue were banished and the trodden
Field-tracks dried under braver footfalls fast.

A map brought me Bridge Court in the tongue-tied
Years after his death. I went there, marked
It a farm in Kingstone, gave it by estimate
To a stalwart yeoman of Cobbett's. But I hear that
Scrub among footfalls yet, my white-faced grand-
Father's. For all his nerves, he was no only son.

179   THE ANCHORITE

Eighteen and one from fosterage
Seventeen men and Diuran
Rhyming for Maeldúin across the bridge
Of glass. Which is that one
Cursed never to get home again
In the same rhyming age?

An island dressed by an anchorite
Tying the sod he came on
Ritually to a tossing site
Of breakers. Maeldúin's men
Noted his nakedness and the vain
Plummet of hair downright.

Their three-skin curragh had a score
Of birds on wing. Maeldúin
Cold of his voyage listened for
Echoes of origin,
Conjured with other islands in
Marking that sodden shore.

Speech must shortly be essayed
With the holy man. But he,
Settling the birds, presently made
The first gesture. 'How many
Souls have you in the company
That journey on afraid?

Each year this sod I stand on grows
By a foot. And gently God
Fastens down trees whose gallows
Days are gone. Abode
Of birds, my kindred, flock of the blood
Treacherous, men whose

Word-wounds I may hold my hands
Up for, the reckoning
Still to be faced – whoever lands
Here shares our horror, turning
The ashes guiltily, questioning
The dead. But your demands

Are different. Can Diuran
Salvage you, rhyme bite back
That vengeance the swart ocean
Promises? Every tack,
Island to island, thundersmack,
Boiling sand, leviathan

In mid-marvel, nudges profanely
Homeward. The seventeen
Not of your blood and leanly
Collared against the sea-green
Oar and the original mean
Tragedy may gainly

Tunnel the wave, breasting like flotson
Their native coast. But the last
Of your foster-brothers, Maeldúin,
Will die in his laugh. Ballast
His known rhymes are, long overcast
With sleep. And what conflation

Of child winds pursing can puff you
Familiarly home? This crumb
Of prayed-upon earth is added to
By grace, an arcanum.
While you, Maeldúin, travel numb
Towards strangers. So adieu.'

The dazzle of winter kept the sea
In leash, the skinny arms
Of the anchorite held the birds drily
Aloft. The aliforms
Of the trees glowed. Expectant harms
Swam out to Maeldúin's company.

180   THE DAMSON TREE

Torrent shouts Manascin in the dark
Setts below, while we, sidling the sheer
Crumble of mountain, crouch out a moment
Of downpour stiff in a quirk
Of reed, beaten as sheep or near.

But such storms pass and, passing, rift
In a blue sworn from another belief:
Quick as a stumble, sudden from ailing cwtch
And river, we reach a cleft,
A roofless hovel, more, a cliff

With a tree of damsons, holding red
To the last shock of its winded parish.
Our pockets fill, the last-minute blackberry
Bag is crammed, but the spread
Of glory persists, its mass a childish

Conclusion to the grim tale of age.
Men were here once, and wilfully, before
Weeks came mechanic or wrapped opinion
Advertised the adage –
Risk gets its fruit from mountainous error.

181   SNIPE'S CASTLE

I can't say I remember you. The truth is
No one does. But in some not too distant
Age you were egregious, Snipe, picking
In seed corn secretly, liming a plot
Or two, grudging the time of day
To countrymen longer billed and taxed than you
A lot.

Not easily defensible this ridge, I
Can see that. But in that backward era
Preseli would come up pat to a Little
England eye (why else a castle?) – so
Possible jackdaws up from off
Might beak in of an evening like the courteous
Near crow.

Entry is simple now. Cold-bowed sycamores
Are the roadside hedge and clumps of tall white
Bells in season edge the old black leaning
Trunks inside. Penetrate far enough
And a cowed outhouse shows, sorry
With brambles. The rest of the secret acre has gone
Back rough.

Someone else's bees quarter the tract lower down
Working the hives. Your tame montbretia,
Snipe, has knives out cunningly on the verge.
Bad times, you'd think, there's never been
Respect. But is that you I see, quiet
And speckled, grubbing a while longer in the dull
Dark rain?

182   ON LLANDEFALLE HILL

Last year this hill was burned,
The bracken stalks
Taken and footed under wintering cows,
All that seemed useful turned
As this poor trackland is, exiguous,
To the advantage of our middling house.

If summer is, then wind
Has made mistake
Of the lush month: the mountains scale the shades
Along bright flanks, behind
Their nearer snorts, a darker rumpus of clouds,
Like shifty serpents waiting for their trades.

Nothing is certain yet
And cannot be:
But these gold thumb-plates in the embittered grass
Are tormentil and wet
Brown felt umbrella-handles are up to address
The sloping weather. All that man was

In history pictures here,
Reluctant light,
Parade of a far terror, wind greyhound
In the mosses. Will he peer
Cunningly from the *hendre* again, chimney-burned,
To catch at summer in its hasty round?

Sheep graze, a cart track shows
Yellower where
The grass is thin and pressed: habit prescribes
The way. If God allows
He spoke once to our fathers, the babes
Will remember it to the wasted tribes.

183   MAY-TREES CLIMBING

It is not the June image, the one month late
To the day, that I cling to, the gulleys slung
With dotted muslin, the voices sunnied
And girlish out of the mountain weather crying
'Look at me!' – 'And me!' and again, in the distance,
'Me!', as the shimmer whitens from Wye bank up
To the almost summit in sight, a delicately
Pearled sky thrown by an obsolete perfectscope
Flat on the travelling hill. It is not beauty
I am looking for, not that beauty at least, nor
The pride of the climber sparing a moment's
Breath. Custom still sounds off sharply
On these, voices going shrill on the top notes,
Cold eyes glittering in the conniving air.
Yet the other eleven months are truer, all
Of them, though dark captains six with misleading
Oaths and five the almost summit clears
And lies to. Arrived there, sopped, in November,
The short grass dragged with mud, the rushy clumps
Spurting with water, I am irresolute, cut
With shears like the season, scarcely aware
Of markers and the human centres of clouds.
Dark by the week or month soon relegates
June to the suspect retina, kitting out
Beauty in its own short weave. Even the eyes
Are purged, the tears of the long winter
Start and well. Diminished, I see the dun
Slope sheering down from me, the rattling
Gulleys begin. The dim world wheels, the weathered
Shapes climb nearer, one close at hand
Already. In the slatey dark what is left
Of courage is caught as it reels by the arms
Of the few and the comely, their storm-roughened bark.

184   SIR GELLI TO R.S.

Even the worst intelligence must needs ride
Some years to reach me where I am, and hardihood
Bids me to leave yours lie. But that I cannot bear

To be held innocent and frail, a touch
For baubles and fine clothes. As well regret
Your verse for simpering at women. All
That I cherished, all, lay in the head –
The secret webs of a Gladestry morning, sun
Lofting at Wigmore or my other house
Of Llanelwedd, the clustered recusants, puritans
And Essex captains waiting on black-browed
Judgement. There was my Wales in thrall, delivered,
Dumb, to the cause. As for the town, man, London,
When was I there more happentimes than you?
I was at Cadiz, sure enough, with the spoils
To divide for my master, I the black pinnace
Roped to the heaving flagship, provisioner
For the extravagant wars. But London's a place
To pass through for a Welshman, always was. And I
Was no Penfro squireling with a perch of squill
On the cliff-top, idling it out in a city
Of coneys. I diced and ran with the Devereux, he
And I at Lamphey, boys of the dangerous covert. My
Black looks defended his bright ones. I
Clothed him with darkness, saturnine, setting the meats
For the rout, pricking him dumb men for sheriffs
Throughout the March, bribing the Assizes' scratch
To a lazy quill for the papists' sake. The magic
Silence there and before my Lord Pembroke's notaries
Was like the spell of Llwyd son of Cil Coed that Manawydan
Knew when he came from plying his trade in Lloegr.

I was always a man of silence. Even at Tyburn
When Cuffe, my cumbersome scaffold fellow, pleaded
To make his peace, I cut him short. It
Was no time for wheedling. The Devereux
Was my master, in treason or out. Why demean
His title a moment for such alien grace?
'Set the axe to,' I said. Yet you aver
I cried for the baubles. Man, when we meet
I'll blood you sharply an you'll not declare
Which of us left an innocence in Wales.

185   MEMLING

What was it brought you, Seligenstadter,
Ambition cursed with smiles, the escalins
All counted and fingered, asking to be taken for
Bourgeois in the staid halls of Brugge?
And why did the Dom of Koln so fret your sky
That Ursula, that little bear of the Celts,
Stepped out of it, a boatload of priests
And maidens fast to her skirts, the white trim
Of innocence to their fold and the flower
Of death? This was an old, preposterous
Story, not meant for your burgher ears. And
Were not the villain Huns the ancestors
You could hardly name without the revilements
Of history? What had you still to exorcise
In your fine stone house on the Vlamingdam?

The gold of this painted reliquary shines
In the poor pilgrims' dark of the Hospital
Of St John, the long tables of poverty
Barely gone from under the arches. What
Is the paradox that has us all by the throat?
That auburn hair, the young girl's unformed
Face, the blue soft sleeves and tiny
Refusing hands, colour and deck our youth as
We like to think it was. And the Hunnish
Tents are elaborate, Burgundian, rigid
Pavilions for Charles the Rash and his
Knights, their arbalests and fluted knee-
Joints and epaulets, the sophisticate
Sheen on their full black armour. It is all
Safely transposed, the ravisher and ravished.
The history we choose speaks largely of ourselves.

186   TO A TOMBSTONE FRAGMENT IN
              THE GARDEN PATH

No, you are not under foot
However my sole muddy the fractured
Word-forms in which they forgot

What your life had been like, the whole
And part of it trodden – wife,
Unwife, daughter, child, the immeasurable
Shifts of a patience that inured
The ribcage of the heart.

But what do I know of you?
I synthesise. One edge breaking
At *Jo* . . . , the islanded meadow
Merch and the last sharp surmise
Of the words *a ragor* cast
Up on the lower shore. This untimed death
Is less than a birth, unmaking
Locus, identity, errand.

But you still have a nation. I
Might have discarded you, turned
You face down rather than save
That slit tongue. Reflect on this
As your cheek lodges beech-nuts, among
Animal eyes. I who would quickly refashion
My stony fathers, had I learned
But how, call you to speak,
Speak.

187   BRECHFA CHAPEL

Not a shank of the long lane upwards
Prepared our wits for the myth, the slimed
Substantiation of the elements. And the coot
With his off-white blaze and queasy paddle
Was an old alarm, the timid in flight
From the ignorant. The lowered shoulder
Of mountain it is, dabbled within the collar,
That shallows and darkens the eye, the first
Slack argent losing the light as bitterly
As the blackened water treads and nibbles
The reeds and bushes afloat in the new
Pool's centre. Beyond, a surviving ray
Points and fondles a reed-knot, the swan
That dreams on it taking no note of stumps

Or visitations. Nearer, however, and shifting
Like pillagers from weed to shore, settling
And starting raucously, hundreds of testy
Black-backs utter their true society, bankrupt
Hatred of strangers and bully unrest whichever
Marge they think themselves forced to. It
Is a militant brabble, staked out by wind
To the cropped-down pasture. Mud and the tricky
Green of the edge contrivingly clap it round
What's left of this latish day that began with love.

Opposite, to the west of the harsh lagoon,
Stands a chapel, shut in its kindred wall
With a score of graves. Legend on one
Cries a minister, dead of the heats in Newport
Before he came twenty-eight, his wife
Rambling on to her eighties. On another a woman
Loosens at thirty, her man afield on the mission
Ploughing till dark. O these stones trouble
The spirit, give look for look! A light from this
Tiny cell brisked in far corners once, the hand held
Steady. But now the black half-world comes at it,
Bleaks by its very doors. Is the old witness done?
The farmers, separate in their lands, hedge,
Ditch, no doubt, and keep tight pasture. Uphill
They trudge on seventh days, singly, putting
Their heads to the pews as habit bids them to,
And keep counsel. The books, in pyramid, sit tidy
On the pulpit. The back gallery looks
Swept. But the old iron gate to the common,
Rusted a little, affords not a glimpse
Of the swan in her dream on the reed-knot
Nor of the anxious coot enquiring of the grasses.
The hellish noise it is appals, the intolerable shilly-
Shally of birds quitting the nearer mud
For the farther, harrying the conversation
Of faith. Each on his own must stand and conjure
The strong remembered words, the unanswerable
Texts against chaos.

188 MADOC

Madoc reputedly sailed from Gwynedd in the year 1170 and is thought to have landed near what is now Mobile, on the Gulf Coast of North America. Leaving most of his followers there, he returned to Wales for reinforcements. He sailed again, probably in the next year, this time from Lundy Island, and was never heard of again. It is not known whether he ever found and rejoined his first party.

In the sixteenth century, however, stories were first heard of a tribe of Welsh Indians encountered, confusingly, in a variety of regions not far from the eastern seaboard. By the late eighteenth century they were being identified as the Mandans, who lived west of Missouri in what is now North Dakota. Their un-Indian characteristics were noted by a number of travellers and George Catlin, the painter of Indians, spent eight years with them at the beginning of the second quarter of the nineteenth century. Meanwhile, however, John Evans, sent out by the London Cymmrodorion Society in 1792 to find and identify them, had denied in his report that they had any Welshness of speech or custom – a report which has made most historians reject not only the 'Welsh Indians' but the Madoc story as a whole. In the year 1838 the Mandans were virtually wiped out by smallpox, now believed to have been shipped to them in a cargo of furs – possibly an act of genocide by some members of the then American government.

The setting of the poem is an Indian heaven to which have come those, whether Indian or European, who died before 1838 and never made effective contact with the new American civilization of the east. Hernando de Soto was murdered after reaching the Mississippi in 1541 and John Evans died of fever in New Orleans in 1799 without ever seeing Wales again. George Catlin enters this Indian heaven 'by licence' and Chief Big White had been once to Philadelphia before he died amongst his tribe on the banks of the Missouri.

The first speaker is Gwenllian, a bitter-tongued noblewoman from Gwynedd who was a member of Madoc's original party.

> *Gwenllian*:
> No, I am not to be comforted
> In any kingdom of trees
> Where the water-rats swim at you
> Out of the shallows and the skinny
> Arm of the pole pushes, pushes
> Slyly into the riverweeds. Heaven –
> *Heaven!* This was the name you pinned
> Like a favour on the sun's
> Fading every day you had meat,

Fire and the means to sleep
Free of the biting Cherokee.
And now, now that my bosom hangs
With age, when clayed-up death
Is only a less interrupted sleep,
You wake me to talk of heaven
Again, a parade of hunting
Nobly in the grey, the spirit
Dawn of the peaceful tribes
Who harried us north from ocean
To narrower, narrower water
And taller wastes of trees.
I cry on waking like a child
Wanting its mother. My eyes
Are globbed with a long night's mucus,
My mouth is dry. I do not see
Well, but I see enough to know
This is not heaven. In heaven
I hope to see my father Llywarch
Rise from his seat to kiss me,
My mother Catrin cease her incessant
Pacing up and down to hold
Me jubilant, clear-eyed, swift
To her rapid breast. O these
And my brothers too, Rhodri,
Rhisiart of the Irish seas
Who would not come with us
For his mother's sorrow. All,
All these, and Gwynedd's court
Would be there, save the foul
Tongue of Dafydd.
                I am awake
Now fully and I know you lie
Saying with even half a breath
That this is heaven, this waste
Of stalking Indians, smoke
Like a thicket fired against
The sun and every token forest
Answering. Where are the great,
The princes, bards of home, the robed
Patriarchs of the Church? I see
White faces peering over

The eastern slopes and in the north
A darker smoke, an ash from fires
Burning more fiercely than
Those of hunting parties. Well enough,
If the Cherokee who hunted us
Run like the deer they are
Before other hunters. But I ask
Much more of heaven than
Justice: my vitals are unwarmed
By fires and silence. Where are
The Welsh, the great inheritors
Of poetry, music, atavistic faith,
The eloquent of the mountains,
Where are they in all this
Yellowing of wood and shadowed water?

John Evans:
I am here, embossed with fever,
Swollen out of this tree
Like a Spain-coloured gourd.
I am John Evans, Evans Waunfawr
In Gwynedd. I understand you
A little, though your tongue
Mourns with less skill than mine
Which Iolo praised and took
Quickly from Gwyrfai's ripple
To the godless ocean. In my life
I was sent to speak to you.

A Voice:
You are a Spaniard and a traitor!
If you were sent to speak
Why did you swear falsely and keep silence?

Gwenllian:
Let him continue swelling
Out of that tree. I need nothing
Of him. I scarcely understand
His language and would rather
My sight were dim than see too well
The outline of such peasant treachery.
Einion, husband, love, you that bled

From an arrow-wound by the broad river
Smelling of fish, the reddened water
That I heard the Indian girls
Call by the name of Coosa – it is all
So long, so long ago: I thought
You woke me now just and called
This clearing heaven. But did I
Perhaps mis-hear? I see you
Moving greyly by my side and, farther off,
Riryd, the great lord of Clochran
Once, who built our forts in the manner
Of Gwynedd, standing aloof
Under that tall pine. Madoc
I do not see: he died so long ago
Trapped on that earliest shoal
That his spirit has re-crossed,
Escaped this Indian forest
And the eternal pleasures, hunting
And being hunted. I close
My eyes again, Einion, choose
The dust that has no promise
To deceive me with. For you, for
The passionate love I bore you,
I cast away wimple, brought
Your buckler after you into the ship,
Stood with the other seven fools
Of women on the deck of Gwennan Gorn
Saluting the long beginning
Of my death. Waves, waves,
Groundswell of distance, going
Back from the bow and over
And breaking, I feared you only
As gangrene, the mountains cut away,
Eryri gone at a heave,
Cold climbing up from the gut
To the heart-cord. And that
Not last: the climbing cold
Encompassed other deaths
And each of them mine, rewardless:
I watched your fearful stagger
By Coosa shore, the bitter drops
In a trail to the granite bluff

Where the redbud is – Einion,
You that are voice and grey
Shadow of speaking, but husband
Then and always my only
True love, do you understand
How I died? How the terrible
Continent closed in on us, rivers
Ran tighter, shelf after shelf
Of pines grew narrower, sun
Tricked our flesh out brazenly,
Hatching a red against the ice
Within? Could we not after this
Creep higher, higher, catch a cool
Breeze off the ocean, glimpse
There a crester running hoisted
And foaming to Gwynedd with tidings?
What's against hope, for fools
And women, irreconcilables dying
With every step? My grave was far
To the north, but I knew the taste
Of it one winter day when Rhun,
The only son I had, brought in
His Indian girl. That grave would be
Red like this soil, death blooded
And clayed like the future. The Welsh
Are always outnumbered. Their men die
And their women leave off bearing
When love dies. Who can recreate
The few and the beautiful
In such a waste of trees?

Riryd:
Come now, Gwenllian. That you knew,
All that, from the beginning,
From the last muster on the quay
At Abercerrig, from that second when
Love, it was plain, brought only
Eight of you against the sea.
Strive to relive that love
In this heady and freer heaven
With Einion, blue and bloodless
Now in the sun and the thin

Sheet of the wind. Speak, speak
To her, Einion, you are too complaisant
Of her opinion. Speak to your faith
In this new heaven.

Einion:
Riryd, brother, and son with me
To the great prince Owain Gwynedd,
I am still weak. The frocked spirit
That carried me from Coosa shore
Has gone back wayward to look
For others, perhaps for Madoc
By that sanded rock the Muskhogees
Crowed to us of, when he landed
The second time. I cannot practise yet
The pride to stomach all regret.

Gwenllian:
True to your nature, Einion. You are like
Madoc in this. He was too mild,
Could not have come so far
With so much fighting. The sea
He loved, and his heart's
Touch on the tiller, and the bow
Wave always halved and true
In the breaking.

Riryd:
You must be silent, Gwenllian, you
Who know so much and no more.
Your choke at death was not his,
Could never be. Half-brothers I
And Madoc, true, as to blood's
Strictures, but in spirit fortunate,
One. Gust and disgust repeated,
Tallied, whether in Gwynedd or
The continent we so long tacked at.
The gale off Abercerrig blew
Fierce from our hearts that hated
Blows, murder, treachery and the sound
Of oaths being broken where Owain
Our father, lord and dear one was

The name to keep. You were a woman,
Could not weep in the same knowledge.

Gwenllian:
All this you have said before
Not once but many times.
For all your oneness, union,
Madoc went back and never came again,
While you are here. Call up Madoc now.
Do you see his spirit running blue
From the spruces yonder? You do not,
Do not, do not. For if there's
One thing sure, it's that he died
Seeking another heaven, one truer
To your first imaginings of peace.

Riryd:
I suffered much from you, Gwenllian,
And from some of the other women
While we were all alive. I do not
Accept that my stubborn portion here
Shall be bitten, spat upon
With the berry-juice and phlegm
You carried in your cheek relentlessly
Up the long river, over the cobs
Of mountains to the spindly
White dogwood where your final
Spleen coughed itself up. I am
The convert – you know that –
The one persuaded, who could not
Disappear, the bleak unfortunate
Who had to execute his brother's
Will, without having understood
It perfectly, much less known
How it would pattern in a half-
Light of overhanging wood.

I was lord of Clochran once,
Young and regardless:
I held *Pedr Sant* whitely
In Madoc's wake:
I made landfall with him

Shouting on the south-facing sand:
I was the first camp's builder
And the blunter of swords:
I waited for the sail between the spider-legs
Month after month, but there came only
Canoes one by one from the south,
Dark heads howling, spiritless
Muskhogees perambulating
A perhaps unfriendly coast. Reinforced
Endlessly, more combative, they talked
And began to paint themselves:
I cried to heaven and Madoc
Like a hound at the grave
Unanswered, and broke camp,
Choosing the eastward swamps
At the river's edge, marking
The trees as I went:
I was the orderer of coracles
On the march, that they should be
Always protected:
I halted by Coosa, calling on hope
And the sound of spears behind us:
I saw blood fill Einion's mouth
When the feathered arrow struck him:
I found the caves by the fall
Of the green river running
In the spine-channel of Mynydd Disgwylfa
And set Rhodri mab Hywel Fychan
And Cynwal the mason to build
The rampart above, Gwenwynwyn
And Geraint arching the caves
In with their groovers:
I smelt the smoke more than
A week before the war-bands came:
I took Cynwal, Geraint and the little
Tuskegee eastward to the great
Mountain and built there a war-camp
Such as I remembered Grono Bach setting
Above Lledr in the farpast realm
Where Owain my father lorded it:
And though there was no mortar
I had them build it cunningly,

Angling the walls so that no Cherokee
Could outflank my throwing arm . . .

Gwenllian (breaking in):
O you heavy-footed Taliesin!
You too too visible boaster
In the one place, you cosmic
Ironlimb! Whom can you say
That you bewitched? What Cherokee
Stopped in his tracks and idly
Played *blerwm, blerwm* with his finger,
A fool within your spear's length?
But if I find quarrelling with you
Easy, Riryd, and bite your speech
Into idiot pieces, a small honesty
Bleats out it was not for this:
Grudging, I grant you played the man
Within walls and without, bitterly
Giving ground when you could not hold it.
I from my bedrock heard you tumble
Stark under three simultaneous
Tomahawks at Muscle Shoals,
Your battle-cry fracted from Madoc
To a watered echo. I give you bravery,
But only as you gave ground
To greater arms than yours, to a weight
Of truth my eye distinguishes.
Where I contend is the heart's vanguard,
The very reason for fighting. Where's
That new island Madoc whispered of,
Set for the Gwyneddigion purposefully
In the west? The countenance,
The songs under the gathered oaks,
The remembering, the note of history
And our high tongue plucked from the orders
In a warmer air? The celebration,
Nobly, of the great among all Britons,
Of Cradoc Freichfras who turned
Even chains into honour, Cunedda
And his dour fist of sons, Arthur,
Artorius dux, and the thirty fat
Henchmen of Maelgwn sitting

Replete at Deganwy?
                    No, alas,
What you have done is break
Our speech from the beginning,
Darken our blood with crowsfeathers,
Trundle these mayhap Indians in
To rock our fires to the morning.
What can poetry, eloquence, do
With such one-syllabled vermin?
And noble blood, how can it bear
The touch and tally hours
With grease? I'll not forgive you,
Riryd, who are Owain's stock direct,
For taking that feckless Osunuka
Rock-faced to your tent, almost
The first of all our warriors.
How could they fail to copy you
In this, as in all hail else?

Riryd:
Plague on you, woman, I had been
Three years of combat lonely then
And it was long after Coosa
And the finding of the caves
When I took temptation straight.
Should I have lain on you, cursed
Tongue and all, after Einion's death?
Is that why you baste me so?

Gwenllian:
Princes are boors and arguments
Fall to insult like a bruise
Discolouring the already darkened
Vein. I spoke to you as one
To whom principle should be dear.
Blood and race and Welshness
Of tongue, with all that they bring
Of glory, song and poems among
The leaves, these are my principle.
I mourn for them in this grey
Void, as I did when alive
And dead in my haggard

Journeyings. Look at this heaven
We have, jagged with pines
And the smoke of the Cherokee
Braves: indicate if you can
What's left of song by this fire
Camped amongst Indian grunts:
Fatherly, praise up the speech
Of these gobblers whitening themselves!
Of the original in word
And life what have you left us?

Riryd:
There's peace. That's what we wanted.
In the end that's what we got.

Hernando de Soto:
I do not understand you, I, Hernando
De Soto, who heard tales
Of the *gente blanco* in the hills
From Chiaha to Tasqui centuries after
You fought and died. Peace is the plain-
Faced need before you build,
Not a thing in itself. It's what
You build that matters.

Einion:
I heard you pass by Coosa
With all your men, de Soto,
And spoke to you in my little Latin,
But you did not answer.

de Soto:
You that are son to a prince,
Einion, should know infallibly
That the first communion is
In death. Though Adelantado
Of Florida, I could not answer
You till I reached Guachoya
And the banks of the greatest
River of all. Treachery, poison,
After these the son of the poor
Esquire who served with Pizzarro

Could speak. But that I choked
In my wine at the last is
Unimportant. I marched,
Marched, over ridge and mountain
I marched, teaching the savages
What it is to run. Cannasauga,
Hiwassee, Coosa, these were rivers
Shod me for Mississippi, mine
To award, to hand to the King
Of Spain, to add to empire.
When I fought I won. And that's
A different sort of peace, de Soto's
Kind, a swift and kindling one
In which the arms and arts
First painted on Castile's tableland
Shield and emblazon the world.

Oconostota:
If I presume to answer you
Whom death has not foiled and daunted,
Nor murder either, let it be
As one who has known victory
And defeat. I am Oconostota,
Chief of the Cherokees. My people,
Vaunted once, the eyes in the south
Of the long-feared Iroquois,
Attacked these Welsh in their hilltop
Walls, fought with them many times
And always won. The Welsh were few,
White men with Indian squaws
And a number of half-breed boys.
They marched away west and then
North before our arrows, turned
And stood at each river. Always
Some died. Amongst our warriors
It is remembered that on an island
Near the falls of Ohio Cynwal,
Who was no lord or chief, when
He had finished burying six of them
In their brief fronts
Of iron, treated with us, gained accord
And leave to take his dozen

White men, all their squaws
And children, many weeks westward
Over the wider river. Wherewithal
That warfare ended. They had fought
Well, these men, but were too few,
Even with buckler and the spear
Arm of despair, to punctuate
Our might. How can those win
Who have no muster? This question
Plagues us, too, the Cherokee,
In our recent wars. The new
Virginians have us now grappled
By the throat. Our shoulders drop
Before their number. Scrabble and
Bite as we may, that memory
We have of battle darkens, turns
To a drab opinion, ends with the brave
Drained like weaklings, husbanding
Women and lost all bloodier mettle.

John Evans:
Let's have no sentiment about
The few and the beaten. Any man's
Aware significance can lie
In choosing a side, and that
The winning one. Come to the wrong
Decision if you must. But I can't
Abide whining. Didn't I
Shuffle to make and unmake plans?
Back in Waunfawr the verdant river-plat,
Indeed the mask of daisied Gwynedd
Whole, exuded my mother's piety,
My father's exhortation strong
On the off-shore breeze. Of all this
What was amiss but a crone or two
Smelling of death? Was I then to guess
The Welsh were catspaws? That old
Fool the skinner from Glyn Myfyr,
His solemn apes of friends, Iolo
The mason and such, sailed me
From London Pool with too little
Money and a charge to find

The Welsh Indians. All of which
Seemed to me then significant,
An act like Madoc's, pictured large
In a new setting. That till I met
With Spain and a pox of fact
In my palm. What should I think,
That New Orleans, and newer still
St Louis, Pueblo, Bernalillo
In the far west, their several
Governors, would not reach up
Missouri to its merest
Trickle, open a traffic
In furs, confine the buffalo
To the hard lands farther off,
And mark all traps, blazing back
The Canucks, one-time French? And why
Should I, to whom England's king
Was nothing, chaffer and wink
Over skins with such new loyalists?
I saw the Mandans, lived with them
For all of six months, swore me
Back to St Louis not a word
On their tongue of Welsh. Who
Abandons the truth for politics
Does not last long. His uses
Are too much used, become assured.

A Voice:
Should *we* be sad about this
Treachery? You left St Louis
On your oath as a Spanish agent.
They would have had your head
At a whisper of Mandan Welshness.
Lies spring in your mouth!

John Evans:
Lies? Truth? Only the simple mind
Bandies this shibboleth about.
I had no need to return, could well
Have blabbed and stayed, or pritheed
North with the Frenchmen, made
A blind way east to Ohio

And Philadelphia, what you will.
My oath – no, not my oath:
That couldn't hold me: I had
Scabbed it already with the old
Simpletons in London – but the scale
Of the thing, my pigeon sense
Of the rival forces facing
Each other, Spain with her feet
On the Gulf, her pale Mexican
Deserts soldiered as far
As Santa Fe, the discredited
French, furring their wounds
Over, and colonial Englishmen
Singular as crows, beating
This side of the mountains, landing
Halfway to the great river. Why
Should I find Wales in the middle,
Stake out Missouri forest English fashion
Because their Longshanks King took right
Of Gwynedd's earth? I tore down
The Union Jack, hoisted the Spanish
Flag the same night. The few,
The beaten – this is mere taradiddle
(These Mandan pigs were not Welshmen
Anyway). I jumped at my birth
A second time, incontinent
In it died. But that's no matter
Here. I served Wales best by never
Going back. And used the real
Powers of the day to make my point.

Riryd:
If I could understand this man
I might respect him. At least
He knows you have to deal
With things as they are.

Gwenllian:
And what they are you make
By knowledge of the highest
Tradition, adherence to it.
The man from Gwynedd called them pigs,

These Mandans. Do I detect
Their odour in the country hereabouts?

Chief Big White:
I have concluded treaties with the whites,
Served Majors Clark and Lewis as my friends,
Kept off the thieving Riccarees and visited
Your chief of chiefs, the Mister
President Jefferson in his stone
Tepee. I am Shahaka, great
And widely known amongst the darker
Men as Chief Big White. And you,
You do not well to insult me
Who have been so gravely entertained.

Gwenllian:
Jefferson? Our chief of chiefs?
I never heard of him. Grossness
Of flesh has overcome your mind.
Where else than here in all this continent
Could any man from Gwynedd have
What passes for his grave?
You are a paler fool than most
Of your thieving kind. But do not
Claim kinship or groundroom
In the hall of my nobles lost.

Chief Big White:
Pale I am not, but white. White.
Accounted so, accepted. Chief
Big White I am. I know what
A treaty means and who my friends
Are. My mother spoke once
Of the life of our tribe very far
To the east, by the stormy shore
Of a great water. And when I speak
To God I say Madoc.

George Catlin:
Madam, before you claim the stage again
And point too clearly at the death
Of what you knew, let me evaluate.

I speak to you by licence. This is
Not my heaven, who will die back east
With my paints around me. But eight years
In the Mandan villages, noting
The language, painting the squaws
With the fairer tresses, reddening
My hog's bristle for the quiffs of braves,
Give me leave to cross the abyss
For a moment, Dives snatching
The crumbs from Lazarus locked
In his own arms that are not Abraham's.
I am George Catlin, painter of Indians.
I have seen the whiter pigmentation
Pass from skin to skin. I have learned
The coracle words. I have heard
The squaws say 'Ach y fi' of their
Darker kinswomen or of Riccarees.
It is there, this pitiful remnant
Of what you knew, and there with reconciling.
They have not fought with whites,
They have peace and in part remember.
Consider, I beg you, whether
The high poetry you knew, the brooding
Music, are not the flames of the few
Igniting the smallness of a place
That is ringed with mountains,
Whether such disciplines could ever
Stretch over plains and through
A multitude, whether a hog-like peace
Should be preferred, the bloodlines
And memories lost, to the sharper
Demands, the divisive pressures
That intellect can make on the many
By too much history and feeling.
I do not contradict you, madam,
In your grief. Perhaps our choice is always
Between a vacuous and piebald peace
And a clash of fiery disciplines.
I would tell you only that the Jefferson
Of whom you have not heard
Is another man of Gwynedd, President
Of those who have freed their names

From the English, living now
Eastward beyond the mountains.
That being so, he has to choose this peace
For his heart and others. A few
Years ago in the green of Monticello
He met Shahaka, held his hand out
For this forgotten of an older
World gravely to shake it.

189   TIDE-REACH

*A Sequence of Pembrokeshire Poems
written for Music*

i
THE GREEN CHAPEL

Stand on the edge and look!
There is weakness and strength,
Strength and weakness. The rock
Is holed right through
But from seaward base makes a leap
To buttress the cliff. Bold
Yet craven at heart, it has the deep
Sea green for its counter, the spray
Cutting age into the rock, and stiff
Against it the span of the keeper, the part
That man clings to for meaning,
That carries abruptly one day
And the pleasures of day in a single
Life. Look down, you have need to see
This leaning chapel, to recognise
The weakness intrinsic to the heart
Of the rock and the harried arch
Of the pillar clinging and shaping it.
Look, look with immortal eyes!

Stand on the edge and look!
There is weakness and strength,
Strength and weakness. The rock
Has needs and is needed.
It denies no sin, no terror,

Yet affirms in its beaded
Sea-sweat that the fear within
Is the worst, the horror of separation
From meaning. This woundhole, yes,
Through which eye orders wave is the first
Mark of where God is, no less
In the sea than the land, no more
In the shapen stillness of rock
Than in the endlessly broken
Effort the water makes, thundering
Again and again as it flies
To the lift of the cognisant hand.
Look, look with immortal eyes!

Stand on the edge and look!

ii
Guénolé

I had not thought to come
Inland, but the sea-turf
Blue with squill and the yellow foam
Of the stunted gorse, all of a will
To keep me, took the laugh
From my heart. I had to deny
Myself the sea.

I began with islands, a
Splinter of granite off
Bréhat, Tibidy in a bay
Farther west. It was close on a bribe,
That aber water, rough
Sometimes at Landevennec,
The longboats there.

My father, with companions
From the estates in Gwent,
Crossed years ago to the Gaulish stations
Assigned to them. One of my cares
Was always, if it were meant
For good, to return and give
The Spirit praise.

But this cliffland has no life.
I must travel east. The few
Men here, their huts and grass slopes rife
With fears of the Irish, scarcely dare
From the double-ditched camp, and new
Farmsteads are emptied at the first
Cowhorn of trouble.

With one man I have compact.
Venetic he calls his people
And I am Wynole in the dialect
Of these parts. Petroc, he says, between
Watch and watch had a cell
Nearby, has followers. I
Pray for as much.

iii
NESTA VOWS TO ESCAPE FROM THE NORMAN HOLD

By this hand,
By the hacked blade of Rhys
My father, by the fireless house
Of Dinefwr, by this hand
There shall be no peace.

In these eyes
Called beautiful, in all these
Dull mysteries of flesh that hide
From the mirror, in these eyes
There can be no peace.

From these lips
Suppled to many pleas
From Beauclerc* (de Windsor my husband curt
And berated), from these lips
There can come no peace.

Cadwgan
Is a canting fool. His lease
Of a kingdom not a Norman means

*King Henry I of England

To survive him. Cadwgan
Can muster no peace.

My one cry
Out of Penbroke, as increase
Its towers, palisades, its balks
Imprison, my one cry
Breaks out to release.

My one hope
Is of counterfeit – the keys
To a sallyport. Owain sends word
He desires me. My one hope
Shapes that release.

Dark comes on.
The castellan decrees
I welcome Beauclerc again, the feast
Is ready. Dark comes on.
There shall be no peace.

iv
WAVE AND FURROW

Voice of the Norsemen:
The wave is our master-force.
Where shall it not take us?
We land with Pebba on this puny cliff
Unhindered. The islands bobbing
In our wake signal the names
We gave them. More arduous
To come by are the sailors' marks off
Ireland, the Orkney stacks
And the passages prised through the tough
Black granites of Léon. But who
Is it claims to match us there
Or in the fiords we remember?
They have a watch beyond Etna
Against our putting in. As for the dukedoms
This side the Pillars no
Frankish vassal questions our origin.

The Poems

What we reap we have not sown.
The sheaves we tie shall not be undone.
Where are the landsmen to withstand the Norse
And the wave their master-force?

Voice of the Flemings:
What can master the furrow
If the cliff protect it?
Our farmsteads, true, were toppled by the wave
That breached the dykes, and pebbly
Roarings came blundering in
Amongst the cornstalks. Bruit
Had us drowned like sedge, wasted save
Ooze and roots. But that
Was in Zeeland, where we have
A soil that is low and vassal. When
Our countrywoman, Queen
Matilda, echoed our cries to Beauclerc
A new fief was given us, a Flimston
Born and dressed behind rock. As for the channels
Leading up and in, the cliff
Funnels and sucks back the water-shock.

We sow our lands as settled men.
The sheaves we bind shall be bound again.
The furrow is safely driven. Now seeps no wave
Fit to damp a Flemish grave.

v
HIS NURSE* TO YOUNG HARRI TUDUR

Come away from the window, my white-faced lad,
Leave the tide to its come and go.
The empty hours that make you sad
Will soon be over. You will wish them back
These days with no playfellow.

Your uncle Siaspar is taut and pine
With the warfare in his blood.

---

*Gwraig Philip ap Howel o Gaerfyrddin (The wife of Philip ap Howel of Carmarthen).

The Poems

But back he will rankle from this campaign
With the Harberts discomfited, their stiff mailed fists
Denied the care of your boyhood.

But I who have second sight discern
For you troubles enough: the long
Cold passage of months in a gruff Breton
Prison at Elven, the suave King of France
Savage to trample a plaything.

Journeys many but the battle one
And valiant is the last I see:
A hawthorn crown, a dragon flag crimson
On green and white sarsenet, an indulgent queen
Sated with quarrelling, easy.

Come away from the window, my white-faced lad,
Leave the tide to its come and go.
Be bright in this moment, be handsome glad
Of these Penbroke battlements, your uncle's gall,
Your nurse's love at your elbow.

vi
THE REMONSTRANCE OF JOHN POYER

Seldom or ever sober
But constantly drunk in the afternoon
A great Swearer
And a stiffe maintainer of the Booke of Common Prayer

   Is that what they said?
   No, that's what Elyot said,
   Elyot of Eareweare, always
   My enemy.

   I drew the short straw in London
   For all rebels. Soldiers
   Like Laugharne and Powell were found
   By other soldiers much less culpable.
   But I, the merchant, whose six or seven
   Barks a year masted up Pennar
   Mouth as far as the Crow, with horses,

Barrel-staves, hides from Ireland,
All of them handled thirstingly
Right up to Pembroke town quay when high
Tide trundled both sides of the walls –
I was the man best fitted of all
To receive the final account.

He owns neither house nor land
Is neither for the King
Parliament nor Army but his own interest
Of freebooting

Is that what they said?
No, no that's what Elyot said,
Or if not Elyot, then the Lorts
Of Stacpoole, Sampson or Roger,
All of them enemies.

Should I have given back the castle?
Let Fleming stalk in the town
Unchecked? It is all lies,
Lies. The market-men gave me
Their produce willingly. The garrison
Had not been paid. And Griffith
White had his doors broken in
At Henllan for harbouring Fleming,
His men and that brace of money-grubbing Lorts.
My soldiers had not been paid,
I tell you. If folk at Pwllcrochan*
Took fright they should marry the blame
To the dribbling, pasty-faced gentry who
Took Poyer for less than a captain.

When he heareth news that pleaseth him
He puts forth bloody colours
Then he is for the King
And the Book of Common Prayer
But if that wind turn
Then he is for the Oath and the Covenant
And puts forth Blue and White

---

*Pronounced *Pullcrawn*

Is that what they said?
Liars, liars, and Goody Elyot most
Of all. I care not what they said.
The account was mine. I paid.

vii
THE ENLARGEMENT OF STACKPOLE HOUSE: HARVEST TIME

A ketch with slates for the roof
Put into Barafundle
Bay half after ten. I had the people
Take all the cargo off
Betimes. Old Tom has gone to fetch
The fiddler.

Bailiff, arms akimbo. Not long to the last gambo.
Must not soon the harvest men be gatheren' round Tom Owen?
Sickles at the ready, wait till she hold steady –
Cut the neck with just one toss and bless the next year's growen'.

On Tuesday morning I rode
Cardigan way to the market.
The harvest people stood and chafed at it,
Sullen that I was abroad,
The sea-fog lifting. Old Tom chose
To cut the neck.

Bailiff, why from home now? The moment it is come now,
The neck is slipped into the house, got in despite the women.
Ride hard if you're able, picture on the table
The plaited neck we're looken' at. It waits only your comen'.

The courtyard is piled with stones
Brought to complete the building.
But the menfolk tripped me quick. Beholden
I was to harvest sons –
And daughters – they said, who had sport
In dancing.

Bailiff, be not narrow. We'll not wait till tomorrow.
The neck is in and we would dance whatever stones encumber.
If gravity's your office, there's still no call to huff us
Who wish to toe it in the yard with women who are limber.

Four quarters of mutton, of beef
Fifty odd pounds, and bacon,
'Buding' twelve gallons and more, a feast to waken
The sea-birds. I'd as lief
Go look at my peach in the gardens, thought
Ten inches round.

Bailiff, now off jerkins! We'll dance you The Three Shopkins.
Inside out and forward, back, the couples trip the long way:
Toe put out and pointed, each pair goes supple-jointed,
Heads the line, trips back again, makes fair this harvest heyday.

viii
THE ARMING OF ABERDAUGLEDDAU

What is that hammering in the fields?
That grating of chains?
Who is it whistles when the short light goes
Sullenly off the water
And this glowering winter day yields
To its nightly consort of rains?

    Adams of Paterchurch has gamed
    These low fields away
    To Meyrick. Now the ships have them, ships young shaver
    Of the line, the few farms limping
    Back to the hill. Re-named,
    The old North Hook, and royally.

    Boney has gone below, but there's
    Likely one or two more
    Will blow us holes at the water-line. *Valorous*,
    Twenty-eight guns, *Ariadne*
    And *Thetis*, our first. Who cares
    If the cry comes 'Tops'ls off shore!'?

What is that lighted rigging stayed upon
A thin tracery of stacks?
As the fog tricks out the flagging day-tasks, whose
Is the horn off the water
Like an ox bawling, gone
Out to some Bashan beyond the rocks?

The sea has contracted. Grey
Tanker hulls loom
Up to Popton* and their oil pipes oozily on
To Swansea. Pwllcrochan** is refining
American crude. From the splay
Skylanes aircraft come.

The bare grass cliffs to Linney Head
Germans engross
With their weaponry in summer. Tanks churn them
To mud. St Govan's lightship,
Seven miles off, is shouting the dead
Sea-field the live shells cross.

Is this your answer? Did we dream
All this when the stick
Plough scored the soil, the skin boat slapped at the wave?
Have we cried our trades loudly
And far in the markets, so to seem
Certain of future wreck?

ix
THE SOUL'S PLAIN SEEING

No, this was not your dream.
Nor are things what they seem.
These heady ways obscure the verities.
Weakness brings folly in
While strength acknowledges the thin-
Nibbed praise intrinsic to obituaries.

Look at the land once more.
Look at the sea. Restore,
No, not this shoreline but the boasting eye
To God who dreamed the dream
For you, though puny you may deem
The humble craft in which the saints came by.

---

*Supposedly *Pebba's ton*
** Pronounced *Pullcrawn*

x
LAUS DEO

The water is hard in the well
But it never fails:
The clifftop fields are infinite salt
When the gales flock and pummel
Roof and farmstack and holt:
But the worm speaks well
Of the earth, the pheasant
Is heavy with praise in the lane:
The sea-birds, for all their grieving,
Gamble and dive at the nape of the storm:
And man embroiders his tales.
Hard hands have not kept it, this puissant
And sacred endeavour, nor high
Heads either this old domain.
It is one engrossing work, this frail
Commerce of souls in a corner,
Its coming and going, and the mark
Of the temporal on it. It is one
Coherent work, this Wales
And the seaway of Wales, its Maker
As careful of strength as
Of weakness, its quirk and cognomen
And trumpet allowed for
The whole peninsula's length.
It is one affirmative work, this Wales
And the seaway of Wales.

ONSET OF WINTER

A thin cataract
Across the mountain's eye
Before the oak
Flocks its last leaves.
Patches of snow attempt the look
Of rigour, hardily
Swearing winter will make it fact.

And the air sharply swears
There shall be no sap
Unfrozen in stem
Or footstep, leave
What you will in dish or crumb
Defiantly. Gossip
Hobbles along with what appears.

But for all the miss
In the steady beat
Of the walking blood
Stopped at the bark
The lamed man keeps his heat
Aware, like the cold, shut clod,
An ancienter oath will answer this.

191   ABER

Is there a bearing to this spot
From where she rises, limned, beyond
The distant stands of light? Or is it not
Permitted, the occasional fond

Recollection, the hastily scribbled note
Of a name, of where the body is
In the black penumbraed mass? Such anecdote
As I have requires the emphasis

Of this tumbled close, the tossing waste
Of hill, the sombre rain coming on
At tea-time. No quicker motion, not even haste
Of words need leap to show. The one

To tell where I've been to, how the dull
Affection aches, quick spine just sensed
Alive in this yard, though drawn straight from the coil
Of wounds, struck free and audienced.

I have no prayers like hers, that sprang
Hard from the laid-down rock, but now,
All lenient muscles tensed, I'll practice long
After dark, if she remember too.

192   TŶ CLYD

A fortnight has gone since her death.
February hangs browned at the edge
Like the snowdrop's sheath.
If there is life still, low in the old drudge
Garden, its crying virtue belongs
With the ground wind, with the weary pokings
At door-jambs, the shuddered gravel
Dry-soled, back and fore, bleak with conscience left behind.

The staid house looks hard at the town,
Elbowed and spry as the hills
Completing the frown.
Builder Meredith capped it, the bills
Depressed by his weight, the deeds held by
Six-foot-six Wilcockson, daily
The Bulwark's barber. O unapt,
It was first dubbed 'The Olives' in the town rate book.

But that day the bluff dead were young,
Sprigs like the house. Dapper world.
David Morgan not long
The rich draper, Arafnah Thomas called
To be minister, booked for the greater fuss
Of marrying his daughter. Part of that choice
Was the house, whether to have
Or to let to a bank-clerk, who cut the new Welsh on the door.

But for thirty-nine narrowing years
My mother it was kept the house
Squared at its peers.
In the master-bedroom the ceiling throws
Off the hills' pale blue: that shade would rouse
Low light awake in the burned-out hollows
Of my father's failing eye, like some
Onset of song near dark, the nightingale returned.

Cosy was rarely its state
Over decades of waiting when *clyd*
White-lettered the gate.
Principled rather, two storeys of deed

Slapped on word, a house with all chance crusades
Abandoned, a crux of definitive shades
Attacking the quiet. Graver
My business when I am hidden from its looks.

193 THE STEWARD'S LETTER

To the Lo. Burghley

Right hon^{or}able
My humble dewtie holden
In minde, please to be adv^{er}tized that yor
Comaund nowe restes secured
In maner folowinge:

It is not easie
To keepe the dead in w^{or}shippe
Who have beene marked by follie in the^{r} lives
But what the formes demaund
Has beene fulfiled f^{r} yor late couzen
William, lest the publicke weale
Dissolve imediatelie in sland^{er}
Or that what is yor hon^{or}s dewe
Tumble with^{t} wille or reputacon
Into anoth^{er}s hande.

Bef^{ore} the coffyn
Wente vi poore men the p^{ar}ishe
Caste as worthie, gowned in suche stuffe of blacke
As suites yor griefe, Herefordes
Prebent nexte, gravelie acompanyed
Wth my uncle P^{ar}ry, yor couzens
Late wifes broth^{er}. Rude scutcheninges
Of Cicilles, P^{ar}rys and H^{ar}batts armes
I had hadde stitched to the coffyn clothe, and
Cladde in wholesome blacke

Vi of my fath^{er}
In lawes mens^{ar}vauntes b^{or}e him
To Churche y^{ar}de, whence from the Churche do^{or} in
Of his viii sonning lawes

In murninge clocks and answerable
Apparel vi bore him on. Three
Nephewes in licke sorte folowed
After, yor couzens sister Ales
In murninge gowne and in licke atyer
Viii doughters folowinge.

I had the nave walles
Hanged all wth blacke and after
Suche concourse as the Church cd not conteyne
Had part dispersed a dole,
Two pennorth of bread and monie both,
The poore attendinge had, their
Number more thanne iv hundred.
And the nexte day another dole
Of halfe as muche a hundred persons
Poore of this parishe each

Had as his dewe. In
Maner so the funeralls
Were compleated, and that the credit might
Attache to yor couzens howse
Of Alterinis I gave oute
The charge to bee yor Lo:shippes,
All of a hundred pownds and uppwardes
As by particulars shalbe shortely
Manifeste. Thus to yor comendacon
Was this sarvice donne.

But it consorted
Ille that Mawde, yor couzens
Wife now livinge, albeit requested, sawe
Fitte not to come, the clothe
Of blacke sent to her roome returned
In silence. Also that Mathew,
My father in lawes sowle hyer, childeles
And unfitted in minde fr preferment,
Throwe wekenes and sinister councell yet allowes
Not his fathers wille

Is ille enowe fr
Or peace. Yet in the writinge

I doe but keepe backe worse, so much dismayed
Am I f^r the int^{er}este
Yo^r hon^{or} has in these Cicill landes.
A bonde nowe f^{or}fayte falleth dewe
By Powell of Llansoy, atte one
Tyme s^{ar}vaunt to her maiestie,
Uppon his fayly^{er} to deliver a rente
On average 80 powndes

Yearlie, the dowry
His moth^{er} should have gotten
In m^{ar}ying yor late couzen William.
Withal that moth^{er} fulle
Of ranc^{or} latelie has conveyed
Plate worthe a hundred markes
To the selfsame Powell, parte
Being the cuppe of silv^{er} and giltte that was
Y^{or} hon^{or}s gifte to my late mast^{er}
As well to defray the charge

Of the funerall doles, as
To yelde some comforte unto
Yo^r late couzens children. Sithens I am
Enformed the said Powell lyes
Abedde and dangerouslie sicke
Wee are licke to have this dette
And muche els f^{or}fayt. I doe beseche
Yo^r hon^{or} makke me a grante of w^{ar}dshippe
Of Powells hyer, his broth^{er} Symonds
Sonne, that haplie wee

May repayre the fortunes
Of the howse conformable to
Yo^r hon^{or}s name and reputacon.
My broth^{er} Mathew lyeth
Sicke of the t^{ar}magauntes and licke
To dye.   Thus I comitte yor
Lo:shippe to the almighties care
This xiiith day of Marche. From my howse
At Preston uppon Wye. Yo^r humble
To comaund, Paul Delahay.

194 THE PATH TO FONTANA AMOROSA

Take this cliff path, no other, let your eye
Wind between sea and flower. It is all
Magic. Cistus and cistus blush
For their mountaining sisters, cyclamen
Flaunting a pallor more chaste are just
Out of the reach. Scent follows ravening scent
To the ultramarine. What does it matter
If Ariosto was never here in the flesh
For all his lushness? Sufficient it was
To know this the white goddess's country,
All the elate ten miles of it, carob
And fig-tree and myrtle, tauntingly to the spring
Where the gush is all women's abandon, the stone
Cloak falling from the pale world's beautiful.
Can it be less than magic as the reckless coast
Unfolds? Conspiracy winking off each blue
Sea-hood's shoulder, each craggier rock
Diverts the step with quickening talk of Akamas,
His wedding to the incandescent slip
Of a girl whose fountain plays ahead. But look
There! Burnet spines are pitting the cistus
Faces, the amorous cliff recedes. By that
Extravagant boulder a lizard big enough
To have known better lies no more
Than bloat. The snake's repellent hiss
Comes back from a sidling crack in the stone.
There is one quick lover the less. Why do you falter
Half a mile on and defer to reach
That legendary fountain? Is your return
Confirmed by the carcases, lizard and snake
Flayed both by a happened wheel since the leap
Of your passing? Onasias, who honoured his father
And mother twenty-five hundred years ago
In Marion, he had this path to take
Or not to take, these blazing flowers
To pick, this shore to travel. But how
To consult such a spirit? Polis, the odd
Vestigial city from which you must
Set out, separates boast from arrival,
The live from the few loving dead. Eucalyptus

Trees, a grove half skirted with bamboo eyots
Cursed in with gravel and sea-water,
Quiver where Marion was. That speaking grave
For all you know despairs with its words
Awash. Whose country it is as the child days
Vanish, stranger, has more to decide than you.

195   INNOCENT DYING

Grey is Nant Iago, grey
With slate planes and break-offs
From the darker roughs
Shot dead in the mines on Cedris. They

Lie flat now, assembled, flat
As the lives of old miners.
Calms immerse
Them, hold them in a cold mercy, set

Grey in their faces, grey
Run weedless, the surface
Clean. It is
Only a skate now to confluence, shy

Death in Dysynni, death
By confusion. Close by at
This gorsy spit
You can see the swathe of green weed beneath

The wave of Dysynni, wave
Going humped with the fields' knap
That's higher up.
A step further shows you Iago, grave

And resistless, hand
His cap in, simple
With years. The full
River swills undyed from his token end.

196 SIGNAL

The corner of an eye pricks
Me. A change? What has happened
Is just out of sight but touching
Somehow, touching. I turn
And catch a leaf in flight
From the wisteria, orange-
Yellow, afloat
In a totally familiar silence.
It parachutes slowly to its far ground
Undeviating, already remote.

Whatever stance I take
There is another in the eye's
Corner and, reckless, another,
Another. Their first take-off
Is secret, and what beck
They jump to who knows either?
I sense no wind.
Must I ghost them downward, follow
Their course to the markers set
For yellow, sudden but disciplined?

197 EXPIATION

I called you cringer, grandfather
Whom I never knew, chooser
Among the aliens. I hedged
The glats to the east of the old
Coedcae, set it at prouder
Slope, recalled it stood leased
From Wales.

But other tales were forgotten, how
At the fairground, stripped, you took
The booth professional
Slam-bang in the second, rather
In duty to mates than fury
Of blood, since you had reckoned
Cardiff

A kick-off for a builder of sorts.
But muscle treated for allies
Briefly. The bouts you lost
Were with coughing, never the pick
Of antagonists. Uphill
The wiseacres gestured, to savour
Banw's

Air. But whose is the choice after
The gullet half-chokes with fears?
Hunching over the fire
You saw your death in a chute
Of ash and cried out louder
Than any comfort. Beneath
Twyn Du

You lie. It is useless to say I am
Sorry. Yours was another
World, its rages all mould
In the present. But to deny
The dead a voice is to falter
In justice. Whatever it meant
Ffynnon

Fawr got me born, and what marks it now
Is the one dark tree you planted
Hard by the quivering
Water.

198 SATURDAY MORNING: APPIN

Storm hit the van roof sharply after dark,
Rain far past midnight rattling on like shot.
But morning came with a calm, all the sky pale
And the paused earth hung with midges. Still
As the weave of water is and the boats
Barely at bob, no jar or slightest pull
On their lines, the picture is not quite
Mirrored. Lismore shafts into sun
In a while, its crofts barred white on the long
Green back the island makes. And the *bheinns*

Of Morven begin to shade and scale
As the cloud-rolls top and break up
From the west, staring like improbable
Giant saurians sated or not yet fully
Awake. In the quiet the foreshore brims:
The piled-up lobster-pots, the cross-braced posts
Once stanchions for a pier, the snub
White lighthouse on its braded rock
In the middle bay, recover poise
After hours of beating. Sad that the heart
Comes back more slowly, peers away
From the flattened sea-loch out to the hairline
Threat of ocean, its ear of blood still cocked
For uneasy combers wickedly raking
A far-off western head that has been
Fixed ever since that fainter coast was laid.

199   THEY, WITHOUT US*

'Voices are voices, when all's said.
Don't witter on about "an urgent tone".
They're soldiers stumping down there on the plat
Where the field edge breaks and before
That river bend winds in. You cock
That ear for no ostensible reason, Crwys.
This is a civilised country.

I don't understand your interest, man.
Let's talk about something else. That trip
To the Gower you were rabbiting on about
For Sunday. All the aqua gear to take
And Baldwin to let know. But Barbarossa not.
Wastes our time with his birds, he does.
The sport's the thing, after all.

They're sure to show up in a minute
Crossing Llangynidr Bridge. For heaven's sake,
Crwys, what's it to us? Some short route march

---

* 'God having provided some better thing for us, that they, without us should not be made perfect.' (Hebrews 11: 40)

> From Cwrt-y-Gollen probably, poor silly
> Buggers that went for soldiers, sweating
> Their follies out. I'm all for doing
> What I want, no harm to others.
>
> What's this you're muttering? Soldiers never
> March up a river bank? And Cynog, damn,
> Who's he? Thomas Coke, Carnhuanawc, Roger Price? Not
> Even names to me. Your lips are white,
> Boy, take hold that post a minute. We'll
> See them swinging as they cross. What *does*
> It matter if they see *us*?'

200   CYNOG

And from which mountain
Did the bald hermit fall? Fan
Oleu or the greater Fan
Where the camp of the iron users was?

At stake is benison
Not history. Which horn
Of Yscir benefits? What crown
Succeeds the boar, stag, fish and the treeful

Of bees that Drichan
Blessed? For they strained and shone,
All four of them, brilliant on
The links of the golden collar

Giraldus was shown
A moment, that Brychan
Set on the dandled infant when
He was brought back muling to the king's

Garthmadryn, the son
Of violation
Decorated. But why enjoin
More mystery? The child in the midst

Of his kin made on
Towards manhood, but unknown
To the chroniclers. The vital one
Conundrum the mountainheads keep to

Themselves, cordon
Like conscience. Five decades on
When raiders came whose pagan
Screams, back winded, had carried too faint

To Uther's column
Flummoxed in darkness upon
Wyebank, no kneeling deacon
Could interpose or cry panic

To the dark farms. In
The osier hut he lay prone
On rags, the startling burden
Of collar hidden under his

Bulking robe. Alien
Howls broke in, a train
Of flame spat out osiers, then
Execration burned in a score

Of voices. More than
One look at the stiff old man
Was witless. To the cliff with the Christian
Skullhead and fire to his lurking

God. Cynog, waxen,
Travelled in silence, a wan
Blessing falling with him. When
Did the true soul go without company?

I stand convinced on
The outer mound of the iron
Users' camp, perhaps mistaken
But unconfronted by adversaries,

Pursuing benison
Down past lichened trees, sodden

Leaves on projecting ledges, on
To the hurtling blur of winter deeps,

Believing ruffian
Ends are baffled, that down
In Yscir the fish breathes patiently in
The river's turbulence and of late

Alder boughs have been
Swarmed by a hive again
Of native bees. Of the hidden
Collar two parts are back in place

And two are stolen.
In this veiled afternoon
By the bed of a pagan autumn
There is time for a holy silence.

201   TERNS AT ROSSNASKILL

Whiter than sand
Is white between
The rock talons brandishing
This promontoried strand
The terns loop, elegant,
Lean, the sea's white
Swallows, embroidering
Up-wind and down the damascene
Showcloth that bright
Evening runs up the lidless
Window. Noonlight
Skies have no such spare
Nonchalance as this.
Down-turned the angled
Bone, the pattern is
Careless, air itself
Has bravado, leaping bare
From such wings
To fresh platforms of height.

The terns banking, cruising,
Occasional raucous
Blasts on their intercom,
Tingle the nerve in us
Of distant war, a shoal
Of kerns in another hemisphere
Marked down for slaughter.
In the rippled fathom near
Black-headed divers already
At work advance the cull
By a minute before the definitive
Stoop begins. It is queer,
This standing within
The envelope, pulse
Beating quicker, while sand,
Rock and all else
Quiver like vertebrates
Caught without hope or luck
By the hundred thousand.

All of a sudden
The first loop breaks. One
Of the terns, not
Having cast so much as a look
From the slit eye over
The hooked, arrogant beak,
Stoops as no pilot does, short
Like a stone to the slack
Between ripples, cutting
The divers apart, a blade-bone
Cleaving the wavelets'
Interface. We distinguish
No victim, though not
Doubting there is one.
An undulation of whites
Marks the ruttish
Inelegance instinct calls
To such rites. As the tern
Angles his wings and kneels
Before take-off, a victor
Making oblation, a poor sort
Of life is conferred

On the scourings, a few short
Minutes for turmoil. Now
As the ripples go over
The mackerel shoal, nothing
Is lost but one pale
Out of the shallows myrmidon.

202 ON DISCOVERING DAUMIER'S 'DON QUIXOTE READING' IN THE NATIONAL MUSEUM AT CARDIFF

It should have been no surprise,
Quixote, this corner turned,
To encounter you burning quietly
As Beltenebros, fitting those
Slashed, interminable bones
With a chary flesh, a faint
New rosy scarring pricked in
By recent dreams. You are back
At your beginning, the book
A refresher course with Amadis
Of Gaul and the other mad
Celts your masters. Old tilts
Are overlaid, Rocinante stalled
At the *Neue Pinakothek*, lean
With comparisons. Nothing
Compels these Iron Age legs
Crossed in the hour of this
Visit but that multi-printed horizon
Where a hundred ills disperse
Barely audible cries of anger
Or distress. You are a skull
Driven by story and the centuries
Of man. It is you who call up
The Lord of Taprobane in a sierra
Dust-cloud, though the Summer Country
Has dried in the leaguered heat
Of Christendom. Illiterate
Dulcinea is no more than
A point of reference on your map
Of charges, inked up with ridicule

And the odd splat of blood. Yet
Those bones twitch from grave
To grave, updating the cerements.
I know when
I turn the corner next
You'll have been long in this dark
And gone.

203   A FIELD AT VALLORCINES

Drops of the rain that tumbled the runnels
Half an hour ago forbodingly hang
From the under-bars of the seat. But abundantly plain

It is that the mountainy drapes so long
Clambered through cannot well be defied
Here where the field cries halt. We can sit and count

The unchemicalled flowers, the red ambuscade
Of clover, the dandelions tall as the grasses
And sorrel policing the burly. For this lush field

Is past season too, the goalpost crosses
Rear woodenly out of the herbage, remember
The game as it was. Away to the left a few

Conifers, planted singly, sombre
The path we took this morning. It
Entices still, its winding masters the slant

Of the brow to the massier trees despite
That knowledge we have of rain. A charm
It has, and promise, and the col above is no less

For the cold of hearts on arrival. Storm
Passes by, flags other, distant alps,
Falls quiet. It is calm here. On the old

Hindmost rushes water gulps
Out jewels and the seep of the field
Is audible. To the right the fenced way pushes

Past garden palings and partly tilled
Vegetable plots to the railway line
Beyond. But the station building, the immediate goal,

Has a kind of grace, a fluted, fine
Semblance of gothic tricked into the metal.
The run down the gorge to the frontier, the silent place

We peered at this morning with so little
In mind, will be full of jerks and slowings
Like the blind climb up. But the station has grace. It has borne

The faces of doubt, the comings and goings
Of millions. We shall stand there solid in
The goodly counsel with which a world back we set out.

204 ON SOUTH LORD'S LAND

On South Lord's Land
Water is slippery
Suddenly, chalybeate,
Staining occasional
Limestone edges dark
Gamboge. This gill drops
Quickly from mind, like
A friend gone off
To the enemy, only
To morse in with chuck
And plop and frank moss
Mischiefed and shot
Garnet-dull as rock.
Whether single or double
Agent this slip means
To try the beaked gardes
Of this bogland, letting go
The patient crannies of origin.
Stop here: these veins
From the past are narrowing:
Only twists of water
Escape. When the Raven
Signals gutter, best we are

Covert allies of Owain's
Or frowsty camp-followers
Not unexpected in Rheged.

SANDERLINGS

That plump little chorus
Tripping balletically,
Leaning delicately into the gale
With the daft precision
Of a collective toy,
Was wound up with a skein
From the ice-cap. This
Is the rude Ardudwy
Station: some skill in
Diplomacy compels
These spasms of wittering,
The tiny side-stepping
Runs that carry the watcher
From foam to deliquescent
Foam and no further, since
The wind postpones take-off
And the chorus ticked in
At Murmansk must whir
Till the Orange River
Groans like a lighthouse
In the craw of survivors.
Naïve of us, then, to cry
Strangers: for a storm in Wales
Trims their flight, not
Their purposes, and wise
We should know whose birds
By right sing here
Before clapping these travellers
Welcome.

RONAN

Ronan
   Lofting in the brake
Scanning the sun
   For recognition
     Of the Immaculate Ego
Collated by thorn
   And a scholarly
      Wind

His back
   Shut to the Menez Hom
Required the black
Wolves of the hillock
   To make his spare offering
And the few spindlestick
   Trees to sharpen
      Thoughts

He played
   Like beads along the week.
The gorse obeyed
Him, birds more afraid
   Of lightning than indignant
Harriers had cried
   His boundaries,
      Crows,

Magpies,
   Bickered beyond the cave's
Approaches, bees
Obliged with honeys
   From herbs on distant commons.
The bare hilltop was
   A discipline
      Struck

Above.
   Below in Kernévé
Wickedness drove
Young women furtive

        In untidiness, fleshly
    Abandon and grave
        Labour of sons.
            Men

Numbered
    Scuffles as the hit
Of their sleazy guard
On honour, toward
    Which few took a dying
Step. It was word
    Of such commonwealth
            Kept

Ronan
    Abhorrent in his cave
Rapt in the mien
Of saint, an opinion
    That love was untouchable
Save for the one
    Alone in the cosmos.
            Time

And no
    Tender humblings on
He stumbled, knew
He was dead. And through
    Forest bogs the bearers
Slithered, blew
    A squat trumpet.
            Now

Ronan
    Buried in his shift
Could bless both kin
And kingdom, common
    As each might be. How better
To light upon
    The clearing where
            He

Should lie
    Than by asking of
  The Spirit. They
  Bundled the body
    Stiffening upon an ox-cart,
  Whipped up the
    Oxen and let
        Them

  Take their
    Churning course as they
  Would. Through the briar
  Thickets, the higher
    Pales of the forest the ox-cart
  Smashed till the bare
    Slopes of the Menez
         Hom

  Came back.
    Ronan in his shift
  Raised himself, spoke
  From the travelling cart-deck
    To his sleeping blood. His body
  Petrified, struck
    Him a monu-
         Ment.

207   CAE IAGO: MAY DAY

  Among these arthritic contours,
  Little atlas and himalaya
  Dip down to cwms of glaciered pasture
  And stiffen, back to the bluff
  Of a new rigidity. Most of the old
  Walls have fallen, the blackthorn
  Splushes have grown out, and each
  Of the half enclosures has its
  Happy trackway up or on behind
  That outburst of rock, beyond
  This bracken hill. Cock
  Pheasants walk these broken

Enclosures, their picking step
Unharassed. The sheep have their
Winter coats round their ears
And the lambs making play by
Tree roots limber and jump
On each other in the brief
Seconds that sun has
To manoeuvre the clouds away.

It is all new! It is not just
Spring hiding behind the snow showers
Or the damson budding again
From its fungused bark. Over
The vanquished summits Ieuan
Appears, his big-wheeled Honda
Trike pursued by sheep, or at
Feeding time rattles a tractor
Down improbable slopes, unbagging
Beet-pulp nuts in trail along
Some shelf of grass, keeping
The hollow bricks of ochred
Minerals topped up. The old
Nomad was right. What has the air
Of cities but obstruction and
The hospital breath of in-fighting?
Up here the men are dead
Who might have argued and the world
Goes on. Snow slants between
This window and Hafotty Ganol's
Ruin across the cwm: the pheasant
Makes his parade: surviving man
Roars up the bounds of his latest kingdom.

GRASSHOPPERS

What is it to grasp,
From this moment, this hasty
Bolt of food on the Rhinerhorn
Where the wimberries thin out
And the few stunts of spruce have
Already reckoned with winter? Patently

It is the grasshoppers I
Must listen to, as they intersperse
A hard leg-music with mad
Travels from tussock to bleaker
Tuft, to broken stick or random
Protuberant stone. Some of these
Rakish frames hark back lime-
Green in talk, some converse
In brown or blue. But every one
Presently makes hard music in
A stop in this Indian summer of his,
Knowing there's no survival
Except in the eggs that instinct
Buried in the entablature at the
Inevitable season. Rightness
Is not in question. It is plainly
Right, here where the trees
On the contour are ellipses, faint
And separate in the transverse sun
Stretching to the strict blue ridge
They will never attain, it is right
To climb as we can, to the limit
Of will. To do less
Is unworthy of such sun, such far
Blue purpose as the distance is,
Folded back and back, fainter
And fainter always, surpassing
Peak with peak, till the day
Is what we can never be and scarcely comprehend.

209   JAZZ FESTIVAL

What I am trying to say
Looks foolish, doesn't it,
With all this noise going on?
The town has been charmed with jazz,
Like a chameleon, putting its mouth
Just so. Have you understood
What it says?

                   Each of us has ears and
Some persuasiveness. Do you think
We need such a rumpus
In the small hours of the afternoon?
Or are we slowly remembering something
Of the vainglorious shapes of riot
Which the shuffling out-island slaves
Would put on when Picton had
The reins in Trinidad.
                     I cross the bridge
Leaving the town. The Usk
Is thin and willowy. The martins
Make their holes in the bank
Just as usual. Why should I listen
More fervently when the town fixes its
Walls around me, though I hear nothing
But the vexed bass?
                     When I was jaunty
And unafraid, the river hill was
Dinas, staining the right bank
With shadow, canvassing the sticks
About the edge. But what is the dismal
Sum of this itinerary? Is there some
Happy issue, of the town as well
As the river? Or should it be this humbling
Bass? Could it be assumed
That time and his friends do not
Make mistakes?

210   THE LAMENTATION OF MARCHELL

My father, Tewdrig, has an unpromising way
With him. He thinks he knows
What the fates are and how they
Can be diverted. The sharpness coming
From the mountains strangles the ferocious
Cold here at Llanfaes, he says,
Making even a princess tremble. But I don't
Understand what the auguries can do
In this savage weather. I would rather have
The cold in the depth of my kirtle

Like a stern reproof, slowing
My blood.

My father's wish, also to be construed,
Looks to Dublin, to Aulach, with
The constraints of travel and the boorish
Hopes of arrival. But that's not how
My marriage will be decided, when the tawniness
Of osiers thickens and the princes,
Like the hazels, will find their
True vocation.

It has happened. Tarell
And Senni are iced all over.
Now I have no choice in the matter.
My father is alarmed, has three
Hundred men from the further region
Of Garthmadrin, beyond the Honddu
And the Yscir Fawr, where the great vicious
Horses are.

My trouble is easy, you will say.
Can the sons of Liathan, swarming the passes
Like ants on the stones of Maes Madoc, test
The mountain ways openly? Do you think
That the Tywi gives a huzza waiting
For my retinue to pass? Yes, there are
Messages always like fibs between
Evil and evil.

All the same, it was a fearsome night
At Glansevin, under the black combs
Of the hills. The sons of Liathan wrestled
A hundred men off the rocks. Was it
The same lank kerns who tried my ranks
At Meidrim in the last cold of the conflict?
I do not know why my step
Should be so bitter, except that my father
Wished it.

Now the auguries in the west are engrossed
And the haven of Porthmawr fits his ambition

I should be content. The rocks are smooth:
I can make my ship live, like Aulach's
In the salty tides of Dublin. The terminal
Cold has gone and my companions
Are rested. But I am distraught
Of ambition: the old heart is not with me
As it was in Garthmadrin. A feather
Will take my eye. Come, see a craning child
Wanting a toy.

211   I SHALL TAKE THE GIG

    From Howell Williams, Ship Street, Brecon, 1 January 1827

'Now if the snow and frost is off, I will
Meet you, dismal as it is, on Wednesday next
At 10 o'clock at Cwm du Turnpike Gate
Half way between Devynnock and Ystradvellte,
Which is nearer and far better for both
Than thro' Ystradgynlais.
                Don't say much about this business.
Bring this letter to meet me.'

    For David Powell, Solicitor, Neath

'On Tuesday night David Jeffreys rode apace from
Ystradwallter, doing his utmost not
To disappoint, but the weather proved unfavourable,
Heavy rain, hail or snow. Consequently
We postponed the journey to next Tuesday
In hope of a dry ride.
                I pray you will do
Nothing till I see you.'

   'Dear Davy,

Mr Powell will be in his office in Carmarthen
This Tuesday. I shall start this evening
To intercept him, leaving this letter at
The King's Head when I pass with the brake.
See Llewellyn Powell, Davy, Thomas Morgan too,

              And Ann Price, certainly.
                        If you are not very bad
With cold, come and see me on Friday.'

        'Think upon this, Davy:

Now that Walter Powell is dead, and all the hope
Of the Clydach Partnership is over,
We should rig ourselves to see John Llewellin at
Caerfilly, respecting the Valuing of the Works
In toto. If you don't like riding long
Journeys, I shall take the gig.
                    Horse hire and turnpikes
And my bedding at The Boat

Should make two days at 12 shillings and 11 pence.
There are others who probably know
Nothing of the Works prospects. Better not
To say anything till I
See what John Llewellin proposes. Yes,
Conjurn yourself to be as brief
                    With Thomas Morgan
Becourse the word goes swiftly amongst
                Cwmdwr people.'

212   THE CLEAR SEA

    Brendan looked down. It was the morning of
    Saint Peter the Apostle's
    Day, moist, sweet-smelling, fragrant,
    Almost a mouth-filling, good-looking
    Day. He looked down again
    To the optical deeps inert
    Beneath the keel

    And saw the fish there, taking the morning off
    Like Saint Peter, tying their
    Heads to their stirring tails. Obliging
    Creatures they were, some of them tiny
    Heads of phosphorus, like
    Two pins on a pincushion, looking
    Tidy on the sea-bottom.

But when Brendan said Mass, breaking into
The Apostle's day with
Intoning, the brothers saw the fish jeering
At them, seeking to invade like
Thin, elongated sword-fish.
How could they not see, fearing
With blunt faces,

That the cocky multitude of racy
Fishes before Brendan's
Nose, flashing with the bible in
Their mouths, would slip into nothingness
Soon, happy to reach
Out into seas dutiful, certain
There may be such?

The fishes swam in bully circles
Like the Apostle's gait
Before the host, passing wide out
Behind the man of God, as he hummed the
Sailor's tune, clement
And accurate along
The sailor's way.

But Brendan had its message straight
In the warm weather
Rejoicing, and the stirring tails are
Spread abroad, swimming paths
Of choice. All the fishes swam
Fantastic shapes there
Above in the clear sea.

213   LOOK AT ME, CALEB

Believe what the land is, whether
It be fat or lean.
See what woods might be on it, ilex
Or olive. This is the first sally
In our beleaguered
Stance.

I see, Caleb, and sometimes with
Oshea, that you do
Misunderstand me. When the others
Grumble at not finding water
That is their silly
Tribute

To me. Think of the children of
Anak, who have the best
Pomegranates. Do you reckon
The next grapes at sunset from
The valley of Eschol
Are sour?

I speak what I believe, and
Do. It is not
Everything that the Lord knows
In his panoply of cloud.
Look at me, Caleb.
It's time.

HALF A DOZEN POEMS FOR THE SPOON RIVER ANTHOLOGY AFTER EDGAR LEE MASTERS

214   DR JOHN JAMES WILLIAMS

When the shepherd laid the fire
At Cwmbanw
I had begun to be weary.
The paper seemed full of court cases
And my children full of Welsh

History. It's years since I left
St Andrews and
Became a member of the College
Of Surgeons and left off doctoring.
I lived in Mumbles, doing nothing

Except keeping the nineteenth-century
Peace. Ten years
Later my household was called
La Parisienne under a lodging-house
Keeper. But that was after I

Built Aberclydach. Then I
Was Captain of the 1st
Volunteer Battalion of the South
Wales Borderers. The rifle range at Slwch
Made my men braggers. Of course

I had the money from my
Grocer father who
Thought only of money. But
I liked to have my fill of farms
Like Elormeirch in the uplands

– And houses in Heolrhydd and
Prospect Row and
Clawygaer and Mount Street
Fields. Some of this came to me from
The railway, the Brecon and

Merthyr. I was one of the
First directors,
And of the Bargoed Coal Company.
But wouldn't it have been better in
My middle years, thinking

Of Mary and that ogre Overton,
If I had somehow
Listened to my wife and told
Her that she need not go to Clifton,
Except to see and comfort Mary.

It was no good at Paddington
And Earl's Court
That Fred and Kate and Alice
Would have me in their company. I am
A slavish fool not to enjoy

My own wife's companionship.
I was once a man
Of luxury, talking always of
Pleasing times. Now I haven't the impetus
To make my villagers talk.

When the shepherd comes to make
My fire at Cwmbanw
I have my daily paper, knowing
That half of my family hates me. Will
It be always as cruel as this?

215   MARY JANE ROBERTSON WILLIAMS

O Mary J. –
I didn't know that the old fellow
Would turn nasty

When we skipped
Around the shooting box.
I was the last

To go. How
Did I know my nails
Would fail me

At the last moment.
I am a childish culprit,
O Mary J. –

216   HOWELL PRICE WILLIAMS

I left Liverpool on the 15th
Of December 1913, on board the Blue
Funnel liner *Aeneas*. I had finished
The refurbishment of Aberclydach
House, pointed in Aberthaw ground-
Lime mortar. Notes of my journey

Through Africa made my name
In the Brecon papers. I knew my trade
As a photographer, passing old Dufile
Where Emin Pasha was made prisoner
Years ago. But, of course, my dreams

Of ground-nuts failed me
In the end. Perhaps my photograph
Did not suit me ('my little beard
Was very small') and the habit
Of playing pianola records to schoolgirls

Was not very seemly. Colonel Snead
Was my companion in Jamaica
When I took yellow fever and died there.

217   WILLIAM RETLAW JEFFERSON WILLIAMS

I tried being a lawyer but was
Broken down at my first defence.

Shy and retiring, I lodged at
Cross Oak House, an inn
Where I thought to have sanctuary

From my father's house. But Mrs
Williams, who used to go huckstering

At Dowlais market, had a daughter
– A fine-looking girl – who undermined
My scattered defences. I was not

A coaxer. Why should I be? I was
Disinherited, as they say, but

Still had my twenty-five thousand
To build Brynoyre half a mile
From my father's house. I always

Despised my father's gentleman-
Like strategy in thinking himself

One of the *uchelwyr*. There was no
Authority for that, in the morose
Sense of the term. He was only

The son of a grocer, after all. I wanted
To be a cynic, *cum grano salis,*

As said by my Latin master. So I
Bought half the legal volumes on
Chancery Lane. It was all grist

To my mill: it was the sort
Of exploit I wanted, to make

A great tome of the Great Sessions
In Wales on the dissertations of
The Welsh Judges. In my study

At Brynoyre I also fashioned 'Old
Wales' before the bank at Brecon

Stopped it. I was always wearing
A black overcoat, obedient and green
With age, irritable when the glum

Children came up to thank Guy
Fawkes for his pennies. I took

My Army Lists to a Cambridge
College, but the Librarian mislaid
Them. When my wife complained after

My death that the Reverend Trevor
Williams at Aber Chapel was always

Preaching at her, she decided to go
To Llanfigan Church. I was
Not a great believer in sermons.

218 GWENFFREDA CATE WILLIAMS
ALICE MATILDA LANGLAND WILLIAMS
(ALIS MALLT)

When Kate Williams began her novelette
'Treverton Hall' she was fourteen. Alice
Was twelve. It was really the officers
From the camp at Slwch that fascinated
Them. Later it was India.

It was a word spoken by Gwenffreda
That made Mallt more refined, both
Of them daughters of 'Brychan', of
The ancient Irish line. They became
Novelists – 'The Dau

Wynne' – pronouncing their Welsh
Names in Aber Chapel with decorum,
With excited cries from the children
Who believed their flaunting robes
As if they were lords

And ladies. Fred was there too, but
Not in the other adventures. The girls
Were getting old, they felt, when
Taldir Jaffrennou and Fransez Vallée
Talked with them on

The canal while the Hon. Mrs Herbert,
'*La grande amie des Bretons*', was
Steering. In the evening Betsy Abadam
Sang with great abandon at Llanover.
It was not an easy

Thing to compose a poem in those
Halls and 'Abherve', as Fransez Vallée
Called himself, went back to Saint
Brieuc to collect himself. In 'The Two
Ways' Cate and

Mallt were supreme in the graces
Of Celtia. 'Playing the spark' did

Something for Breton voices too. It
Was two years later when 'A Maid
Of Cymru' was

Published. Perhaps it was Cate rather
Than Mallt who thought an Englishman
Would make Elormeirch his home. One
Cannot tell. At least it was not
The Dyffryn, anyway,

In its pages. But that was the end
Of the faded contents, for Cate died
Fourteen years later. Mallt persisted in
Going to Brittany and Ireland,
Always bountiful

With prizes and doing her Welsh
As she could. It was in Frederick's
House that she made her home in
The Towy valley, till limited means
Made her brother

Most unhappy. Could there be
Fortune for such a lady when
The last post was Plas Pontsaeson?
But that's not the reason for disquiet.
There was a place

That was sacred, the house of
Aberclydach, once the home of
John James Williams. Do you see
The tablets in the graveyard corner?
Shall it be to

Dismiss the *uchelwyr* as ever
Censorious? And for Mary Jane
Robertson Williams, should she
Turn back and, heart-whole, visit
Her father in

His costly estrangement. Who
Thinks of Brynoyre now? Does

William Retlaw Jefferson Williams
Think of it, despite his wife's pleas
From the hundred

And seventh psalm? Is there not
An answer, it may be, beyond
The vale of tears? Gwenffreda Cate
And Alis Mallt Williams have
Raised a token

Indiscretion. Were they not
Authoresses, Kinswomen to
All Celts, daughters of Brychan
In the Gorsedd of Britain? Did
They speak of poetry

And the watchword that many
Cowards would not put out? It
Was still a sad story, but the Celts
Were good at judging sad stories,
Don't you feel?

219   FREDERICK GEORGE ROBERTSON WILLIAMS

I was very good at timing the trains
To Talybont station, but especially if
Mabel Bridgewater, my Richmond friend,
Was due on the line. True, I was

Sometimes at Earl's Court or Paddington
When Mabel came on visits, when
Gwenffreda guested us, but I was not
The cheery partner Mabel would have

Me be. I wrote my diary, with its inked
Letters, sometimes at Aberclydach, often in
London. 'Ho! I idd ilke ti os hwne
Hse iwnkde ta em', the girl from

The chorus in the Prince of Wales' Theatre.
But I was never brave, not even with

Mabel. Outside the Iron Church she patronised
Me, always talking of Richmond. I began

To think of my landowning interests, Berthlwyd
Fawr and Nantllanerch, that lack of prosperity
I had not foreseen, and so went up to Llanwrtyd
To find a bride. Nevertheless, I became

A rentier in the Teifi valley, dispirited,
Looking with anger at dogged obstacles.
Yet I was the last male of the family,
Believing how children might accomplish

Much if only the money lasted. Don't you
Remember me at Aberclydach, riding
My bike, looking to see if the trains are
Late? It was then I was a true spirit.

220   PETER HAS BEEN DIGGING

Peter has been digging the beds, swaying
Under forget-me-nots, as he always
Does, but there is no honour nor contentment
Since Molly has gone. Each of these days
Has its parley on, its heredity buried in
The summer. The Buff Beauty roses are perking
Now, defining the beds. But this is a conceit, a gipsy
Wandering, to make magical these petering last
Ragged days, looking for appetite to answer
Those blackbirds singing like incendiaries.
This is what summer does, stops and tries
Out old habits, girds the visitor with crumbs.
No, this is not what Isidore of Seville may say
In the old world, nor the notary at the gate,
This is Molly's garden, schooling for the arrival of
The right and quiet assertion that it formerly was.

Appendix

The poet considers the poem published here incomplete, yet 'God is not Mocked' has the appearance of a fair copy and is accompanied by a note of the date and place of composition or transcription: '24 April 1943; Tŷ Clyd, Brecon'. It is immediately preceded at the back of Notebook I by 'London Welshman' (dated 22 April 1943), which was published in *Break in Harvest*. It takes its imagery, in the main, from the war and farming and *seems* to be concerned with love and morality (among other issues of the day, perhaps). In these respects the poem has a good deal in common with others in *Break in Harvest*. However, it has the appearance of automatic writing and uncertainty prevails where references are highly personal and the language is so tightly compacted. Read aloud, it reveals that sonorous array of rhetorical devices characteristic of much of Mathias's poetry. Indeed, it has a good deal in common with 'Fulwell', which, though dated almost nine months later (8 January 1944), is the next poem in the Notebook.

GOD IS NOT MOCKED (A Modern Morality)

More than the integer, no more
Provincial callowness before
Dressing for the metropole,
Artifice apple whole
Enter the Paris of the year
The leer depressed
The deerlike eyes
Loving deceit (love lies), the shiny suit
Walking flesh-sentimental-wise beside
The recruit weakness, antennae
For the myopia well-slicked
And sensitive, many the most
Foregone, the cornucopia mobile
Acclerating
To retreat (O hope here)
Or out flank
Some undefended wadi at the waning time.

O wise and grim nothing, millipede
Milting your simultaneous campaigns
Your gains rank from the freshfield with a rake –

A fake machine, no binder –
Before the blinder regulars could break their reins.

The hour that understudies fear
The hour, come pity, O the hour
The night, the day, the evil hour
Harrowing.

The last dilettante
Surpassed sentiment, the well-meant, you're helper
Now. And helper you are
And are to keep. (Ho, guards!)

Now grounded, knowing the air the power
Nearing a Rotterdam hour in your bones
Kicking the chocks the stones, not a new part
In the old model, heart,
The old lame corrigenda
Last line patter defender, knowing the names
The implemented strains of crows you know
Percentage odds you know, the hundred targets hit
Fast in the pit how does it feel
Forcing the crate to death.

Fool, breath and sentiment
Have sent your skill to care
What chance the average will permit:
Impenitent, watch the fit stripling wave
Tippling his happy take-off, brave, no odds
Dock his first message to the gods, slump
In the cockpit.
Well heart, live, thump on –
You know and only you.
Thump on and shiver too. See
The after-tea invaders lean
Over the white map of your womanhood
Detail the ground they would, go confident
And bent return
Stroking their stern report with smiling face
Into its place among the base intelligence –
White, dearest undone white
In death, but fighting not to die happy,
Die possessed, no therapy and no defence
Against the vitals. Hence and die –
Take off and fly the requital minute
Sideslip and in it die!

Appendix

The hour, the overstudied hour
Dying.

Now curtain, jocunds, cordon off.
And in antennae, call in Photo Joe,
Frequent your Talus, nine miles dark to boats
With the right brazen query for the blast.

And observe so
Young green concordat in a field ex-oats –
The Lord God give you camouflage at last.

Editorial Note

In preparing the poems for publication, I have consulted three Notebooks in which the poet gradually acquired the habit of copying poems as they were nearing completion. The earliest (Notebook I), covering the period from February 1941 to October 1947, has short stories at various stages of development at the front and poems at the back. It was in part a working notebook and contains some early and abandoned drafts in addition to substantially finished poems. Many, but not all, of the finished are accompanied by annotations revealing the date and place of composition and, occasionally, the magazine in which they were first published. Notebook II contains poems only and is more consistently a 'fair copy' book (though further slight amendments were often made after copying). Its entries date from January 1948 to February 1972. The annotations in Notebook III (March 1972 to July 1995) are generally more refined and detailed. In every case where it is provided, the annotation is included verbatim at the beginning of the Notes on the poem that follow.

Poems were usually placed in the various books published by the poet in the order in which they were written. With the odd exception, that order has been retained in this volume, but the Notes provide a check on the chronology of composition for the great majority.

This volume also contains a small number of poems that have not previously appeared in book form and a few previously unpublished. Among the former are poems written since the publication of *A Field at Vallorcines*. All have been placed as nearly as possible in the correct chronological position and are marked with an asterisk in the list of poems and in the Notes. A poem from Notebook I that, though substantially complete, the writer considers unfinished is included in the Appendix.

Textually, the vast majority of the poems are as they appeared in book form or, in those cases referred to in the previous paragaph, as published in magazines or transcribed into the Notebook. A few typographical errors among the printed poems have been amended silently.

Notes

DAYS ENDURING (Arthur H. Stockwell Ltd, 1942)

7. To My Uncle David
The first of a handful of poems about the poet's favourite uncle, his father's brother, David, who lived in Sennybridge (see also 'Parting' and 'Youth').

8. On Hearing Richard II, Broadcast by the O.U.D.S.
The poem describes a family scene. In the first section, the 'huddled figures' are those of the poet and his brother, perhaps his father too. The one with 'plaited hair' who persistently 'parries sound' (from the wireless) with 'sound / More empty' is the poet's younger sister. The one who 'had left the room / Bent on the common round' is their mother. The O.U.D.S. is the Oxford University Drama Society.

10. In Frimley Woods
Frimley is about fifteen miles south-east of Reading and some four miles north of Aldershot. The poem was written when the Mathias family home was at Aldershot, which explains the military imagery used in the first stanza to describe the pine trees.

11. Sunset Over the Sea
The first poem with a clearly identified Welsh subject.
l. 4 *Cardigan Bay* – the great bay that extends between the Llŷn peninsula in the north of Wales and the Pembrokeshire peninsula in the south.
l. 5 *coracles* – small, round boats traditionally made of hides over a wicker frame, still used for river fishing.
l. 7 *Trevor* – [Trefor] on the north coast of Llŷn, about twelve miles from Caernarfon.
l. 8 *Bardsey* – a small island off the tip of the Llŷn peninsula. Its Welsh name is Ynys Enlli.
l. 18 *New Quay* – on the coast of Cardigan Bay, about fifteen miles south of Aberystwyth.

12. Memories
In his *Artists in Wales* essay the poet recalls the time during his childhood when the family lived 'in an Army hut at Sling, the upper or more rural limit of Bulford Camp: directly above us the grass slope of the hill rose steeply past the Kiwi which the New Zealanders had cut in the chalk during the war to a cowboys and Indians wood at the top'.
l. 4 *Porto-Pi* – the fishing port of Palma, Majorca (and scene of a battle in 1229, when Palma was attacked by James I of Aragon).

Notes

13. Rissersee
The lake that gives the poem its title is to the north and west of two notable mountains, the Kreuzeck and the more formidable Zugspitze, in the Garmisch Partenkirchen region of Germany, thirty to forty miles north-west of Innsbruck, which the poet visited during a walking tour with an Oxford friend in the summer of 1935.

14. Against Jericho (June, 1936)
Jericho is the famously walled town that was destroyed by the Israelites under the leadership of Joshua (Joshua 6). The poem is based in part on *The Foundations of Bible History: Joshua, Judges* (1931) by the noted archaeologist John Garstang (1876–1956), who excavated places associated with the passage of the Israelites into Canaan. His fieldwork at Jericho concluded in 1936.
l. 1 *the plain of Esdraelon* – also called the valley of Jezreel; it extends about twenty-five miles from the hills of Lower Galilee to the north to the Samarian Hills in the south.
l. 5 *the scarped heights of Ramleh* – [Ramlah] from AD 716 capital of Palestine, the region south of the Plain of Esdraelon, after the defeat of the Byzantine power by Muslim forces under Caliph 'Umar in 636.
l. 24 *Moab* – in the book of Numbers, chapters 20 and 21 tell of events leading up to the entry of the children of Israel into the plains of Moab, outside Canaan, including God's promise to bring forth water from the rock at the word of Moses. Because Moses struck the rock twice with Aaron's rod rather than speaking to it, neither was allowed to enter the Promised Land. Chapter 32 deals with the settlement east of Jordan.
l. 27 *It is no land of full fertility* – in Deuteronomy 6: 3, the Israelites are promised a land 'that floweth with milk and honey'.
l. 37 *The East at last!* – the east bank of the Jordan.

15. Sundew
The title refers to sunlight on dew, not the bog plant.

16. Hiraeth
The second poem in the collection to make direct reference to Wales: the word 'hiraeth' means longing for home.

17. Days Enduring
The poem expresses the poet's emotions as a holiday in Wales nears its end. It has stylistic features that become characteristic, such as the transposition of a word to preserve the rhythmic integrity of a line, and unconventional use of language.
l. 3 *Teifi* – the river that enters the sea at Cardigan (Aberteifi), on the southern edge of Cardigan Bay.
l. 4 *the Island* – Cardigan Island, close to the headland that forms the northern extension of the Teifi estuary.
l. 6 *Mwnt* – a small headland and bay, accessible only via steep, narrow lanes, on Cardigan Bay, between the town of Cardigan and Aberporth, now in the hands of the National Trust. The poet sometimes bathed there in his youth.

Notes

l. 11 *Preselly's southern stride* – [Mynydd Preseli], an upland area of northern Pembrokeshire, which runs roughly west to east and, from Cardigan, appears to 'stride' across the view to the south.

18. Sea-moods
l. 4 *saxifrage* – a species of mostly dwarf plants with small white, yellow or red flowers.
l. 7 *Cemmaes bluff* – [Cemaes] Head, the headland that forms the southern seaward extension of the Teifi estuary.

20. Parting
The relationship alluded to, which the poet described to the editor as his 'first adventure into happiness', was real enough.
l. 2 *the Forest* – [Fforest Fach] a mountain to the south of Sennybridge.
l. 10 *Salem* – the chapel in Sennybridge that the poet's Uncle David (see 'To my Uncle David') served as secretary.
l. 44 *Cwm Clydach* – a small valley whose stream rises on Fforest Fach and joins the Senni (a tributary of the Usk) a mile or so south of Sennybridge.

22. October Sun
l. 1 *levée* – an assembly held by a king at which men only are received.
l. 3 *conscious chequer style / Of field display* – the pattern on the well-mown grass.
l. 8 *the presence* – the presence of death.

23. Now Starlight Knows You Not
The subject of this poem, as of 'Dusk' and 'The Stars Above', which follow it, is also the young woman of 'Parting'.

26. Knapweed
The poet considers this the first poem in which he consciously tried to incorporate that verbal texturing he had learned from his reading of Edith Sitwell's *Aspects of Modern Poetry*. It is a recollection of early childhood and the family's second home in Germany, at Marienburg, a suburb of Cologne.
l. 1 *knapweed* – common name of a wild flower (*Centaurea*) with a hard stem and light purple flowers on a dark globular head.

28. The Past
The theme is the powerful hold of history and legend on the writer's mind.
l. 4 *temeraires alight upon the tide* – the *Temeraire* was the second ship in Nelson's line at the Battle of Trafalgar. The allusion here is to J. M. W. Turner's painting of *The Fighting Temeraire* in 1838, on her way to her last berth to be broken up. Though wonderfully effulgent, the pictured ship is not *alight* in the usual sense.

31. The New Miracle
The poem compares the sights of the countryside in early spring when it still bears the marks of winter (in terms that will become increasingly familiar) with London streets. Like 'Knapweed', it is seen by the poet to foreshadow a new direction in his writing.

Notes

l. 18 *coronation* – that of George VI.

33. Youth
An early piece of critical self-analysis: the poet concludes that he has been protected from the harsh realities of life for long enough and must stir himself to action.
l. 1 *my birthday* – the poet's twenty-first. He stayed at his Uncle David's home during summer holidays and walked with him on the mountains near Sennybridge: see 'To my Uncle David' (7).
l. 2 *Penwaundwr* – a mountain location in the Brecon Beacons close to Cray Reservoir, overlooked by Fan Bwlch Chwyth.
l. 6 *the Fan* – Fan Bwlch Chwyth, one of the lesser peaks of the Brecon Beacons.

35. 'O World Intangible'
The title of the poem provides a clue to its inspiration: it is taken from the second line of Francis Thompson's 'The Kingdom of God', which also contains the memorable phrase 'many-splendoured thing' and the image of Jacob's ladder 'Pitched betwixt Heaven and Charing Cross'. Like Thompson's poem, it begins with a stanza metrically different from the remainder. It also contains the kind of self-admonishment that becomes familiar in the poet's later writing.

36. On Newport Reservoir
In Notebook I the poem is annotated 'August 11, 1938 / Fairhaven, Cranmore Lane, Aldershot'.
The setting of the poem is described in Roland Mathias's *Artists in Wales* essay ('My birthplace was ... high up on Glyn Collwn under the old Brecon–Merthyr railway line. At a slant above it was the halt of Pentir Rhiw'), and in the late short story 'The Only Road Open'. Glyn Collwn is the name of the valley of the River Caerfanell, near Talybont-on-Usk, Breconshire, once a community of scattered farms, which was flooded to provide water for the port and industrial town of Newport, then in Monmouthshire.
l. 15 *mammonites* – worshippers of Mammon, those devoted to the acquisition of wealth.
l. 27 *Tyle's fields* – an example of poetic licence: Tyle-Clydach was a cottage with little land. What true memories are in the poem are of Aber Farm, close to the village of the same name. It was to this farm, tenanted by his mother's brother (Uncle Emlyn), that the poet moved as a small child with his mother and grandmother following the death of his grandfather, Joseph Morgan. It was there too that his brother, Alun, was born.

37. New Year, 1939
A melancholy poem on the heavy prospect of the year ahead, with the threat of war looming.

38. Evening in Saundersfoot
The poem describes an actual event.
Saundersfoot – a seaside town in Pembrokeshire, near Tenby, on the western curve of Carmarthen Bay.

Notes

39. The Forest
l. 15 *spindle-tree* – tree or shrub of the genus *Euonymous*, with hard, fine-grained wood formerly much used in the manufacture of spindles. This is a memory of childhood: there were spindle-trees near the army hut that was the family home at Bulford Camp.

41. Lines Written on Hearing of the Invasion of Poland (September 1st, 1939)
With war imminent, the poet thinks of those pursuits and pleasures (teaching, rugby football, choir, hill-walking, a car) he had anticipated in his fourth term as a teacher in St Helens. His pacifist convictions are alluded to: 'all I do, / And have done, has no point, no blade to bend / To war'.

41. Declaration of War (September 3rd, 1939)
Observation of preparations for war at close quarters near the barracks at Aldershot.
l. 15 *Oudenarde* – barracks named after one of the Duke of Marlborough's victories in the Netherlands in the War of the Spanish Succession (1708).

42. Dream
The implicit theme is the war and the poet's response to it: he must come to terms with the realities of existence.
l. 14 *Frigga* – also Frigg or Freyja, wife of Odin (supreme god and god of war) in Scandinavian mythology.

43. Tower on an Evening Sky
Annotated 'April 4, 1940 / Tŷ Clyd, Brecon' in Notebook I.
The poem is a prayer for strength to withstand whatever may chance.
l. 8 *Hatto's tower* – Hatto is known to history as a tenth-century archbishop of Mainz. Legend says he invited the famished poor to take grain from his barn, but once they were inside secured the doors and set fire to the building. Having dismissed his victims as mice who consumed the corn, he was himself pursued by a plague of mice. They followed him to his tower on the Rhine, where they devoured him. The story is told in Southey's ballad 'Bishop Hatto', but Mathias knew it from his childhood in Germany.

44. Pax Nobiscum
Included in Notebook I, but without annotation. The title is a variation on the words 'Pax vobiscum' (Peace be unto you) in the liturgy, from Christ's greeting to his apostles on the first Easter morning. It means 'Peace be unto us'.
l. 1 *Finger Post* – on the highway from Manchester to Liverpool.
l. 2 *Dentons Green* – the location of Cowley School, St Helens, where the poet taught.
l. 4 *Cribyn* – a rocky escarpment near the considerable peak of Pen-y-fan in the Brecon Beacons. That this feature is mentioned rather than Pen-y-fan is due to the peculiarity of its being clearly visible from the front garden of Tŷ Clyd, the home of the poet's parents.

45. Blitz in Manchester
Included in Notebook I, but without annotation. The poem alludes to a brief relationship conducted against the background of turbulent events.

46. Nepotism
In Notebook I the poem is annotated '5. II. 41 / 116 Harris St., St Helens'.
Nepotism – the practice of showing special favours to relatives or friends.

47. Lament for Cassandra
The poem appears as 'Cassandra' in Notebook I, with the annotation: 'Begun in 1937. Finished April 16, 1941'.
As its Breconshire setting indicates, this is another poem concerned with the poet's early relationship with a young woman from Sennybridge.
Cassandra – prophetess daughter of King Priam of Troy in the *Iliad*.
l. 9 *the arming Allt* – Yr Allt (literally 'the hill' or 'the slope', often wooded) is a forested mountain (now crowned with a radio mast) that rises immediately to the north-west of Sennybridge, an area long used for military training.
l. 22 *Cray* – [Crai] name borne by a river, its valley and a village a few miles south-west of Sennybridge in the Brecon Beacons.

48. For Marjorie
The poem appears as 'To Marjorie' in Notebook I, with the annotation: 'April 22, 1941 / Tŷ Clyd, Brecon'.
'Marjorie' is not the young woman of the previous poem.
l. 1 *the Skerries* – small islands, one with a lighthouse, a short distance off Carmel Head, the promontory at the northern end of Holyhead Bay, Anglesey.
l. 9 *Richmond* – Marjorie's London home.
l. 9 *old mother Môn* – Anglesey (Môn in Welsh) is traditionally referred to as 'Mam Cymru' (mother of Wales).

49. Café Parting
The scene of this poem, about yet another relationship, is the Italian café on the square at Tonyrefail, Glamorgan.

50. Inter Tenebros (Even Here)
The poem is written in red ink in Notebook I, and annotated: 'Walton Gaol, Sept. 1941'.
Inter Tenebros – 'In the midst of darkness'.
l. 5 *pourboire* – a gratuity or 'tip'.
l. 7 *nether lines* – lower depths; in a note to the editor, Mathias added 'Satan's kingdom'.

51. Vista
Not in Notebook I. It is about the routine of washing the prison lavatories.

52. Bars
Written in red in Notebook I, with the annotation: 'Walton Gaol, Sept. 1941'.

Notes

l. 12 *seven-squared days* – an allusion to the block of the prison building and its daily routines and seven times seven days' incarceration.

l. 18 *hugs the tack* – an amendment in the published version of the poem of the Notebook's 'alters tack', adding the sense of an affectionate embrace to that of holding a course.

53. Wishes from Walton
Not in Notebook I.

l. 6 *Descanting* – the beginning of a short sequence of terms or images drawn from music, especially that of the pipe-organ. The word can mean either a treble accompaniment to the melody or, for a speaker, to go on at length about a subject. The second meaning predominates here.

l. 6 *swells and stops* – a swell is a device on an organ used by the player to vary the force of a tone; a stop is the handle or knob by means of which the player can turn a set of pipes on or off.

ll. 6–7 *Bootle . . . Penny Lane* – well-known addresses in Liverpool, where Walton Gaol is situated.

l. 23 *wired cockerels* – the prisoners, confined by wire, are like cockerels in a chicken coop in which there are no hens. The poet says the image is of prisoners exercising in the prison yard; *wired* also carries the entirely appropriate modern connotation of 'nervously tense'.

l. 36 *Blundellsands* – Mathias knew this part of Liverpool, having played rugby there. It was the home of Waterloo RFC, then a notable team.

l. 37 *Lister Drive* – The poet comments: 'I moved to Lister Drive, an ordinary sort of street in St Helens [a few miles north-east of Liverpool], when the authorities got at me.'

54. Cries in the Night
Not in Notebook I. The sounds of prison left a strong impression on the writer (see also the short story 'Take Hold on Hell').

l. 2 *Stafford* – Mathias spent part of his sentence at Stafford Gaol.

l. 7 *jeremiad* – lamentation or sorrowful complaint.

55. Fagenbaum
Written in red ink in Notebook I and annotated: 'Walton Gaol, Sept. 1941'. A portrait poem of a character observed in prison, identified in the short story 'Take Hold on Hell' as 'Fagenbaum, the Hoxton fence, with the perpetual pitted sneer'.

l. 11 *the inner round* – prisoners who were the cause of trouble in the exercise yard walked the 'inner round'.

56. Night on the Brecon Road*
The last of the group of prison poems, heretofore unpublished. It describes the poet's return to Brecon following his release from gaol.

57. The Close*
This previously unpublished poem appears in Notebook I without date and place of composition but it follows directly after 'Bars' which, like the other prison poems, is annotated 'Walton Gaol, Sept. 1941'.

Notes

58. Credo*
A previously unpublished poem dated '5 January 1942' in Notebook I.

59. Oxford Castle*
A previously unpublished poem dated '6 January 1942' in Notebook I.

60. Slow Meeting*
A previously unpublished poem dated '9 January 1942' in Notebook I.

61. Maesyronnen
The poem has a number of features associated with the poet's mature writing, including his preoccupation with history and with religious belief. In a note to the editor he observed: 'My father took me to Maesyronnen.'
Maesyronnen – literally 'ash-tree field' – was originally a plot of land donated by Charles Lloyd (d. 1698), squire of Maes-llwch in Radnorshire, and notable Dissenter, for the founding of the first Congregational meeting-house in Wales – the 300-year-old chapel that bears the same name.
l. 4 *their Babylon* – as the later reference to *the Church and . . . Her Popish springs* signifies, this allusion has its origin in the Puritan epithet for the Roman Catholic church – 'the whore of Babylon'. The established Anglican church was similarly viewed by the Dissenters who founded the chapel at Maesyronnen. The poet's attitude to Roman Catholicism changed considerably in the decade that followed. Largely as a result of reading the Salisbury Papers at Hatfield House, in connection with his research for *Whitsun Riot*, he developed a sympathetic interest in recusancy.
l. 8 *tenebrate* – a rare, obsolete word meaning 'darkened' or 'dark'; here it represents the round, black stove-pipe rising to the roof. Its use demonstrates the poet's readiness to draw upon archaic language in the pursuit of historical texture and to employ his large resources of language creatively.
l. 12 *incubus / Of braver days* – that the chapel would fall into disuse, as evidenced by its dilapidation and the dusty hymn books, would have been a nightmare to the congregations of the past.
ll. 24–5 *In controversial quorum, face to face, / The leaders of the faith* – the chapel deacons, seated in their own enclosed pew beneath the pulpit.
ll. 36–9 *serving-men . . . who flung the gage / Downhill across the Wye* – the ministers who proclaimed the challenge of their faith from this hillside chapel to the English-speaking parts of Breconshire and Herefordshire.

62. Worm in the Brain
l. 6 *gambo* – the Welsh term for a heavy farm cart.
l. 7 *drashings* – the poet identifies this as a dialect word. It possibly derives from the obsolete 'drast', meaning husks or waste materials, often gathered from hedgerows.
l. 13 *my aunt* – Aunt Gladys (his mother's sister), who lived at Tydu, Llanilltern, in the Vale of Glamorgan. It is at this farm (where the young Roland Mathias spent part of his vacation while awaiting his degree result in the summer of 1936) that the journey in the old van begins in the short story 'One Bell Tolling'.

Notes

63. Pastorale

The poem is connected with a brief essay entitled 'The Shame of Youth', published in the Spring–Summer 1943 issue (17) of *New Vision: The International Review*, edited by G. B. Pittock-Buss:

> Behind his urn little Caesar's temper was none to good. On this sullen day the sun of Italy had settled behind clouds, too. At his third ungraciousness, I was driven hastily into the red and white bus already filling with passengers.
>
> Soon, with a wide swing of the driver's arms, we turned and roared at the Cefn road. The little climbing rows of miners' cottages slid past; the years they had spent in stumping up the hill were all softened into the hum of tyres, their toil into a slight sizzling heat and the early buzzings of a bemused fly upon the pane. This well-sprung flight into the mountains, I could see, left them humble, stubborn and resentful. Below and to the left appeared rows and rows of crosses. They started up in serried lines all the way up the opposite side of the cwm. On this side, too, they stood below the trees. To this, then, I felt, it was to this narrow pass that we had come so quickly. Father and son, Cefn colliers had had to hew and blast their way from dark to dark, from cottage to pit and home again, and then take their last long walk, feet first, up the mountain. They had not come as far as this without the final labour of all. But I – I had come too quickly, too effortlessly. I could never know those men down there until I, too, had walked with the bearers up that long road and eased the muffler round my neck. No, my country lay on, on, beyond the towering ridge and across the bare shoulders out in front.
>
> The smooth hurrying of the bus brought us bounding along the hummocks over against the three reservoirs. Little waves raced us; at every lift a giant roller passed underneath. Up on the brown slope of Corn Du were vague patches of green. A little restless wind climbed the cleft with us. The mountains looked strange and ashamed. Suddenly it seemed amazing that the ageing things of the world should share in the childhood of spring, share in it painedly, almost unwantingly, as though it were a piece of frolic beneath their dignity. Like birds in moult, the bald old hills had hidden their grim outlines in embarrassment at the childish breakings-out they were suffering. They had understood no more than we that everything was new and shy and young again.
>
> And then I knew I had come home. Home to a gift I had not earned, home to a joy my hands had never made nor my brain sufficiently remembered. Munificent, I knew, too, that I should share it with those who had borne the burden of the day and earned no more than I. For we would be the sheen on the shoulders of the Beacons; for them the sunbeams through the smoke and the miracle of green around their clambering tops.

Phrases like 'little Caesar', 'rows and rows of crosses', 'well-sprung flight', 'sizzling heat', 'bare shoulders out in front', 'smooth hurrying of the bus', 'sheen on the shoulders of the Beacons' all link with and, in some cases, help to explain the origins of images in the poem. The emotional response of the poet to his realization of the harsh lives of the miners and his own unworthiness of the favours that, without the effort of physical labour, had come to him, points to an important development in his thinking and his poetry.

l. 1 *from Merthyr by the Cefn road* – the route is the A470, which, soon after leaving Merthyr Tydfil, passes through Cefncoedycymer before crossing the Brecon Beacons and descending into Brecon.

Notes

l. 21 *the Twmp* – a south Wales colloquialism for 'hill', here applied as the name of a farm.
l. 27 *Storey Arms* – an inn (now an outdoor education centre) at the highest point on the route described above.
l. 40 *Libanus* – a hamlet on the A470 a few miles outside Brecon.

64. Balloon Over the Rhondda
In Notebook I it is annotated: '8 September 1942 / Tŷ Clyd, Brecon. / Published in *Life and Letters To-day* – July 1943, in *Modern Welsh Poetry* ed. Keidrych Rhys (Faber & Faber) June 1944'.
l. 1 *Tabor* – a chapel in Penygraig, Rhondda, which derives its name from Mount Tabor, near Nazareth, where the Transfiguration took place (Matthew 17: 1–9).
l. 5 *diaconate* – the group of men who hold the office of deacon at the chapel.
l. 9 *Forced down* – a wartime phrase describing an aircraft damaged in aerial combat and forced to land.
l. 15 *Suborns of bigger men had gone adrift* – not the verb 'suborn' (to induce or bribe someone, usually to perform an illegal act), but an abbreviation of 'subordinates', a synonym here for that tool of the 'bigger men' in the Air Force, the balloon.
l. 19 *silver elephant with wings* – an apt description of barrage-balloons, tethered close to key targets as an obstacle to the attacks of enemy warplanes.
l. 33 *pine end* – a south Wales colloquialism for the usually blank end wall of a house; here it is the end of the balloon opposite the winged front.
l. 35 *Spitfires* – famous Second World War fighter plane.
l. 47 *Duw* – 'God', used colloquially (if inappropriately in the hearing of the deacons) to give force to the expression.
l. 47 *Whitley* – Second World War heavy bomber also equipped with the first-ever power-operated rear turret carrying four machine guns.
l. 53–5 *old Arafna John . . . black* – a notable member of the chapel diaconate and railway signalman, who wears his company's uniform trousers with a thin red line at the seam.
l. 58 *Whose son is this?* – addressed to the poet's father, Revd Evan Mathias, who was himself from time to time the visiting preacher at Tabor.
l. 59 *pregethwr* – 'preacher'.

65. March on the Mountains
l. 1 *Llanfrynach pool* – Llanfrynach is a village a mile or so south of Brecon town.
l. 2 *Caerau* – the name of a farm.

BREAK IN HARVEST (Routledge, 1946)

67. The Bearers
In Notebook I it is annotated: 'December 29, 1943 / Tŷ Clyd, Brecon. / Published in the *Welsh Review*, Sept. 1944'.
l. 4 *the text from Maccabees* – an unspecified quotation from one of the four books of Jewish history (two in the Apocrypha) that tell how Judaea was freed from occupation by Syrian regime of Antiochus Epiphanes – see also 'Judas Maccabeus' (102).

l. 9 *Something there is that turns me to the hills* – reminiscent of Frost's 'Something there is that doesn't love a wall'. Mathias wrote 'Robert Frost: An Appreciation' for the first number of the magazine *Here Today*, which he edited jointly with Pierre Edmunds in Reading, 1944–5.

l. 18 *An Eginhard over the unfallen snow* – in his *Artists in Wales* essay the poet wrote 'At eight years of age I . . . knew far more of Hatto's Tower, of Charlemagne, of Eginhard and Emma, than I did of the Wales that bore me'. He still has his childhood copy of the eighth edition of *Legends of the Rhine* by Wilhelm Ruland (published in Cologne for English readers), where he met these tales. 'Eginhard and Emma' is a story of passionate love that oversteps the barriers of parental disapproval and anger but survives long suffering and quietly triumphs in the end. Early in the story, Emma carries Eginhard on her back across the snow-covered yard of her fortress home to leave only her footsteps so that her father, Charlemagne, will not suspect Eginhard has visited her chamber.

68. Beacons
In Notebook I it is annotated: '22 April 1943 / Tŷ Clyd, Brecon'.
l. 1 *Bevel* – set at an angle.
ll. 3 / 4 *two black fancies . . . hangers* – the silhouettes of birds.

69. London Welshman
In Notebook I it is annotated: '22 April 1943 / Tŷ Clyd, Brecon. / Published in *Wales*, Summer 1944'.
The story of Uncle John, brother of the poet's father, and like him born on the Rhos, who had been a carpenter on the Stepney Estate in Llanelli before going to London (at the instigation of his wife) to seek his fortune as a dairyman, is also told in the short story 'Block System'.

70. Llyn Bodgynydd
In Notebook I it is annotated: '1 May 1944 / 184 Wantage Road. / Published in *Here Today*'.
Here Today was the 'review [edited and] published in Reading' by Mathias and his friend Pierre Edmunds. The three undated issues appeared in 1944–5. 'Llyn Bodgynydd', 'Kidmore End' (80) and 'Mirror' (84) were in the first number.
Llyn ('Lake') Bodgynydd is one of the smaller lakes of Snowdonia, in the upper Gwydyr forest not far from Betws-y-coed.

71. Drover's Song
Annotated '31 May 1944 / 184 Wantage Road' in Notebook I.
l. 9 *Bachan* – 'little [one]' or a colloquial form of the Welsh 'bachgen' ('boy'), a familiar mode of address, especially to a younger person.
l. 10 *Butty['s]* – in the south Wales vernacular especially, a familiar term for friend and fellow worker; identified in dictionaries as an English dialect word.
l. 11 *Haiptrw ho!* – Welsh rendering of a traditional cattle call used by drovers.
l. 14 *Dafi Jones o Caio* – [Dafydd Jones o Gaeo]. Dafydd Jones (1711–77) of Cwm Gogerddan, Caeo, Carmarthenshire, a cattle drover by trade, was converted at the Independents' meeting house at Troedrhiwdalar (near Builth, Powys) on his way

Notes

home from a cattle-drive into England. Although he had little formal education he became a notable hymn-writer and translated into Welsh the hymns and psalms of Isaac Watts.
l. 25 *Jacky Bint in the Drover's Arms* – an invented character in one of the many inns so named that mark the routes once taken by drovers.
l. 27 *Farnboro* – [Farnborough] a town in southern England (north-east Hampshire) on the drovers' route.

72. The Ballad of Barroll's Daughter
Annotated '22 May 1945; 184 Wantage Road' in Notebook I.
This narrative poem draws on the family history of the poet's mother. Her father, Joseph Morgan, subscribed to a family tradition that they were descended of English gentry, whose ancestral home was 'Bridge Court' in Herefordshire. His grandson discovered the family line led back to the 'Barrolls of Byford', Herefordshire. 'Bridge Court' was indeed the home of Farmer Barroll; it exists today, a farm of modest size on the edge of the village of Kingstone in south Herefordshire. 'Blue Blood and Englishmen' (178) and 'Expiation' (197) explore the same theme.
l. 3 *Skirrid rocks* – the Skirrid [Ysgyryd Fawr] is a rocky outcrop that overlooks Abergavenny from the north-east. In the context of the poem, it is a deliberately misleading location.
l. 21 *Margaret* – the poet's great-great-grandmother.
l. 28 *Where the long-dead horsemen are* – the poet declares this to be an invention unrelated to any fact, contemporary or historical. There is a similar example in 'The Lamentation of Marchell' (210): 'beyond the Honddu / And the Yscir Fawr, where the great vicious / Horses are'.
l. 30 *childless Saturn* – Saturn, Roman equivalent of the Greek god Kronos (time), was said to have eaten all his children except Jupiter (air), Neptune (water) and Pluto (the grave).
l. 33 *Tom Lenthall* – the name, which appears in the poet's carefully constructed family tree, is not uncommon in Herefordshire. A Lenthall was Speaker of the House of Commons in 1642.
ll. 47–8 *He spoke her hotly in a phrase / Across the old convention* – he proposed marriage to the daughter without the knowledge of her father.
l. 137 *The feckless child* – Emma, Margaret's daughter, who eventually became the wife of James Morgan and mother of Joseph, the poet's grandfather.
l. 140 *Mrs Nicholls Jarvis* – a fictitious name.
l. 142 *saturnine lover* – one of 'dull and glowering' temperament, but also one born under the influence of Saturn, thought to be an evil planet.
l. 149 *Battle churchyard* – near Brecon; Margaret died in 1841 and is buried there.

73. Whitewater
Annotated '9 April 1943 / Tŷ Clyd, Brecon' in Notebook I.
The poem's imagery derives from a walk in the Thames valley near Reading.

74. Enstone Rock
Annotated '8 April 1943 / Tŷ Clyd, Brecon. / Published in *Poetry London*' in Notebook I.

The poet's wife, Molly (Hawes), was a farmer's daughter from Church Enstone, not far from Woodstock and ten miles or so south-west of Banbury, Oxfordshire, on the eastern edge of the Cotswolds. The significant topographical feature identified by the title is not a rock, although there might once have been one, but a spring (see 'mosaic rock' below).

l. 4 *Bushell* – as a result of visiting Enstone, the poet discovered Thomas Bushell, 1594–1674, speculator and mining engineer. Bushell was page to and protégé of Francis Bacon, who taught him what was then known about mineralogy. The walks and fountains he created at Enstone were visited by Charles I in 1636. Having successfully appealed for royal patronage, he worked the royal mines in Wales in 1636–7. The short story 'Digression into Miracle' is a version of Bushell's venture at Aberystwyth, where he became Master of the Mint in 1637. A stalwart supporter of the Royalist cause, he was at Shrewsbury in 1642 and at Oxford in 1643. He held Lundy for Charles I till 1647 and then went into hiding. In 1652, having given security for good behaviour, he leased Crown mines from the Protector. Hoping to raise a little money by them, he wrote pamphlets about his schemes, including the waterworks at Enstone.

l. 2 *wold* – open, rolling country.

l. 5 *Lean from the Calf of Man* – Bushell lived on the Calf of Man (the small island off the southern tip of the Isle of Man) 1626–9, and returned from there poor.

ll. 9–10 *Charles, the noble slipmaster / Irritant* – this play on the familiar 'paymaster general' portrays a 'slippery' king who, annoyingly, does not pay his debts.

l. 10 *catspaw* – dupe.

l. 10 *envoi voyant* – loud or gaudy dedication.

l. 14 *mosaic rock* – a reference to Moses striking the rock with Aaron's rod to produce water – see 'Against Jericho (June, 1936)' (14).

l. 18 *minting with the plume of three* – coins stamped with the Prince of Wales's feathers.

l. 27 *nardus* – a rare synonym for spikenard (or 'nard'), the aromatic ointment of the ancients derived from a plant of the same name.

l. 30 *Ditchley* – Ditchley Park is a grand country house about three miles south of Enstone, see also 'A Prospect of Ditchley' (94).

l. 37 *adit* – a tunnel into a mine.

l. 49 *Glyme* – a stream that runs from Church Enstone to the nearby village of Enstone and feeds the lake known as Queen Pool in the Great Park of Blenheim Palace, about seven miles to the south.

75. Ladysmock*
A previously unpublished poem dated '17 April 1943' in Notebook I.

76. Fulwell
In Notebook I, it is annotated: '8 January 1944 / Tŷ Clyd, Brecon. / Published in *Life and Letters To-day*, May 1944'.
Fulwell is a hamlet, which has a well and is barely a mile from Enstone. In the poem the well is a metaphor for love.

Notes

77. For M.A.H.
It appears in Notebook I annotated '8 January 1944 / Tŷ Clyd, Brecon'. M.A.H. are the initials of Mary Annie Hawes, who would become the poet's wife.
l. 5 *Wychwood runnels* – a runnel is a brook; Wychwood Forest is situated about two miles south of Enstone.
l. 8 *Arraigning an andante opening* – calling to account a slow beginning (to the relationship).
l. 10 *the rows at Tew* – rows of trees at Great Tew Park, about four miles to the north of Enstone.
l. 12 *Lucius Cary* – 1610?–1643, second Viscount Falkland. He succeeded to the estate at Burford (about a dozen miles south-west of Enstone) c.1630 and later lived in retirement at Great Tew. He served as an MP 1640-2, accompanied Charles I to York and was sent to negotiate with the Parliamentary forces in September 1642. He was present at the siege of Gloucester in August 1643. Despairing of peace, he threw away his life at the battle of Newbury in September of the same year. He was a philosopher and wrote poetry and has a special appeal for Roland Mathias as a courageous lover of peace.
l. 13 *Hampden* – John Hampden 1594–1643. Of a staunchly Puritan Buckinghamshire family, he was a strong opponent of Charles I and the most popular member of the Short Parliament of 1640. He moved the resolution giving control of the militia and the Tower to Parliament, raised a regiment of foot and was an active field commander. He was mortally wounded in a skirmish with Prince Rupert at Chalgrove Field (a few miles east of Abingdon) and died at Thame (where Molly Mathias went to school).
l. 14 *Chiselhampton* – a village about four miles north-west of Chalgrove, near Oxford.
l. 15 *Bushell* – see 'Enstone Rock' (74).
l. 19 *reaves* – breaks.
l. 20 *windrush* – a suitably onomatopoeic word but also a Cotswold allusion: a river and a village about fifteen miles west of Enstone bear the name 'Windrush'.
l. 21 *hangdog[s]* – of downcast appearance but also a play on 'firedogs'.

78. Prayer Before Marriage*
A previously unpublished poem dated '11 January 1944' in Notebook I.

79. Last Happiness
Annotated '11 January 1944 / Tŷ Clyd, Brecon' in Notebook I.
Another love poem involving much wordplay and a complex stanza form that incorporates internal rhyme. Love sets a challenge to the poet's skill.
l. 14 *Penoyre* – a mansion near the village of Cradoc, two miles or so north-west of Brecon.
l. 20 *ember day* – the lovers' last day together before parting for a while but also, in the Christian year, a day of fasting and prayer and, by extension, a special day in the calendar of their love.
l. 23 *We joined the poor jargon of points* – 'we returned to everyday things'. The 'points' are those needed to obtain food during the Second World War.

Notes

80. Kidmore End
Annotated '31 May 1944 / 184 Wantage Road, Reading' in Notebook I.
Kidmore End is a village just north of Reading, roughly between Pangbourne and Sonning Common.
l. 1 *agrimony* – plant of the genus *Agrimonia*, having compound leaves, long spikes of small yellow flowers and bristly fruits.
l. 3 *mullein* – plant of the genus *Verbascum*, having tall spikes of yellow flowers and broad hairy leaves.
l. 15 *Planes prayed like pharisees* – The peaceful appearance of warplanes on the ground is a kind of hypocrisy. The simile is consistent with the poet's (and especially his mother's) conscientious objection to war.

81. Requiescat
Annotated '13 May 1944 / 184 Wantage Road' in Notebook I.
The title means 'May he/she rest in peace'. The poem is about a visit, soon after their wedding in 1944, to the grave of Molly's mother, who had died in 1937. The experience starts a meditation on death and grief.
l. 15 *Trealaw* – a former mining village in the Rhondda Fawr (near Porth and the junction of the Rhondda Fawr with the Rhondda Fach), which has a large cemetery. Mathias had relatives from his father's side of the family in the Rhondda.
ll. 24–5 *the break in understanding . . . cautery* – this is the first poem in which the poet expresses a sense of guilt at the comfortable distance of his life from that of his 'dark cousinhood'. It is, however, foreshadowed in his essay 'The Shame of Youth'; see the notes to 'Pastorale', p. 302.
l. 44 *wimpey* – wartime slang for the Wellington, a famous bomber aircraft.
l. 50 *preposing* – a coinage from the Latin *praepositio*, meaning 'to place before'. It has the sense here, in the context of the evidences of war 'over the hedge', of bringing peace forward.
l. 60 *Heythrop* – a village in Oxfordshire between Chipping Norton and Great Tew, a few miles from Enstone.

82. The Cauldron of Diwrnach Wyddel (A Poem for the D-Days)
Annotated '20 July 1944 / 184 Wantage Road, Reading' in Notebook I.
The story of the cauldron of Diwrnach Wyddel appears in the tale of Culhwch and Olwen in the *Mabinogion*. As one condition of allowing Culhwch to marry Olwen, her father, the giant Ysbaddaden, demands the cauldron to cook meat for the wedding feast. Arthur's men travel to Ireland, kill Diwrnach, who is steward to the King, and take the cauldron by force. On D-Day (6 June 1944) Allied forces invaded occupied France, beginning the final stage of the Second World War in Europe.
l. 6 *asseveration* – solemn declaration.
ll. 1–12 *Monte Cassino . . . Benedict* – a reference to the great Benedictine monastery above Cassino in central Italy, destroyed in 1944 by Allied bombing.
ll. 15–17 *Bermondsey . . . the street names were changed* – a London docklands district that suffered large-scale destruction in the Blitz, the German bombing campaign of the early 1940s. Whole streets were destroyed, many civilians were killed and thousands made homeless.

l. 37 *cruseward* – guardian of the 'cruse', an archaic term, borrowed from the *Mabinogion*, for a vessel used to contain liquids.

83. The Lament of Little Gwion
Annotated '15 August / Fulwell Farm, Enstone' in Notebook I.
Gwion bach, servant of the goddess Ceridwen in the mythological 'Hanes Taliesin', swallows drops from the magic cauldron intended for her son Morfran. Thus he acquires the gift of poetry and is pursued by Ceridwen through various metamorphoses until, as a grain of wheat, he is eaten by her in the form of a hen. Then, however, he is reborn of her and in such beauteous form that she cannot kill him but casts him adrift on the sea. He is discovered and adopted by Elffin ap Gwyddno Garanhir and renamed Taliesin.

84. Mirror
Annotated '16 August 1944 / Fulwell Farm, Enstone. / Published in *Here Today*' in Notebook I.

85. Evening: Unloading Wheat
Annotated '17 August 1944 / Fulwell Farm, Enstone' in Notebook I.
See Introduction p. 15.

86. Grace Before Work
Annotated '18 August 1944 / Fulwell Farm, Enstone' in Notebook I.
This is a key poem in the development of the poet's sense of indebtedness to his forebears from Rhos Llangeler and his self-admonishment never to forget them.
ll. 10–11 *Kept / The chapel bare* – Saron, the Independent chapel at Rhos Llangeler.
ll. 15–16 *Maengwyn . . . Our elder Thomas* – Thomas Mathias (b. 1778) was, in the poet's own words 'the first antecedent'. He built the squatters' cottage on the Rhos and named it 'Maengwyn' ('white stone').
l. 17 *tenter* – a frame on which cloth is stretched in manufacture to ensure it keeps its shape. The image of cloth, its constituent threads and the emerging pattern of the finished article, is used again by the poet in his *Artists in Wales* essay (1970).
l. 28 *the first builder* – Thomas Mathias again. In Wales, the trade of the 'saer' (carpenter) traditionally extended far beyond woodworking. The word 'pensaer' (literally 'chief carpenter') means 'architect'.

87. Pontwillim Plough
Annotated 'January 1945 / 184 Wantage Road, Reading' in Notebook I.
The poem is characteristically self-critical. The poet is the 'artist . . . in error', dissatisfied with the scene before him, and also one of the 'critics' who should purge themselves of their ill-humour. Pontwillim [Pontgwilym] is on sloping ground at the foot of the sharp hill surmounted by Pen-y-crug, to the west of the river Honddu and immediately north of the town of Brecon.
l. 3 *broken hills* – those of the Eppynt, to the north-west of Brecon.
l. 12 *Coldcrops keep the bellon* – an image borrowed from the poet's research into lead and silver mining near Aberystwyth. 'Coldcrops' are crops on land poisoned by mine waste; 'bellon' is lead colic, the effect of the poison on farm stock, vividly described in the short story 'Digression into Miracle'.

Notes

88. *Subite*
Annotated '29 April 1945 / 184 Wantage Road, Reading' in Notebook I, where it appears under the title 'Winter Scene'.
The Latin title means 'suddenly'.
l. 2 *Carrying the hardships of the heart / Into this last phase* – a reference to the war and signs that it was at last drawing to a close.
l. 4 *The white lines of our former rulings* – the clearly drawn lines of the poet's pacifism beyond which he determined not to move.

89. *Hillside*
Annotated '15 May 1945' in Notebook I.

90. *In This Cold Room*
Annotated '19 May 1945' in Notebook I.
In a note to the editor the poet writes: 'This is part of my thinking in the war years. You have to know what it feels like to understand the "communion of death". It [life] must be proffered to death.'
ll. 1–2 *pictures / Of night in the arena* – the note also reveals that the 'pictures' are of Roman scenes by Alma Tadema, which hung in the dining room at Fulwell Farm.
l. 11 *the two fir trees* – trees that stood on the lawn beside the house.

91. *Lowbury Hill*
Annotated '26 June 1945 / 184 Wantage Road' in Notebook I.
Lowbury Hill is a landmark about five miles south-east of Didcot. All the locations mentioned in the poem, with the single exception of Liddington/Liddington Castle (which is some twenty miles due west of Lowbury Hill) are closely grouped. That they have Saxon names confirms the identity of the victors in the battles that were fought there. The tank tracks mentioned in the poem are a reminder of the Second World War. The same area is the site of those military operations of the 1940s and the swathe of poppies referred to in Harri Webb's poem 'A Crown for Branwen'. That it was a battleground in distant ages, particularly at the time of the Saxon invasions, and has manifest connections to modern warfare holds the interest of a poet constantly alert to connections between past and present.
l. 15 *anchusa* – plant with rough hairy stems and leaves and blue flowers.
l. 18 *tumuli* – prehistoric grave mounds.
l. 26 *balebird* – coinage for bird of ill-omen, referring to 'the cowardly kite' in l. 10.
l. 28 *Haggard* – The multiple meanings of the word all have some allusive force: broadly it describes action that is wild or unruly; it is also a farm or barn, and, like 'balebird' above, a synonym for hawk.
l. 31 *scathe* – an archaic word meaning 'hurt', 'damage'.
l. 53 *Woden* – Anglo-Saxon name of the Scandinavian god Odin, who was (among other attributes) the god of war. His 'blessing' is obviously ironic.
l. 54 *Ambrosius* – Ambrosius Aurelianus, a legendary fifth-century battle leader of the Britons in their resistance against the Saxon invaders, said by the historian Gildas to be the last of the Romans in Britain.
l. 64 *this antlered hill* – a hill associated with the cult of Cernunnos, a pagan Celtic god.

l. 69 *sainfoin* – medicinal plant with pale pink flowers.
l. 71 *Kai* – the Arthurian knight, foster-brother and seneschal to the king.
l. 76 *Badon* – the (unknown) location of a great victory that the Britons, under Arthur, won over the Saxons.

92. Crossing into Peace
Annotated '17 May 1945 / 184 Wantage Road' in Notebook I.
The poem marks the end of the Second World War.
l. 10 *Sulham* – a village between Reading and Pangbourne.
l. 20 *And the Pang between* – the Pang is both the river and the keen emotion of the occasion – a pun.

93. Break in Harvest
Annotated '9 August 1945 / Fulwell Farm, Enstone' in Notebook I.
In a note to the editor the poet writes, 'This is about the war and how the beginning must indemnify the result.'
l. 7 *willow-herb and sorrel* – common plants. The former, of the genus *Epilobium*, has narrow leaves and clusters of (usually) pink flowers; the latter, of the genus *Rumex*, has acid-tasting leaves often used in salads and sauces.

94. Prospect of Ditchley
Annotated '20 August 1945 / Tŷ Clyd, Brecon' in Notebook I.
Ditchley – the early eighteenth-century mansion and great park of Ditchley lie barely two miles south of Enstone. The description shows the neglect of the property during the war years.
l. 5 *Capability Brown* – Lancelot Brown (1716–83), landscape gardener, known as 'Capability' from his habit of telling clients that their gardens had 'capabilities of improvement', was the leading figure in the development of a characteristically informal English style of park landscape. He came to Ditchley about five years after the building of the house and had a part in the planning of the gardens, including the damming of a stream to make the lake.
l. 9 *silverweed and John's wort* – common plants. The former, of the genus *Potentilla*, is a creeping plant with silvery leaves and yellow flowers; the latter, St John's wort, of the genus *Hypericum*, has bright yellow flowers.
l. 12 *Gibbs's italian* – the architect of the mansion, James Gibbs, spent some years in Italy and brought back with him Italian craftsmen and ideas influenced by the simplicity of Palladian architecture.
l. 16 *Heythrop* – a village about five miles to the north of Ditchley.

95. Going
Annotated '4 September 1945 / 35 Empire Way, Gretna. / Completed, all but the last few lines, at Tŷ Clyd, Brecon, before 31 August' in Notebook I.
The poem is about the journey from Reading, via Brecon, with a few sticks of furniture, to the new home in Gretna that Mathias and his family would occupy for the school year 1945–6.
l. 35 *Kiwi* – another reference to a childhood memory of the poet: the kiwi cut in the chalk above Bulford camp by New Zealanders in the First World War.

Notes

ll. 49–50 *the grave on the hill / Untended* – see 'Requiescat' (81).
l. 55 *Hypatia* – a novel by Charles Kingsley which appeared in book form in 1853; it is based upon the Greek Neoplatonic philosopher of the same name, who was reputedly the first woman mathematician.
l. 75 *The Quiet Woman* – an Oxfordshire inn where the Enstone road turns off towards Stow-on-the-Wold, a route leading to Wales.

THE ROSES OF TRETOWER (Dock Leaves Press, March 1952)

96. Solway
Annotated '28 September 1945 / 35 Empire Way, Gretna' in Notebook I.
The poem was first published in *The Listener*, 1 January 1948. The Solway Firth is the west-coast inlet that separates the Lake District from Scotland. Its shoreline is heavily silted, at its narrowest easterly point by the rivers Sark and Esk. The Scottish village of Gretna stands close to the northern shore.
l. 6 *Paul Jones* – [John] Paul Jones (1747–92), a naval adventurer of Scottish descent. His adventures included slave-trading and smuggling before he joined the American navy. As commander of the 'Ranger' he captured the fort at Whitehaven and led the combined French and American force that threatened Edinburgh in 1779. Subsequently he served the French and then achieved the rank of rear-admiral with the Russian navy at the Battle of Liman in 1798. His career with the Russian fleet was ended by a quarrel with Potemkin, favourite of Catherine the Great. He died in Paris.
l. 10 *Galeenies* – guinea-fowl (from the Latin *galina*).
l. 14 *Sark* – the river flowing south through Gretna into the tidal mudflats of the Solway Firth.
l. 17 *Skiddaw* – the nearest peak in the Lake District, almost due south of Gretna.

97. New Year's Day 1946
Annotated '1 January 1946 / 35 Empire Way, Gretna' in Notebook I.
In a note to the editor, the poet described Gretna as 'a sad and hopeless place'. The poem is a sombre meditation on the uncertainty of his life in a temporary teaching post, with the responsibility of a wife and two children not quite a year old. It was one of five poems by Mathias set to music for voice and piano in 'Canticle No. 2' by the composer David Harries.

98. The Lurking Ancestor
Annotated '3 January 1946 / 35 Empire Way, Gretna' in Notebook I.
The epigraph is from Donne's *Devotions upon Emergent Occasions* (1624), 'Meditation XXI', which begins: 'If man had been left alone in this world at first, shall I think that he would not have fallen? If there had been no woman, would not man have served to have been his own tempter? When I see him now subject to infinite weaknesses, fall into infinite sin without any foreign temptations, shall I think he would have none, if he had been alone?'
ll. 19–20 *The mark of the beast in the furrows, / Of God in the fight* – the concluding lines are an expression of the Puritan belief that man's response to his condition is his own choice. He can follow the path of God or the way of the Beast.

Notes

99. From a Bus at Crosby, Cumberland
Annotated '15 May 1946 / 35 Empire Way, Gretna' in Notebook I.
Mathias associates the poem with a friend and fellow poet, Roderick Webb, who died, still in his twenties, in 1948.
l. 13 *Try John Peel on the wall* – a sign on the drystone wall advertising a local ale.
l. 20 *Lickserpent* – an invented compound word to convey the 'coiling' reflection of the mountain in the waters of the firth.
l. 20 *Criffel* – (misspelled 'Crifell' in *The Roses of Tretower*) a modest peak on the Scottish side of the Solway Firth, rising quite steeply from the muddy shoreline.
l. 22 *faithless rover* – a further allusion to John Paul Jones – see 'Solway' (96).

100. In Offenham Church
Annotated in Notebook I: 'Roughed out at Offenham about April 24, 1946. Completed 35 Empire Way, Gretna, 17 May 1946. / (*Writers of Tomorrow*).'
Offenham is a village a little to the north of Evesham, where Molly Mathias's sister lived. The poet and his wife often spent holidays there.

101. Evening
Annotated in Notebook I: 'Roughed out at Offenham, April 1946. Completed 1 June 1946 at 35 Empire Way, Gretna.'
First published in the *Milford Haven Arts Club Annual*, 1949.
l. 11 *bypassed peaks* – identified by the poet as those viewed from Brecon. He suggests they are 'excursive' because they are some distance from the town or because the cool of evening makes them seem so.

102. Judas Maccabeus
Annotated in Notebook I: 'Roughed out at Offenham, 22 April. Completed 18 May 1946 at 35 Empire Way, Gretna. / (*The Welsh Review*).'
In describing the singing of Handel's oratorio at The Plough chapel in Brecon, the poem comments on both the musical performance and the opposing forces of good and evil. The writer undertook a similar exercise in prose in the early short story 'Saturday Night'. Judas Maccabeus was the leader of a Jewish revolt (166–161 BC) against the kingdom of Antiochus IV of Syria, which led to the recapture of Jerusalem and the rededication of the Temple.
l. 12 *the Syrian yelp* – a reference to the homeland of the occupying forces.
l. 13 *'How vain is man'* – from 'Part the Second' of the oratorio. In the opening scene, as described in the score, the Israelites are celebrating the return of Judas from the victories over Apolonius and Seron. The first 'Air' has the following text: 'How vain is man who boasts in fight / The valour of gigantic might, / And dreams not that a hand unseen / Directs and guides this weak machine'.
l. 13 *Mattathias* – a priest of the village of Modi'im, some seventeen miles north-west of Jerusalem who, in 167 BC, began the Jewish resistance against the regime of Antiochus. He was the father of Judas Maccabeus, who took over leadership of the cause when Mattathias died *c.*166 BC.
l. 35 *the rodlike serpent raised* – both the conductor's baton and the foe of God.
l. 59 *Against the pit the pillar and in the pillar sign* – The allegory of the poem requires that 'pit' be interpreted as both the musicians, following the conductor's baton, and Satan's realm. The pillar is a biblical image, from Exodus 13: 21 'And

the Lord went before [the people of Israel] by day in a pillar of cloud, to lead them the way; and by night in a pillar of fire, to give them light.'

103. *The Path to Dinas*
Annotated in Notebook I: 'Roughed out at Tŷ Clyd, Brecon, about 14 April 1946. Much altered and completed 25–26 May 1946 at 35 Empire Way, Gretna. / (*Tribune*).'
The publication date in *Tribune* was 26 July 1946. Dinas was the nineteenth-century mansion home of Sir John Lloyd, a noted local historian and benefactor, who established the museum in Brecon and the Brecknock Society. The house, close to the banks of the Usk to the south of the town, became dilapidated and was demolished soon after the Second World War to make way for the Brecon bypass. The tall trees of the park that surrounded it can be seen from the bypass and there is still a path leading to the site the house once occupied. It is also referred to in the poem 'Jazz Festival' (209), from Mathias's last book, *A Field at Vallorcines*.
l. 15 *tree-creeper* – a small songbird of the family *Certhiidae*, with a downward curving bill. It gains its name from its habit of creeping along tree trunks in search of insects.
l. 17 *toothwort* – a plant of the genus *Dentaria*, which has creeping underground stems covered with tooth-like projections.

104. *Lochmaben Stone*
Annotated in Notebook I: 'Roughed out at Gretna. Completed 28 December 1946 at 49 Northumberland Road, North Harrow, Middlesex. / (*Tribune*).'
The publication date in *Tribune* was 31 January 1947. The Lochmaben Stone is an ancient site on the edge of the Solway Firth very near Gretna. Kirtle Water is the river that flows into the firth close to the stone. In common with the other poems set in this borderland between northern England and Scotland, the setting is bleak and spirits correspondingly low. There is a Lear-like savage despondency about the piece, a notion reinforced by the use of 'houseless', but as a whole the diction is loaded with bitterness – *wastrel, disparages, simper, wizened, cowering, thinning and harsh, blood, shelterless, slaughter, stupid wounds, evil, houseless sticks, cold, aghast, cold scoured shore, ragged, shadow.*
l. 3 *idle marriages* – those at Gretna Green, traditionally (and still) the destination of youthful elopers.
l. 7 *bents* – stiff grass or sedge.
l. 17 *whin[s]* – gorse.

105. *The Mountain*
Annotated '3 January 1947 / 49 Northumberland Road, North Harrow. / (*The Welsh Review*)' in Notebook I.
In a note to the editor, the poet termed the first fifty-seven lines a jeremiad, and it is indeed a long, mournful complaint which finds an answer in the section of the poem beginning 'Comfort ye . . .' – see Introduction p. 21. The poem refers to the fields and the mountain visible from the poet's Gretna home, but in this poem the topographical features have a symbolic force. His note mentioned that, in addition, Skiddaw, the mountain of this poem as of 'Solway' (96), was a direction marker,

pointing back, as it were, to the Lake District and St Helens beyond, where he had begun his career in teaching and had his first experience of independence.

ll. 11–12 *Thrift . . . Pink growing wickedly* – thrift is a low-growing flowering plant also called sea pink, but the reference here also carries overtones of the more usual meaning of 'thrift', that is, caution in the management of money (see also l. 71).

l. 58 *Comfort ye, comfort ye my people* – Isaiah 40: 1.

ll. 71–2 *greys of government / Walling the tenement* – a reference to the school where the poet taught at Carlisle.

l. 73 *Adam's collar galling* – the image derives from George Herbert's poem 'The Collar' – see the next note.

ll. 88–90 *the unbowed / Neck flushing fashions the collar anew . . . Pushing the burden of passions back* – another reference to Herbert's 'The Collar' which, like 'The Mountain', begins by railing at the constraints that prevent us from attaining a life of ease and ends with renewed acceptance of God's yoke.

l. 99 *polluted hand and prescient eye* – the foreknowing eye is that of the soul which apprehends God; the polluted hand is the earthly part of man.

l. 112 *O I am growing old* – Mathias was thirty-one. T. S. Eliot was about twenty-nine when he wrote 'I grow old, I grow old' in 'The Love Song of J. Alfred Prufrock'.

106. Searching Spring

Annotated '9 April 1947 / Tŷ Clyd, Brecon' in Notebook I.
First published in the *Milford Haven Arts Club Annual*, 1949. At one level the poem is about the poet's first efforts to turn the garden. Much of the text describes the scene (Gretna still) but in terms more frequently used in connection with ills of the body: *haggard, gash, (ragged) shoulders, grave wound, vein, sick, flayed*.
ll. 13–14 *I had no notion till the fork dug in / My chiefest covenant was with my skin* – according to Mathias these lines were probably the starting point of the poem. They refer to an unidentified human pain, physical, psychological or spiritual, that emphasizes the primacy of self-preservation.

107. Bablockhythe

Annotated in Notebook I: 'Roughed out, first two verses, at camp at Standlake, 29 July–5 Aug. Completed 23 August 1947 at Tŷ Clyd, Brecon. / (*Now*).'
Standlake is a village near the confluence of the Windrush and the Thames some ten miles west of Oxford, a part of the Thames valley where, on their holiday, the poor drink (at 'The Chequers') alongside moneyed locals. The poem is largely descriptive.

108. On the Grave of Henry Vaughan at Llansaintffraed

Annotated in Notebook I: '28 June 1947 / 49 Northumberland Road, North Harrow. / Published in *Wales*.'
Llansaintffraed (Llansanffraid) is a village near Mathias's birthplace, Talybont-on-Usk, Breconshire. The first stanza sets the scene in the graveyard with the sun declining and the lengthening shadows of yew trees immersing rows of gravestones. The language of the poem is compacted and the versification, involving internal rhyme, is typically complex. The use of assonance and alliteration, not least of sibilants, and the emphasis on 'light' in the third stanza are reminiscent of Vaughan's poetry.

l. 6 *In this blind parcel* – Henry Vaughan's grave is a distinct 'parcel' of land. Its 'blindness' is a matter for conjecture but, most obviously, it lacks the power of the senses and the consciousness of the poet interred there.

l. 8 *prostrate* – submissive.

l. 9 *light* – Mathias has argued (in an article in the Henry Vaughan special issue of *Poetry Wales*, 11, 2, Autumn 1975, pp. 6–35) that Vaughan's use of words like 'light', 'white', 'ray' and 'beam' reveal his interest in Hermetic philosophy.

l. 13 *Peccator maximus* – the stone which covers the tomb is inscribed, at Vaughan's direction, with the Latin words *Servus Inutilis: Peccator Maximus / Hic Iaceo* (meaning 'A useless servant: the greatest of sinners / here I lie'). In the same article mentioned in the note above, Mathias describes the inscription as 'a supreme expression of Christian humility, conviction of sin and faith in the sacrifice made by Jesus Christ on the cross'.

l. 15 *Pisgah* – the mount from which Moses viewed the Promised Land: Deuteronomy 34: 1–4.

109. Drought

Annotated in Notebook I: '31 August 1947 / 49 Northumberland Road, North Harrow. / (*Tribune*).'

The poem appeared in *Tribune*, 19 September 1947. A description of the River Honddu, which joins the Usk in the town of Brecon, during a drought affords an opportunity for a meditation on death.

l. 16 *Lethe* – one of the rivers of Hades in Greek mythology. By drinking its water the dead forgot their previous life.

110. Olchon

Annotated in Notebook I: 'Begun at Tŷ Clyd, Brecon, before 27 August 1947. Completed 31 August at 49 Northumberland Road, North Harrow.'

First published in *Poetry (Chicago)*, October 1949. The Olchon Brook rises in the Black Mountains a few miles south of Hay-on-Wye and eventually joins the river Monnow. The border between Breconshire and Herefordshire, in this part running north to south, is very close and parallel to its valley. Joshua Thomas in *Hanes y Bedyddwyr* ('History of the Baptists') (1778) writes of the appearance of the sect at Olchon in 1633. This would have been in keeping with a tendency for Puritanism to infiltrate where ecclesiastical jurisdiction was relatively weak, as in the border region, because conflicting authority between Marcher lords left gaps to be exploited. The poem is one of religious affirmation, although in a note to the editor the poet acknowledges that 'the answer is not always "Come"' (l. 22).

l. 3 *Crib y Garth* – a ridge with a rocky summit overlooking the Olchon Valley, also known as the Cat's Back.

ll. 28–9 *The worldling's cassock . . . long doubt* – the cassock identifies members of the Anglican clergy; a 'worldling' is one who is primarily concerned with material things of this earth rather than those that are spiritual and of the life to come.

111. Craswall

Annotated in Notebook I: 'Completed 3 September 1947 at 49 Northumberland Road, North Harrow. / (*Poetry Commonwealth*).'

Notes

The poem appeared in *Poetry Commonwealth*, Summer 1948. Craswall is a village a few miles south-east of Hay-on-Wye, very near Olchon, just at the border with Herefordshire. It has a ruined priory, which was not, however, visited by the poet. The poem is about the emotion he feels at being at 'the gate of Wales' (l. 12). It was one of three poems by Mathias set to music by the composer Mansell Thomas.

l. 5 *canting neck* – the downward slanting groove of the brook that rises from the spring.

l. 9 *This is the boundary* – the boundary between Wales and England.

l. 9 *different burrs / Stick* – punning use of burr (bur) meaning both the sticky seed-heads and speech accents.

112. Camp by the Windrush

Annotated in Notebook I: 'Completed 27 Sept. 1947 at 49 Northumberland Road, North Harrow. / (*The Listener*).'

The poem appeared in *The Listener* on 23 October 1947. The Windrush is a tributary of the Thames, which it joins near Standlake, about twelve miles west of Oxford. It was the site of the annual camp of St Clement Dane's School, where Mathias taught 1946–8.

l. 27 *Stentor* – a Greek herald in the Trojan war famed for his loud voice.

113. Thomas ap Richard of Doier to the Tower, These

Annotated in Notebook I: 'Completed 5 October 1947 at 49 Northumberland Road, North Harrow. / (*The Listener*).'

The poem appeared in *The Listener* on 16 October 1947. It is closely based on the poet's research for *Whitsun Riot*. The locations are in that part of Herefordshire close to the border with Monmouthshire known as Archenfield; the time 1605, not long before the Gunpowder Plot. The poem is concerned with the 'commotion' of 1605, an uprising among Catholic recusants in that area. This began on 21 May, the Tuesday of Whitsun week, at the village of Allensmore, five miles south-west of Hereford, with the early morning burial in the Papist manner of a known Catholic woman who had been refused burial by the vicar of the parish. The vicar could not prevent the interment, but he hastened to report the names of several among the large burial party to the bishop of Hereford.

Thomas ap Richard (or Prichard) lived at New Grange in the parish of Dore, which was situated only a mile from Treville Park, the home of William Morgan. On 4–5 June 1605, he mustered the men to ambush the Bishop of Hereford's party on its way to seize Morgan. For reasons impossible now to determine, the ambush was called off and Morgan was taken into custody. The men involved in the fiasco dispersed and Thomas ap Richard was one of several ringleaders who were not subsequently apprehended.

l. 1 *Morgan* – William Morgan of Treville Park, a gentleman of some means and standing, whose Catholic sympathies were proved by documents found by magistrates at his house. He was imprisoned in the Tower. Under interrogation, by Attorney General Coke – see 'Indictment' (155) – among others, he eventually confessed but gave little away. Official interest in him seems to have cooled quite rapidly and he did not long remain in gaol.

l. 5 *Sir Scudamore* – Sir James Scudamore of Holme Lacy, who accompanied the bishop of Hereford on the mission to seize William Morgan of Treville Park. He had been knighted before Cadiz in 1596 and appears as 'Sir Scudamore', a model of knightly virtue, in Spenser's *Faerie Queene*.

l. 6 *the bishop* – Robert Bennett, bishop of Hereford.

l. 7 *valletts* – a local dialect word for a dell, usually wooded; it appears on Ordnance Survey maps showing the South Herefordshire district attached to woodland near Wormbridge, just north of the Abergavenny–Hereford road.

l. 13 *Arkston* – Arkstone Common and the manor house, Arkstone Court, are situated north of the Abergavenny–Hereford road, six miles or so south-west of Hereford.

l. 15 *Treville* – the manor house of Treville was located a few miles south of Arkstone and west of the village of Thruxton. The 'black whaleback of Treville wood' features in *Whitsun Riot*.

l. 18 *weavers of Hungerstone* – Hungerstone is a small village bordering Arkstone Common to the east. Two weavers of the village, James Coles and William Chadnor, identified as leading members of the burial at Allensmore, were the first to be arrested by the local High Constable on a warrant from the bishop of Hereford.

l. 21 *Wormbridge* – a village on the A465 between Abergavenny and Hereford.

l. 22 *Quarrell* – Thomas Quarrell of Wormbridge, one of the leaders of the planned ambush, who, like Thomas ap Richard, got clean away.

l. 29 *Vaughan of New Court* – a reliable ally of the bishop of Hereford, Rowland Vaughan was the second son of Watkin Vaughan of Bredwardine and Joan Parry of New Court. After marriage to a second cousin, he became known as Vaughan of Whitehouse. His mother was a daughter of Miles Parry and Blanche Parry, Queen Elizabeth's 'bedchamber woman'.

l. 30 *his receipt from hell* – on Wednesday 19 June, the justices and a strong party led by Rowland Vaughan among others conducted a thirty-mile search along the borders of Monmouthshire, finding substantial evidence of Catholic usage but hardly any of the inhabitants, who had fled. A strong (but probably inaccurate) oral tradition persists that they caught an outlawed priest named Ainsworth in his hideout in the Darren woods and beheaded him. Bright red spots on stones at the 'Priest's Well' near Skenfrith are said to have been stained with his blood.

ll. 31–2 *evil . . . With book and bell* – 'bell, book and candle' is a phrase asssociated with excommunication from the Catholic church, but here it stands for execution, the closing of the book of life and the tolling of the bell for one who has died.

114. The Roses of Tretower

The first poem to be copied into Notebook II, where it appears with the annotation: '11 January 1948 / 49 Northumberland Road, North Harrow, Middlesex.'

The narrative, derived from a local Breconshire tale, is also the basis of the short story which bears the same title. The poem differs from the story, most notably in the strong religious imagery towards the end of the second section. In the original book publication, this poem and 'The Riddle' (like the dust jacket) were illustrated by Mathias's friend Eric Peyman.

l. 2 *cant* – a slope.

l. 5 *water rail* – a small long-legged wading bird seen on marshes.

l. 7 *on the nail* – on the spot (usually applied to payment), but 'nail' stands for Lewis throughout the poem.

Notes

l. 11 *Cynghordy Uchaf* – the full name of the farm, literally Upper Council-house, or perhaps more properly 'counsel house'. It suggests an old building that at one time may have been regularly used by local farmers as a meeting place.
l. 16 *livid behind his knees* – an image suggesting a difficult man, quick to anger.
l. 30 *a hedge-matter* – a gap in the hedge needing attention.
l. 39 *helpless feather bed* – one of several examples of transferred epithet: the drunken Lewis is helpless.
ll. 40–41 *stale / With drink* – foul (but 'stale' also means to urinate).
l. 49 *The ark of gopher wood* – Noah's Ark is thus described (Genesis 6: 14), though the context suggests the Ark of the Covenant carried by the Hebrews on their journey to the Promised Land, the construction of which is described in Exodus 37: 1–5.
l. 54 *point-device* – an archaism meaning 'perfection'.
l. 58 *bar sinister* – of illegitimate birth (heraldry).
ll. 62–3 *dead serf had full defence / Against all but his lord* – an aphorism meaning those in whom you trust for protection can undo you.
l. 80 *gammer* – an old woman (archaic).
l. 106 *crying like rods on the stairs* – 'like stair-rods' more often used colloquially of heavy rain.
l. 111 *puling thorn* – 'puling' means whimpering. Eleanor's emotions are transferred to the roses.

115. *Hawk*
Annotated '20 April 1948 / Tŷ Clyd, Brecon' in Notebook II.
First published in *The Listener*, 20 May 1948.
l. 4 *Jehu-crack* – a sound like a whiplash: 'Jehu the son of Nimshi . . . he driveth furiously', II Kings 9: 20.
l. 10 *squireen's cavil* – a 'squireen' is a petty squire, the local lord. The word is also imitative of the hawk's cry, here termed its 'cavil' to stand also for its disputatious attitude.
l. 12 *master-pinion* – an ambiguous image: 'pinion' suggests wing feather in this context, but 'master-pinion' prompts the idea of cogwheel (as in rack and pinion) and thus an allusion to the colloquial 'big wheel' of the place, which fits with the appositional 'nemesis over the heath'.
l. 12 *nemesis* – an agency of vengeance.
l. 20 *cloudgallant* – a coinage suggesting both 'gallant among the clouds' and, because of its echo of 'topgallant' (an extension of a ship's topmast or the sail carried on it), of great height.
l. 24 *unshrives* – 'to shrive' is to confess sins in order to obtain forgiveness, especially when death is imminent. Here the lambs 'unshrive' one another because the threat of death has been removed.
l. 25 *laverock* – a northern English dialect word for skylark.

116. *The Flooded Valley*
Annotated in Notebook II: '21 May 1948 / 49 Northumberland Road. Begun at Brecon during April: 2nd stanza virtually completed there.'
The poem has its basis in the drowning of Glyn Collwn, the valley above Talybont-on-Usk, Breconshire, formerly a community of scattered farms (one the birthplace

of the poet), to create a reservoir for the supply of water to Newport, on the southeast coast of Wales.

l. 8 *My pounds are slipping away and will not wait for the end* – the farmers' scant compensation for their drowned land. Those who were tenants, rather than owners of their farms, received only £280.

l. 11 *Caerfanell* – the stream that once flowed through Glyn Collwn and now feeds the reservoir.

l. 13 *Grwyney, both your rivers are one in the end / And are loved* – the Grwyne[y] Fawr, which rises in the Black Mountains not far from Capel-y-ffin, is joined by its tributary the Grwyne Fechan a few miles from Crickhowell, shortly before entering the Usk at Glangrwyney.

l. 16 *Patricio* – Partrishow is a small church, dating from the eleventh century, which stands high on a ridge above the Grwyne Fawr. It is famed for its rood screen. The church is dedicated to the martyr Ishow, and has a number of ancient wall paintings, including one, in red, of a skeleton.

l. 17 *Senni* – the Afon Senni flows north from the Fforest Fawr watershed of the Brecon Beacons not far from Fan Gihirych to join the Usk at Sennybridge. The poet's favourite uncle, David, lived at Sennybridge.

l. 20 *Kedward, Prosser, Morgan* – the poet speaks for all the dispossessed families, whose memorial stones stand in the graveyard of Aber chapel, just above the reservoir. Prosser was the maiden name of his mother's mother.

117. Morning: New Jerusalem
Annotated in Notebook II: 'Roughed out during the summer in various places. Completed 22 December 1948 at 10 Argyle Street, Pembroke Dock.'

The original title of the poem, 'Beulah' (a Hebrew word meaning 'married woman'), gives a clearer sign of the poet's satirical intent. In Isaiah 62: 4, God promises Israel: 'Thou shalt no more be termed Forsaken; neither shall thy land any more be termed Desolate; but thou shalt be called Hephzi-bah, and thy land Beulah: for the Lord delighteth in thee, and thy land shall be married.' The 'talkers' in the poem are women and, with the final line of the poem, we see that their quotidian concerns are at odds with the religious significance of Christmas.

118. A Winter's Day
Annotated '31 December 1948 / 10 Argyle Street' in Notebook II.
This is one of the poems set to music by David Harries.

l. 2 *the elder towns on either hand* – Pembroke Dock and Milford Haven.

l. 7 *the planes afloat* – Sunderland flying boats. A squadron remained in the Haven after the Second World War to assist with air-sea rescue.

l. 10 *destroyer[s]* – a small fast warship. Several that had been taken out of service at the end of the war were moored upriver.

l. 15 *A youngster who did not smile, or smiled, / Could lose himself a friend* – another example of aphorism. Its meaning is clear enough: a stranger cannot be sure what kind of expression will be best suited to gaining acquaintance, a feeling the poet might have had as a new arrival in Pembroke Dock.

Notes

119. Pas Seul
Annotated '5 February 1949 / 10 Argyle Street' in Notebook II.
First published in *Poetry (Chicago)*, October 1949. It was originally entitled 'Solitaire' (a game played, either with a pegboard or cards, by one person) and was set to music by David Harries.

120. Pas de Deux
Annotated '5 February 1949 / 10 Argyle Street' in Notebook II.
First published in *Poetry (Chicago)*, October 1949. In discussion with the editor, the poet said that death is the theme of both this poem and 'Pas Seul'.
l. 7 *The scarab's ball breaking* – alludes to the iconography of ancient Egypt. The scarab beetle, which makes and rolls a ball of dung, was seen as a symbol of the solar deity, representing in particular solar rebirth.
l. 10 *bedeguar* – a kind of gall on rose bushes (the word is Arabic in origin).

121. Towards Pencombe
Annotated '10 February 1949 / 10 Argyle Street' in Notebook II.
Pencombe is situated in the border country, a few miles south-east of Leominster. The poem links the rural border setting with the story of the illicit love of Lancelot and Guinevere and the betrayal of King Arthur.
l. 11 *The Defence of Guinevere* – *The Defence of Guinevere and other poems* (1858) was William Morris's first book, many of the poems having first appeared in the *Oxford and Cambridge Magazine*, of which he financed the first dozen issues while working for the Gothic revivalist architect, G. E. Street.
l. 12 *double of blood* – having connections with both Wales and England.
l. 28 *Camlann* – [or 'Camlan'] King Arthur's final battle, in which he was mortally wounded by his nephew, Mordred.

122. Spring in Weggis
Annotated in Notebook II: 'First draft – Hotel National, Weggis. Completed 11 May 1949 at 10 Argyle Street.'
Weggis is a town on Lake Lucerne in Switzerland.
l. 2 *the brothers Grimm* – Jakob Ludwig Karl (1785–1863) and Wilhelm Karl (1786–1859), German philologists and folklorists, who collaborated on the collection known as *Grimm's Fairy Tales*.

123. Freshwater West
Annotated 'Completed 25 June 1949 at 10 Argyle Street' in Notebook II.
First published in *Poetry (Chicago)*, October 1949. The sound and movement of the sea are graphically conveyed in the poem's rhythm and imagery. In answer to a number of questions about the poem, Mathias said that what mattered to him was the feeling it communicated. Its theme is mutability and it seems to express emotions close to the Keatsian condition of being 'half in love with easeful death'. The final line has an echo of Donne's 'No man is an *Iland* . . . if a *Clod* be washed away by the *Sea*, *Europe* is the lesse, as well as if a *Promontorie* were, as well as if a *Mannor* of thy *friends* or of *thine owne* were; any mans *death* diminishes *me*, because I am involved in *Mankinde*.'

124. *Afternoon in Water Street*
Annotated 'Completed 1 July 1949 at 10 Argyle Street' in Notebook II.
Water Street is in Pembroke Dock.

125. *A Letter*
Annotated 'Completed 3 September 1949 at 10 Argyle Street' in Notebook II.
l. 6 *bakestone* – the round, flat cast-iron implement placed on an open fire (or a stove), typically for cooking Welshcakes.
l. 9 *scrallion* – not in OED. The poet identifies it as a Pembrokeshire dialect word meaning 'lean', 'scraggy'.
l. 24 *'tisty-tosty, how long shall I live'* – 'tisty-tosty', more usually an ejaculation of triumph or exultation, is also the name used in parts of Dorset and Somerset (the 'home' the letter-writer refers to in the previous line?) for a bunch of flowers made into a ball by children. Here it also seems to signify a game played with the flowers.

126. *'Remember Charlie Stones, Carpenter'*
Annotated 'Completed 6 September 1949 at 10 Argyle Street' in Notebook II.
The setting is Capel-y-ffin, on the banks of the river Honddu in the Vale of Ewyas, which runs south-eastwards from Hay-on-Wye to Llanthony Priory and beyond. Eric Gill was the leader of a small colony of fellow artists and craftsmen, which for a time included David Jones, that settled there 1924–8. Gill himself carved the inscription on the tombstone that became the title of the poem.
l. 19 *Prating as ill as I?* – 'to prate' is to talk idly and at length.
l. 19 *Over this valley is a well* – St Mary's Well at Partrishow (see 'The Flooded Valley'), where Ishow is said to have been murdered by a traveller to whom he had given shelter and hospitality. Partrishow is somewhat to the south of Capel-y-ffin in the next valley to the west.

127. *O Tihuanaco*
Annotated in Notebook II: 'First draft about 1945. Altered many times. Almost definitive version produced January 1950. Completed 28 March 1950 at 10 Argyle Street.'
The poem purports to be a prayer or chant by Eoi, a priest to Tihuanaco, but the names used in the poem are drawn from a variety of sources. None of them is a deity. Tihuanaco (Tiahuanaco) is a great ceremonial centre that grew up about AD 900 in the southern highlands of Peru, near the Bolivian side of Lake Titicaca, and gave rise to a distinctive style in art and artefacts.
l. 6 *Toxodon* – one of the largest of an extinct group of grass-eating mammals, found as fossils, mostly in South America, and dating from the later Paleocene (about sixty million years ago).
l. 19 *Kayappia* – [Kayapo] one of a number of South American Indian peoples who inhabit eastern and southern Brazil and part of northern Paraguay.
l. 21 *Titicaca* – the highest large lake in the world, between southern Peru and western Bolivia in the Andes.
l. 37 *Illimani* – a peak of over 21,000 feet in the Cordillera Real, the Bolivian section of the Andes. It is about seventy miles from Lake Titicaca.
l. 39 *Copak* – [Capac or Qhapaq] the brother of Pachacuti Inca Yupanqui, who had set himself up as emperor at Cuzco in succession to his father Viracocha Inca.

Notes

l. 50 *Chamak-pacha* – [Pachacamac] an earlier (about AD 600) ceremonial centre of the Tiahuanaco culture with its own variety of pottery, frequently decorated with a griffin-like creature with a winged feline body, human hands and an eagle head.

128. Argyle Street
Annotated in Notebook II: 'Completed at 10 Argyle Street on 14 April 1951.'
l. 3 *house in chancery* – a dwelling of which the ownership is in doubt pending decision of the Lord Chancellor's court.
l. 9 *the haven* – Milford Haven; oil refining and other industries are, in the main, located on the other side of the waterway from Pembroke Dock, near the town of Milford Haven.

129. Riddle
Annotated in Notebook II: 'Completed 4 September 1950 at P.D.G.S. [Pembroke Dock Grammar School].'
The broad answer to the riddle is 'Man'.
l. 3 *crupper* – the part of a horse's rump behind the saddle.
l. 4 *a damned outsider* – this is, at one level, a reference to horse-racing, which is extended forward to the next line and back to 'bucked' and 'crupper' and to 'seahorse' in the first line. Here, however, the 'outsider' is the newborn child, outside the womb and damned because born into original sin.
l. 5 *nap* – a tipster's selection of the horse likeliest to win a race.
l. 5 *An enemy had done this* – from the parable of the wheat and the tares (Matthew 13: 28) 'The kingdom of heaven is likened unto a man which sowed good seed in his field: But while men slept, his enemy came and sowed tares among the wheat', etc. The parable is about good and evil and the final judgement; 'seed', 'sowing' and growth and the mingling of wheat and tares are apt hidden metaphors in this context.
l. 7 *earliest element* – water; see Genesis 1: 2: 'And the earth was without form, and void; and darkness was upon the face of the deep. And the Spirit of God moved upon the face of the waters.'
l. 9 *urban tower* – grown man in his home (his 'castle', as the saying goes).
l. 12 *brass and counterpeace* – anger, strife and war.
l. 13 *Decent an age older* – a variation on the colloquial saying 'a decent age' with transposition of words, that is, 'a decent age' older.
l. 16 *his newest park* – a new house and garden.
l. 19 *Wreathe me with berries and I give back blood* – the berries are those on a bramble.

130. Coed Anghred
Annotated 'Completed at 10 Argyle Street on 14 April 1951' in Notebook II.
The title locates the scene as overlooking Skenfrith, near Abergavenny, from the west. Exploration of the area was an aspect of the research undertaken for the poet's study of the 'Commotion amongst Catholics in Herefordshire and Monmouthshire in 1605', published as *Whitsun Riot* in 1963.
l. 5 *spurge* – plant of the genus *Euphorbia*.
l. 6 *craving stone* – one that bears an inscription wishing that the interred may rest in peace; 'craving' also echoes both 'grave' and, visually, 'carving'.

Notes

l. 9 *cuckoo-comer* – a 'comer' is one who comes, as in 'newcomer'; a cuckoo is an interloper. The description is self-referential: the poet, a Nonconformist, does not belong in the place.

l. 10 *the priest's house* – the use of the definite article in 'the priest's house' indicates particularity, explained in *Whitsun Riot*. The priest was Father Robert Jones, 'chosen instrument of the Counter-Reformation in Wales ... [who, by 1605] ... not infrequently said mass ... at The Darren ... [which] may be identified either with a cottage nowadays called The Sand House, or with one of several other nearby cottages now in ruins, all of them some four hundred yards from the main Skenfrith–Ross road ... Opposite, westwards, stands Coed Anghred Hill' (pp. 22–3).

l. 22 *Robin Caffrey* – refers back to the description of the bird 'with an Irish eye'.

131. The Tyle

Annotated in Notebook II: 'Completed at The Norvals, Offenham 17 August 1951.'

The Tyle (pronounced 'tiller') is a cottage and smallholding overlooking the hamlet of Aber, just above the Talybont reservoir, which Joseph Morgan, the poet's grandfather, took as a tenant in 1895. It survives, unlike Ffynon Fawr, the farm the family occupied subsequently and where Roland Mathias was born. The poem was one of those set to music by David Harries.

ll. 1–2 *In the proud season penitence / Droops* – the poet's admission of guilt, that in his pride he neglects to express his regret.

l. 2 *haulm* – the stem or stalk of a plant (such as potatoes, beans, etc.).

l. 5 *Pressure of water in the ear* – from the nearby presence of Cwm Clydach stream.

l. 10 *cosened stone* – from the archaic 'cosen(ed)', that is 'cousin(ed)' or related.

132. Returning

Annotated in Notebook II: 'Completed at Tŷ Clyd, Brecon 24 August 1951. First verse written at 10 Argyle Street, second at The Norvals immediately previous.'

The poet recounts events on a visit to The Tyle accompanied by his own children.

l. 3 *spindle-trees* – see the note on 'The Forest' (39), p. 298.

l. 9 *the first elements* – the poet's children.

l. 20 *unaccomplished blots* – faults and misdeeds as yet unrecorded.

l. 26 *the missioner's box* – the *Artists in Wales* essay supplies an explanation; recalling his early childhood, the poet writes: 'When I was four and a half and had filled my missionary box more than twice, we left Glyn Collwn ... to join my father in Cologne.'

Notes

THE FLOODED VALLEY (Putnam, 1960)
The following poems included in *The Flooded Valley* had already been collected in *The Roses of Tretower*: 'The Flooded Valley', 'The Path to Dinas', 'Searching Spring', 'Craswall', 'Bablockhythe', 'Camp by the Windrush', 'On the Grave of Henry Vaughan at Llansaintffraed', 'Drought', 'Thomas ap Richard of Doier to the Tower, These', 'A Winter's Day', 'Hawk', 'Pas Seul', 'Pas de Deux', 'Morning: New Jerusalem', 'Afternoon in Water Street', 'Freshwater West', 'A Letter', 'Remember Charlie Stones, Carpenter', 'Argyle Street', 'The Tyle', 'Riddle', 'Coed Anghred', 'Returning'.

Four more poems written after the publication of *The Roses of Tretower* which were not included in *The Flooded Valley* have been inserted in this volume roughly in their chronological positions: 'To the Muse, Wrongheadedly', 'Building a House (in Four Movements)', 'The Lost Kingdom' and 'Friends I Have'.

133. An Age
Annotated in Notebook II: 'Begun 20 October 1954; completed 22 October at 4 Park View Crescent.'
First published in *Dock Leaves* in 1954 (5, 15), this typically autumnal poem reflects a growing awareness of the passage of time. In a note to the editor, the poet described the Pembrokeshire background to the poem as a 'blackberrying day in Cosheston (with the children)'. The setting is near the Neyland–Burton ferry across the estuary of the Cleddau.
l. 7 *The envelope* – a metaphor for the containing air, light, atmosphere of the described scene or event; it is used in other poems by Roland Mathias and in the short story 'The Match'.
l. 9 *Old as Mabon ... wall* – in the tale of Culhwch and Olwen from the *Mabinogion*, one of the tasks set the hero is to rescue from captivity Mabon, who was stolen from his mother's bed when only three days old. The name 'Mabon' is ancient, being derived from Maponos, a Celtic sun-god.

*134. To the Muse, Wrongheadedly**
Annotated in Notebook II: 'Completed 24 August 1953 at Tŷ Clyd, Brecon. First draft, now much altered, about 12 August at 4 Park View Crescent.'
Although not previously published, the poem was read in a BBC radio broadcast, *A Modern Anthology of Poems by Welsh Poets*, 4 March 1954. In discussion with the editor, the poet said it was 'about failing to do better in my poetry'.
l. 1 *A neap tide* – when the high-water level stands at its lowest point.
l. 3 *rout* – disorderly company or occasion.

*135. The Lost Kingdom**
Annotated in Notebook II: 'Begun November 1954. Completed 6 June 1955 at 4 Park View Crescent.'
The poem has not been previously published. Though not readily identifiable in the opening section, its theme is stated in the title. It concerns the poet's Breconshire home and relations, the region of his youth, from which, in 1954, he seemed still in exile. It is a poem about looking back from the autumn of age to the eternal summer of youth.

Notes

l. 2 *the drowned kingdom of our stars* – reference to Cantref y Gwaelod, the fertile land said by legend to have existed where Cardigan Bay now is ('between Cardigan / And Lleyn'), but lost for ever when Seithenyn, the drunken guardian of the sluice gates, allowed the sea to inundate it.

l. 7 *barbary* – north Africa.

l. 19 *Salem . . . The Plough* – chapels attended by the poet and members of his family, the former at Sennybridge, where his uncle David lived, the latter in the town of Brecon.

l. 22 *leagured* – beleagured or besieged.

l. 23 *mummering mouth* – a 'mummer' is one who mutters or murmurs; the phrase suggests youthful inarticulacy.

l. 24 *Senni['s]* – the stream that flows north from the Brecon Beacons to join the Usk at Sennybridge.

l. 53 *Trephilip* – a farm near Defynnog, a mile or so from Sennybridge.

l. 55 *knout* – a stout whip.

l. 58 *bastinadoed* – tortured by having the soles of the feet beaten.

l. 62 *champaign my midgets till* – 'champaign' is an archaic word for open countryside. From the distance of his observation, those who work this land appear 'midgets'.

l. 70 *Lady fain* – one who would be pleased to be (considered) a lady.

136. Scithwen Valley

Annotated in Notebook II: 'Written and completed 27/28 September 1955 at 4 Park View Crescent.'

The valley described is near Crickadarn, on Mynydd Eppynt, roughly midway between Brecon and Builth. The poem is a revised version of 'Scithon Valley', which appeared in *Dock Leaves* in 1955 (6, 18) and was then a straightforward celebration of landscape. The final lines fixed the scene and the denizens of it in the poet's perceptions and art:

> My lambs, my chug away
> In the valley, kestrels bitter after food,
> Mine in this halt to gather and grass in sun for good.

The revision reconstructs the occasion and imposes on the same scene a mood of bitter self-analysis.

137. Conversation on Stackpole Head

Annotated in Notebook II: 'August 1953, Tŷ Clyd, Brecon. First draft earlier, August 4 Park View Crescent.' Lines 2 and 3 were 'Altered 1 February 1954'.

The two lines referred to in the annotation above originally read: 'In the sky wheeling some two score / Gulls mew out their patience near the cut-back cliff'. The poem was read on the BBC radio broadcast, *A Modern Anthology of Poems by Welsh Poets*, 4 March 1954. Stackpole Head is a promontory in Pembrokeshire, about five miles south of the town of Pembroke.

ll. 6–8 *the lame / Emmet will always trundle in the hoppling last / Flax grain of the nine hestors* – 'hoppling' ('hobbled') refers to the ant ('emmet') rather than the flax grain, one of the many examples of transposed epithet among the poems. The lines

Notes

refer to one of the tasks that Ysbaddaden, Chief Giant, sets Culhwch for the hand of his daughter Olwen, in the tale of Culhwch and Olwen from the *Mabinogion*. The giant demands nine hestors of flax seed from which to grow the white linen veil for Olwen's wedding. It seems an impossible challenge until Gwythyr, one of the chosen band of Arthur's knights helping Culhwch, saves a colony of ants from the fire attacking their anthill and in gratitude the ants bring in the nine hestors – all save one seed, which a lame ant brings in before nightfall.
l. 24 *anchusa* – a hairy-stemmed plant akin to borage.

138. Building a House (in Four Movements)*
Annotated in Notebook II: 'First drafts of Parts I and III in 1952. No other work done till February 1954. The whole completed 22 February 1954 at 4 Park View Crescent, Pembroke Dock.'
The poem was published in *Dock Leaves* in 1954 (6, 16). It is about the house in Park View Crescent, the poet's second address in Pembroke Dock. What appears to be a response (making extensive use of colloquial expressions) to the criticism he encountered from some quarters in the town the poet now says was a *jeu d'esprit*.
l. 3 *wirepuller* – one who gains an advantage by exploiting personal connections.
l. 13 *Convolvuluslike* – a compacted simile; convolvulus, commonly termed 'bindweed', twines about its host, often another plant, and produces white, funnel-shaped blooms.
l. 15 *Barrack Hill* – a prominent landmark in Pembroke Dock.
ll. 30–1 *a work . . . Of supererogation* – one that exceeds requirements.
l. 33 *collied syllables* – the syllables in the word 'supererogation' have been gathered together as a collie sheepdog does sheep.
ll. 48–9 *cloudbreath / Mongers* – those who deal in gossip.
l. 51 *Sodom* – one of the 'cities of the plain' destroyed by God because of its wickedness (Genesis 19: 24–6). Angels warn Lot, 'Escape for thy life; look not behind thee, neither stay thou in all the plain; escape to the mountain, lest thou be consumed.'
l. 56 *cully* – mate.
l. 57 *occipitally* – an adverb formed from 'occipital', meaning relating to the back of the head.
l. 59 *The raf come in, the triumvirs* – 'raf', usually capitalized, 'RAF', the Royal Air Force. The 'triumvirs' in Roman history were three men who shared high office, here a flight of three Sunderland flying boats (for air-sea rescue) stationed in the haven off Pembroke Dock during the war years and for some time after.
l. 63 *cumuli* – rounded masses of cloud, an indicator of fair weather.
l. 64 *Preseli*[s] – mountains in north Pembrokeshire, about thirty miles north of Pembroke Dock.
l. 65 *the oil-veined hill* – one adjacent to the oil terminal at Milford Haven.
l. 69 *Gath* – a city of the Philistines, the home of Goliath (I Samuel 17).
l. 71 *cosmopoles* – cosmopolitans, those familiar with many parts of the world.
l. 74 *Concord* – here a verb with the sense of 'harmonize'.
l. 79 *shrublace* – a shoot or branch rooted to produce a shrub, as in layering.
l. 79–80 *byboot / Babylonica* – 'byboot' is an epithet applied to objects or species of uncertain or illegitimate origin, colloquially 'bastard'; *Salix Babylonica* is the weeping willow.

Notes

l. 81 *rue* – shrub with evergreen leaves and a small yellow flower, also known as 'herb of grace'.
ll. 88–9 *God of the Caucasus / And of the Barrack Hills* – the Caucasus is a mountain range between the Black Sea and the Caspian Sea. Here it represents remotely distant places, in contrast to the 'Barrack Hills'. Briefly, God is everywhere.
l. 96 *Rab upon rab* – the poet thought of 'rab' as the red soil or a red hillock.

139. Marston Sicca
Annotated in Notebook II: 'First draft 20 August 1954 at The Norvals. Completed 27 August 1954 at 4 Park View Crescent.' The third stanza, which reads:

> What the poor scholars mutter, the poor I laid
> In the garden, I hardly know.
> Their function is simply to utter
> My alphabet and grave it deeply. The first undertaker only is paid.

was changed on 4 September 1954 to the version as published.

The civil parish corresponding to Marston Sicca (or 'Dry Marston') is called Long Marston. It is situated about five miles south-west of Stratford-upon-Avon and about six miles east of Offenham, where Molly's sister lived in a house named 'The Norvals'. Long Marston once had a famous band of morris dancers. Its church has a number of memorials to members of the Tomes family.

This poem, like the one before it, is a meditation on death. It has, too, that quality of dramatic utterance, like 'A Letter' (126), for example, and its diction is archaic: 'I feel my free soul bounden'; 'its habit bones'; 'unread / Apprentice gravelled in his piece'; 'cry covenant'; 'Graves every mound'; 'mort and unmade'. The impression made by the sound of the poem, read aloud, is important. The poet, who is uncommonly harsh in his judgement of his own work, thinks it a good poem.
ll. 6–7 *the apostles / In their yards* – the 'yards' are the six feet of earth in which they are interred.

140. Orielton Empty
Annotated in Notebook II: 'Begun some time in the summer of 1954. Completed 6 June 1955 at 4 Park View Crescent.'
The poem describes the mansion and park of Orielton, situated about two miles south-west of the town of Pembroke. It was the seat of the Owen family that played a major part in Pembrokeshire life from the seventeenth century until the twentieth. Sir Hugh Owen, b. 1604, a Nonconformist and a notable Parliamentarian in the Civil War, was grandson of Sir Hugh Owen of Bodowen, Anglesey, whose marriage to Elizabeth Wyriott in 1571 began the dynasty. Owens continued owners of the property until 1857 when, in the midst of building a wall round the estate, they ran out of money. Thereafter, a succession of owners and tenants occupied the house and during the 1920s it was sadly neglected. In 1954, it was purchased by R. M. Lockley, the naturalist and writer, author of *Orielton: The Human and Natural History of a Welsh Manor* (1977). Lockley sold it to the Field Studies Council, an independent educational charity, in 1963 and it has since functioned as a field studies centre.

l. 16 *Durgi and Soda* – gundogs whose gravestones at Orielton commemorate them.
l. 16 *Rosebery* – the sixth earl of Rosebery (1882–1974), famous racehorse breeder and owner.
l. 24 *a beldame and her pack* – 'beldame', an archaic word meaning 'old woman' or 'virago', refers to a profligate owner of the estate, while the metaphor 'pack', referring to the crowd of hangers-on, fits the context both of hunting and gaming.

141. Cascob
Annotated in Notebook II: 'Begun at Builth Easter 1955. Completed 25 March 1957 at 4 Park View Crescent, Pembroke Dock.'
The poem was first published in *The Dragon* (the magazine of UCW Aberystwyth), summer 1958. Cascob is a hamlet a few miles west of Presteigne and Offa's Dyke, on the edge of Radnor Forest. It has an ancient church where the Revd William Jenkins Rees was once rector. The poem is a meditation on the ancient past and the ever present fact that life ends. In its various oppositions of ancient and modern, pagan and Christian, life and death, its creation of an atmosphere of mystery and just-concealed horror, and its shaft of colloquial levity – 'For two pins / I'd leave in a hurry' – it resembles the short story 'One Bell Tolling'.
l. 11 *Raised on a druids' mound* – the site was once pagan. This knowledge provides the motive and, to a large extent, the theme of the poem.
l. 12 *a brass of familiars* – the brass plaques placed in the church by friends and relations to commemorate the dead (like that to 'our sister / Elizabeth Lloyd'), but there is a play on words, 'familiar' being also the demon that attends a witch.
ll. 12–13 *habit of clergy* – the liturgy and/or clerical garb and customary repetition of prayers.
l. 13 *pater . . . noster* – 'our father' (repeated).
l. 14 *Three times for Saturn* – reference to Saturnalia, the Roman festival marked by debauchery that was the predecessor of modern Christmas-tide.
l. 18 *Who is it coming?* – the poet says that we do not know the answer. It might be a contemporary Christian or an ancient pagan, God or the devil.
l. 21 *Night follows day* – In a further note to the editor, the poet comments, 'Everything happens, but you don't know how'.

142. Friends I Have*
A previously unpublished poem annotated in Notebook II: 'Effectively written January 1959 at Thorpe House, Coxbench. Final version 27 March 1959.'
l. 6 *the dried poll in fog* – the head, but not out of doors and wet; 'fog' is a metaphor for uncertainty.
ll. 6–7 *Blessing the well / Is customary* – reference to a Derbyshire custom.
ll. 10–12 *pumps / From old levels . . . shift . . . damps / And falls* – sustained mining metaphor to reinforce the sense that the writer constantly draws on his connections with and memories of Wales.

143. For Warren Davies, Two Years Dead
Annotated in Notebook II: 'Completed 30 April 1959 at Thorpe House, Coxbench.' Further slight amendment occurred on 12 November 1959.
  This poem begins a sequence of elegies to significant individuals, his father and

uncle David among them, that continued in Mathias's next book *Absalom in the Tree*. Warren Davies, who attended the same Congregational chapel as the poet, was a carpenter and boatbuilder.

l. 4 *Magnus* – Magnus Barelegs Haraldsson (the son of Harald Hardradi), who led a Viking fleet into the Irish Sea in 1058.

l. 6 *South Hook* – near Dale, on the northern shore of the seaward end of Milford Haven.

l. 13 *Hakin Point* – another location on the northern shoreline of the Haven, adjacent to the oil refinery on the outskirts of the town of Milford Haven.

l. 19 *Chathamward* – to Chatham, a dockyard and former naval arsenal on the estuary of the River Medway, Kent.

l. 21 *Pater tackle* – [paternoster tackle], the tackle of a paternoster line in sea fishing, which has hooks or groups of hooks attached at intervals.

l. 22 *spinnaker* – large triangular sail for running before the wind.

ll. 23, 30 *Church Street . . . Lewis Street* – streets in Pembroke Dock.

l. 37 *Lawrenny* – a village on a point of land between the estuaries of the Cleddau and the Creswell, at the inland end of Milford Haven.

l. 37 *plat* – a plot of ground.

l. 40 *Cleddau* – a river rising on Mynydd Preseli flowing south via a long inlet into Milford Haven.

l. 54 *White-collar jobbers and casuists* – people in white-collar jobs who enjoy argument for its own sake: the poet has himself in mind.

ll. 56–7 *hullabaloo / Break on my chest* – refers to the conversational habit of poking the chest with a finger.

144. The Last Days of Heat
Annotated in Notebook II: 'Completed 7 October 1959 at Thorpe House, Coxbench.'

l. 12 *rhine* – an open ditch.

ABSALOM IN THE TREE and other poems (Gomer, 1971)

145. Chinon
Annotated in Notebook II: 'Drafted 27 August 1960, completed 30, at Thorpe House, Coxbench'. Further amendments were made at 'Tŷ Clyd, 27 October 1961'. The poem was inspired by a visit to Chinon, on the banks of the river Vienne in France, and the recollection of a line from an old textbook, 'Shame on a conquered king'. The castle at Chinon overlooks the river. In the eleventh century it passed into the hands of the counts of Anjou, one of whom, Henry Plantagenet, became Henry II of England in 1154. Chinon, at the heart of his French possessions, was one of his favourite residences. In 1185 he fought against his sons Henry and Geoffrey on behalf of his third son Richard (known as the Lionheart), and later, when he sought to advance instead his youngest son, John, against Richard and Philippe Auguste, King of France, whose claims he was finally obliged to acknowledge. These are the causes of the 'shame' on him. He died at Chinon, 6 July 1189.

l. 9 *Aquitaine, England* – Henry II was heir to Anjou, Normandy and England, and ruler of Aquitaine by virtue of his marriage to Eleanor of Aquitaine in 1152.

Notes

146. Brynafan: First Light
Annotated in Notebook II: 'Drafted August / September 1961. Completed 11 November 1962 at Thorpe House, Coxbench. / *The Anglo-Welsh Review* No. 31 (entitled Another Dawn).'
The poem appeared in The *Anglo-Welsh Review* in 1963 (13, 31). It is discussed in the Introduction, page 34.
l. 1 *cruck* – exposed traditional curved-beam structure supporting the roof.
l. 9 *tod* – a traditional name for a fox.
l. 11 *the recovery of tricks* – an extension of the casual greeting 'How's tricks?'
l. 30 *methusalem with a wish* – [Methuselah] is the Old Testament patriarch said to have lived 969 years and thus a symbol of longevity. The idea expressed here is the human desire for survival, 'until the call comes', the poet added in discussion with the editor, 'and the hounds are after him'.

147. A Last Respect
Annotated in Notebook II: 'Drafted some time in the winter of 1962/63. Polished up 20–24 October 1963, at Thorpe House, Coxbench. Corrected again 30 April 1964. *London Welshman* July 1966; *Welsh Voices* 1967.'
l. 17 *Cantref* – a shoulder of hill between the Usk and Pen-y-fan in the Brecon Beacons.
ll. 18–19 *the pinnacles / Of Sion* – the holy hill of ancient Jerusalem and so the heavenly Jerusalem or the kingdom of heaven. Here the visible hill is transformed into a vision of heaven.

148. Sarnesfield
Annotated in Notebook II: 'Begun after a visit to Sarnesfield on the return north after the Easter holiday 1962. Pottered at several times since, and finally polished up on 4 & 5 January 1964 at Thorpe House, Coxbench.'
Sarnesfield is an English village about ten miles north-west of Hereford, close to the Welsh border.
l. 10 *butt[s]* – several meanings of the word are relevant: those connected with the imagery of warfare at the beginning of the poem (target and rifle-butt), and the colloquial (especially American) abbreviation of 'buttocks'.
ll. 24–8 *The cock was a gold achievement, as full / Of himself and breasted every way at once / As if the sun had left its quartering. / An hour at stand: York Herald in the north-east corner / With a grass-train of Marshalls forming* – words used to describe the scene have double meanings, one set being drawn from heraldry. An 'achievement' is a coat of arms; 'a quarter' is one of the four quadrants into which an armorial shield is divided; the college of heralds, incorporated by Richard II in 1483–4, has an Earl Marshall and includes six heralds, one of whom is York Herald. The 'grass-train of Marshalls' is also a row of graves of the Marshall family.
l. 31 *John Abel* – John Abel (1577–1674), an architect of timber houses, built the old town halls of Hereford, Ledbury and Leominster, and was loyal to the monarchy. When Hereford was attacked by Parliamentary forces in 1645, he constructed cornmills for the use of the besieged townsfolk.
l. 42 *the five travellers* – the poet, his wife and their three children.
l. 44 *mistery* – a skilled craft, in medieval times often regulated by a guild. The involvement of guilds in cycles of religious dramas led to the latter's being termed 'mistery' (now Mystery) plays.

l. 44 *aery vat* – like 'envelope' in other poems, a metaphor for the surrounding scene and atmosphere.

149. Departure in Middle Age
Annotated in Notebook II: 'Written for the East Midlands Eisteddfod at Leicester on 14 March, 1964. Actual date of composition some time at the end of January. Thorpe House, Coxbench. / *Poetry Wales* Vol. 2 No. 2 / *Welsh Voices* 1967 / *The Lilting House* 1969 / Professor H. M. Waidson (UC Swansea) 8th May 1974. "Departure in Middle Age" *Swiss Journal*.'

It is not clear what the final reference in the note means. The original title of the poem was 'Leaving Wales'. Its theme parallels the short story 'The Only Road Open', in which the narrator travels the snowbound route south from Brecon past the entrance to the valley where he was born and recalls the burial of his father in the chapel graveyard there.

150. Freshwater West Revisited
Annotated in Notebook II: 'November 1964, Quarry Bank. / Published in *Poetry Wales* No. 1 Spring 1965. / *Welsh Voices* 1967.'

See 'Freshwater West' (123). The penultimate line tells us it is six years from the experience that produced the earlier poem. The writer's winter of the spirit persists, or has come again.

l. 5 *socius* – Latin for 'fellow'. Sea and land, mutual antagonists, remain nevertheless in company, one with the other.

l. 12 *girds* – an archaic use of the word, meaning 'invests with strength'.

l. 18 *bloodwreck* – a coinage for the terrible results of conflict, echoing 'bladderwrack', a seaweed that strews the dividing line between sea and land.

151. For an Unmarked Grave
Annotated in Notebook II: 'Begun at Tŷ Clyd, Brecon, August 1965. Completed 25 & 26 November at Quarry Bank, Inkberrow.'

Another October poem, for and about the poet's Uncle David, his father's brother, to whom he was particularly close. The grave is unmarked because there was insufficient money to raise a headstone.

l. 6 *hard-tack* – the notoriously tough ship's biscuit, meant to keep.

l. 11 *Cwmcamlais* – the valley of a stream that flows north to meet the Usk at Abercamlais, a few miles east of Sennybridge.

l. 14 *since your loins were water* – a biblical-sounding expression meaning 'since you were a boy'.

ll. 16–18 *companied / A nephew wide over Senni and the nearer / Hill of day* – in a note to the editor, the poet explained: 'My uncle took me to Pen-y-waun-dwr (near Fan Frynych) where we consumed bacon and eggs in a mountain cottage. It was my twenty-first birthday.'

152. The Least Echo
Annotated in Notebook II: '19–28 August 1966. Tŷ Clyd (19–20) and Quarry Bank. / *Mabon One*, May 1969.'

It is a poem *à clef*, about a teacher at Pembroke Dock who was in various ways remarkable. As we see from the final stanza, he had received a gallantry award for war service in Burma, achieved a First in Greats and made himself a mathematician. But he also had a flaw – ambition, which expressed itself as a constant need to bring the least job done to the attention of the headmaster. There is an element of unflattering self-portraiture in the first stanza in the scorn and distaste shown by the Head's reception of the teacher's ingratiating demonstration of the latest of those 'thin / Victories' that others would not bother to mention, and, in the second stanza, in the Head's (poet's) description of himself as others might view him, 'a talker, incontinent, fill- / Dyke in every month, chewing the fat / Of my colleagues' achievements'.

ll. 37–51 *True but strange . . . At 9 Victoria Terrace* – identification of a parental home in Hopkinstown is authentic, though the address is not. These lines suggest an explanation for the teacher's behaviour: having gained a first-class degree, he returned home and, in a momentary aberration, anticipated the joy of telling his parents of his success, forgetting they were dead and buried. The final two lines of the poem reinforce the suggestion and add a measure of understanding.

l. 53 *Fifty-One in the Quarter* – fifty-one seconds in the quarter-mile, an achievement then.

l. 55 *dusty ball without echo* – compare 'the illimitable ball of existence' in the short story 'Take Hold on Hell', which explains the metaphoric use of 'ball' in the poem.

153. Absalom in the Tree

Annotated in Notebook II: 'Drafted at Swansea, circa 8–18 March. Revised at Quarry Bank 22–29 March 1967. Dispatched 30 March as entry for the Redditch Festival of Arts. 2nd Prize, Redditch Arts Festival, June 1967. / BBC Midlands Poets Radio 4: 8 August 1968.'

The poem takes as its starting point the Bible account of Absalom, the third of the six sons of King David, all by different wives, who were born in Hebron (II Samuel 3: 2–6). His story is told in II Samuel 13–18. Absalom kills his brother Amnon because he ravished Absalom's sister, Tamar. After the murder, Absalom flees to another country where he remains for three years, returning only as a result of the (devious) intervention of Joab on his behalf. But two years pass and he is not allowed into his father's sight. In chapter 14, much is made of Absalom's beauty and especially the length and thickness of his hair. In the same chapter Absalom sends for Joab to ask him to intercede on his behalf with David and, when Joab fails to come, orders his servants to set fire to Joab's field of barley. Then Joab does as he is bid and David and Absalom are reconciled. In chapter 15 we learn how Absalom intercepts all those who come as supplicants to the king and gradually 'stole the hearts of the men of Israel'. Under the threat of the conspiracy David and his entourage and the priests of the temple flee into the wilderness. David's spies persuade Absalom to lead an attack against his father in person. With the battle imminent, his people beg David not to participate in the fight. In a long day of slaughter David's forces are victorious. Chapter 18: 9 and 10 bring us to the opening of the poem: 'And Absalom met the servants of David. And Absalom rode upon a mule, and the mule went under the thick boughs of a great oak, and his head caught hold of the oak, and he was taken up between the heaven and the earth; and the mule that was under him went away. And a certain man saw it, and told Joab.'

l. 32 *David* – anointed king over the house of Judah following the death in battle with the Philistines of King Saul and his son Jonathan, David's friend.

l. 48 *Mephibosheth* – the lame son of Jonathan and a supporter of King David, who sends a servant, Ziba, to him in the wilderness bearing food and wine for his host.

l. 53 *Joab* – son of Zeruiah and brother of Abishai, David's less than scrupulous ally, who would have killed King Saul as he slept (I Samuel 26: 8). Joab himself is unforgiving and vengeful. David has sent Abner, another potential enemy, away in peace, but Joab does not forget that Abner killed his brother Asahel in battle and bides his time: 'And when Abner was returned to Hebron, Joab took him aside in the gate to speak with him quietly, and smote him there under the fifth rib that he died' (II Samuel 3: 27). Although David mourns Abner and recognizes that 'the sons of Zeruiah be too hard for me' (II Samuel 3: 39), in the battle against his own son, Absalom, he appoints Joab and Abishai to lead two of the three parts of his force, admonishing them before they set out: 'Deal gently for my sake with the young man, even with Absalom' (II Samuel 18: 5). Joab's response comes in the same chapter, verse 14: '. . . he took three darts in his hand, and thrust them through the heart of Absalom, while he was yet alive in the midst of the oak'.

154. Some Tight-lipped Wave

Annotated in Notebook II: 'Written out first on 13 October 1967 (ten days after the disaster, which was at 4.17 am, on 12 October) completed 15 October at Quarry Bank, Inkberrow. / *Anglo-Welsh Review* No. 39 & *Poems '69*.'

Hugh and Lily Griffiths were friends of the poet killed in the destruction of a Comet airliner by a terrorist bomb en route for Nicosia, Cyprus, 13 October 1967.

l. 2 *undulant* – 'moving in waves', an adjective used as a noun.

l. 6 *Kastellorizon* – a small Greek island (also known as Megisti), east of Rhodes, very close to the Turkish coast.

l. 8 *Minoan savageries* – 'Minoan' is the name given to the civilization of Bronze Age Crete; here, however, it signifies the unscrupulous politics of the regime of the infamous military junta ('the Generals') in Greece, which came to power in 1967 and countenanced acts of terrorism.

l. 10 *Slade* – a hamlet near Cosheston, a few miles from Pembroke Dock.

155. Indictment

Annotated in Notebook II: 'Written first and completed 3 January 1968 at Quarry Bank, Inkberrow.'

The poem is based upon Mathias's research for *Whitsun Riot*. The historical background of the poem is the struggle for influence at court between the faction led by Robert Devereux, earl of Essex, who was for some time favourite of Elizabeth I, and that led by Robert Cecil, Viscount Cranbourne, later Elizabeth's Secretary of State, who was the victor. The family origins of both Essex and Cecil were partly in lands on the Welsh border, the former in Archenfield, the area around Ewyas Harold in Herefordshire, the latter in Monmouthshire. Their rivalry was represented in the Welsh Marches by Paul Delahay of Allt-yr-ynys, a manor house in the parish of Walterstone, steward of the Cecil lands in Monmouthshire, and John Arnold of Llanthony, a supporter of the earl of Essex. In the latter half of 1600, Essex began to plan a coup designed to end the ascendancy of Cecil. If it had succeeded, this would have secured patronage for his followers, including several Catholics who were later to be involved in the Gunpowder Plot. The coup, on 8 February 1601, collapsed within the day. Essex was seized, tried and executed shortly after. Among those followers executed with him was his steward, Sir Gelly (or Gelli) Meyrick, who had extensive lands in Radnorshire and the March, and had sought financial backing for his master among Herefordshire squires with Catholic sympathies. The substance of the interrogator's utterance is a series of questions drafted by the historical Delahay at the height of the turmoil in 1601.

l. 1 *John Arnallt* – 'Arnalt' in texts of the period; today he would be known as John Arnold.

l. 7 *the treasoned Earl* – Robert Devereux, earl of Essex.

ll. 10–13 *Sir Robart Cicill / A Cook by his mother, my Lord / Bacon a Cook by the same / Error* – Robert Cecil, like his father, William Cecil, became Secretary of State, both to Elizabeth I and to her successor, James I. He was responsible for securing the accession of James (VI of Scotland) to the English throne. As earl of Salisbury, he built Hatfield House, where Mathias undertook research for *Whitsun Riot*. Robert Cecil's mother was a daughter of Sir Anthony Cooke of Gidea Hall, Romford, Essex. Another daughter of the same family married Sir Nicholas Bacon, attorney and (in 1558) Lord Keeper of the Great Seal. These were the parents of Francis Bacon (1561–1626), the statesman, writer and philosopher, first Baron Verulam and Viscount St Albans. Francis Bacon was one of those appointed to investigate the causes of Essex's revolt and was largely responsible for the earl's conviction.

l. 41 *the Council at Ludlow* – the Council in the Marches of Wales, first appointed under Edward IV and Henry VII to administer estates of the Prince of Wales, and based at Ludlow. In the reign of Henry VIII, Thomas Cromwell made it a permanent part of Welsh administration. It was finally dissolved in 1689.

156. They Have Not Survived
Annotated in Notebook II: 'Very largely written on Sunday, August 11, 1968 at Quarry Bank. Finally amended August 18. / *Transatlantic Review* / Peter Finch's anthology (India) / *Poems 1970*.'
First published in *Poet: An International Monthly* (Illinois, USA), April 1969. This is a key poem presenting a perspective of the poet's father's family history back to its origins on the 'melancholy Rhos' and a view of himself as an outsider who, unlike them, has survived and prospered.

l. 2 *cenedl* – in this context perhaps best translated as 'clan'.

l. 3 *tallut* – a Gower variant of the west of England dialect word 'tallet', meaning the loft formed by laying boards on the joists over a stable, cowshed or the like.

l. 5 *porringer* – an archaic word for a small basin.

l. 10 *Rhos* – moor; here Rhos Llangeler, Carmarthenshire, not far from Llandysul.

l. 18 *milgis* – greyhounds.

ll. 27–8 *Coughing in terraces above / The coal* – one branch of the family settled in the Rhondda.

157. Testament
Annotated in Notebook II: 'Completed 10 / 1 / 68 at Quarry Bank. / *Anglo-Welsh Review* No. 41 / *Poems 1970*.'
In a note to the editor the poet commented, 'Many other people can't remember exactly what made them grow. I cannot be sure what I remember . . . I was not a

rebel [against the traditional forms and practices of the Nonconformists] . . . I was the child of belief.'

l. 17 *old Model Army* – a metaphor for those older values of Nonconformism referred to above which the poet supported. It derives from the 'New Model Army' formed under Sir Thomas Fairfax and Oliver Cromwell in 1645 that defeated English and Scots royalist forces.

158. God Is
Annotated in Notebook II: 'Largely written in August 1968: the last two lines and the title finally decided 1 January 1969, at Quarry Bank.'
See Introduction, p. 35.

159. A Letter from Gwyther Street
Annotated in Notebook II: 'First draft early November 1968, at Quarry Bank after the half-term visit to Pembrokeshire. All other drafts and final version worked on at Deffrobani 2 October 1969.'
Gwyther Street is in Pembroke Dock; Siân, Herbie, Doc and Elis are all friends from the poet's days there. The poem is about change and death but it is devoid of the usual expressions of Christian hope and faith in an afterlife where friends are reunited. The dead are out of reach of companionship and give no sign from beyond the grave.
l. 2 *Barafundle* – a bay between Stackpole Quay and Stackpole Head on the coast of Pembrokeshire south of Pembroke Dock.
l. 8 *deckspar* – rubbish cast up on the beach.
l. 12 *Llanion* – an outlying part of the town of Pembroke Dock.
l. 13 *W.V.S.* – Women's Voluntary Service (now WRVS).

160. Not Worth the Record
Annotated in Notebook II: 'Written in answer to a request from the Arts Council / Dial-a-Poem. Drafted 4/1/70: altered and completed 5/1/70 at Deffrobani. Recorded 7 August 1970 at Museum Place. / *Poems 1970*.'
The poem attempts to engage and challenge the listener, and to shock with its confessional mode and brusque tone – see Introduction p. 35. It is characteristic of the self-castigating stance of the poet that its theme is the recognition of personal failure, even in carrying through the evil wish to the sinful deed.
ll. 23–4 *Hard by the pillar / I willed down evil* – as in the story of Samson, who brought the roof down upon his Philistine captors by toppling the pillars that supported it (Judges 16: 25–31).
l. 26 *shearling choir* – a 'shearling' is a sheep that has been shorn once, therefore, the young; the poet considers his role as a headmaster. In the short story 'Incident in Majorca', Mallinson, the ill-fated headmaster who has brought a party of boys on an expedition to the island, ponders the essential natures of his pupils in these terms: 'Not one in all those four hundred souls, he knew, could contend with the fiend. They were all souls like his, helpless, weak, mischievously wicked, often kindly or cruel in a small way.' This has a good deal in common with the present poem and with others (like 'Brynafan: First Light' and 'God Is', for example) that allude to man's, or more often the writer's own, weakness and propensity to sin.

Notes

161. *For Jenkin Jones Prisoner at Carmarthen, These*

Annotated in Notebook II: 'First three stanzas roughed out in 1968. Remainder, rough, 1969. Final version save a few points, early January 1970. The above version completed and copied 28 January 1970 at Deffrobani. / *Poems 1970*.'

Another poem based upon a historical episode and historical characters. The period is that of the Civil War and its aftermath, more specifically 1660, the year of Charles II's return as king. The 'H.V.' at the end of the poem is Henry Vaughan, physician in and around Brecon and supporter of the king's cause in the Civil War. Jenkin Jones, whose upbringing and education were close in time and place to Vaughan's, is a Puritan, from his youth militantly for the people and the Nonconformist faith. Yet he prevented the denunciation of Vaughan as a royalist, as 'Mathew Havard told me, choking / Behind his hand'. In the last stanza the return to England of Charles II is alluded to, and the report that Jenkin Jones had fired pistol shots into the church door at Llanddetty ('Talybont' is preferred in the text to preserve the rhythm of the line) and ridden off. He was apprehended and imprisoned at Carmarthen, but H.V. cannot rejoice in the fall of an enemy 'Who troubles my heart in failing'. The poet referred to the same story in his earlier prose essay, 'Take Me Over the Border', published in *The London Welshman* (January 1961):

> Tŷ Mawr, the birthplace of Vaughan's co-student, the Jesus servitor Jenkin Jones. Oxford men, all of them, Henry [Vaughan] and Leander [Jones, 'Archbishop Laud's room-mate at St John's who came from his long exile in Rome to tempt his contemporary with a cardinal's hat'], but separated at the last towards the ultimate poles of belief. Too beautiful a country for warfare, even the warfare of ideas, one might think; but beautiful only in the gold of its trees, the dark coil of its river and the plotted fertility of its bottom acres. Behind are the bald heads of the hills, the heads that look different as the light changes and yet never really change. It was in their communion that Jenkin made his last rebellion, fired his two shots into the church door and rode off, inflexible as ever, into the unhistoried night.

An important source of the poet's knowledge of the era is *The Puritan Movement in Wales, 1639 to 1653* by Thomas Richards, published by the National Eisteddfod Association in 1920, but it does not contain the more colourful details of the life of Jenkin Jones.

l. 5 *Approver[s']* – Jenkin Jones was an 'Approver', under the 'Act for the Better Propagation and Preaching of the Gospel in Wales' of 1649. This meant that, along with twenty-four others so nominated, he could recommend for approval and certification by Parliament's appointed Commissioners 'that godly and painful men, of able gifts and knowledge for the work of the Ministry, and of approved conversation for Piety, may be employed to preach the Gospel'. As 'pastor of a congregated church', he was admitted to the rectory at Llanddetty on 18 November 1657. Though mainly associated with the Brecon area, he preached more widely.

l. 12 *Sions Tŷ Mawr . . . servitor at board* – Jenkin Jones, employed at Vaughan's Oxford college to wait at table.

l. 25 *Werin* – [gwerin], folk, the common people of a place.

l. 25 *faze* – a synonym for 'lose'.

l. 30 *Morlais brook* – above Vaynor, near Merthyr Tydfil.

l. 32 *Courage Gronow* – a typical Puritan name, but the character and event are imagined.

l. 34 *Capten Shinkin* – Jenkin Jones, who also had the task of enlisting troops for Parliament.
l. 41 *catabaptism* – It was alleged that Jones 'dyd speake and hold oppynyon against the baptisme of children'.
l. 51 *Llanddetty* – a neighbouring parish to Talybont, near Brecon.
l. 52 *comfit* – a sweet.
l. 53 *Mathew Havard* – an imaginary character.
l. 55 *Breda* – a town in Holland where Charles II lived in exile and where, in 1660, he issued a 'Declaration'. This offered a general pardon and amnesty for all offences committed during the Civil Wars and promised that as king he would rely on the advice of a free parliament and allow a measure of religious freedom. The declaration paved the way for the Restoration.

162. Under Quinag
Annotated in Notebook II: 'Completed at Deffrobani New Year's Day 1970: first draft 28 December 1969. / Professor H. M. Waidson U.C. Swansea 8th May 1974 / 'Under Quinag' *Swiss Journal*.'
Quinag is a mountain a short distance inland on the far north-west coast of Scotland, about twenty-five miles south of Cape Wrath, which has a view to the west of islands in Eddrachillis Bay. The theme of the poem (in the poet's words, 'about free will and choice') emerges in the second stanza.

163. The Fool in the Wood
Annotated in Notebook II: 'First written draft in my room at the University of Brest, April 1970. Stanzas 1–4 virtually completed July 1970 at Deffrobani. Stanza 5 and the last quatrain 19 August 1970 at Deffrobani (after my return from the Br. Council course at Swansea.) / *The Anglo-Welsh Review*, Spring 1971 / *Poems '71*.'
l. 11 *hest* – behest, call.
ll. 14–15 'O / *Itroun Gerhez Mari*' – the Breton means 'O Lady Virgin Mary'; the dialect is that of the Léon region in the north-west of Britanny.
l. 24 *Cozenage* – the practice of deception.
l. 46 *Montfort* – Simon de Montfort, a minor baron from the Île de France whose piety was matched only by his ruthlessness. In due course he led the Albigensian Crusade which despoiled much of the south of France.
l. 46 *Auray* – a town in southern Brittany, on an inlet of the Golfe du Morbihan, a few miles west of Vannes.
l. 48 *architrave* – the moulding around a door or window, here used metaphorically.
l. 70 *March* – border, frontier.
l. 71 *Anatomy* – body, or, in older usage, a skeleton.
l. 72 *king's . . . evil* – scrofula.

164. Au Cimetière de Brest
Annotated in Notebook II: 'First draft April 1970 at the University of Brest (written and part typed). This abandoned October 1970 (*c*.26) and a fresh start made. Completed 30 October 1970 at Deffrobani. / *Poetry Wales*, Winter 1970.'
Brest is a major military and mercantile port on a bay at the tip of the Brittany peninsula. Many of those buried in its cemetery were seamen and the commanders

of ships. Several of the commemorated dead are named. The poem is a 'dance of death' with its own stately rhythms occasionally intruded upon by the blare of loudspeakers calling consumers into the nearby shops. In a note to the editor, the poet commented on the great difficulty he had in framing the poem: 'My first feeling was hopeless. Decided to take Vernon Watkins's advice in "Ophelia" (Sapphic stanza) "Stunned in the stone light, laid among the lilies".'

l. 6 *auger* – a tool with a helical cutting edge for boring holes in wood.

l. 7 *coign* – projecting corner.

l. 10 *Rade* – harbour; 'Rade de Brest' is the name given to the bay at the end of the Brittany peninsula.

l. 14 *Temeraire[s]* – in this context the French word 'temeraire' is perhaps best translated as 'reckless'. It is famously the name of the ship in a painting by Turner, *The Fighting Temeraire* (see the note on 'The Past' (28), p. 296).

l. 22 *Capitaine de vaisseau* – ship's captain.

l. 29 *L'Amiral* – admiral.

l. 39 *Monoprix . . . Sigrand* – large department stores.

ll. 45–6 *Ce qui / Reste de l'honneur* – what remains of honour.

165. Channel Saint

Annotated in Notebook II: 'Completed, all but the word 'braces', at the University of Brest in April 1970. Final form 6 December 1970 at Deffrobani.'

In the Notebook, the poem is entitled 'Saint (Across) Over the Water'. The Celtic saint named in this poem is particularly attractive to the poet because he voyaged from Brittany to Pembroke. In the former he is known as Guénolé and in the latter as Winwaloe. (The later poem entitled 'Guénolé', in 'Tide-reach' (189, ii) offers further detail and gives the Welsh version as 'Wynole'.)

l. 1 *Ohé* – 'Hullo' or 'Ahoy' ('Ohé du bateau' is 'Ship ahoy').

ll. 2–3 *Guénolé / Tower* – Guénolé was said to have come to Pembrokeshire 'swimming', and he made a tower there.

l. 4 *Landevennec* – a small town on the estuary of the Aulne in the south-eastern corner of the Rade de Brest. Visitors can gain admission to the grounds of the famous abbey founded by Guénolé, said to have been the burial place of King Gradlon in the sixth century. The abbey was pulled down at the Revolution.

l. 8 *Pardieu* – an exclamation (literally 'By God').

166. A Celtic Death

Annotated in Notebook II: 'Completed 18 November 1970 at Deffrobani. First draft at Brest in April. Worked on 11–18 November. / *Poetry Wales*, Summer 1971 / *Poems '71*.'

The poem, originally entitled 'L'Ouessant', decribes the harsh landscape of the Île d'Ouessant and the weekly haemorrhage of loved ones off to school or work on the mainland.

l. 1 *the Latin* – that is, the word *Finistère*, 'end of the land', taken directly from the Latin.

ll. 11–14 *the shadowy / Ness long drowned . . . seas of myth* – a 'ness' is a promontory; the lines allude to the legend of the drowned city of Ys, off the coast of Finistère, which has an almost exact Welsh parallel in the story of Cantref-y-Gwaelod.

l. 15 *Léon* – the coastal zone to the north and west of Brest with innumerable offshore reefs and islets.
l. 20 *Roman wall* – The poet explains that 'the whole of Celtdom' was once part of the Roman Empire except Léon and outlying parts like Ouessant. Although no sign of it remains, a wall would have kept the 'uncivilized' out.
l. 21 *Oeussant* – the Île d'Ouessant, a rock-bound island, about five miles long and two miles broad, some twelve miles off the tip of Finistère, at the end of the Brittany peninsula. It is known as Enez-Huessa (Isle of Terror) in Breton because of its long history of shipwrecks.
l. 26 *tamarisk* – an evergreen shrub with feathery branches that bears small white or pink flowers. It is often planted on coasts.
l. 38–9 *Bugel Eussa* – the name of a ferry plying between Ouessant and the mainland.
l. 40 *Baie du Stiff* – a bay on the eastern coast of Ouessant, its mouth facing the mainland, where the island's ferry port is located.
l. 59 *Grandmothers, stiff with the coiffe / And rheumatics* – the coiffe is the traditional lace headress worn by Breton women, its pattern varying from place to place. Even thirty years ago it was worn only by the old in remoter areas and it is rarely seen now except on religious and other festivals.

167. New Lease
Annotated in Notebook II: 'Completed 10 December 1970 at Deffrobani. / *Spirit* (USA).'
The poem marks the early stages in the acquisition by the Mathiases of a dilapidated cottage, known as The Wells, at St Twynells, Pembrokeshire, which the sanitary inspector who surveyed the property declared 'Done for'. The poet's analysis of his own motives in buying the house is characteristically harsh: he sees himself as 'Mercenary, a wanderer with an eye / For walls like yours'.
ll. 8–9 *Llifiau / From beyond Bannog* – Llifiau was the Pict who, in the *Gododdin*, joined the warriors setting out to attack Catraeth (Catterick). 'Bannog' is the name given to hills near Stirling in Scotland, famed, much later, as the scene of the Battle of Bannockburn.

SNIPE'S CASTLE (Gomer, 1979)

168. After Christmas
Annotated in Notebook II: 'Roughed out (all but stanza 4) early in January 1972.'
The poem's four four-line stanzas have a regular half-rhyme pattern (*aabc*) at the ends of lines; in addition, the penultimate syllable of the second line in each stanza rhymes with the final syllable of the last line. Repetition is a feature of the first line in each stanza. Also, line length is fairly regular – mostly six syllables in the first three lines and five in the last. In sum, the poem is an example of complex patterning. There are only two punctuation marks – the colon used twice – between the first word and the final full-stop, but there is no enjambement at the ends of stanzas. In a note to the editor, the poet said the poem came to him 'above Garthbrengy [about half way along the narrow mountain road between Brecon and Builth] past

the church. It became a difficult poem only because the feeling of sloes in sticks came back to me on the next day.' Though coloured by the religious significance of the season (hence the references to 'virgin' and 'maiden', 'Protestant' and 'catholic' – with a small 'c' – and 'the Child'), it is essentially descriptive.

l. 2 *scantlings* – small morsels, in this case the few remaining berries and leaves in hedgerows.

l. 3 *a bone from the lost tribe* – a metaphor for 'twig'.

l. 4 *Convivial song* – the phrase needs to follow 'hang' in l. 2.

ll. 13–14 *All humours and all wills / Consult the dark* – all mankind is obliged to accept the dark that winter brings.

ll. 15–16 *except fools / Trading a whisper that the Child / Is back from Egypt* – except those, considered foolish, who believe in the light of Christ.

169. A Stare from the Mountain
Annotated in Notebook II: 'Completed 18 November 1971 at Deffrobani, in response to an urgent request for a poem for the 21st issue of *Poetry Wales*.'

The poem describes sky and landscape viewed from a mountain. As is so often the case, it is a late autumn scene, red ploughed soil already stiff with frost. The appearance of a horse, its outline illuminated by the setting sun so that it seems 'marked with redemption', prompts the poet's self-examination for similar signs, with typically unsatisfying results. But down below, paradoxically, a rubbish tip and the sunstruck ancient town have for a moment their share of glory.

l. 2 *trug* – a shallow oblong basket made of wood strips (see also 'the struts', 'the wicker rents' in the next line).

l. 12 *Yscir mountain* – Mynydd Aberysgir, a few miles north-west of Brecon, on the western slopes of the valley of the Afon Ysgir, which joins the Usk at Aberyscir.

l. 28 *fining* – making fine, or refining.

ll. 29–30 *the town, taken by the sun and arked . . . Domesday Book* – The poet sees in these lines images that are almost contradictory. They suggest either 'man again doing things to destruction, or man hoping to find the new ark of promise'.

170. Squirrel-path
Annotated in Notebook III: '*c.*March 18, 1972 at Deffrobani. / *Dragon's Hoard* [an anthology for schools], 1976.'

l. 2 *zany* – a clown.

l. 16 *Reduncle* – another squirrel.

l. 42 *catamountain* – literally 'mountain cat' (puma or lynx), but metaphorically a wild, quarrelsome person.

171. Porth Cwyfan
Annotated in Notebook III: '10 November 1972 at Deffrobani. / Poetry Now programme, BBC Radio 3, 1 March 1973 / *Poems '73*.'

Porth Cwyfan is a walled, Celtic-church-crowned islet near Aberffraw, Anglesey, accessible at low tide. The poem is in the confessional mode of Mathias's later work. In part, it is prompted by nationalism and the kind of Anglophobic attitude that characterizes certain poems by R. S. Thomas, but it comes to a different conclusion. See Introduction, p. 41.

ll. 1–2 *wind / Bluffing* – a verbal form used in the figurative adjectival sense of 'bluff', that is, 'big, surly, blustering'.
l. 5 *fribbles* – trifles, small pieces.
l. 7 *I can call nothing my own* – a brief, simple sentence that expresses a world of alienation from this particular place and, by extension, from Wales and Welshness.
ll. 8–9 *the branchy / Shifts of voyage everywhere* – cast-up litter.
l. 11 *marram* – sea reed or bent grass which binds together the sand on a shore.
l. 17 *Cwyfan* – a monk who accompanied St Beuno to north Wales in the early seventh century.
ll. 18–19 *belled / Wetherlike towards God* – a bell-wether is a sheep with a bell about its neck that leads a flock; 'bell-wether' is sometimes used satirically of the leader of a group. The lines suggest that faith was simple in the primitive church and believers sheep-like, in contrast with the poet's complex response to God and belief.
l. 21 *Porth China* – a small bay to the north of the church.
l. 24 *Beuno* – widely commemorated in Powys, his birthplace, and north Wales, where he is particularly associated with Clynnog Fawr. He is said to have restored to life Gwenfrewi (St Winifred) and Digiwg after they had been beheaded. A spring that started from drops of blood shed at the beheading of Gwenfrewi is known still as St Winifred's Well, Holywell, Flintshire (the well of G. M. Hopkins's 'The Leaden Echo and the Golden Echo' – see Introduction, p. 12).
l. 26 *a few wild settles* – toppled wooden benches in the church.
ll. 27–8 *Roger Parry, / Agent to Owen Bold* – a name and description on a tombstone.
l. 29 *skew-whiff* – a colloquialism, meaning askew or slanting out of line.

172. Fool's Fingers
Annotated in Notebook III: 'Begun 1 March 1973 at Deffrobani: completed 4 March ditto. / Dial-a-poem January 1974 / *Poems '74* / *Poetry Wales* Summer 1974.'
ll. 14–15 *Soar's / Unheeding backs* – the phrase serves to identify the location of the poem. Soar is a hamlet on the banks of the Nant Bran, a stream that flows south-eastwards from the army's 'Sennybridge Training Area' to join the Usk near Aberbran, a few miles west of Brecon. The 'backs' are those of cottages backing on to the stream.
l. 31 *Struwwelpeter* – the shockheaded, long-fingernailed creation who figures in a series of gruesome narrative poems for children written and illustrated by medical doctor and artist Heinrich Hoffman, first published in 1844. The poet encountered the stories as a child in Germany.
l. 32 *fat shilling digits* – 'shilling' here has the force of 'substantial', derived from the Latin equivalent coin *solidus*, also the root of 'solid'.

173. In the Swiss Jura
Annotated in Notebook III: 'Begun 31 July 1973: completed 7 August 1973 at Deffrobani. Alterations 8/viii/73 after a day in bed with fever. / *The Anglo-Welsh Review* No. 50.'
The poem was published in *The Anglo-Welsh Review* in 1973 (22, 50). It telescopes the emotion of a holiday with the writer's daughter, in 1972, before she left for a

two-year stint in Madagascar as a 'volunteer' teacher, to a single mountain walk. The ants' nests they see both foreshadow (at least in the father's expectations) the experience of famine his daughter will encounter and recall shared experiences of her childhood, the stories of giants and beanstalks and of 'Culhwch and Olwen'.
l. 17 *tarquiniad* – a nonce word, coined from the legendary line of early Roman kings, the Tarquins.
l. 27 *Gwythyr* – another reference to the character in the story of 'Culhwch and Olwen', see 'Conversation on Stackpole Head' (137). 'Gwythyr' is the subject of the sentence that extends over the remaining fourteen lines of the poem.
l. 34 *luff coast of Africa* – 'luff' means 'weather side', here the east coast.
l. 37 *emmets, pismires (red truculents moreover)* – two dialect words for 'ants' followed by a descriptive phrase for aggressive red ants.

174. La Tène
Annotated in Notebook III: 'August 1973 at Deffrobani. / *The Anglo-Welsh Review* No. 50.'
First published in the same number of *The Anglo-Welsh Review* as the previous poem. La Tène is a shallow area at the northern end of Lake Neuchâtel (or Neuenburg to German-speakers) in Switzerland where, in 1858, an amateur archaeologist, Colonel Schwab, recovered almost two thousand Celtic artefacts, many of which were intricately decorated in ways scholars had not previously seen. The find inspired a search over a wider area and the place gave its name to a culture. The La Tène culture originated in about the mid-fifth century BC, when the Celts came into contact with Greek and Etruscan influences from south of the Alps. It came to an end about 15 BC under the constant pressure of Germanic peoples from the north and the Roman Empire from the south.
ll. 14–16 *Celts . . . pull out and intertwine the tips / Of marsh quakers* – the quakers are quivering tendrils of vegetation; in Celtic art the forms of flowers and creatures were twisted into intricate knot patterns.
l. 21 *armed entrepôt* – a commercial centre to which goods are brought for distribution, a function served by the Celtic settlement at La Tène. The Celts were a warrior race and many of the finds had a military function.
l. 25 *the Vougas, father and son* – original discoverers of signs of Celtic settlement in the lake as successive hot summers reduced the water level.
l. 26 *fouilles* – archaeological excavations, digs.
l. 28 *bêtise* – a foolishness; the lake was foolish to betray its secrets.
l. 32 *Biel, Genève, Neuchâtel* – towns in Switzerland where there are substantial museum collections of Celtic artefacts. Biel is at the northern end of the Bieler See, Neuchâtel nearby on the shores of Lake Neuchâtel, and Genève on Lake Geneva (Lac Leman).
l. 33 *commote* – [commot] neighbourhood.
l. 35 *setts* – stones, cobbles.
l. 35 *the Thielle* – [La Thielle] a Swiss river that enters Lake Neuchâtel at its south-western end and issues from it at its north-eastern end.
ll. 35–6 *the language- / Line* – that which separates French- and German-speaking Switzerland.
ll. 36–7 *Vandal, / Hun . . . Goth* – Germanic peoples who invaded large parts of Europe and north Africa and sacked Rome in the fifth century.

Notes

l. 38 *rhine* – a large, open ditch – see also 'The Last Days of Heat' (144).

l. 41 *Wotan* – the supreme god in Germanic mythology.

ll. 43–4 *over and under / Worlds touching and not touching* – the description of the poet's walk along the breakwater echoes the indistinct separation of life in this and the otherworld characteristic of Celtic mythology.

ll. 45–6 *fract / Back* – a coinage: refract, or reflect.

l. 54 *unguents* – ointments.

ll. 65–6 *Celts . . . uncompromised chasers* – reference to the Celtic skill in chasing metal.

ll. 58–9 *earth-god horns the stag, Esus / Become Cernunnos* – in Celtic art and mythology, the attributes and identities of Cernunnos, stag-horned god of the underworld, and Esus, god of plenty in this world, are sometimes merged.

ll. 62–3 *Vix . . . Lassois* – Vix is a village near Chatillon-sur-Seine in the department of Haute-Marne, France. In 1929, excavation of the hill where the village is located, Mont Lassois, revealed that it was the site of a substantial Celtic trading centre.

l. 66 *Cub-lipped Etruscan jars* – receptacles with spouts in the form of animal mouths made by the Etruscans, an ancient people of central Italy. Their civilization influenced the Romans, who destroyed them in about 200 BC.

175. Burning Brambles
Annotated in Notebook III: 'Completed 27 December 1973 (draft some weeks earlier) at Deffrobani. / *Aquarius* No. 8 February 1976. / *Poems '76*.'
See Introduction p. 41.

176. Is it the Same Country?
Annotated in Notebook III: 'Completed *c.*14 January 1974, at Deffrobani. / *Poetry Wales*, Summer 1974.'

The poet pictures himself 'deer-stalkered . . . in my vented coat / And earflaps', the cartoon-like epitome of the moneyed exile who has bought a small piece of the land his forebears sweated over for negligible returns. He sees himself also like a tramp, 'toes stubbing out vilely from gravelled socks', a traveller without a true home of his own, scrabbling for a toehold in a place where 'the prophet / Walked common and scatheless'. The poem ends with a typically dramatic utterance that extends the biblical conceit of the prophet in the wilderness and combines it with a clear reference to his peasant ancestry among the squatters who cultivated the harsh soil of Rhos Llangeler. The title of the poem is an incomplete question: is it the same country that bore the peasantry on the Rhos?

l. 2 *mirror's bevel* – the edge of the mirror set at an angle to the surface – see also 'Beacons' (68).

ll. 10–11 *gwair / Rhos cwtta* – [cwta] literally 'short hay of the moor', that is, poor harvest.

ll. 20–3 *the prophet / Walked common and scatheless, all forty days and nights / To Horeb, crying that every bush by the squatters' / Verge has a boast, is messaged and hugely on fire* – these lines combine the story of the squatters on the moor who built their homes at the side of the road (the 'squatters' / Verge') with that of Elijah, who, unlike the poet, dressed humbly and, when Jezebel threatened to kill him, went at the Lord's command forty days and nights into the wilderness (I Kings 18 and 19). Fire is strongly associated with the miraculous deeds of Elijah, but the allusion to the bush 'messaged and hugely on fire' is from Exodus 3: 2, when the Lord calls on Moses.

177. Pwll Llong, Pwll Whiting
Annotated in Notebook III: 'Completed *c.*20 January 1974 at Deffrobani. / *Poetry Wales*, Summer 1974.'
Pwll Llong and Pwll Whiting, literally 'Ship's Pool' and 'Whiting Pool', are neighbouring rocky inlets approximately half way between Strumble Head and St David's Head on the north Pembrokeshire coast, near Abercastle. This is essentially a descriptive poem, but with strong contrasts in its imagery between the brightness of the first stanza and the sombre allusions to war and suffering in the second.
ll. 7–8 *Strumble . . . Tyddewi* – two notable Pembrokeshire headlands at the far southern edge of Cardigan Bay.
l. 9 *fallen faces* – cliff faces.
l. 12 *reiver* – [Scottish dialect] bandit, plunderer, despoiler: here, the waves undercutting the coast and causing cliffs to crumble into the sea.
ll. 15–16 *the skeletal aspect / Two Poles had* – eye-like features of the shattered cliff face recall images of the suffering caused by the war.
ll. 17–18 *this no more than exuberant / Noise in the distance* – from the military installation at Trecwn or the rocket-firing base at Aberporth; either could be the origin of a warlike rumble which reminds the pacifist poet of the horror of war.

178. Blue Blood and Englishmen
Annotated in Notebook III: 'Completed 14 February 1974 at Deffrobani. / *Planet*. / *Poems '76.*'
The poem was first published in *Planet* 24/25, August 1974. It tells the story of the poet's mother's father and chiefly concerns (1) his grandfather's bitter suspicion that local farmers had conspired against him in Welsh when he was buying equipment and livestock at auction for his first farm tenancy and the lifelong mistrust of all to do with the language that flowed from it; and (2) his fruitless search for an aristocratic ancestry in Herefordshire, a claim that his grandson subsequently found had been exaggerated.
l. 3 *Todmorden* – a town in Lancashire where the poet's grandmother taught as a young woman.
l. 6 *the Ffawyddog* – Y Ffawyddog is a village on the hillside above the Usk overlooking Crickhowell.
ll. 6–7 *stony white / With trade* – he worked as a mason and small builder in a family concern in Cardiff, before ill health drove him to return to the cleaner air of Breconshire and life as a farmer.
l. 16 *gambos* – heavy farm wagons.
l. 32 *Glat* – a gap in a hedge.
l. 33 *Glottis* – the opening between the vocal cords, here a metaphor for language.
l. 36 *Bridge Court* – the name of the ancestral home, preserved in the family.
ll. 38–9 *a farm in Kingstone, gave it by estimate / To a stalwart yeoman of Cobbett's* – the grandson, poet and historian, found Bridge Court on the Ordnance Survey map of south Herefordshire on the edge of the village of Kingstone, an area he

researched for his book *Whitsun Riot*. William Cobbett (1763–1835) prolific writer on political and economic affairs, is perhaps best remembered for his *Rural Rides*, a collection of essays published in 1830. Bridge Court then dates from about the beginning of the nineteenth century when it was the property of a yeoman, that is, a respectable farmer who owned his land.

179. The Anchorite
Annotated in Notebook III: 'Completed 13 June 1974 at Deffrobani, as an entry for the Stroud Festival. Alterations 24 December 1974. / *Poetry Wales*.'
The poem was first published in *Poetry Wales* 11, 4, Spring 1976. Its source is a book the poet acquired in 1956, *Myths and Legends of the Celtic Race* by T. W. Rolleston, first published by Harrap in 1911. Rolleston summarized the narrative of Maeldúin's 'wonder-voyage' from a nineteenth-century translation of an Irish manuscript of about 1100, *The Book of the Dun Cow*. The poem deals freely with only part of this summary. It focuses on the voyagers' landfall on the Island of the Anchorite, and adopts the device of allowing the anchorite (or hermit) to foretell some of the adventures that will befall them.
Stanza 1:
ll. 1–3 *Eighteen and one from fosterage / Seventeen men and Diuran / Rhyming for Maeldúin* – the number of voyagers is significant because Maeldúin, who has set out to avenge the killing of his father, has been warned by a Druid that he must take only seventeen companions. At his departure, however, his foster-brothers plead to be allowed to go with him. For his transgression in permitting them aboard, all are doomed to a long and dangerous voyage. One of the party, who has an active role in various adventures, is named 'Diuran the Rhymer'.
ll. 3–4 *the bridge / Of glass* – They are delayed on one island by a bridge of glass, leading to a fortress, that throws them backwards when they seek to cross it.
Stanzas 2–11:
l. 7 *An island dressed by an anchorite* – on a wooded island full of birds, they find a hermit, whose only clothing is his hair. He tells them that he put to sea with a sod of his native country (Ireland) under his feet and that God turned the sod into an island that grows by a foot's breadth and one tree every year.
l. 13 *three-skin curragh* – an ancient Irish boat of wickerwork covered with hides. At the advice of the Druid, Maeldúin's has skins 'lapped threefold, one over the other'.
l. 40–4 *Every tack . . . leviathan . . . nudges . . . Homeward* – a 'leviathan' is a sea monster. Their long journey is circular in that they will at last return home, where the mission of vengeance does not end bloodily but with Maeldúin forgiving his father's assassin.
ll. 47–8 *the original mean / Tragedy* – the murder of Maeldúin's father.
l. 49 *flotson* – an archaic form of 'flotsam'.
ll. 50–2 *the last / Of your foster-brothers, Maeldúin, / Will die in his laugh* – it falls to one of Maeldúin's foster-brothers (the last survivor of them) to explore the Island of Laughing Folk. As soon as he lands he begins to laugh and play with the inhabitants and refuses to leave.
l. 55 *child winds* – light winds.
l. 58 *arcanum* – a hidden thing, a profound secret.
l. 64 *aliform[s]* – an adjective meaning 'wing-shaped', here used as a noun.

Notes

ll. 65–6 *Expectant harms / Swam out to Maeldúin's company* – they have more dangers to face before they achieve the end of their quest.

180. The Damson Tree
Annotated in Notebook III: 'Completed 14 October 1975. Alterations 24 October 1975 & later. / SEWAA [South-east Wales Arts Association]: Dial-a-poem 20/ix/76.'
l. 1 *Manascin* – [Nant Menasgin] a stream that rises near Fan y Big in the Brecon Beacons and joins the Usk at Llanfrynach a few miles south-east of Brecon.
l. 2 *Setts* – stones, cobbles, here used broadly to denote the rocky valley bottom.
l. 9 *cwtch* – a place to shelter or hide.

181. Snipe's Castle
Annotated in Notebook III: 'The Wells, 15 & 16 February 1977. / *The Times Literary Supplement*, 4 March 1977. / *Poems '78*.'
In a note to an American friend, Michael J. Collins, the poet provided some background to the poem: 'The ruins of a cottage near The Wells in Pembs. Nobody locally could tell me the origin of the name. Preseli – in north Pembs 30 miles off. "up from off" is Pembs dialect for "a stranger".'
Although there is half-submerged criticism of interlopers, better-off than the locals, not belonging to the place and not fitting in, there is a good deal of playfulness in the man/bird imagery, the colloquial diction and the tone of the poem. In the absence of more information, the poet gives Snipe, who is a stranger and therefore 'egregious', that is, he stands out in a way that is not particularly likeable, some characteristics associated with the bird – 'picking in seed corn secretly', because, though their food usually consists of worms and molluscs, snipe also eat seeds, and 'grudging the time of day', because they are mainly twilight birds and not so often seen in the open as other waders. The outstanding feature of the bird is its long bill, used for grubbing in mud. Punningly, the locals, also partaking of the bird image, are said to be 'longer billed and taxed than you / A lot'. The final image of the speckled figure 'grubbing a while longer in the dull / Dark rain' is more bird than human.

182. On Llandefalle Hill
Annotated in Notebook III: 'First draft Jubilee Tuesday, June 7, 1977, on Llandefalle Hill. Worked on at The Wells June 11 and 12. Completed at Deffrobani June 14, 1977. / ACGB [Arts Council of Great Britain] *New Poetry* 4.'
Llandefalle [Llandyfalle] Hill is rather less than four miles as the crow flies north-north-east of Brecon. The poem is about the passage of the seasons and the unseasonableness of weather (a familiar theme), the historical place of man in this environment and God's constancy to mankind.
ll. 5–6 *exiguous / To the advantage* – of scant advantage to.
l. 16 *tormentil* – a low-growing, trailing herb with bright yellow flowers.
l. 17 *Brown felt umbrella-handles* – the shoots of bracken.
l. 23 *hendre* – winter dwelling; originally the homestead of farming folk who had their 'hafod' or summer house with their beasts in the hills.
l. 30 *wasted tribes* – ourselves.

183. May-trees Climbing
Annotated in Notebook III: 'Drafted and altered several times during December 1977 at Deffrobani. Final version 27 December 1977.'
The point of the poem, the poet explained in a note to the editor, is that he is not looking for beauty. The title was originally accompanied by a dedication – 'For Molly'.
l. 8 *perfectscope* – a stereoscope, an optical instrument allowing photographs to be seen as though in three dimensions.

184. Sir Gelli to R.S.
Annotated in Notebook III: 'Begun at The Wells, September 1977. Completed at Deffrobani, 15 December 1977. *Planet* 42, April 1978.'
In the persona of Sir Gelli, Mathias responds to 'Sir Gelli Meurig', a poem by R. S. Thomas (in *Not That He Bought Flowers*, 1968), which depicts him as a dupe, misled into conspiracy and treason alongside the earl of Essex by the promise of pecuniary rewards. The poem thus takes its place among those spun off by his research for *Whitsun Riot*, notably 'Indictment', in which Sir Gelli's propensity for violence in support of his master is alluded to. In the present poem he protests his manliness as well as his conviction of the rightness of his cause. Sir Gelli, who had extensive lands in Radnorshire and the March, and had sought financial backing for his master among Herefordshire squires with Catholic sympathies, was one of the followers of Essex who were executed with him. 'Lamphey' and 'the Devereux' will be familiar to readers of Mathias's short story 'The Palace'.
l. 1 *intelligence* – in the archaic sense of 'information' or 'news'.
ll. 6–7 *All / That I cherished, all, lay in the head* – Sir Gelli was beheaded.
ll. 8–10 *Gladestry . . . Wigmore . . . Llanelwedd* – places in the March where Sir Gelli had residences: Gladestry is about six miles north of Hay-on-Wye; Wigmore is a few miles south-west of Ludlow; and Llanelwedd is now that part of the town of Builth on the Radnorshire side of the Wye.
l. 10 *recusants* – those Roman Catholics who, from the sixteenth century to the eighteenth, did not attend services of the Church of England, as was required by law.
l. 10 *puritans* – Christians, particularly in the sixteenth century, who adhered to strict moral and religious principles.
l. 11 *Essex captains* – those who, like Sir Gelli, commanded forces under the earl of Essex.
ll. 11–12 *waiting on black-browed / Judgement* – that is, Sir Gelli's judgement.
l. 14 *happentimes* – chance occasions.
l. 15 *Cadiz* – a port in south-west Spain, sacked by a naval force under Essex in 1596.
l. 17 *pinnace* – a small, usually two-masted, vessel that attended a man-of-war, supplying it with stores, dispatches, etc. The description also serves as an image of Sir Gelli's relationship with Essex.
l. 21 *Penfro squireling* – a minor landowner in Pembrokeshire.
l. 21 *squill* – a coastal plant bearing small blue or purple flowers.
l. 23 *coneys* – rabbits, but used here in the archaic sense of fools or dupes.
l. 23 *the Devereux* – Robert Devereux, earl of Essex. He inherited the earldom at

the age of nine and later became ward to William Cecil. His widowed mother married Robert Dudley, earl of Leicester, who subsequently brought him to court and, in 1586, took him on a campaign to the Netherlands. There, his cousin, Sir Philip Sidney, died, leaving Essex with the ambition to succeed him as an icon of Puritan chivalric virtue. For a time, particularly in the 1590s, his charm and good looks made him the favourite of Elizabeth I, but after a succession of military failures he fell out with the queen. Finding himself in debt and, as he thought, surrounded by enemies at court, he gathered a group of would-be heroes and attempted a *coup d'état* in February 1601, which failed miserably and at once. Essex and many of his fellow conspirators were tried and executed.

l. 24 *Lamphey* – the palace near Pembroke, which was one of the Welsh residences of the earl of Essex.

l. 26 *saturnine* – of gloomy temperament.

ll. 31–2 *the spell of Llwyd son of Cil Coed that Manawydan / Knew when he came from plying his trade in Lloegr* – a character from the *Mabinogion* identified in the tale of 'Culhwch and Olwen' as one of Arthur's uncles. He appears in 'Manawydan Son of Llŷr' to explain that he cast the spell upon the seven cantrefs of Dyfed that caused all the dwellings and people and flocks and herds to disappear and imprisoned Pryderi and Rhiannon. Manawydan had been a shoemaker in Lloegr (England).

l. 33 *Tyburn* – the place of public execution in London until 1783.

l. 34 *Cuffe* – another of the Essex faction.

185. Memling

Annotated in Notebook III: 'Completed 24 December 1977 at Deffrobani.'

Hans Memling (?1430–94), a German-born painter of religious works and portraits, noted for the beauty and harmony of his style. He was very successful during his lifetime: Bruges city records show that by the 1480s he had amassed a fortune sufficient to become a moneylender. The poet visited the Hospital of St John in Bruges (the Memling Museum), where among the treasures displayed are a number of his paintings, including those decorating the shrine of St Ursula, an object of exquisite beauty incorporating six panels by Memling that tell the story of Ursula's voyage and martyrdom.

l. 1 *Seligenstadter* – Memling was born in Seligenstadt am Main.

l. 2 *escalins* – coins of the period.

l. 4 *Brugge* – the Flemish name of Bruges, a city in north-west Belgium, centre of the medieval European wool and cloth trade.

l. 5 *Dom of Köln* – the cathedral of Cologne.

l. 6 *Ursula, that little bear of the Celts* – a fifth-century Celtic British princess who is said to have set out on pilgrimage to Rome accompanied by eleven thousand virgins. All were massacred by the Huns at Cologne. The saint's name is derived from the Latin 'Ursa', meaning 'bear'.

l. 11 *burgher* – respectable citizen of a medieval town.

l. 12 *Huns* – barbarian peoples of Asiatic origin who invaded the Roman Empire in the fourth and fifth centuries AD.

l. 15 *Vlamingdam* – a street in Brugge (Bruges).

l. 16 *reliquary* – a repository for relics, particularly those of saints.

Notes

ll. 17–18 *Hospital / Of St John* – a building dedicated to St John where in medieval times pilgrims rested on their journey.
l. 20 *the paradox that has us all by the throat* – characters and events that legend tells us belong to the fifth century are portrayed as though they belong to the fifteenth. Examples are given in ll. 24–9.
l. 26 *Charles the Rash* – also known as Charles the Bold, of Burgundy, brother-in-law and ally of the English king, Edward IV. He was eventually defeated by the Swiss and lost his life at Nancy in 1477.
l. 27 *arbalest* – a large medieval crossbow.

186. To a Tombstone Fragment in the Garden Path
Annotated in Notebook III: 'Begun 24, completed 27 January 1978 at Deffrobani.'
ll. 12–13 *Merch . . . ragor* – 'daughter . . . and also'.
l. 16 *Locus* – the place (where she lived).

187. Brechfa Chapel
Transcribed in Notebook III without note of date or place of composition.
Brechfa and Brechfa Pool are some nine miles north-east of Brecon, on the mountain above the village of Llyswen.
ll. 3–4 *coot / With his off-white blaze and queasy paddle* – waterbird with black plumage and a distinctive flash where the upper part of the white beak extends in a plate between the eyes and on to the forehead (hence 'bald as a coot'). If disturbed, it paddles for the nearest cover.
l. 18 *Black-backs* – lesser black-backed gulls, scavengers that occasionally nest in colonies in moorland bogs.
l. 21 *brabble* – a rare synonym for 'squabble', which has the onomatopoeic force of 'discordant babble'.
l. 26 *kindred wall* – one that enfolds chapel and graveyard in a kind of kinship.
l. 27 *Legend* – the words carved on a gravestone.

188. Madoc
Transcribed in Notebook II without note of date or place of composition. Most of the fair copy of this long poem 'commissioned by the BBC in 1971 at the instance of the Welsh Arts Council' appears under the title 'An Act of Significance' in that earlier notebook, between 'New Lease' (10 December 1970) and 'A Stare from the Mountain' (18 November 1971), where space appears to have been left for it. The space was not big enough, however, and some of the lines of Gwenllian's seventh speech and what remains of the text following are written on the blank flyleaf at the back of the book. The poem was first published in *Webster Review* (magazine of Webster College, St Louis, Missouri, USA), Spring 1974.

The poet's interest in this topic was of long standing, substantially predating his scholarly review of Richard Deacon's *Madoc and the Discovery of America* in *The Anglo-Welsh Review*, 38 (1967), in which he asserted that Deacon had made a case for the Welsh origins of the Mandan Indians 'that simply cannot be pooh-poohed'. Despite the doubts cast subsequently by historians like Gwyn A. Williams, he remains convinced of the historical basis of the story of Madoc and the pre-Columbian settlement of America by voyagers from Wales led by Madoc and his half-brother Riryd. The introductory paragraphs give a brief account of the voyage and the story of the search for the Welsh Indians. Among the sources for the poem are Richard Hakluyt's *Voyages* (1582), David Powel's *The Historie of Cambria* (1584), *The Discovery and Conquest of Terra Florida by Don Fernando de Soto* in the translation of Richard Hakluyt, published by the Hakluyt Society in 1851, *The Journals of Lewis and Clark*, edited by Bernard DeVoto (Boston, 1953), and Richard Deacon's *Madoc and the Discovery of America* (London, 1967). A number of the characters who speak or are mentioned in the poem are historical (details are given in the notes that follow); others, including Gwenllian, Einion, Llywarch, Catrin, Rhodri mab Hywel Fychan, Rhun, Rhisiart, Cynwal, Gwenwynwyn, Geraint and Gronw Bach, are imaginary.

l. 11 *Cherokee* – an Iroquoian Indian nation who inhabited eastern Tennessee and the western Carolinas. Some commentators have linked them with the 'Welsh Indians'.

l. 40 *Dafydd* – Dafydd ab Owain Gwynedd, a half-brother of Madoc.

ll. 70–1 *John Evans, Evans Waunfawr / In Gwynedd* – in 1792, John Evans (1770–99), who came from the village of Waunfawr, near Caernarfon on the coast of north Wales, agreed to accompany Iolo Morganwg on a quest to find the Welsh Indians reputed to inhabit the upper reaches of the Missouri. When Iolo withdrew, Evans proceeded alone and became one of the first white men to ascend the Missouri, some 1,800 miles above its junction with the Mississippi. In the course of his long journey he was imprisoned by the Spanish governor of St Louis and eventually entered the service of the Spanish government. While acting on behalf of Spain, he spent the winter of 1796 with the Mandans before returning to St Louis in July 1797. He remained loyal to Spain until his death in New Orleans in May 1799. His report to the Honourable Society of Cymmrodorion, which had sponsored his original venture, categorically denied that the Mandans had any Welsh roots. It has been argued that he falsified this finding because he was in the pay of Spain. Gwyn A. Williams in *Madoc, the Making of a Myth* (1979) concluded that Evans had made a significant contribution to the exploration of the American West and that he had reported accurately to the Cymmrodorion Society.

ll. 51–2 *White faces peering over / The eastern slopes* – settlers from England.

l. 74 *Iolo* – Iolo Morganwg (Edward Williams, 1747–1826), poet and antiquary, a major contributor to the later development of the Madoc myth.

l. 75 *Gwyrfai* – a river in Caernarfonshire near Waunfawr.

l. 91 *Coosa* – a river in the state of Alabama, USA.

l. 97 *Riryd, the great lord of Clochran* – another half-brother of Madoc, who features in both Irish and Welsh stories about seafarers who disappeared on voyages of exploration. Clochran is in Ireland, where Riryd is said to have inherited or acquired his lordship. In a note to the editor the poet said that Gwenllian's speech, from which this phrase is taken, is indebted to David Jones's *In Parenthesis*, Part 4, pp. 79–83, 'This Dai adjusts his slipping shoulder straps . . .'

l. 114 *Gwennan Gorn* – the name of the vessel that carried Madoc and his followers to America, derived from tales of a magical ship said to have sailed from the old harbours at Abergele and Afon Ganol and associated with the hero's departure from Wales.

l. 111 *Eryri* – Snowdonia, the heart of the kingdom of Gwynedd in the Middle Ages.

Notes

l. 134 *crester* – a sailing ship riding the crests of the waves.

l. 151 *Abercerrig* – an unidentified port in north Wales from which Madoc is said to have set sail. Deacon (p. 96) quotes an ancient manuscript of port records listing ships missing at sea. Those from 'Aber-kerrik-guignon' include Madoc's 'Gwennan Corn' and Riryd's 'Pedr Sant'. He argues that 'Aber-kerrik' is the modern town of Abergele, a few miles from the Caernarfonshire–Denbighshire border.

l. 163 *Owain Gwynedd* – king of Gwynedd (*c*.1100–70), an able statesman who, though forced to pay tribute to Henry II, laid the foundations of the pre-eminence enjoyed by Gwynedd under his grandson Llewelyn Fawr.

l. 168 *Muskhogees* – [Muskogee] another name for the Upper Creek Indian nation (and also for the language of a wider grouping), who originally occupied the plains of Georgia and Alabama. Their first verifiable contact with Europeans was in 1538, when Fernando de Soto invaded their territory. They too have been linked with the 'Welsh Indians'.

ll. 204–6 *[Madoc] died / Seeking another heaven, one truer / To your first imaginings of peace* – Powel's *Historie of Cambria* declares that, after the death of Owain Gwynedd, several of his sons fought for the succession. Madoc left them in contention and sought peace for himself and his followers across the ocean.

l. 214 *cobs* – ridges.

l. 216 *dogwood* – a tree of the genus *Cornus*, which has dense clusters of white flowers. There is a fine specimen in the poet's garden.

l. 228 – *Pedr Sant* – [Saint Peter] the name of the second vessel in Madoc's little fleet (see 'Abercerrig' above).

l. 248 *coracles* – small, basket-shaped boats made of wickerwork and covered with skins or other waterproof material.

l. 257 *Mynydd Disgwylfa* – a translation into Welsh of 'Lookout Mountain', at De Soto Falls, Alabama. It is the site of of one of three pre-Colombian forts, originally built of stone, within a radius of seventy miles of the town of Chattanooga.

l. 266–7 *little / Tuskegee* – a fictitious Indian. The poet borrowed the name from the city of Tuskegee, seat of Macon county, east-central Alabama. Some eight miles to the north-west is Fort Decatur, once headquarters of John Sevier (see the note on l. 395, below) while he acted as commissioner determining the boundary of the Creek Indian lands. Tuskegee, with a population of about 12,000, might reasonably be described as 'little'.

l. 269 *Lledr* – a tributary stream of the River Conwy, near Dolwyddelan, Gwynedd.

l. 275 *you heavy-footed Taliesin* – Taliesin is the famed Welsh poet of the late sixth century, one of whose boasts was that he spoke 'perfect measure'; Riryd is being accused of talking too much.

l. 181 *blerwm, blerwm* – child-like sound and gesture with finger to lips, again suggesting Riryd talks too much. The phrase is taken from Charlotte Guest's translation of *Hanes Taliesin*. The bards and heralds of the court of Maelgwn approach the king to sing his praises and earn largesse. As they pass the corner where he has hidden himself, 'Taliesin pouted out his lips after them, and played "Blerwm, blerwm", with his fingers upon his lips.' The bards and heralds cannot prevent themselves from repeating this gesture before the king.

l. 292 *Muscle Shoals* – Oconostota, chief of the Cherokee nation (see above l. 11), told of a battle between his people and the 'White Indians' at 'Muscle Shoals', in the

Chattanooga area, as a result of which the Whites agreed to quit the place and find a new home.

l. 293 *fracted* – broken off.

l. 301 *Gwyneddigion* – an influential literary and cultural society, consisting mostly of men from north Wales. It was this society that collected money to send John Evans in search of the Welsh Indians.

l. 308 *Cradoc Freichfras* – a figure of Welsh origin, said to have been the first king of Silurian Gwent after the departure of the Romans, who became a legendary hero of the Arthurian cycle. Here, however, the poet has in mind the Caradoc (Caractacus) who fought against the Romans about the middle of the first century AD and was eventually defeated and taken in chains to Rome, where his pride and noble bearing won him the admiration of his captors.

ll. 309–13 *Cunedda. . . Deganwy* – Cunedda, *fl. c.*450, a chieftain of the Gododdin, a British tribe from the area around present-day Edinburgh, travelled south to help expel the Irish from what is now Wales. He was accompanied by his eight sons, each of whom is said to have established a dynasty in Wales. The only credible one, however, was that which had its seat at Deganwy, near Conwy, in the reign of Maelgwn, King of Gwynedd, the grandson of Cunedda.

ll. 310–11 *Arthur, Artorius dux* – legendary battle-leader ('dux') of the British in their attempts to repel the invading Saxons, whose name may be derived from the Latin Artorius. The real Arthur belongs to the late fifth–early sixth century.

l. 325 *Osunuka* – Riryd's Indian bride; an imaginary figure.

ll. 362–3 *Hernando / de Soto* – *c.*1496–1542, Spanish explorer, the son of one of Pizzarro's conquistadors who sought to extend Spain's New World empire on the north American continent. He received information about 'White Indians' from fellow countryman Juan de Ortiz and others.

l. 364 *gente blanco* – white men.

l. 365 *Chiaha to Tasqui* – Chiaha, a location mentioned by de Soto, has been placed by researchers who have traced his journey in what is now the state of Georgia, on the Eluwee branch of the Coosa river. 'Tasqui' [Tascaluca] is another spot on de Soto's route some fifteen miles south of Chiaha in what is now Alabama.

ll. 377–8 *Adelantado / Of Florida* – chief administrator or governor of the province, an appointment de Soto received from the King of Spain.

l. 379 *Guachoya* – a village on the Mississippi, about twenty miles below its confluence with the Arkansas river, where de Soto died on 21 May 1542. A number of his men were glad to see him die because they hoped his successor would lead them home.

ll. 380–1 *the greatest / River of all* – the Mississippi, discovered by de Soto in 1541.

l. 383 *Pizarro* – Francisco Pizarro (?1475–1541), Spanish conqueror of Peru 1532–3. De Soto's father had proved an outstanding captain for Pizarro and amassed great wealth in the course of the conquest of Peru.

l. 389–90 *Cannasauga, Hiwassee* – rivers in North Carolina and Tennessee.

l. 398 *Castile* – a former kingdom comprising most of modern Spain.

l. 395 *Oconostota* – a chief of the Cherokee nation who, when questioned by John Sevier, founder of Tennessee, in 1782, reported that the forefathers of his tribe had fought against the white people in what is now Carolina and that when hostilities ceased the whites left, to settle eventually on some of the branches of the Missouri.

Notes

l. 398 *Iroquois* – a group of Indian tribes with a common language who occupied territory around Lakes Ontario, Huron and Erie in what has become the states of New York and Pennsylvania and the southern parts of Ontario and Quebec in Canada. The Iroquoian tribes shared a distinctively warlike culture.

l. 417 *the wider river* – the Missouri.

ll. 425–6 *The new / Virginians have us now grappled by the throat* – by 1838 (the given date at which these voices are speaking from their various vantage points in time) the Cherokees had fought and lost numerous battles against white settlers. Their power was effectively broken after defeats in 1776 and they surrendered vast tracts of territory in North and South Carolina.

l. 449 *catspaw[s]* – a person used by another as a dupe.

l. 450 *the skinner from Glyn Myfyr* – Owen Jones (Owain Myfyr, 1741–1814), co-founder of the Gwyneddigion Society in 1770 and editor of *The Myfyrian Archaiology of Wales* (1801 and 1807), which brought into print and preserved a great volume of ancient Welsh poetry and historical texts that until then existed only in manuscript. He was born in Llanfihangel Glyn Myfyr, Denbighshire and, having learned the trade of skinner, set himself up in business in London with considerable success.

ll. 451–2 *Iolo / The mason* – Iolo Morganwg (Edward Williams, 1747–1826), who was born at Llancarfan, Glamorgan and for much of his life worked as a stonemason while acquiring a reputation as a poet and immense antiquarian knowledge. He helped to edit *The Myfyrian Archaiology*, invented the Gorsedd of bards and had a great influence on Welsh letters and culture.

l. 462 *Pueblo* – a town about 120 miles south of Denver in the state of Colorado.

l. 462 *Bernalillo* – a town north of Albuquerque in the state of New Mexico.

l. 470 *Canucks* – Canadians, especially those of French origin.

l. 474 *Mandans* – among the most easterly of the Plains Indian tribes, they occupied territory along the Upper Missouri, lived in large fortified villages and had developed a number of features (such as their wickerwork and skin boats) that bore a resemblance to Celtic settlements. They were virtually wiped out by two smallpox epidemics, in 1781 and 1837.

l. 493 *Philadelphia* – in south-east Pennsylvania, today the fourth largest city of the USA. Founded by Quakers in 1682, it became the financial and cultural centre of Britain's American colonies.

l. 503 *Santa Fe* – a city in north-central New Mexico, USA, and one of the oldest European settlements in North America.

l. 503–4 *the discredited / French* – a reference to the loss of the French possessions in North America. This came about as a result of the extension of the 'Seven Years' War' (1756–63, in which Britain was allied with the Prussia of Frederick the Great against France, Austria and Russia) to India and the continent of America. Between 1758 and 1760, the British won repeated victories in what is now Canada and the United States. As a result, the Treaty of Paris (1763) gave Britain all of North America east of the Mississippi, including Florida, which had belonged to Spain. In recompense for the loss of the latter territory, the western Mississippi valley was ceded to Spain.

l. 511 *Longshanks King* – Edward I (1239–1307), nicknamed 'Longshanks'. In two campaigns, 1276–7 and 1282–3, he defeated Llywelyn ap Gruffudd and conquered Wales, granting it as a principality to his eldest son.

ll. 517–19 *I jumped in my birth / A second time, incontinent / In it died* – Evans says he was reborn as a Spaniard and that over-indulgence in his new life precipitated his death: he died of drink.
l. 534 *Majors Clark and Lewis* – William Clark (1770–1838) and S. Merriweather Lewis (1774–1807), explorers. They led an expedition in 1804–6 overland from St Louis to the Pacific Ocean using a copy of the map made by John Evans.
l. 535 *Riccarees* – the Arikaras, one of the Indian tribes occupying territory neighbouring that of the Mandans. Lewis and Clark, who refer to them in their journals as 'Rickorrees' or 'Ricares', encountered the tribe at the confluence of the Moreau and the Missouri (South Dakota) early in October 1804; they met the Mandans some three weeks later. The Riccarees gradually took over Mandan villages as their populations dwindled and eventually enslaved the few who survived the smallpox of 1838.
l. 537 *President Jefferson* – Thomas Jefferson (1743–1826), third president of the United States (1801–9) and chief drafter of the Declaration of Independence (1776).
l. 538–40 *Shahaka . . . Chief Big White* – principal chief of the Mandan tribe, head of a village named Matootonha, which was surrounded by a walled embankment of clay and a ditch, on the west bank of the Missouri a few miles below the mouth of the Knife River in what is now North Dakota.
l. 573–5 *Dives . . . Lazarus . . . arms that are not Abraham's* – a reference to the parable of the rich man and 'the beggar named Lazarus, which was laid at his gate full of sores' told in Luke 16: 19–31.
l. 576 *George Catlin* – (1796–1872), American artist and author. From 1832 he spent eight years among the Indians. His painting, drawing and recording of the Mandans persuaded many of their Welsh origins. He thought he detected traces of their ancestry particularly in their coracle-like boats, the 'whiteness' of their skin, their method of making blue glass beads and their language.
l. 611 *Monticello* – a town in Albemarle County, Virginia, where Jefferson lived.

189. Tide-reach – A Sequence of Pembrokeshire Poems Written for Music
Annotated in Notebook III: 'Written May–July 1978 at Deffrobani.'
The composer David Harries invited the poet's collaboration on a cantata for the Fishguard Festival in July 1979 but no performance took place.
Locations in the poems are on the Angle–Castlemartin peninsula in the extreme south-west of Pembrokeshire (many within easy walking distance of Mathias's cottage, The Wells), but they are seen at points in time between the fifth century ('Guénolé') and the present ('The Arming of Aberdaugleddau'). In a note to Michael J. Collins, Mathias explained: 'The whole sequence is an attempt to give a religious connotation to the interaction of sea and land in this peninsula.' The work is responsive to music in its variety of technical devices: patterns of rhyme and repetition, long and short lines, questions and answers, choruses, contrasting moods and voices.

i The Green Chapel
The natural arch formation of the rock (a Pembrokeshire landmark known as 'The Green Bridge of Wales' on the Castlemartin peninsula) becomes a parable about the paradox of strength in weakness and the omnipresence of God. 'The Green Chapel'

here expresses the belief that we can recognize the presence of God in landscape and seascape.
l. 36 *cognisant hand* – a hand that has knowledge: God's hand.

ii Guénolé
A second poem dedicated to the Breton saint – see also 'Channel Saint' (165). Writing to M. J. Collins, Mathias says: 'I imagine him landing on this then desolate coast in the late fifth century.'
l. 10 *Brehat, Tibidy* – islands just off the north coast of Brittany, west of St Brieuc.
l. 12 *aber* – Welsh for a river-mouth or estuary, in this case that of the Aulne in Brittany.
l. 13 *Landevennec* – a coastal town at the mouth of the Aulne in the south-eastern corner of the great inlet guarded by Brest, Finistère.
ll. 15–18 *My father, with companions / From the estates in Gwent, / Crossed years ago to the Gaulish stations / Assigned to them* – the saint's ancestors were in the second wave of migration to Brittany, about AD 460.
l. 25 *fears of the Irish* – marauding Irish threatened coastal areas in all parts of Wales.
l. 28 *Cowhorn of trouble* – the alarm sounded on a cow's horn when an enemy threatens.
ll. 29–30 *With one man I have compact. / Venetic he calls his people* – the Venetae were the Gauls of southern Brittany; Guénolé is referring to a companion who, like him, is a Breton.
l. 32 *Petroc* – the hamlet of St Petrox is little more than a mile to the east of St Twynells, where the poet had his Pembrokeshire cottage.

iii Nesta Vows to Escape from the Norman Hold
Nesta or Nest (*fl*.1100–20), the daughter of Rhys ap Tewdwr, the last king of Deheubarth (that part of Wales between the rivers Teifi and Tawe, which fell to the Normans when Rhys was killed in 1093). She was renowned for her beauty. About the year 1100 she married Gerald of Windsor, appointed castellan (keeper or governor) of Pembroke castle by Henry I. Gerald de Barri (Giraldus Cambrensis) was one of their grandchildren. She is also reputed to have had many lovers, including Henry I (see stanza vii), and to have borne at least seventeen children.
l. 4 *Dinefwr* – a castle near Llandeilo, which was the seat of the rulers of Deheubarth.
l. 13 *Beauclerc* – Henry I, third surviving son of William the Conqueror, was well educated, hence his nickname, the English version of which would be 'the learned'.
l. 16 *Cadwgan* – Prince Cadwgan ap Bleddyn, who fought for many years against Rhys ap Tewdwr before warring against the Normans.
ll. 17–19 *His lease / Of a kingdom not a Norman means / To survive him* – Cadwgan ap Bleddyn fought against the Normans but was forced to flee after a battle in defence of Anglesey in 1094. On his return from exile in 1099 his lands in Powys and Ceredigion were restored to him, but at the price of vassalage to the Norman rulers. Nest means that his reputation of having come to an agreement with the Normans will survive.
l. 22 *Penbroke* – an early form of the name, derived from Pen Fro.

Notes

l. 28 *sallyport* – an opening in a fortification from which troops may make a sudden violent excursion, a sally.
l. 28 *Owain* – Owain ap Cadwgan, who is alleged to have abducted Nest in 1109, though she may have been his accomplice.

iv Wave and Furrow

In the first stanza, the Vikings celebrate their seafaring triumphs from Orkney to Sicily. In the second, the Flemings, who were settled in the northern parts of the lordship of Pembroke about 1108, hail their quieter success as farmers in a new land less prone to flooding than their Zeeland home.
l. 3 *Pebba* – a Viking leader who settled his people near Angle in AD 877; Popton (Pebba's-ton) is named after him.
l. 10 *Léon* – a region of Brittany, now part of Finistère.
l. 15 *Pillars* – the Pillars of Hercules, that is, the Straits of Gibraltar.
l. 16 *Frankish* – the Franks, a West Germanic people, spread east into the Roman Empire in the late fourth century AD, gradually conquering most of Gaul and Germany. They were the dominant presence in France at the time of the Viking settlements.
l. 26 *Bruit* – rumour.
l. 29 *Zeeland* – a province in the south-west of the Netherlands, mostly reclaimed land below sea level.
ll. 31–2 *Queen / Matilda* – Matilda (1102–67), only daughter of Henry I and wife of Geoffrey of Anjou. After her father's death in 1135 she unsuccessfully waged war against Stephen, grandson of William the Conqueror, for the English throne. Her son succeeded as Henry II.
l. 32 *Beauclerc* – Henry I (see the note on l. 28 in the previous poem).
l. 33 *Flimstone* – an abbreviation of 'Flemings' town'.

v His Nurse to Young Harri Tudur

l. 6 *Siasper* – Jasper Tudor (*c*.1431–95), Earl of Pembroke. One of the five children of Owain Tudor and his wife Catherine de Valois, widow of Henry V, he became the ward of his brother Edmund's son, Henry (*Harri*) who therefore spent his childhood at Pembroke Castle. Edmund (*c*.1430–56) married Margaret Beaufort, a descendant of John of Gaunt, who, after the death of Henry VI in 1471, was the main Lancastrian claimant to the throne of England.
l. 6 *pine* – 'long eagerly for'.
l. 9 *the Harberts* – an extensive clan founded by William Herbert (d. 1469), leading supporter of the Yorkist cause in Wales during the Wars of the Roses. In 1461, he contributed to Edward of York's victory at Mortimer's Cross, near Leominster, after which Owain Tudor (see the note on *Siasper* above) was executed. Following the victory he attacked the remaining Lancastrian strongholds in Wales, including Pembroke Castle, and for a time held the young Henry Tudor prisoner.
ll. 13–14 *a gruff Breton / Prison at Elven* – Henry Tudor spent the years 1471–85 in exile with his uncle Jasper in Brittany. Elven is a small town near Vannes in Morbihan.
l. 14 *the suave King of France* – Charles VIII, known as 'l'Affable' ('the affable'); he succeeded his father Louis XI in 1483 and reigned until his own death in 1498.

When he realized Richard III faced mounting opposition, he freed Henry Tudor from jail and made a fleet available to carry the invasion force gathered in France to the Pembroke coast. So began the campaign that led to the Battle of Bosworth.
l. 16 *the battle* – the Battle of Bosworth, fought near Market Bosworth, Leicestershire, which settled the conflict between Lancastrians and Yorkists in favour of the former. In the battle, Henry Tudor, having gathered support from loyal Welsh nobles en route from Pembrokeshire, defeated Richard III.
l. 18 *A hawthorn crown* – according to tradition, after the battle, Richard III's crown was retrieved from a thorn-bush and placed on the victor's head. This is borne out by the use subsequently of the crown and thorn-bush as a Tudor emblem.
l. 19 *sarsenet* – a fine fabric.
ll. 19–20 *an indulgent queen / Sated with quarrelling,* – Henry Tudor appealed to Yorkists by marrying Elizabeth of York, daughter of Edward IV and Richard's niece.

vi The Remonstrance of John Poyer
Poyer (d. 1649) a staunchly anti-Catholic merchant and military commander, committed Pembroke to the Parliamentary cause when the Civil War began in 1642. As a former mayor of Pembroke and captain of the local militia he seized Pembroke Castle and prepared it for defence. With Rowland Laugharne and Rees Powell he took part in the defeat of the Royalists in 1644 and went on to capture Carew Castle. The latter action aroused the animosity of a group of turncoat Royalists led by Roger Lort and John 'Elyot of Eareweare' (l. 7), that is, Amroth, Pembs., whose successful intrigues in London precipitated his downfall. Poyer claimed that he held on to the Carew lands in order to pay the expenses of his military activities and when, in 1647, he was ordered to disband his men and surrender Pembroke Castle to Colonel Fleming, who had been appointed Governor by Cromwell, he refused. Royalist agents seized the opportunity to stir trouble and, in April 1648, Laugharne and Powell joined Poyer in open resistance to Parliament. Defeat of the combined former Parliamentary and Royalist forces at the battle of St Fagan's in May 1648, and the fall of Pembroke Castle to Cromwell in July of the same year were decisive. Laugharne, Powell and Poyer were all condemned to death, but Cromwell decided to execute only one. The 'short straw' (l. 9) fell to Poyer, who was shot at Covent Garden on the morning of 25 April 1649.
ll. 14–15 *Pennar / Mouth* – on an inlet of Milford Haven south of Pembroke Dock.
l. 15 *the Crow* – a location, possibly an inn, near Pennar Mouth.
ll. 32–8 – *Fleming ... Griffith White ... At Henllan* – the Whites of Tenby and Henllan were among the most prominent of Pembrokeshire families. As pillars of the Parliamentary cause they threatened Poyer with legal action for embezzlement. Colonel Fleming, appointed governor of Pembroke Castle by Parliament, arranged to meet loyal members of the Pembrokeshire gentry at Henllan Hall (near Pwllcrochan), but Poyer's men prevented the meeting and surrounded the house.
l. 41 *Pwllcrochan* – a village close to the southern shore of Milford Haven, a mile or so as the crow flies from Pembroke Dock.
l. 50 *Covenant* – the 'Solemn League and Covenant' of 1643 between Scotland and England to defend Presbyterianism.
l. 51 *Blue and White* – the colours adopted by the Parliamentary forces.
l. 53 *Goody Elyot* – a jibe at John Elyot's rigid style of Puritanism.

Notes

vii The Enlargement of Stackpole House: Harvest Time
In his notes for Michael J. Collins, the poet explains: 'Authentic, early eighteenth century, based on bailiff's letters. The Three Shopkins, a dance now well authenticated but then brand new. The longer stanzas match the line. The bailiff's shorter-lined ones are deliberately broken and unmusical, to indicate his unease and dislike for the proceedings.'

l. 2 *Barafundle Bay* – a bay between Stackpole Quay and Stackpole Head, south of Pembroke Dock (see also 'A Letter from Gwyther Street').

l. 7 *gambo* – a heavy farm cart, a dray.

l. 10 *Cut the neck with just one toss and bless the next year's growen'* – a plait of straw simulating the neck that in primitive fertility rites would have been cut so that the blood is spilled on the ground.

l. 30 *limber* – agile, pliant.

l. 33 *'Buding'* – the poet (who consulted a journal of the period for many of the details in the poem) says this is 'pudding'.

viii The Arming of Aberdaugleddau
'Aberdaugleddau' is the Welsh name of Milford Haven.

l. 7 *Paterchurch* – the former name of what became Pembroke Dock.

l. 13 *Boney* – Napoleon Bonaparte, who despatched the last invasion fleet to Britain, famously repelled at Fishguard by women whose tall black hats deceived the French into thinking the place well defended.

ll. 15–17 *Valorous . . . Ariadne . . . Thetis* – 'ships of the line' in the days of sail.

l. 24 *Bashan* – a place renowned for its rich pasture: Deuteronomy 32: 14.

l. 27 *Popton* – a fort near Angle Point, the headland to the west of the town of Pembroke; see also the note on 'Pebba' in 'Wave and Furrow' (183 iv).

l. 31 *Linney Head* – the southern boundary headland of Freshwater West, south of the entrance to Milford Haven.

l. 32 *engross* – occupy wholesale.

l. 34 *St Govan's lightship* – stationed off St Govan's Head, the most southerly point of the Pembrokeshire peninsula.

ix The Soul's Plain Seeing
ll. 5–6 *strength acknowledges the thin- / Nibbed praise intrinsic to obituaries* – poem viii above describes the changes that have overtaken the rural landscape and the seascape of the peninsula in modern times. These lines acknowledge two certainties: firstly, that all that has gone before in the sequence is of the nature of elegy, for the simple peasant past of the peninsula is dead; secondly, that the poet's praise has been insufficient and that he needs to admit as much.

x Laus Deo
'Laus Deo' (Latin) means 'Praise God'.

l. 12 *puissant* – powerful.

l. 15 *engrossing* – holding the attention, absorbing.

ll. 20–2 *its Maker / As careful of strength as / Of weakness* – the lines recall the parable of 'The Green Chapel', the first poem in the sequence.

l. 22 *quirk* – individual peculiarity of character.

l. 22 *cognomen* – originally the term for an ancient Roman's third name or nickname, which later became his family name.

A FIELD AT VALLORCINES (Gomer, 1996)

190. Onset of Winter
Annotated in Notebook III: 'November 1978 at Deffrobani / *Helix* [deleted] Brigham Young University May 19 1986.'
l. 19 *The lamed man* – mankind, not a personal reference.
l. 21 *An ancienter oath* – that spring will come.

191. Aber
Annotated in Notebook III: 'Deffrobani 27 December 1979. Alterations in st. iv 1 March 1980 / *Helix*? [deleted] Brigham Young University May 19th 1986.'
Note in *A Field at Vallorcines* (1996): 'Aber, near Talybont-on-Usk, is where my mother's grave is situated.'
l. 2 *limned* – embellished.
l. 7 *penumbra[-ed]* – a partly shaded area around the denser dark of an opaque body.
l. 9 *tumbled close* – the sloping graveyard on its hillside.

192. Tŷ Clyd
Annotated in Notebook III: 'Deffrobani 29 July 1980. First drafted in June, but worked on seriously 28 & 29 July. / *Poetry Wales*.'
Note in *A Field at Vallorcines* (1996): 'Tŷ Clyd is the name of the house where my parents lived in Brecon. Arafnah Thomas was once minister of the Plough Chapel. "Two storeys of deed" / Slapped on word' describes the conflict between my mother's independent, uncompromising pacifism with its rejection of organised "established" religion and my father's position as a Congregational minister, formerly an army chaplain.'
  The poem was first published in *Poetry Wales*, Winter 1980 (16, 3). The complexity of the stanza form signals the emotional intensity involved in writing about the tensions in the relationship between the parents and the poet's relationship with them. The detached 1909 house, which Evan Mathias rented from Arafnah Thomas on his retirement from the army, stands in Alexandra Road, on a slight rise above the former cattle mart (now occupied by a supermarket). It overlooks much of the town, and is a few hundred yards from the bungalow into which Roland and Molly Mathias moved on his own retirement from teaching.
l. 1 *A fortnight has gone by since her death* – this places the date of the initial impulse to write on the subject at about mid-February 1979.
l. 15 *The Bulwark* – the square in Brecon.

193. The Steward's Letter
Annotated in Notebook III: 'Deffrobani (completed) 10 January 1980. Line found missing and added 12/1/80. / *The Anglo-Welsh Review*.'
The missing line was in the seventh stanza, 'atte one / Tyme servaunt to his majestie / Upon'.

Note in *A Field at Vallorcines* (1996): 'Alltyrynys is a mansion (still standing) in Walterstone, which is in the corner of Herefordshire adjoining Breconshire and Monmouthshire. From the thirteenth century it was the family seat of the Sitsillt family whose name subsequently became Cecil. The most famous member of that family, William Cecil, Lord Burghley, Secretary of State to Queen Elizabeth I, acquired the property in the 1590s when it passed to him from his cousin William, because of outstanding debt.

'The poem is closely based on a letter written by Lord Burghley's steward in the area, Paul Delahay. The letter describes the funeral which he has organised for the deceased, William Cecil of Alltyrynys. William Cecil had nine children, of whom only one was a boy, Matthew, apparently "unfitted in mind fr. preferment". The second daughter married Paul Delahay.

'Apparently, William Cecil had not led a blameless life, since Paul Delahay had to organise a lavish funeral to maintain the reputation and social standing of the family (and, by his family connection, of Lord Burghley himself).

'William Cecil's first wife was Olive Parry whose brother is mentioned as being in the funeral procession. Maud Herbert, William's second wife, refused to come to the funeral. The funeral seems to have taken place over two days – a custom of Monmouthshire at the close of the sixteenth century.'

Paul Delahay is a significant figure in *Whitsun Riot* – see also the notes on 'Indictment' (155). Drafts of the poem reveal that the archaic spelling and the characteristic abbreviations of sixteenth-century texts were late additions and that the poet was much concerned about the impact of the letter when read aloud: he carefully noted the pattern of stresses in each line.

l. 1 *To the Lo. Burghley* – William Cecil (1520–98), baron Burghley (1571), secretary of state to Elizabeth I 1550–3 and 1558–72; Lord Treasurer 1572–98.

ll. 20–1 *Herefordes / Prebent* – the canon of the cathedral at Hereford.

l. 23 *Rude scutcheninges* – roughly drawn escutcheons; the steward is claiming no great skill on the part of those who made these shield designs bearing family coats of arms.

l. 30 *viii sonning lawes* – eight sons-in-law, the husbands of William Cecil's eight daughters.

l. 101 *tarmagaunt[es]* – termagant, a shrewish woman.

194. *The Path to Fontana Amorosa*

Annotated in Notebook III: 'Worked on intermittently 16–26 June. Deffrobani 26 June 1980. / China.'

Note in *A Field at Vallorcines* (1996): 'The poem describes a walk to the Baths of Aphrodite in the far north-western corner of Cyprus. The walk takes the poet past the islet of Ayos Georgios.

'Ludovico Ariosto (1474–1533) was author of "Orlando Furioso" (1532), the greatest of Italian romantic epics.

'Polis is a small town near the Turkish frontier in Cyprus. There is an inscribed tablet in Paphos dedicated to the parents of Onasias, once one of the inhabitants of Marion, a settlement which flourished some 2,500 years ago on the same site as the present town of Polis.'

The poet's sources of information (revealed by transcribed notes accompanying the MSS of the poem) were *The Traveller's Guide to Cyprus* by Hazel Thurston and

Colin Thubron's *Journey into Cyprus*. He noted Ariosto's advertisement of the beauty and sexual abandon of the local women and, in the midst of a poetic prose description, a quote from an eighteenth-century British traveller that Thubron had borrowed from another guide book. The poem provides a commentary and meditation upon what is described in *The Blue Guide* to Cyprus as 'a pleasant short excursion' that may be made from Polis (about twenty miles due north of Paphos, at the centre of the curve of Khrysokhou Bay), the main town of that western corner of the island, to the so-called Baths of Aphrodite, rather more than five miles to the west, under the ridge of the Akamas peninsula. 'A few minutes' walk along a path to the left brings us to a spot where the goddess Aphrodite took her bath before marrying Akamas ... The right-hand track climbs parallel to and some distance above the sea through a still unspoilt land and seascape ... to (6 km) the Fontana Amorosa.' Polis is further described as 'a small place of slight intrinsic interest but growing importance', not least as a citrus centre. To the south-east of Polis, 'on an eminence stood the city of Marion, said to have been founded in the seventh-century BC by Athenians. It was an important copper-mining centre, but was destroyed in 312 BC by Ptolemy I ... The whole area is surrounded by a necropolis, the tombs of which have yielded abundant artefacts to various excavators.' The guide adds the story of Alexander Drummond, British consul in the eighteenth century, who did not taste the water of the Fountain of Love because the effect 'upon old people like me, is said to be that of making the spirit willing while the flesh continues weak'.

l. 3 *Cistus* – the shrub also known as 'rock rose'.

l. 11 *carob* – a large evergreen tree, native to the eastern Mediterranean, which bears long black bean-shaped seed pods that are sweet tasting.

l. 21 *Burnet* – a plant of the rosaceous genus; here the burnet rose is indicated, a very prickly variety.

l. 41 *eyot[s]* – an obsolete synonym for 'island'. In discussion with the editor, the poet recalled that there are eyots in the Thames near Richmond.

195. Innocent Dying

Annotated in Notebook III: 'Drafted on shore of Tal-y-llyn, 27 August 1980. 2nd draft 3 September 1980. Completed 6 September. / *Poetry Review* and *Scottish Mountains Anthology*.'

Note in *A Field at Vallorcines* (1996): 'Nant Iago is a stream which flows down from the former lead-mines of Mynydd Cedris. It joins the River Dysynni half a mile above Abergynolwyn.'

The poem was first published in *Poetry Review* in 1982 (72, 2); the anthology referred to in the annotation is *Speak to the Hills* eds. Brown and Berry, 1985.

l. 12 *a skate* – a very short distance, an easy journey.

ll. 21–2 *hand / His cap in* – another variation on a colloquial expression conveying Iago's yielding of separate identity as it joins the larger stream.

196. Signal

Annotated in Notebook III: 'First draft Autumn 1980. Completed 4 February 1982. / *The Anglo-Welsh Review*.'

The poem was first published in *The Anglo-Welsh Review* in 1982 (72). The MS shows the poet (as usual) concerned with the number of stresses in each line and to introduce subtle patterning by the use of internal rhyme. The rhyming of *sight/ flight* appears in the first draft and may have arisen by happy accident; subsequent drafts develop this into a formal structure.

197. Expiation
Annotated in Notebook III: 'Deffrobani, Brecon. Completed 27 October 1981. / *The Anglo-Welsh Review*.'
A few slight amendments are dated 14 March 1982.
Note in *A Field at Vallorcines* (1996): 'My grandfather was born in Llangattock and began trade as a builder in Cardiff before being advised for the sake of his health to move to the clearer air of the mountains to farm. This poem will be better understood if the poem "Blue Blood and Englishmen" (*Snipe's Castle*, 1979) could be read first. Coedcae is a rough piece of ground partly covered by trees and gorse bushes. Ffynnon Fawr was the farmhouse where I was born, near the Caerfanell stream (or Crafnell as it is now beginning to be known). The valley has since been flooded for a reservoir, and all that remains of Ffynnon Fawr are a few stones and a conifer near the edge of the reservoir.'
  The poem was originally entitled 'An Expiation of Sorts' and remains 'A Kind of Expiation' in the Notebook – the title under which it first appeared in *The Anglo-Welsh Review* in 1982 (72). Subtlety in the use of internal rhyme is a feature of the poem.
l. 4 *glat[s]* – a gap in a hedge.
l. 21 *banw* – Blaen Cwm Banw is high in the Brecon Beacons to the west of Aber village, close to the headwaters of the Clydach stream which joins the Caerfanell (now as it emerges from Talybont Reservoir) at Aber village, near Talybont-on-Usk. The cottage known as Tyle-Clydach (where the poet's grandfather lived first, when he left Cardiff to seek healthier air in the Brecon area) was some distance up this same valley. See 'On Newport Reservoir' (36).
l. 28 *Twyn Du* – a mountain to the north-west of Talybont reservoir and forest.

198. Saturday Morning: Appin
Annotated in Notebook III: 'Draft: Port Appin, 12 Sept. 1981. Finished: 2 February 1982. Alterations: lines 14 & 23 – 10 June 1982. *Spirit* (USA).'
The poem first appeared in *Spirit* (the magazine of Seton Hall University, South Orange, New Jersey, USA) in 1982. Appin is on an inlet of Loch Linnhe on the north-west coast of Scotland.
l. 8 *Lismore* – a long, thin island at the mouth of Loch Linnhe.
ll. 10–11 *the bheinns of Morven* – [Morvern], mountain peaks, Creach Bheinn and Fuar Bheinn, on the other side of the loch.
l. 26 *that fainter coast* – the coast of Wales.

199. They, Without Us
Annotated in Notebook III: 'First draft Seefeld [Austria], June 1981. Completed 4 February 1982 at Deffrobani. / *The Anglo-Welsh Review*.'
Note in *A Field at Vallorcines* (1996): 'I was reminded of the poet "Crwys", whom I knew as an old man (William Crwys Williams, 1875–1968).

'Baldwin, king of Jerusalem (died 1118), and Frederick Barbarossa of Germany (1121–90), took part in the Second and Third Crusades.

'Cynog was a sixth-century saint of Breconshire. Thomas Coke (1747–1814), born at Brecon was a Methodist evangelist in Britain and America. Thomas Price ("Carnhuanawc") (1783–1848), another Breconshire man, was a Church of England cleric and a proponent of the Welsh language. Roger Price (1834–1900), also a native of Breconshire, became a Congregational missionary in South Africa, and was known as the "Lion of Bechuanaland".'

The poem was first published in *The Anglo-Welsh Review* in 1982 (72). It seems to have emerged virtually complete at first draft; the MS has only a few small amendments, notably, 'Peredur' becomes 'Crwys'. The epigraph from Hebrews accompanied the draft. Chapter 11, about the power of faith, is largely composed of examples of Old Testament figures such as Noah and Abraham who, having heard the promise of God, believed and had the faith to act in accord with that promise, and then of others who, 'died in faith, not having received the promises, but having seen them afar off'. The final four verses (37–40) close the argument: 'They were stoned, they were sawn asunder, were tempted, were slain with the sword . . . And these all, having obtained a good report through faith, received not the promise: *God having provided some better thing for us, that they without us should not be made perfect.*' These final words take up the theme of the opening of the Epistle: 'God, who at sundry times and in diverse manners spake in times past unto the fathers by the prophets, / Hath in these last days spoken unto us by his Son.'

l. 3 *plat* – patch of ground by the river.

l. 6 *Crwys* – in discussion with the editor, the poet made the further observation that, in his view, Crwys was 'a would-be Christian'.

l. 16 *Llangynidr Bridge* – a notable arched stone bridge over the Usk at Llangynidr, a small village just off the Abergavenny–Brecon road, near Bwlch.

l. 18 *Cwrt-y-Gollen* – an army camp off the same Abergavenny–Brecon road, near Crickhowell.

200. Cynog

Annotated in Notebook III: 'Completed at Deffrobani 23 February 1982 and worked on for the best part of a week previously, but for no more than an hour a day. Alterations 25/2/82. Printed alterations 10/vi/82. / *Spirit* (USA).'

The poem appeared in *Spirit* (the magazine of Seton Hall University, South Orange, New Jersey, USA) in 1982.

Note in *A Field at Vallorcines* (1996): '(From the Cotton MSS in the British Museum: Vespasian A. XIV. Of the Situation of Brecknock).

'St Cynog (*fl*.500) was the son of Brychan Brycheiniog, the king of Brycheiniog (formerly Garthmadryn) after the death of his father, Aulach. Drichan was tutor to both Brychan and his son Cynog.

'Legend has it that Cynog had a decorated torque given to him by his father, and after Cynog's death the torque became a most precious relic. It has not survived, but Giraldus Cambrensis saw it and gave a detailed description.

'Cynog's place of death is uncertain but the story is told that Irish raiders hurled him from the top of a cliff into one of two streams, the Yscir or the Yscir Fechan.'

Notes

The typescript drafts of the poem include notes from *Lives of the Welsh Saints* by W. J. Rees, Theophilus Jones's *History of Brecknockshire* and T. R. Roberts's *Eminent Welshmen*. Although the text is extended over five drafts, in essentials the poem emerged in the first.

ll. 2–4 *Fan / Oleu or the greater Fan / Where the camp of the iron users was* – Fan Oleu, to the east of the Ysgir Fawr, also overlooks the village of Lower Chapel, a short distance further east. The 'greater Fan' is Corn y Fan, which rises steeply from the bank of the Ysgir Fechan a mile or so to the west of Fan Olau. On the summit of Corn y Fan is an Iron Age fort.

ll. 6–7 *Which horn / Of Yscir benefits* – the Afon Ysgir joins the Usk at Aberyscir a few miles west of Brecon. In the mountains to the north it divides into the Ysgir Fawr and the Ysgir Fechan. Merthyr Cynog, the hamlet named after its church dedicated to the martyr, is situated between them.

l. 29 *Uther's column* – the fighting men of Uther Pendragon.

ll. 63–4 *Of the hidden / Collar two parts are back in place* – it was at least known about in the twelfth century: Giraldus Cambrensis mentions it in the course of his 'Journey through Hay and Brycheiniog', the second section of the *Itinerary Through Wales*.

201. Terns at Rossnaskill

Annotated in Notebook III: 'Completed 28 August 1982 at Deffrobani. Worked at, as time allowed, for some weeks previous. / *The Honest Ulsterman*, Oct. 1982.'

Rossnaskill cannot be traced in map or guide book, but the poet recalls its being located on the coast of County Galway, with islands offshore and the mountains known as the Twelve Bens (or 'Twelve Pins') to the east.

l. 25 *kerns* – lightly armed foot soldiers in medieval Scotland or Ireland: a continuation of the military metaphor with which this section of the poem begins.

l. 33 *The envelope* – a late use of Mathias's characteristic metaphor for the scene, the land and sea and the containing sky.

l. 66 *myrmidon* – adjectival use of the word used in the plural to name the warlike people of Thessaly who followed Achilles to the siege of Troy. It suggests shallows seething with movement.

202. On Discovering Daumier's 'Don Quixote Reading' in the National Museum at Cardiff

Annotated in Notebook III: 'Finished about 25/x/82 and re-copied here on 1 December 1982. / *Poetry Review*.'

The double page preceding this entry in the Notebook has a cancelled earlier version of the entire poem with the annotation 'Completed 8 October 1982 at Deffrobani'. The poem first appeared in *Poetry Review* in 1983 (73, 2).

Note in *A Field at Vallorcines* (1996): 'Beltenebros was Amadis of Gaul, a fictional character in one of the prose romances written by the Portuguese Vasco of Loberia (died 1403) – and others – which made up fourteen books altogether.

'The Lord Taprobane is thought to have been overlord of Ceylon. Ptolemy in the second century AD and Isidor of Seville (*c.*560–636) thought it was a Celtic country, part of the Summer Country where the Celts lived long before the northerners or the Persians came. It is often spelt "Deffrobani".'

Notes

l. 4 *Beltenebros* – (the word means 'darkly beautiful') a love-child of Perion, King of Gaula (Wales) and Elizena, Princess of Brittany, who was cast away at birth and became known as the Child of the Sun. He is represented as a poet and musician, a knight-errant and a king and, above all in this context, as a model of chivalry. Many of the details in the tales of Amadis of Gaul (who is of course a Celt) are derived from Arthurian legend.

ll. 4–6 *fitting those / Slashed, interminable bones / With a chary flesh* – the gaunt appearance of Don Quixote is depicted in unnumbered illustrations of Cervantes' hero.

ll. 9–10 *the book / A refresher course* – the simple-minded Don Qiuxote is so crazed by reading romances of chivalry that he sets out as a knight-errant to right all the wrongs of the world.

ll. 12–14 *Old tilts / Are overlaid, Rocinante stalled / At the Neue Pinakothek* – illustration of the adventures of Don Quixote is a theme of the poem. One of the adventures most often pictured is his tilting at windmills. His equally boney nag, grandly named Rocinante, is as frequently illustrated; here the poem refers to a particular picture in the gallery at Munich.

l. 16 *Iron Age* – the age of the Celts in Europe.

l. 28 *Dulcinea* – Don Quixote's lady love and object of his knightly homage.

203. A Field at Vallorcines

Annotated in Notebook III: 'Completed and entirely written at Caeau Capel Hotel, Nefyn, 14–16 September 1983. / *Fine Madness* (Seattle).'

In a note to the editor, the poet wrote, 'This poem I worked on in the bedroom of the hotel. My wife did several pictures in the week that we were there. I came down at lunch each day and after lunch some of the artists asked me to produce my poem. One of them said that she fully understood what I was getting at; all the others said that they had no idea what I was doing.' Vallorcine (the spelling 'Vallorcines' does not appear on current maps) is a village in the Alps approximately fifteen kilometres north of Chamonix, just over the Swiss border.

l. 9 *burly* – as in 'hurly-burly'.

204. On South Lord's Land

Annotated in Notebook III: 'Completed 18 July 1984 at Deffrobani. First two drafts made at Bryn Tanat Hotel, Llansantffraed-ym-Mochnant (150 yards inside Powys) 10–12 July 1984. / *Fine Madness* (Seattle).'

A few later amendments are dated '30 March 1985' and '15th February 1995'. The poem first appeared in *Fine Madness* in Spring 1986 (vol. 3, 1).

Note in *A Field at Vallorcines* (1996): 'On a mountain pasture near Dent, in Cumbria. See "Brigantia: A Mysteriography" by Guy Raglan Phillips (Routledge and Kegan Paul, 1976), which gives useful information about the legends of the kingdom of Brigantia (the area of present-day Yorkshire, Lancashire and Cumbria).

'The cult of the raven may long have persisted in the Rheged area of north-west Brigantia. In "The Dream of Rhonabwy" from the Mabinogi, the Prince of Rheged, Owain ab Urien (though probably not of Arthur's vintage), is described as playing *gwyddbwyll* (a game like chess) with Arthur. Arthur's men attack Owain's ravens and Arthur ignores Owain's pleas, insisting that he must continue the game. The

ravens then attack Arthur's men, but a truce is finally called. It would seem that Arthur's soldiers often kept an uneasy and untrusting peace with Rheged.'
l. 3 *chalybeate staining* – the 'rusting' of rock exposed to water impregnated with iron.
l. 6 *Gamboge* – a yellow pigment.
l. 16 *beaked gardes* – the ravens; 'gardes' (guards) is taken from the book *Brigantia*.

205. Sanderlings
Annotated in Notebook III: 'Completed 19/vii/1984 at Deffrobani. First two drafts made 10/13 July at the Bryn Tanat Hotel, Llansantffraed-ym-Mechain, Powys. / *Poetry Australia*.'
The poem first appeared in *Poetry Australia* in 1985 (102). In a note to the editor, the poet emphasized the nationalist sentiment of the final eight lines.
l. 8 *Arduduy* – the area around Harlech, between the rivers Glaslyn and Mawddach, which reach the sea in the far north of Cardigan Bay.
l. 14 *deliquescent* – melting.
l. 18 *Murmansk* – a town in northern Russia close to the Arctic Ocean and the border with Finland.
l. 19 *Orange River* – in southern Africa.

206. Ronan
Annotated in Notebook III: 'Most of this was written at Esgir Wen, Cwmystwyth, in October 1984. Completed at Deffrobani 22 March 1985. / *Orbis* No. 75, Winter 1989.'
Note in *A Field at Vallorcines* (1996): 'The story of Ronan appears in "Legendes traditionelles de la Bretagne" by O.-L. Aubert.
Ronan was an Irishman who received a call to go to the province of Cornouaille in Brittany, becoming a hermit in the highlands. Menez Hom is the highest hill in Brittany.'
Surviving drafts of the poem, half-a-dozen typed sheets, suggest that its complex form emerged virtually at once. While the poem was extended, it changed little in substance in the successive drafts.
l. 5 *the Immaculate Ego* – Ronan himself.
l. 14 *spindlestick* – a late echo of 'spindle trees' in the wood at Sling, on Salisbury Plain, where the poet spent part of his childhood. See also 'The Forest' (39) and 'Returning' (132).
l. 22 *Harriers* – falcons.
l. 34 *Kerneve* – according to the writer, a village in Finistère near Menez Hom.
ll. 87–8 *Menez Hom* – the most imposing hill in Brittany, standing 330 metres above sea-level. It overlooks the inlet of the river Aulne, a few miles south of Landevennec in western Finistère.

207. Cae Iago: May Day
Annotated in Notebook III: 'Most of this was written at Deffrobani in May 1985. With a few emendations, the fair copy was made in March 1991. / *Poetry Wales* Vol. 28 No. 2.'
The poet found 'Cae Iago' (James's Field) near Bala, Gwynedd.

ll. 6-7 *blackthorn / Splush[es]* – blackthorn is the thorny shrub *prunus spinosa*, also known as sloe; 'splush' is a dialect word suggesting vigorous growth.

l. 17 *limber* – verbal use of the adjective meaning 'agile', or an abbreviated form of 'limber-up'.

ll. 33-4 *The old / Nomad* – Abraham, whose way of life (in Genesis 18) is contrasted with that of the inhabitants of 'the cities of the plain', Sodom and Gomorrah.

l. 40 *Hafotty Ganol['s]* – a ruined farm; its name, a colloquial form of 'hafod-tŷ ganol', literally 'middle (canol) summer house', harks back to a period when flocks were taken up to the high mountain pastures during the summer months and their shepherds stayed with them in a summer dwelling.

208. Grasshoppers

Annotated in Notebook III: 'The idea of 'Grasshoppers' came to me whilst having lunch by the Rhinerhorn, in September 1982. The third copy was the one which was tucked in my Poetry Notebook III in October. I didn't feel that it was quite the thing that I wanted. In September 1989 we climbed the Rhinerhorn again and we found the grasshoppers exactly in the same place. In 1991 I tried to make the whole design work, but my ability was not sufficient to make any changes. In June 1991 a fair copy was made in Deffrobani.'

Note in *A Field at Vallorcines* (1996): 'The Rhinerhorn is a mountain south of Glaris, near Davos in Switzerland.'

l. 20 *entablature* – in architecture, that part of a building that is above the shaft of a column or, here, a raised platform.

209. Jazz Festival

Two versions appear in Notebook III. The first (cancelled) version is annotated: '4th December 1991. The beginning of this poem followed the Brecon Jazz Festival. I tried every Wednesday before lunch (12-1) to make a poem, which I have not done before since my stroke. Except when we went to Venice (14th – 21st October), I tried a line or two each Wednesday and the resulting poetry is here.' The fair copy of the second, as published in *A Field at Vallorcines*, follows 'Look at Me, Caleb' in the Notebook and is annotated: 'Tuesday, February 7 1995 (My father's birthday). / *Poetry Wales* July 1995.'

ll. 15-16 *when Picton had / The reins in Trinidad* – Sir Thomas Picton (1758-1815), younger son of Thomas Picton of Poyston, Pembs. A soldier, he first saw active service at the capture of St Lucia in 1796 and became military governor of Trinidad. He died at Waterloo.

l. 27 *Dinas* – site of a mansion about half a mile down river from Brecon: see 'The Path to Dinas' (103).

210. The Lamentation of Marchell

Annotated in Notebook III: '18th November 1992. / *Poetry Wales* Volume 29 Number 2 (October).'

Note in *A Field at Vallorcines* (1996): '"The Lamentation of Marchell" is part of the account of Brychan of Brycheiniog (see Poem 11 [i.e. 'Cynog' (200)]).'

'Marchell was the daughter of Tewdrig, king of Garthmadrin. Her father saw an alliance with the men of Dublin as a way of countering the influx of other Irishmen coming over the mountains. At her father's command, she was to cross to Ireland to marry Aulach of Dublin.

'The Ui Liathain (Sons of Liathain) had already settled in the south of Glamorgan. Historically it is debatable which group from Ireland first settled the area of the Black Mountains of Carmarthen and Brecon Beacons, the Ui Liathain or the men of Leinster (Dublin), or possibly even the Deisi, from the area of Gower, whom Marchell had to repulse on her way to Porthmawr, near St David's, before embarking for Ireland.'

l. 6 *Llanfaes* – now a part of Brecon town west of the Usk.

l. 10 *kirtle* – a woman's gown or skirt.

ll. 21–2 *Tarell / And Senni* – tributaries of the Usk, which the Tarell joins at Llanfaes, and the Senni at Sennybridge.

ll. 26–7 *Garthmadrin, beyond the Honddu / And the Yscir Fawr* – the Ysgir Fawr (which, after joining the Ysgir Fechan, becomes the Afon Ysgir that flows into the Usk at Aberyscir) and the Honddu, another tributary, which meets the Usk in Brecon (or Aberhonddu). Both rise on Eppynt Mountain, to the north of the town. Garthmadrin was then the whole of the region of the Usk as far as the Brecon Beacons and north to the Eppynt.

ll. 27–8 *where the great vicious / Horses are* – an invention of the poet.

l. 31 *Maes Madoc* – adjacent to Nantmadog, on the A4067 a few miles south of Sennybridge.

l. 33 *Tywi* – the river Tywi now flows south-west from the Llyn Brianne reservoir to the sea near Carmarthen.

l. 38 *Glansevin* – a former mansion house, now a hotel, a mile or so east of Llangadog, Carmarthenshire.

l. 42 *Meidrim* – a village on the B4298 about six miles west of Carmarthen.

l. 47 *Porthmawr* – otherwise known as Whitesands Bay, a short distance from St David's, Pembrokeshire, a point of departure for Ireland.

211. I Shall Take the Gig*
Composed in 1999, this is substantially a 'found' poem in the manner of 'The Steward's Letter'. It has not been previously published.

212. The Clear Sea
Annotated in Notebook III: '24th March 1993 (The Voyage of St Brendan). / *The New Welsh Review*.'
Amendments affecting six lines are dated '23 April 1993'.
Note in *A Field at Vallorcines* (1996): 'From "The Voyage of St Brendan: Journey to the Promised Land", translated from the Latin by John J. O'Meara: p. 21, "The Clear Sea".

'St Brendan was born around AD 489 and died sometime between 570 and 583.'
First published in *The New Welsh Review* in 1993 (6, 2).

213. Look at Me, Caleb
Annotated in Notebook III: '5th January 1995. / *The New Welsh Review*, 29 Summer 1995.'
Note in *A Field at Vallorcines* (1996): 'Numbers 13. The Holy Bible, Authorised King James Version.'

In this chapter, Moses and Aaron and the children of Israel are in the wilderness of Paran. Moses, 'by the commandment of the Lord', sends out heads from each of the tribes to reconnoitre Canaan and report on the strength of its inhabitants and the fertility of the land, which they are to prove by bringing back samples of its fruit. The spies find Hebron occupied by 'the children of Anak' but rich – in proof whereof they cut clusters of grapes and pomegranates and figs. After forty days' reconnaissance, they return to Moses, Aaron and their people to report that the land 'floweth with milk and honey' and to show the fruit they have taken from it. However, they add, the peoples that live in it are very strong. When Caleb urges 'Let us go up at once, and possess it' his fellow spies insist that the opposition is beyond the Israelites' power to match, referring particularly to the sons of Anak, who had 'come of the giants', so that they felt themselves 'as grasshoppers in their sight'. The speaker in the poem is Moses.

l. 7 *Caleb* – identified in Numbers 13 as 'Caleb the son of Jephunneh' of the tribe of Judah.

l. 8 *Oshea* – identified in the same source as 'Oshea the son of Nun' of the tribe of Ephraim, who is called Jehoshua by Moses.

l. 17 *Eshcol* – Numbers 13: 24: 'The place was called the brook Eshcol, because of the cluster of grapes which the children of Israel cut down from thence.'

Half a dozen poems for the Spoon River Anthology after Edgar Lee Masters
Annotated in Notebook III: 'June 1995 / July 1995. The six poems composed were made in June 15th and July 12th.'

Note in *A Field at Vallorcines* (1996): 'These poems are based on the lives of members of the Williams family of Aberclydach.

'William Retlaw Jefferson Williams (1863–1944) was a historian and editor who, after his failure in his first case as a lawyer, retired to live for the rest of his life at Brynoyre near Talybont. He published four books on the parliamentary history of Wales and one on the history of the Great Sessions of Wales, all at his own cost. Between 1905 and 1907 he published the journal "Old Wales" but his family inheritance was by then exhausted. He had to sell most of his valuable library to pay for his last great work, a full list of the officers of the British armed forces, but the manuscript was lost and never published. Gwenffreda Cate and Alis Mallt, sisters of William Retlaw Jefferson Williams, were novelists who together wrote two novels under the pen name of "The Dau Wynne". In 1899 the sisters met the Breton poets Abherve (François Vallée) and Taldir (François Jaffrenou), and this inspired their lifelong interest in the Breton language. Alis Mallt, who lived long after her sister, was also a supporter of women's rights and one of the earliest and most generous supporters of Plaid Cymru.'

Edgar Lee Masters (1869–1950) was born in Kansas but grew up in rural Petersburg and Lewiston, Illinois. He, too, was a lawyer but, unlike Williams, practised for twenty-five years. From his teens a prolific writer, he was entirely unregarded until his free-verse 'Spoon River' poems, based upon the area where he had been brought up, began to appear in a weekly magazine published in St Louis. *Spoon River Anthology*, a collection of sketches of the people he knew as a boy and young man, was published in 1915 and was an immediate success. The poetry is casual, laconic and bare of ornament, almost the polar opposite of Mathias's 'textured' writing, and, though often ironic, it is straightforward and lucid. *Spoon River Anthology* contains many epitaphs, uttered by the dead themselves, in which they expose their lives, their thoughts and, unwittingly, their human failings.

214. Dr John James Williams

Williams was a medical doctor but had no practice. He became a director of the Brecon and Merthyr Railway, which served the Talybont area from 1863 until it became part of the Great Western Railway in 1922.

l. 2 *Cwmbanw* – the name given to the upper reaches of the valley of the Clydach stream, which joins the Caerfanell (the river whose valley was dammed to create the Talybont Reservoir) at Aber village.

l. 7 *St Andrews* – the Scottish university.

l. 10 *Mumbles* – coastal suburb of the city of Swansea on Mumbles Head, at the western end of Swansea Bay.

l. 16 *Aberclydach* – a fine country house built by Williams just outside Aber village in the 1860s. In 1950 it was acquired by Newport Corporation for use as a guest-house and is now a Buddhist retreat.

l. 19 *Slwch* – a hillside below the fort just to the east of the town of Brecon. The name probably derives from the English word 'slough'.

l. 25 *Elormeirch* – (the name means 'stallion's bier'), a farm (no longer extant) a few miles to the north of Brecon.

ll. 26–9 *Heolrhydd and / Prospect Row and / Clawygaer and Mount Street / Fields –* addresses in and around the town of Brecon. Heolrhydd is now known as Free Street (a direct translation of the Welsh); Prospect Row, now Prospect Close, is just outside the town to the north-west; Clawygaer [Clawdd-y-gaer] is named after the ditch below the old town walls; Mount Street Fields, an euphemistic Anglicization of the Welsh Heol Llygoden ('Mouse Street'), were within the town, a little to the east of the cathedral.

l. 36 *Mary and that ogre Overton* – his daughter and the man who raped her (see 'Mary Jane Robertson Williams' below). Overton was associated with Williams in the railway company.

l. 39 *Clifton* – a suburb of Bristol.

l. 43 *Fred and Kate and Alice* – his other children.

215. Mary Jane Robertson Williams

Mary was raped by Overton when she was little more than a child. Shame prevented the family from referring the offence to the police. Her mother took Mary away to Clifton to have the baby in seclusion and did not return to the family home other than at intervals to see her children.

216. Howell Price Williams

l. 5 *Aberthaw* – between Barry and Llantwit Major on the coast of the Vale of Glamorgan, a location with a long and continuing history in the manufacture of cement.

l. 9 *Dufile* – a village in Uganda, now part of a game sanctuary.

l. 10 *Emin Pasha* – the name adopted by Eduard Schnitzer (1840–92), a German explorer. While exploring near Lake Tanganyika, he was murdered by Arabs.

Notes

217. William Retlaw Jefferson Williams
l. 4 *Cross Oak* – a hamlet near Talybont-on-Usk; the house of that name still exists.
l. 8 *Dowlais* – part of Merthyr Tydfil in old Glamorgan, a former mining district.
l. 14 *Brynoyre* – a house, still standing, about halfway between Aber village and Talybont-on-Usk, built by William Williams when he became estranged from his father.
l. 18 *uchelwyr* – Welsh term for the highest social rank, the nobility.
l. 22 *cum grano salis* – Latin: 'with a grain of salt'.
l. 25 *Chancery Lane* – home of the Chancery Division of the High Court, which deals (among other things) with property disputes.
l. 42 *Aber Chapel* – the small chapel in the hamlet of Aber, on the hillside overlooking Talybont Reservoir. The chapel graveyard is the last resting place of the poet's mother and father and his maternal grandparents.
l. 44 *Llanfigan* – a Breconshire parish; the church is at Pencelli, a village a mile or so north-west of Talybont-on-Usk.

218. Gwenffreda Cate Williams / Alice Matilda Langland Williams (Alis Mallt)
l. 8 *Brychan* – a chieftain of Irish stock who founded the kingdom of Brycheiniog, roughly corresponding to modern Breconshire.
ll. 10–11 *'The Dau / Wynne'* – the pen-name the sisters used in their collaboration as novelists.
l. 21 *the Hon. Mrs Herbert* – wife of Sir Ivor Caradoc Herbert, grandson of Lady Llanover, who was an outstanding supporter of the Welsh language and culture in the nineteenth century.
l. 22 *'La grande amie des Bretons'* – 'the great friend of the Bretons'.
l. 23 *Betsy Abadam* – of Middleton Hall in the Towy Valley, Carmarthenshire, a member of the gentry and friend of Lady Llanover.
l. 24 *Llanover* – Llanover Court was home of Lord and Lady Llanover (Benjamin Hall, 1802–67, and Augusta Waddington, 1802–96).
ll. 29–30 *Saint / Brieuc* – a town near the coast of north Brittany.
l. 40 *The Dyffryn* – Dyffryn Crawnon, the next valley to the south of the now largely drowned Glyn Collwn. The Afon Crawnon joins the Usk at Llangynidr.
ll. 47–8 *Frederick's / House* – 'Plas Pontsaeson' near St Dogmaels, north Pembrokeshire. Frederick George Robertson Williams (see below) bought the Pontsaeson estate. After the death of Gwenffreda in 1914, he invited Alis to live with him.
l. 49 *Towy Valley* – the river Towy, or Tywi, flows westward to enter the sea a little to the south of Carmarthen town.
ll. 70–1 *the hundred / And seventh psalm* – the theme of the psalm is God's mercy to the righteous: 'they cry unto the Lord in their trouble, and he bringeth them out of their distress' (verse 28).
l. 79 *Gorsedd of Britain* – the assembly of the bards of Britain, a society of Welsh poets, musicians and antiquaries founded by Iolo Morganwg (Edward Williams) in 1792.

219. Frederick George Robertson Williams
l. 11–12 *'Ho! I idd ilke ti os hwne / Hse iwnkde ta em'* – 'Oh! I did like it so when / She winked at me.'

l. 15 *the Iron Church* – a 'chapel of ease' at Talybont where services were held regularly and often used instead of St Meugan's, the parish church of Llanfeugan, during the dark winter months.
ll. 17–18 *Berthlwyd / Fawr* – a property about half a mile to the south-west of Aber village.
l. 18 *Nantllanerch* – a mountain property on the southern side of the valley of the Clydach, west of Aber.
l. 19 *Llanwrtyd* – a town some fifteen miles north-west of Brecon on the further side of the Mynydd Eppynt.
l. 21 *rentier* – one whose income comes from property investments.
l. 21 *the Teifi valley* – the Teifi flows south from its source in the mountains to the east of Aberystwyth and then curls westwards to enter the sea at Cardigan (Aberteifi).

220. Peter Has Been Digging
Written in 2000, Roland Mathias's most recent poem is both elegiac and celebratory.
l. 13 [Saint] *Isidore of Seville* – AD ?560–636, Spanish scholar and archbishop.

Select Bibliography

REVIEWS
Days Enduring
Patricia Ledward in *Poetry Review*, July/August 1943, pp. 244–5.

Break in Harvest
Times Literary Supplement, 19 April 1947.
Naomi Lewis in *Tribune*, 25 April 1947, p. 20.
E. P. Thompson in *Our Time*, 1 June 1947.

The Roses of Tretower
R. S. Thomas in *Dock Leaves*, 3, 8, pp. 34–5.
A. G. Prys Jones in the *Western Mail*, 20 August 1952.
Norman Nicholson in *British Weekly*, 25 December 1952, p. 2.

The Flooded Valley
Times Literary Supplement, 30 September 1960.
Elizabeth Jennings in the *Guardian*, 21 October 1960.
Glyn Jones in *The Anglo-Welsh Review*, 10, 26, pp. 71–3.
Al Alvarez in the *Observer*, 18 December 1960.

Absalom in the Tree
Jeremy Hooker in *Poetry Wales*, 7, 3, Winter 1971, pp. 97–101.
Robin Fulton in *Planet*, 10, February/March 1972, pp. 80–2.
Thomas Crawford in *Lines Review*, 41, June 1972.
Peter Abbs in *The Anglo-Welsh Review*, 21, 47, pp. 201–4.

Snipe's Castle
Peter Elfed Lewis in *Poetry Wales*, 15, 3, Winter 1979, pp. 130–8.
Leslie Norris in *The Powys Review*, 6, Winter/Spring 1979/80, pp. 86–8.
Richard Swigg in *The Literary Review*, 12, 21 March–3 April 1980, p. 25.

Burning Brambles
Anne Stevenson in *The Anglo-Welsh Review*, 75, 1984, pp. 96–100.
Jeremy Hooker in *Poetry Wales*, 21, 1, 1985, pp. 94–101.

A Field at Vallorcines
Robert Minhinnick in *The New Welsh Review*, 36, Spring 1997, pp. 85–6.
Mercer Simpson in *Poetry Wales*, 33, 1, July 1997, pp. 65–7.

ARTICLES

Jeremy Hooker, 'The poetry of Roland Mathias', *Poetry Wales*, 7, 1, Summer 1971, pp. 6–13.

M. Wynn Thomas, '"All lenient muscles tensed": the poetry of Roland Mathias', *Poetry Wales*, 33, 3, 1998, pp. 21–6.

OTHERS

The autobiographical essay 'Roland Mathias' in *Artists in Wales*, ed. Meic Stephens (Gomer 1971).

'Anglo-Welsh bards and metropolitan reviewers – a letter from Roland Mathias', *Poetry Wales*, 9, 4, Spring 1974, pp. 4–8.

A Note by Roland Mathias (on Edward Thomas) in *Poetry Wales*, 13, 4, Spring 1978, pp. 112–14.

A Note by Roland Mathias (on the state of criticism of Anglo-Welsh poetry) in *Poetry Wales*, 15, 2, Autumn 1979, pp. 25–7.

'Roland Mathias: an interview' (by Cary Archard), *Poetry Wales*, 18, 4, 1983, pp. 58–63.

Index of Poem Titles

A Celtic Death 166
A Field at Vallorcines 203
A Last Respect 147
A Letter 125
A Letter from Gwyther Street 159
A Stare from the Mountain 169
A Winter's Day 118
Aber 191
Absalom in the Tree 153
After Christmas 168
Afternoon in Water Street 124
Against Jericho (June, 1936) 14
An Age 133
Argyle Street 128
Au Cimetière de Brest 164

Bablockhythe 107
Balloon Over the Rhondda 64
Bars 52
Beacons 68
Blitz in Manchester 45
Blue Blood and Englishmen 178
Break in Harvest 93
Brechfa Chapel 187
Brynafan: First Light 146
Building a House (in Four Movements) 138
Burning Brambles 175

Cae Iago: May Day 207
Café Parting 49
Camp by the Windrush 112
Cardiff 202
Cascob 141
Channel Saint 165
Chinon 145
Coed Anghred 130
Conversation on Stackpole Head 137
Craswall 111
Credo 58
Cries in the Night 54
Crossing into Peace 92
Cynog 200

Days Enduring 17

Declaration of War (September 3rd, 1939) 41
Departure in Middle Age 149
Dr John James Williams 214
Dream 42
Drought 109
Drover's Song 71
Dusk 24

End-piece 66
Enstone Rock 74
Evening 101
Evening in Saundersfoot 38
Evening: Unloading Wheat 85
Expiation 197

Fagenbaum 55
Fool's Fingers 172
For an Unmarked Grave 151
For Jenkin Jones Prisoner at Carmarthen, These 161
For M.A.H. 77
For Marjorie 48
For Warren Davies, Two Years Dead 143
Frederick George Robertson Williams 219
Freshwater West 123
Freshwater West Revisited 150
Friends I Have 142
From a Bus at Crosby, Cumberland 99
Fulwell 76

God Is 158
God is Not Mocked *Appendix*
Going 95
Good-Friday 29
Grace before Work 86
Grains of Sand 21
Grasshoppers 208
Gwenffreda Cate Williams/Alice Matilda Langland Williams (Alis Mallt) 218

Hawk 115

Index of Poem Titles

Hillside 89
Hiraeth 16
Howell Price Williams 216

I Shall Take the Gig 211
In Frimley Woods 10
In Offenham Church 100
In the Swiss Jura 173
In This Cold Room 90
Indictment 155
Innocent Dying 195
Inter Tenebros (Even Here) 50
Is it the Same Country? 176

Jazz Festival 209
Joy and Faith 2
Judas Maccabeus 102

Kidmore End 80
Knapweed 26

La Tène 174
Ladysmock 75
Lament for Cassandra 47
Last Happiness 79
Lines Written on Hearing of the Invasion of Poland (September 1st, 1939) 40
Llyn Bodgynydd 70
London Welshman 69
Long Abed 4
Look at Me, Caleb 213
Lowbury Hill 91

Madoc 188
Maesyronnen 61
March on the Mountains 65
Marston Sicca 139
Mary Jane Robertson Williams 215
May-trees Climbing 183
Memling 185
Memories 12
Mirror 84
Moorland Thunder 5
Morning: New Jerusalem 117

Nepotism 46
New Lease 167
New Year, 1935 1
New Year, 1936 6

New Year, 1939 37
New Year's Day, 1946 97
Night on the Brecon Road 56
Not Worth the Record 160
Now Starlight Knows You Not 23

O Tihuanaco 127
'O World Intangible' 35
October Sun 22
Olchon 110
On Discovering Daumier's 'Don Quixote Reading' in the National Museum at Cardiff 202
On Hearing Richard II, Broadcast by the O.U.D.S. 8
On Llandefalle Hill 182
On Newport Reservoir 36
On South Lord's Land 204
On the Grave of Henry Vaughan at Llansaintffraed 108
Onset of Winter 190
Orielton Empty 140
Oxford Castle 59

Parting 20
Pas de Deux 120
Pas Seul 119
Passers-by 30
Pastorale 63
Pax Nobiscum 44
Peter Has Been Digging 220
Pontwillim Plough 87
Porth Cwyfan 171
Prayer Before Marriage 78
Prospect of Ditchley 94
Pwll Llong, Pwll Whiting 177

'Remember Charlie Stones, Carpenter' 126
Requiescat 81
Returning 132
Riddle 129
Rissersee 13
Ronan 206

Sanderlings 205
Sarnesfield 148
Saturday Morning: Appin 198
Scithwen Valley 136
Sea-moods 18

Index of Poem Titles

Searching Spring 106
Signal 196
Sir Gelli to R.S. 184
Slow Meeting 60
Snipe's Castle 181
Solway 96
Some Tight-lipped Wave 154
Spring in Weggis 122
Squirrel-path 170
Storm 32
Subite 88
Sundew 15
Sunrise at Even 3
Sunset Over the Sea 11

Terns at Rossnaskill 201
Testament 157
The Anchorite 179
The Ballad of Barroll's Daughter 72
The Bearers 67
The Cauldron of Diwrnach Wyddel (A Poem for the D-Days) 82
The Clear Sea 212
The Close 57
The Damson Tree 180
The Fall of the Year 19
The Flooded Valley 116
The Fool in the Wood 163
The Forest 39
The Lament of Little Gwion 83
The Lamentation of Marchell 210
The Last Days of Heat 144
The Least Echo 152
The Lochmaben Stone 104
The Lost Kingdom 135
The Lurking Ancestor 98

The Mountain 105
The New Miracle 31
The Past 28
The Path to Dinas 103
The Path to Fontana Amorosa 194
The Roses of Tretower 114
The Stars Above 25
The Steward's Letter 193
The Tyle 131
The White Poplar 34
They Have Not Survived 156
They, Without Us 199
Thomas ap Richard of Doier to the Tower, These 113
Tide-reach 189
To a Tombstone Fragment in the Garden Path 186
To My Uncle David 7
To the Muse, Wrongheadedly 134
Towards Pencombe 121
Tower on an Evening Sky 43
Tŷ Clyd 192

Under Quinag 162
Under the Shadow 27

Vista 51

White Peonies 9
Whitewater 73
William Retlaw Jefferson Williams 217
Wishes from Walton 53
Worm in the Brain 62

Youth 33

Index of First Lines

A bronze fish breathing a fountain of trees 103
A fall, a season running into sleet 142
A fortnight has gone since her death 192
A half hour since 29
A man with a blowlamp clambers opposite 128
A neap tide tops my heart, needlessly 134
A plane like a fish, leap finished, drops 93
A purse of silver is lying 120
A quarter mile it was the signpost said 13
A smile 7
A thin cataract 190
About the sill the gritting of the leaves 144
Above the elderberry bushes and the banks where hens 132
Across the field, beyond the lordly hedge 61
After six years this winter has not changed 150
Among these arthritic contours 207
And from which mountain 200
And so tonight another door will open 6
As knapweed, bitter like the plague 26
As on my birthday, many days ago 33
As short a while ago as seven hours 40
As the sun slants, the best of it over 169

Beech-dark each day, brought down 163
Before the earth was round, or man was tired 11
Believe what the land is, whether 213
Bevel and plume of a graveyard yew 68
Beyond me and between 10
Beyond this contour 74
Blow hot and cold 35

Brendan looked down. It was the morning of 212
Can it be night? 32
Comfort in centuries with broken feet 91
Concourse of tents on the plat 112
Cool is the plot of evening, consolation 101

Did a dog bark in Olchon? 110
Did you, John Arnallt 155
Down at the station there are pickets set 41
Down Kendrick hill I must admire 60
Drops of the rain that tumbled the runnels 203

Eastward there's only the world to see 21
Eight years ago come Tuesday now I walked 125
Eighteen and one from fosterage 179
Embalm these memories and build 57
Even the worst intelligence must needs ride 184
Evening is grey with us, Morgan 113

Finished, yes. Complete and in order now 152
First to the ford tonight 71
Foam at the Skerries heel 48
Follow the ponderous tailor, mark 55
For once the Latin has an edge 166
Four days remain to me, but four – and then 17
From Howell Williams, Ship Street, Brecon, 1 January 1827 211
From copse to copse I leap and hollo 39

God is who questions me 158
Gone is the plain of Esdraelon 14
Gravelgreat are the hills and perching 106

Index of First Lines

Grey is Nant Iago, grey 195
Greying of suds upon an earthy white 51

He doesn't know 170
Hearing the news from Idris, hoarse 154
Here in the huddle of the lowest room 50
Hey, friend, I have been here a long time 153
High founts that play in the sun 46
How best remember? Shipwright you, quiet, wry 143
How sombre lies the earth against the white! 4

I called you cringer, grandfather 197
I came from Merthyr by the Cefn road 63
I can't say I remember you. The truth is 181
I cannot be sure what 157
I have been here in the fields a year 105
I have had no great acquaintance 81
I have no stick to poke down in the tank 136
I have prayed askance in the slow cold air, in the cave 127
I left Liverpool on the 15th 216
I remember agrimony. And the tall 80
I saw you yesterday in the high hedge 75
I see a ripple on a thoughtless arc, and then 36
I travel back to joys unmixed with pain 12
I tried being a lawyer but was 217
I was very good at timing the trains 219
I watch the muster of grasses between the stones 139
I would have said 45
If I could see that all my miseries of heart 27
If you were dead, as I 135
In that white country 84
In the grass gold rings 119

In the late cousinhood of country ways 114
In the proud season penitence 131
In the wet pageantry tonight deploys 79
In this cold room, with the pictures 90
Is there a bearing to this spot 191
It came from those trees there, that rapid 148
It is ill dying in the wind 72
It is not the June image, the one month late 183
It should have been no surprise 202
It was night at last when he grew weak 151
It's a dead house, he said. Done for 167

Joy is the substance of delight in all things 2
June, but the morning's cold, the wind 171
Just here's the middle of a silence that 141

Last year this hill was burned 182
Like the lost cheesecloth talent in the parable 100
Llanfrynach pool is clear again! 65
Look 162
Looking down 73

Maybe in days to come the sun will shine 15
Met at the high table of history 82
Money you'll never see, Shon 69
More than the integer, no more *Appendix*
My father, Tewdrig, has an unpromising way 210
My first is like a sea-horse, scaled 129
My grandfather, white-faced son of the water- 178
My house is empty but for a pair of boots 116
My sun, capricious, holds its heaven. I cannot wish you 161

No great tide 99
No, I am not to be comforted 188
No, you are not under foot 186

Index of First Lines

Not a shank of the long lane upwards 187
Not everything is named, either 172
Now that my morning window sees the fields 19

O Mary J. 215
O mine, O tension in the main 76
Off the low fields the lagging pools 96
Ohé 165
Old berry and old sun 168
On South Lord's Land 204
One day of wind (it was my last) 20
One of the afternoon, misted over the death glass 164
Only the sob of raindrops in the grass 5
Out of a day the wastrel wind disparages 104
Out of the pallor of a dream 25
Over, break white and wash swiftly 123
Over the stubble the gulls steer 97

Pain, you come out of this patch 98
Peter has been digging the beds, swaying 220

Rain in the trees 62
Red fresh-turned plough across the gate 87
Ronan 206

Scarves pull at the throat, a gale 117
Sesame, word of logic, or wild guess 85
Sharply towards the evening, sharply 89
Sir Benfro's silver beaches whisper sweet 16
Softly, softly down the carpet of eventide 3
Stand on the edge and look! 189
Storm hit the van roof sharply after dark 198
Sun at arm's length, infant cajoling ball 108
Sun blinding back from glass cases, eyes that see black 174
Sun-in-my-window-shine 52

Take this cliff path, no other, let your eye 194
That edge of rose – there! – to the tender 176
That frail asbestos finger 42
That peradventurer who breaks at last 78
That plump little chorus 205
The ancient pirouette of trees 94
The blue singleness of summer was in that air 133
The blue tide like a lively child 118
The corner of an eye pricks 196
The days pass quicker than my finger slow 30
The gallery of faces is a cloud 102
The gate is open and the green ride ends 121
The gaunt old cheek of earth 31
The groves are feverish as a dream 109
The heat that blistered Finger Post 44
The hedges are dazed as cock-crow, heaps of leaves 149
The hollows are full 83
The house is already building 138
The humping bridge that spanned 92
The lamps are trimmed again upon my doom 23
The lees of life 24
The lizards on the wall move 145
The mood of many nights 47
The oldest building in the town, they said 59
The red importance of the winter sun 124
The scent of peonies in June 9
The sea at a distance glints now and again, as though 175
The sea's blue eye and the lobster boat 177
The slope is taken with a jerk 95
The soaking rucksack at the table leg 49
The still punts with fishers watching 107
The stream is sultry and a short haze mulls it 126
The sun, disinterested, summer on either side 147

Index of First Lines

The sun, the railings, and the coping shine 37
The track is invisible 88
The train that whinnies at me in the night 54
The tree-flanks are meek 173
The world a waste of days 70
The year's last levee was a-throng today 22
Then in remembering I do not enough 86
There are marks of snow on the goitred neck 115
There has been burning, identifiable still 140
They have not survived 156
This morning, the rain pucker over 159
Time, if we had a watch, would point to four 137
To the Lo. Burghley 193
Torrent shouts Manascin in the dark 180
Tower on an evening sky 43
Turbulent, unbecoming, how this head goes on 56

Up seven green steps, around a moist 130
Upon the humbled ear 53

Vacant were we, and dull of eye 8
Voices are voices, when all's said 199

We had gone down to Tabor, to the door 64
We have remembered now the myth 58
We know that time slips on unseen, unheard 1
Wet in the field 67
What I am trying to say 209
What is it that you expect, caller? 160
What is it to grasp 208
What was it brought you, Seligenstadter 185
What's done I cannot do 66
When I remember how I met the man 38
When Kate Williams began her novelette 218
When the shepherd laid the fire 214
When walls are down and through the wide of air 28
Whiter than sand 201
'Who laughed?' said a wind from the west in the dawning 34
Wind like a trollop darting eerily out of the woodpile 122
Wind-whispers 18
With a long stirrup under fern 111
Within the cruck the night 146

You move in history now and in my gain 77